F. Hollich, Th. Otter,
H.-D. Scheuermann

Shared Services – Foundation, Practice and Outlook

A comparison study of
Shared Service implementations

Martin Meidenbauer »

Die Deutsche Bibliothek verzeichnet diese Publikation in der Deutschen Nationalbibliografie; detaillierte bibliografische Daten sind im Internet über http://dnb.ddb.de abrufbar.

Printed in Germany

Gedruckt auf
chlorfrei gebleichtem, säurefreiem und
alterungsbeständigem Papier (ISO 9706)

ISBN 978-3-89975-123-9

Verlagsverzeichnis schickt gern:
Martin Meidenbauer Verlagsbuchhandlung
Erhardtstr. 8
D-80469 München

www.m-verlag.net

Table of Contents

1 Introduction

Most multi-national and global companies run Shared Service Organizations or intend to do so in the near future. Globalization and dynamic, accelerated changes of products, markets and technologies - and other corporate environmental influences - force companies to focus on their *competencies* and especially on their core competencies. Managing the core competencies allows them to differentiate themselves from competitors and so their supporting processes become critical. Shared Service Organizations are a way of *organizing and managing supporting business processes*. A whole chain of process steps, or the entire chain of business processes, may need to be reengineered, simplified, harmonized, consolidated, centralized and standardized. This applies especially to the *administrative part of operational business processes* with its different type of *information processing,* from purely human based to interactive information and communication system support, to full automation. The increasing capabilities of information and communication technology are the main drivers for the breakthrough of the Shared Service concept.

One of the principal Shared Service design guides is reassigning the administrative part of business processing, which is mostly information processing execution, to an internal centralized unit. Sourcing of business processes is not limited to internal execution resources. Instead, there is an emerging trend to outsource activities to an external service provider. The Shared Service concept is an approach that realizes the benefits of centralization and market orientation. Performing market mechanisms are the most efficient coordination form because of efficiency and effectiveness. From an end-to-end business process flow perspective, the involvement could be in the early stages of processing (for instance, a centralized financial credit limit check), at the end of the process chain (invoicing and payment) or even customer-facing tasks (such as. customer order taking) or in a contact/interaction center. The Shared Services approach is not limited to any special categorization of business tasks (front or back-offices[1]; employee, customer or supplier facing processes) but can be used at any stage.

[1] Front and Back-Office: Front-Office deals with customer facing activities. Back-Office functions are not part of the core business of a corporate, they are supporting processes to manage the company company itself. Thus information and communication technology application software is often often categorized according to these two categories as front-office and back-office applications.

From an industrial corporation perspective, many processes are labeled back-office functions: Finance and Accounting (F&A), Human Resources (Human Capital Management), Information and Communication Technology Management (ICT, or in short IT), Procurement and generic corporate services like Facility and Real Estate Management, Travel and Expense/Entertainment Management. Apart from ICT, F&A and HCM are the two leading *business function* categories that first implemented the Shared Service concept first. Now, with this all the experience available, and the value it can add, all business processes within a corporation could, in principle, enjoys the benefits of Shared Service optimization.

Most contributions to Shared Service knowledge focus on pragmatically listing business cases or providing results of empirical surveys, without science-based, methodical and theoretical reflection on the foundation beneath the different approaches. This book should serve as a conceptual frame for systematically and methodically evaluating current and upcoming business practices with regard to shared services and the use of ICT. After presenting an introduction into the origin and nature of Shared Services, the books focuses on *how* shared service benefits are achieved, in these major areas:

- Introduction to Shared Services (What are Shared Services? What are the reasons to introduce a Shared Service concept? What are the key benefits which can be achieved?)
- Benefit Levers of Shared Services (What are the levers to achieve Shared Service benefits?)
- Business Process Suitability (What kind and type of business activities are suitable for Shared Services?)
- Resource Capabilities (How can Shared Service business processes be resourced?)
- Organization and Management of Service Delivery (What is the optimum way to organize business processes and execution resources?)
- Operation Model of Shared Services (How can coordination be achieved? How are agreements handled?)
- Implementation, transformation and transition (What are the challenges of transforming to Shared Services?)
- Practices (What kind of practice examples can be found?)
- Evolution of Shared Services (How can Shared Services evolve in the future?)

These areas shape the book's chapters. For easier navigation, the following diagram shows the relationship among the chapters and recommended reading flow.

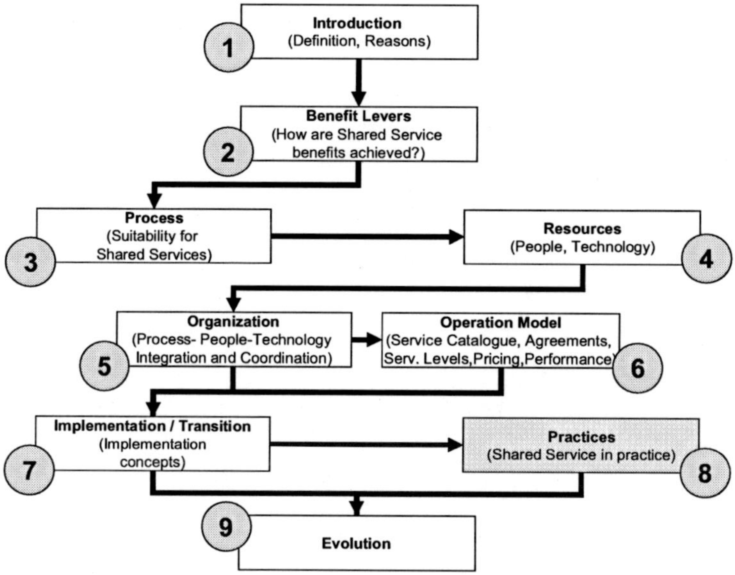

Fig. 1: Content structure of this book

The book provides a conceptual frame to assess today's and future business practice in Shared Services, complemented by current practices derived from interviews with the heads of well established Shared Services Organizations of large enterprises. The theoretical conceptual chapters are also enriched with practical chapters, as well as interesting views and practices.

1.1 What is a Shared Service Center?

Shared Services are not a new concept. The concept goes back to the differentiation and separation of work. There are many ways to characterize and split work, either according to products or product groups, geographical areas or functions. Companies began separating administrative tasks from core operational tasks during the industrial revolution in the nineteenth century. Frederick W. Taylor elaborated on the *functional specialization of operations,* with the goal of increasing productivity of personnel resources within a serialized production line.

Looking back at how companies were organized in the past, we find that most of them were more or less organized as independent business units serving local markets or as suppliers for a central or regional headquarters. The relationship among them was purely based on capital and hierarchical coordination by the headquarters. In a first wave, the concept of *centralization* allowed greater economies of scale. However, central organizations became slower in reacting to dynamic market changes. Losing sight of the customer led to implementation of the reverse concept of *decentralization*. The decentralized units were better able to assess customer needs and to respond faster to changing market conditions. However, this resulted in redundancy in effort, function, departments and technology usage. Centralization of such supportive and administrative tasks seems to be the logical consequence. But companies needed to approach centralization differently in order to avoid these negative effects.

American companies were the first to exploit an approach during the mid-1980s which tried to combine the positive effects of both approaches and tries to make back-office functions work in a more competitive and business-like environment. The goal was to achieve an internal client-vendor-relationship where multiple business clients would be *served*. A new type of organizational structure was born – the 'Shared Service Center'.

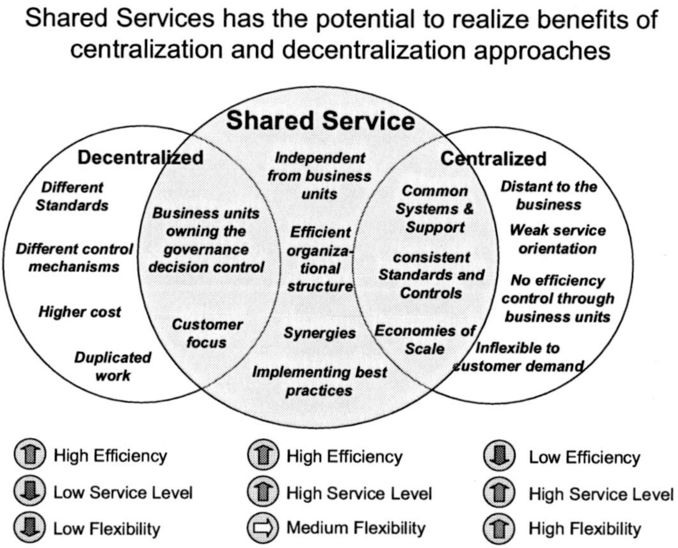

Fig. 2: Shared Services – An approach to realize benefits of centralization and decentralization

Source: Daley (2003, 108).

Shared Services tries to provide better services using both centralization and decentralization and to leverate the significant benefits, especially that of lower cost.

It is important to have a common understanding of the terminology in use to avoid misunderstanding and confusion. The label of this type of organizational model contains the two words *shared* and *service*. Shared refers to multiple requestors obtaining the same service from one source by sharing process ownership and responsibility. The word service refers to making the service delivery professional with a customer-vendor relationship and high performance service-culture in mind. By doing a literature review and browsing the internet, you will find many definitions and perspectives on Shared Services.

Selected Examples of Definitions:

"Shared services is a collaborative strategy in which a subset of existing business functions are concentrated into a new, semiautonomous business unit that has a management structure designed to promote efficiency, value generation, cost savings, and improved service for the internal customers of the parent corporation, like a business competing in the open market."

Source: Bergeron (2002)

"Shared Services … is the organization that provides non-core Services to the business, employing a specialist team, geographically unconstrained, and focusing on the requirements of the customers. This involves a philosophy and approach totally unlike traditional Corporate-driven centralisation. The goal of Shared Services is to provide high quality, non-core services (which can include both repetitive common processes and more specialised professional services) to the business at lower cost and more efficiently than the business could otherwise provide for itself. Shared Services achieves cost savings and higher quality of service by leveraging economies of scale, core technology, standardised processes, best practice and end-to-end process re-engieering."

Source: SBPOA (2004)

"Shared Services are the convergence and streamlining of an organization's functions to ensure that they deliver the organization the services required of them as effectively and efficiently as possible. This often involves the centralizing of back office functions such as HR and Finance but can also be applied to the middle or front offices. A key advantage of this convergence is that it enables the appreciation of economies of scale within the function and can enable multi function working (e.g. linking HR and Finance together, where there is the potential to create synergies). A large scale cultural and process transformation is often a key component of a move to Shared Services. … Shared Services are more than just centralization or consolidation of similar activities in one location. Shared Services mean running these service activities like a business and delivering services to internal customers at a cost, quality and timeliness that is competitive with alternatives."

Source: Wikipedia Shared_Service (2007)

An overall, and generally accepted, definition doesn't exist. The following set of characteristics describes the basic concept of Shared Services:

- Shared Service is the *intelligent distribution of (information processing) work* which leads to better process performance, less personnel effort and better financial results.
- Selection, separation (isolation) and bundling of similar *subset of non-core common business functions/processes*.

- Selected business functions are mostly *supportive, administrative repetitive tasks.* Specialized professional tasks where competence, judgment and expertise are required can be organized as a Shared Service as well.
- Processes are mostly *reengineered* (standardized, consolidated) and streamlined with an end-to-end process chain in mind for high performance.
- Activities are *managed as business services* like a marketable service offering with a defined service description (definition) and formal or informal *contractual agreements* on services and their associated *service levels.*
- Shared Service clients are (ideally) *charged based on usage* and agreed negotiated price.
- Service delivery will be out of a *semi-autonomous processing hub* to recipients (multiple business service consumption units, such as business units, local subsidiaries or central enterprise headquarters) based on a long term supplier-customer relationship.
- The service processing hub is *geographically unconstrained.*
- Service consumers are mostly *internal customers* of a parent entity (or sometimes external partners or joint venture partners).
- The key basic value benefit (or strategic benefit and success factors) of a Shared Service approach is to achieve *lower cost, improved service quality (accuracy and timeliness), shorter performance time with a productivity increase (duration, execution), better risk management* and higher responsiveness to dynamic changes (*flexibility).*

Based on the grouping of business activities in *core and non-core activities (processes, tasks)*, the non-critical ones can be executed by someone else. Those activities can be performed in a central organizational processing unit or even outsourced to an external party.

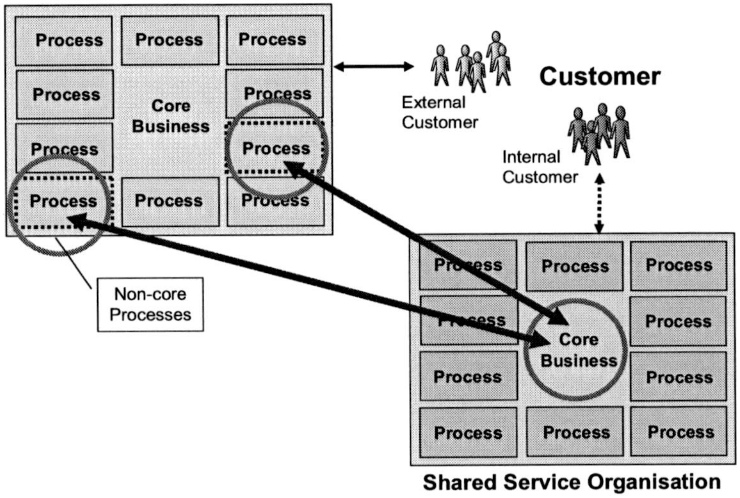

Fig. 3: Shared Service approach

Assigning activities to a central unit requires a more formal specification of the processes. This becomes mandatory if the workload is shifted to an external partner. Here, the business process execution is treated as a *'business service'*. Regardless of whether they are within or outside the corporate boundary, services can be viewed as a well-defined intangible product that is implicitly assumed to be for multiple clients. In order to achieve the desired results, companies must rigorous apply:

- Consolidate *demand* (volume aggregation of back-office, non-revenue generating functions to achieve economies of scale)
- Harmonize and streamline *business processes* (standardizing and eliminating redundancy work)
- Consolidate supply side *resources* (service delivery infrastructure of people and IT systems; centralized service delivery organization)
- Simplify business processes by means of technical *automation* (changing the proportion of person to machine work)
- Relocate to lower the *factor costs* (relocate people's workload to achieve labor arbitrage effects)

The following quote underlines exactly what the intentions of a Shared Service concept are: "Never have a Back-Office – let it be another one's Front-Office" [2].

An *industrial enterprise* Shared Services should include support functions of Human Resources (HR), Finance & Accounting (F&A), Information and Communication Technology (ICT), Procurement and other corporate support activities like facility management, travel and expense management, real estate, and so on.

During the early adoption stage, most implementations established a central physical location and called it Shared Service Center (SSC). This covered one or more business functions. There are also Shared Service center structures which operate more as virtual organizations, so the more neutral term 'Shared Service Hub' could be more appropriate. Shared Service centers could operate out of multiple physical locations under the *governance* of one organizational roof. In today's world we find multiple distributed locations processing Shared Services on a national, regional or global basis. If there is central governance for all (or part) of the distributed shared service centers in place, then it is better labeled a Shared Service Organization (SSO). SSC is the older term and widely used. For our purpose we use SSC, SSO and Shared Service Hub as synonyms.

1.1.1 Shared Services versus centralized corporate service

Collecting common tasks and centralizing it in a central processing unit looks similar to establishing a central organization unit. The difference with a Shared Service unit is the required mind-set change.

[2] Walsh Jack, former CEO General Electric, quoted by: Hans-Dieter Scheuermann, Transforming the Finance Function and Finance Operations, SAP Business Solution Architects Group CFO Roundtable, Budapest, 5. April 2005

Tab. 1: Differences between Shared Services and centralized corporate services

	Shared Services	Centralized Corporate Service
Goals	Superior business service/process performance (cost and quality) and continuing improvement	Cost reduction and central control
Customer/ Demand orientation	Customer oriented (focus on client needs, business partnering), client = business units,	Delivery oriented (headquarter focused), client = corporate entity,
Core/non-core business view	Offered services are viewed as their core business (operates as an own business)	Support activities, weak service attitude
Organizational setup	Separate business unit, or even external business partner; operating as a centralized, decentralized or virtual unit	Corporate / Central department
Financial organizational status (financial governance type)	Ideally profit or revenue center; in practice mostly cost center	Cost Center
Specificity of services	Customer specific services, market orientation (market principles) driven by demand and requirement; individual and customized service delivery	Delivery/supply of activities/tasks (viewed as support tasks) determined by central corporate entity
Formal agreement / arrangement	Bilateral service offering (scope, quality, cost); Service level agreement (SLA), possible customer contractual agreement, use of key performance figures	No/seldom formal arrangement agreement, use of service level key performance figures not common
Charging of services	Agreed price arrangement or full cost; allocation approach; charging business units based on performance and utilization (usage)	Full cost; overhead costs not dependent on usage
Operational Distance	Greenfield (in an ideal situation); usually away from headquarters	Brownfield (located at headquarters)
Governance / Controlling	Governance stays with the client, more partner relationship; planning and controlling remain in the business units	Tight alignment between headquarters and business units (clients); centralized planning and controlling
Responsibility	Full responsible for cost, quality and potential profit.	Low responsibility for cost, quality

Shared Service Centers allow the business units to concentrate on their core operational business and take over the non-core activities. Such an aggregation of common activities provides a platform for leveraging the economies of scale and may even forma critical mass of skills and expertise.

1.1.2 Shared Services and Outsourcing

Establishing a Shared Service center provides a variety of options. The most common one is set up as an internal organizational service unit. Or there is the option to separate it legally as an external servicing company. From a sourcing point of view, the latter is called internal outsourcing (outside the enterprise corporation boundary). But there is still a dependency between the two legal entities which belong to the same concern. Legal separation is not necessarily a clear criteria to distinguish between in- and outsourcing. Outsourcing is characterized by a high degree of independence, such as own governance and no presence of ownership conflicts.

Tab. 2: Differences between Shared Services and external outsourcing

	Shared Services	External Outsourcing
Goals	Superior business service/process performance (cost and quality) and continuing improvement	Cost reduction and central control
Customer/ Demand orientation	Customer oriented (focus on client needs, business partnering), client = business units	Delivery oriented (headquarter focused), client = corporate entity
Core/non-core business view	Offered services are viewed as their core business (operates as an own business)	Services are core business; key competencies;
Organizational setup	Separate business unit, or even external business partner; operating as a centralized, decentralized or virtual unit	External business partner
Financial organizational status (financial governance type)	Ideally profit or revenue center; in practice mostly cost center	Independent legal entity
Specificity of services	Customer specific services, market orientation (market principles) driven by demand and requirement; individual and customized service delivery	Market and customer driven (individualized and standardized services)
Formal agreement / arrangement	Bilateral service offering (scope, quality, cost), Service levels (SLA), possible customer contractual agreement	Customer legal binding contractual agreement with service scope, quality and pricing. Service Level Agreements (SLA)
Charging of services	Agreed price arrangement or full cost; allocation approach; charging business units based on performance and utilization (usage)	Market price based between contracting parties
Operational Distance	Greenfield (in an ideal situation); usually geographically away from headquarters	Outside enterprise boundaries; mostly geographically separated
Governance / Controlling	Governance remains by the client, more partner relationship; business planning and controlling remain in the business units	Governance and service execution at service provider; internal and external agreed combination; intervention is difficult
Responsibility	Full responsible for cost, quality and possible profit	Full responsible for own profit

1.2 Why Shared Services?

The reasons or motivation for setting up a Shared Service Organization are multifaceted, since these tend to be complex and interdependent. Extracting the multiple factors and determining their single contribution to either cost savings or more process transparency, for example, is a challenging task. It is hard to distinguish between a reason for setting up a Shared Service Organization and the benefits achieved, projected or anticipated.

Tab. 3: Reasons for setting up a Shared Service Organization

Better service, improvement in quality, accuracy, timeliness of info	69 %
Reduction of general and administrative costs	47 %
Financial cost savings (such as working capital, cash management)	36 %
Headcount reduction	25 %
Reduce duplication in functions	25 %
Platform for flexible business growth at incremental cost	24 %
Grouping of similar activities and expertise for critical mass	23 %
Easier roll-out and support of standard IT infrastructure	15 %
Standardization of services	15 %
To be able to service the geography as one uniform market	5 %
Intermediate step toward outsourcing of non-critical functions	4 %

Source: Kris (2002)

The reasons articulated have a visible or hidden correlation to an assumed *benefit* (from the provider point of view). In economic terms, fundamental *key value benefits* like cost savings, performance improvements (duration and execution time/productivity), quality improvements (accuracy and timeliness) and better risk management are the measurement criteria or categories. The reasons articulated for implementing shared services are single or multiple depending on those assumed key value benefits. Nevertheless corporations are using shared service as a *catalyst for business transformation*. Accelerating the speed of post-mergers integration emerges as a reason for implementing the shared service concept.

The easiest measurement of benefit is cost. Empirical studies show that the introduction of shared services has a remarkable reduction on operational costs.

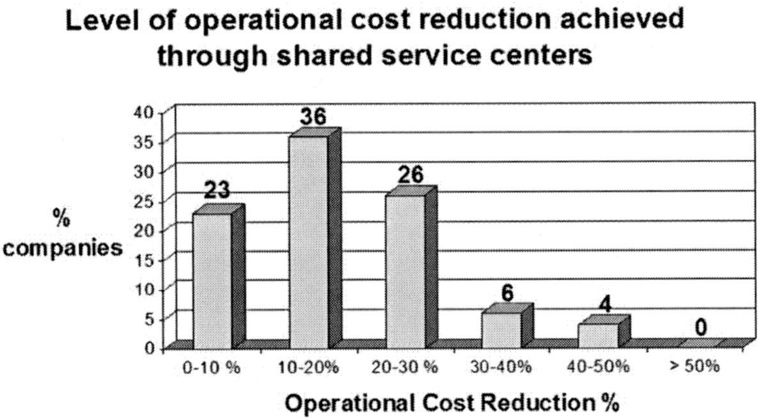

Fig. 4: Level of operational cost reduction achieved through shared service centers

Source: Kris (2002)

Interpretation should be carried out carefully because the percentage of savings depends on the starting position of each Shared Service center. Poor performance in the past, low labor cost at the Shared Service center location and how the implementation project is managed all have a significant impact on the cost performance of a Shared Service center. Important aspects in managing an implementation of a Shared Service Organization include a trustworthy, sound business case with accurate figures and controlled change management that matches the new requirements.

Information Technology, Finance, Human Resources and Procurement are the main business function groups that implement Shared Services. The benchmarking figures show a huge difference between world class performers and poor performers.

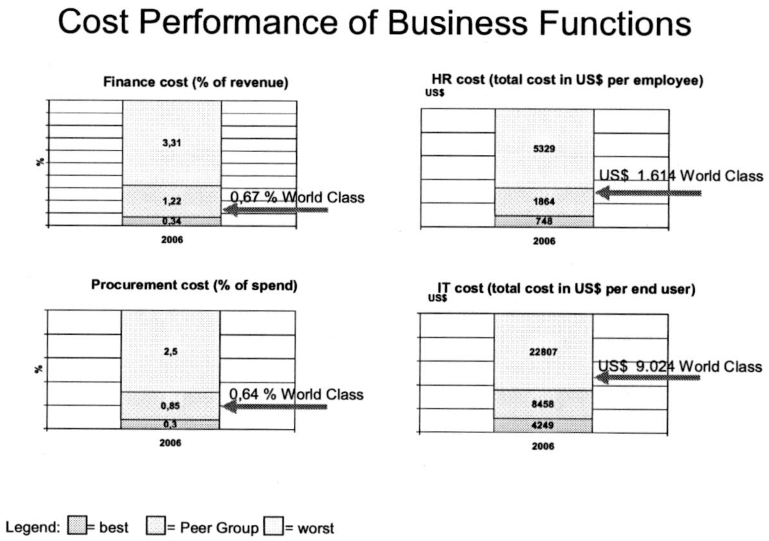

Fig. 5: Cost categories in relation to associated reference criteria
Source: Bangemann (2007)[3]

1.2.1 Finance & Accounting

The Finance & Accounting (F&A) business function is currently undergoing a fundamental transformation from a purely back-office function into the demanding role of acting as a business partner. Environmental changes and pressures like increased regulatory requirements and compliance issues, higher flexibility required due to more mergers and acquisitions, ongoing pressure in reducing the operational cost in F&A, better supporting operational businesses, assessing and implementing emerging information and communication technologies, have led advanced organizations to launch a F&A transformation program. These cover activities like business process reengineering and questioning the sourcing of the processes. New service delivery models like Shared Services, Business Process Outsourcing and self-services become compelling alternatives.

[3] Definition: World-Class = In Hackett's empirically based methodology, a company is considered to be world-class when it ranks in the top 25 % both in efficiency and effectiveness metrics.
Peer Group = Represents the median of non-world-class companies (Hackett (2007, 88)

According to a study conducted by SharedXpertise in association with Hewlett Packard (December 2006)[4] cost reduction is still the main driver of change.

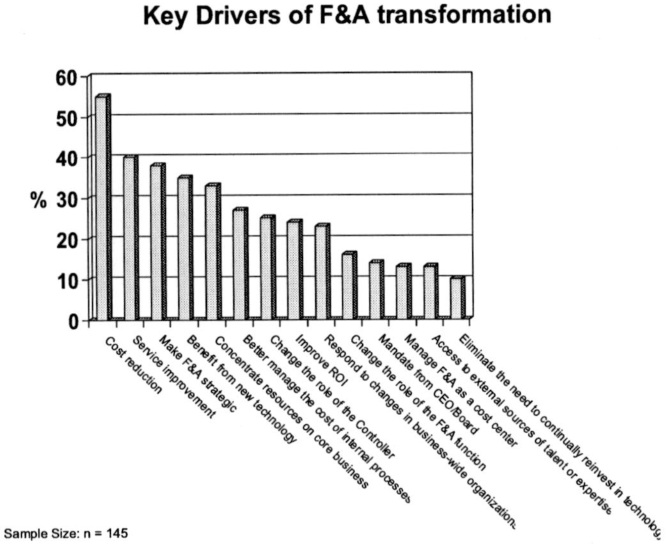

Fig. 5: Key Driver of F&A transformation
Source: Searle (2006)

Although cost is the main driver in the F&A transformation other value drivers like service improvement, focus on strategic direction and on core business (such as decision support and strategic guidance) rank quite high alongside the efficient delivery of the business finance function.

Looking at the F&A cost curve as a percentage of revenue, substantial cost reductions have been achieved in the last 15 years.

---

[4] Searle: F&A Transformation Survey – How shared services and outsourcing are impacting the F&A operation 2006, SharedXpertise, 2006; n=145 respondents, 2/3 of respondents operate in more then 10 countries, revenue range from less than $50 million (17,1%) to $1 – $5 billion (29,3%) and over $10 billion (19,5 %): headcount with 8,1% having less than 500 employees, just under 30% having 500 – 5000 employees and nearly 11% have more than 100 000 people.

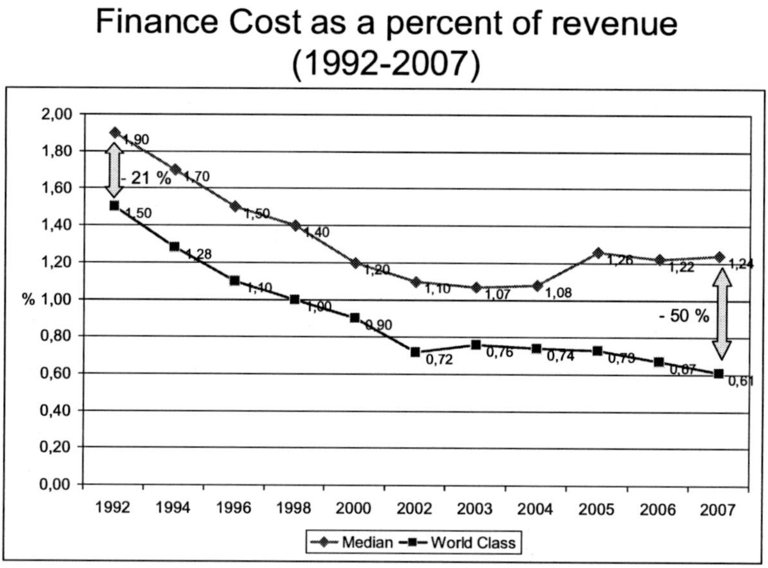

Fig. 6: Development of Finance & Accounting costs as a percent of revenue

Source: Value figures from Hackett (2006) and Weller (2007)

The diagram shows that the pressure on F&A will increase dramatically. The gap between the median and world class companies in F&A seems to be increasing (1992: 21 %, 2007: 50%). The increase in costs during 2004, caused by Sarbanes Oxley (SOX), shows that world class companies were better prepared for extended management of internal controls.

A change of the role of F&A is necessary. F&A has to evolve into a business partner for the business, and its future challenges are the increasing demand for decision support and cost reduction.

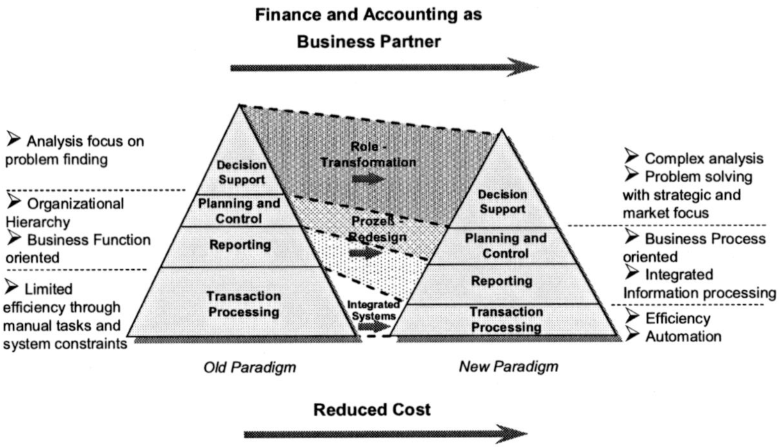

Fig. 7: Future Challenges of Finance & Accounting

1.2.2 Human Resources

HR shared service is now a significant trend. Over 90% of the European 500 is considering some form of shared service, with HR second most prevalent function (after finance). Many multinational companies have implemented HR shared service centers, some on a national basis, others on a regional basis and fewer on a global basis. Examples of organizations deploying HR shared service include IBM, Siemens, Gillette, SAP, Ford, HP, Leeds City Council, Centrica, Procter & Gamble, Henkel, Vertex, BP, Shell, RBS, Nestle, Motorola, Ericsson, Compass, Eastern Health Services, Philips, Zurich Financial Services and Barclays to name a few. Shared service has gained traction across all industries, and shared service is becoming the predominant model of HR service delivery in large organizations. It is also interesting to note that the majority of large consulting organizations that sell shared services have implemented them internally.

In the UK, the government sector has embraced shared service, Surrey County Council, Leeds City Council, Stafford shire, Westminster and other London boroughs, Salford, Hertfordshire and a number of others as well as the health services are all moving to a shared service model. At a central government level shared service is also having an impact. Examples of shared service best practice can be readily found in the UK public sector. The decision has partly been driven by the Government's

2005 e-delivery initiative, but also by a need to cuts costs and improve service.

Indeed over a decade ago Ulrich (Ulrich 1995) noted:
The concept of shared service has suddenly and without much fanfare, become a model for the organization and delivery of staff operations, including Human Resources. He went on to note. The impetus for shared services is the intersection of five management concerns: productivity, reengineering, globalization, service, and technology. Over the last decade this has moved from model to reality, and Ulrich's HR transformation model remains a key part of the drivers behind HR Shared Service. It could be argued that the move to shared services is as much about freeing HR management from its perceived administrative shackles as it is about pure cost reduction and process improvement.

Despite this significant move to shared service, there is limited academic research available on HR administration and shared service, at least that we have been able to uncover. Much of the HR research has been focused on how HR can become more strategic Human Capital Management, HR as business partners and such like. There is little on the more prosaic components of HR. Stripping costs out of administrative processes, while maintaining or improving service levels has received relatively little attention. Strategy is more fun it seems. However in the UK the Institute of Employment Studies has some interesting research. This study is well worth reading, as it is well researched and bereft of any subliminal sales message. It is several years old, but prescient. However, given the impact that shared service has on both the business and the HR function, and its cost implications, more empirical research on best practice would be welcome. Most of the research is vendor and consultant driven. A Mercer study [Mercer 2002] noted most of the business impact surveys suggest that the potential savings from shared services are between 15 percent and 40 percent of labor cost.

The drive to shared services in HR is part of a broader HR transformation process. Over the last decade, HR departments been under significant pressure to reduce costs and deliver more tangible business benefits. The scope what HR is doing has grown significantly over the past decade.

Over the period between 1996 until 2005 the total cost per employee increased.

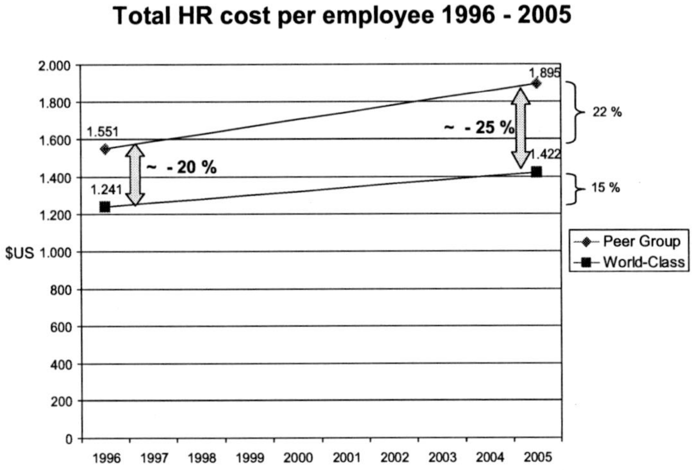

Fig. 8: Total HR cost per employee 1996 – 2005

Source: Values retrieved from Hackett (2005e, 13)

Similar to the finance business function is the gap of total HR cost per employee between the peer group and world-class over time period is widening. High performance HR organizations operate with lower staff, have a higher retention rate and have access to a better information and communication technology infrastructure environment. They are achieving better results with a lower cost level then companies of the peer group (which represents the median on non-world-class companies).

1.3 Resons for Shared Service

1.3.1 Reasons and Benefits - Introduction

Shared Services are often set up for administrative and support functions (transactional processes). Those back-office functions will be transformed into flexible, responsive, effective, customer-oriented processes and *offered as a service* to clients. The following figure summarizes some of the reasons allied to strategy, business processes, resources and overall organization. Many of the reasons are interrelated and have a tight or loose correlation to some basic benefits like cost reduction or quality improvement.

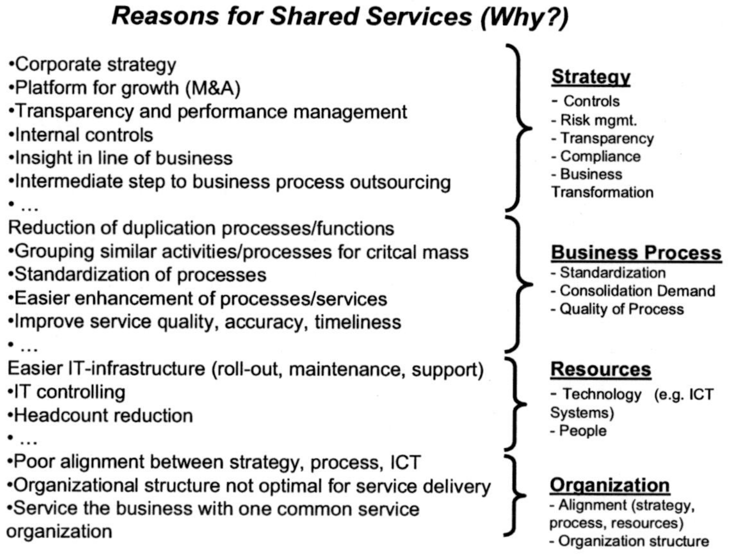

Fig. 9: Reasons for shared services

It is difficult to distinguish between *reasons for implementing* Shared Services and the *key value benefit* expected. Fundamental *key basic value benefits* for Shared Service (by which we mean *strategic success factors for Shared Service*) are:

- Cost savings
- Quality improvements (such as accuracy and timeliness)
- Time performance

We can distinguish them from the above list of reasons because they are directly linked to *all* the reasons and secondly, because each group has a main distinctive *measurement category.*

Most studies mention only three to four key value benefits: *Cost, Quality, Time-Performance and sometimes Risk*[5]. Cost, Quality and Time are the

[5] Risk should not be seen in isolation. The triple governance, risk and compliance (GRC) forms an integral part. Governance (here in the sense of corporate governance) deals with the control and steering structures of a political-social unit regardless if it is a privately or publicly entity. This covers legal as well as non-legal strategic directives. Risk deals with the calculation of a probability of possible negative impact (e.g. damage, danger) on the corporate business. The possible positive impact on the business is called chance. Risk assessment depends on the value propositions. Risk

three *classical* measurement categories with a typical operational focus. We would like to enhance and adapt the picture with:

- Better *risk* management as an explicit additional key value
- Higher responsiveness (flexibility, agility, adaptability) to *dynamic change*

The following figure shows the interconnection between all these benefit categories.

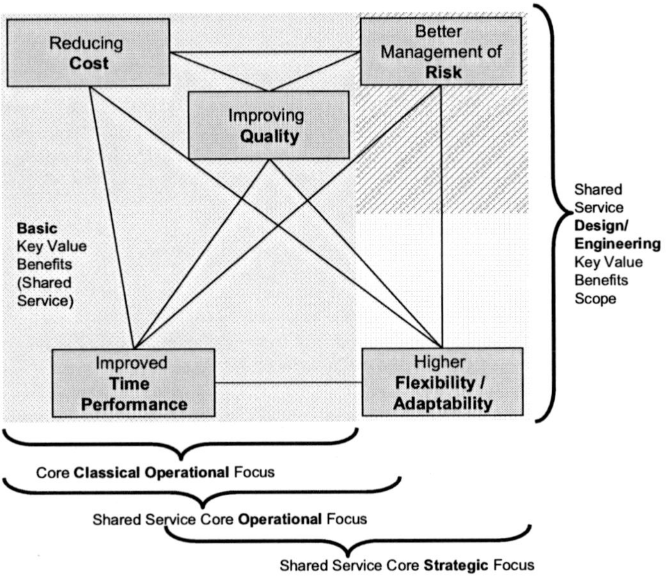

Fig. 10: Shared Service Key Value Benefits

The Shared Service key value benefit categories (including risk) and the core classical operational focus (Cost, Quality and Time) can be applied to assessing *any information processing sourcing decision* regardless if the service delivery is *internal or external*. Evaluating Shared Services should include configuration criteria which focus on structural and strategic aspects as well. For Shared Services we have added the *risk management* and *flexibility/adaptability* as key value drivers.

Sourcing business processes to an external service provider (with an internal service consumption view) is less about HOW the provider achieves service commitments in the short, medium and long term.

Management deals with the conscious planning to deal with risks. Compliance deals with the obeying of rules regardless if they are erected by law or other sources.

Innovation (productivity improvements through advanced ICT technology) and the capability to react flexibly on dynamic changes will also become crucial factors for internal Shared Service Organizations. From the external service provider view time performance and flexibility/adaptability of the service delivery (as well as a competitive price, quality and risk) are highly ranked goals.

Key value benefits are the ultimate single, identifiable, extractable measurement categories. These are based on:

- Monetary values (cost and working capital)
- Quality measures (qualitative or quantitative measures, such as types of error, error rates, timeliness of execution)
- Risk exposure measures (probability measures)
- Quantity units (time measures or input/output relations of productivity measures)
- Flexibility and adaptability indicators to measure the capability and response to dynamic change

Measuring only makes sense if the boundaries of the *measured system* (or the contextual environment) are clear. Those can be *structural boundaries* (such as the organizational corporate level) or *process boundaries* (business processes such as Order-to-Cash). Both can be broken down into more granular structures and processes. Structural and process boundaries together with the key value benefits provide a frame into which all the articulated reasons can be grouped. Theoretically, all key value benefits can be applied to any level of boundaries.

Each key value benefit category, with regard to its context, has its own level of focus. Operational and strategic aspects may overlap.

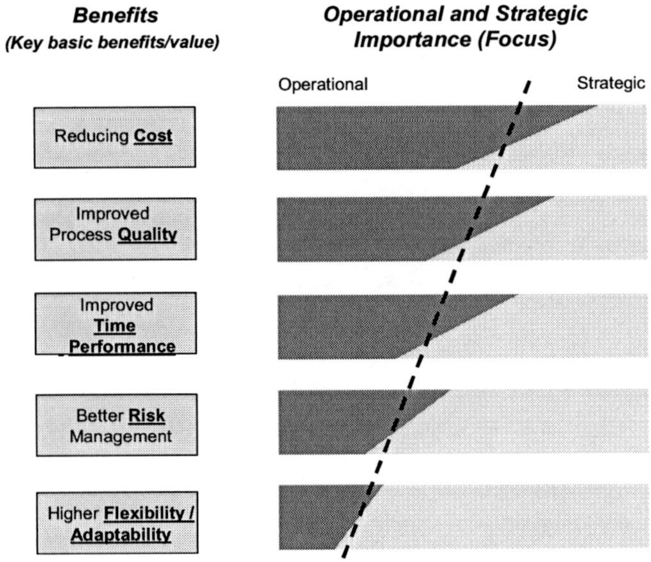

Fig. 11: Operational and Strategic Focus of Key Value Benefits

The range shown in the figure is for illustrative purposes only. Operational and strategic focus may change over time. For instance, early Shared Service implementations were heavily determined by cost cutting approaches. After the initial launch of Shared Service the second wave concentrated on quality and productivity improvements.

1.3.2 Practice: Reason for introducing Shared Service

Henkel:

"When I joined the process in 2002, we thought about how we could improve financial accounting at the company. We noticed two things; a) we didn't know how expensive we were. We were hearing in the markets, and from Hackett, that companies with Shared Services had roughly 35% lower financial costs than companies without them. And b), that a paradigm had collapsed, the idea of lower costs with higher quality through standardization, simplification and optimization." [Interview with Dr. Carlo Mackrodt, Henkel]

SAP:

"We think of the Shared Service itself as a significant motor and catalyst for the change in the finance sector. You can see that in the fact that the skills profiles of the CFOs are changing, the demands made on employees are changing. They are changing because we are extracting the

transactional issues out of the activity portfolios of individual employees in our country organizations and are pushing them a bit to make them shift their focus. The whole thing is ultimately a driver for change in the finance sector, but also at SAP, as we get used to working with virtual finance sectors.
The ultimate aim from the CFO point of view is achieving better governance and increased transparency, but quality is also an aspect, of course – we want things to be posted quickly, done quickly, and at the end of the day we want to be as efficient as possible, both in terms of operational excellence and cost. Those are our main drivers, so to speak."
"… And then of course there is the finance transformation issue, one which is becoming more and more obvious because it is turning the organization on its head, as well as altering mindsets." [Interview with Peter Rasper, SAP]

Solvay:
"We were relatively late to the game of the shared services center. Officially we started in 2005, but we started to study it in 2003. The reason it took a little bit longer is that Solvay decided to follow a strategy of BPM, business process management. That means the first priority was put on "redesign first and transform after." [Interview with Guy de Mercier, Solvay]

Surrey County Council:
"I think there were two key drivers, one was obviously the service delivery. It was critical that we continue to deliver a service philosophy. And in these days we got to deliver Swedish style services with American prices. In simple terms it means more for less. When we looked at our operations, they were very diverse, very split off, and one of the most obvious solutions was to get things into one place and deliver. And I think the other driver behind it was of course technology itself, it was coming clearer and clearer to us that one of the big 21st-century catalysts of the local government is going to be technology. So we wanted to make sure that we were putting in place all the best practice we can find." [Interview with Graham White, Surrey County Council]

1.4 Shared Services Benefits and Obstacles

1.4.1 Benefits

Former non-core business processes become core business processes of the Shared Service Organization. The range of reasons for implementing Shared Services varies. Some of them are directly related to the key value objectives like cost, performance time, risk or flexibility needs. Thus, when trying to find answers to reasons and key value objectives the picture is blurred. Out of the many different lists of reasons and empirical studies, reduction of cost and improving quality (regarding timeliness and accuracy of tasks, error reduction) are the most important and frequently mentioned factors for implementing Shared Service. The concentration of expertise (employees) at one location provides the opportunity to leverage the economies of scale and to improve and streamline business processes. Centralizing and specializing suitable tasks (such as highly repetitive, non-value adding transactional tasks) leads to lower duration and execution time and thus to higher productivity.

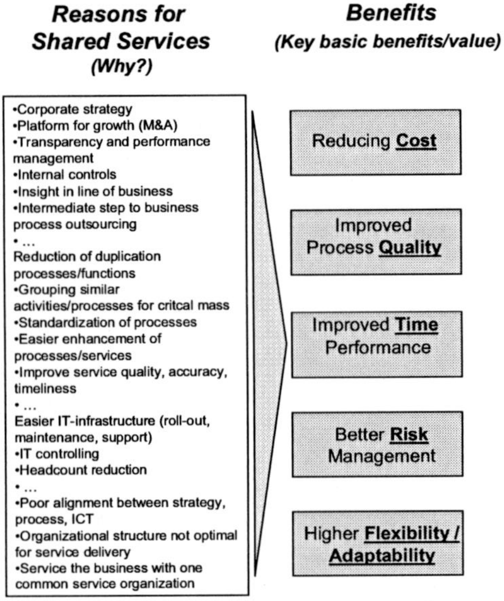

Fig. 12: Reasons and key basic benefits for introducing Shared Services

We live in a highly dynamic environment with high-speed changes (economic, jurisdictional, social, technical). Structures and processes have to adapt quickly to those changes. Flexibility in changing business processes and/or their sourcing assignments is a critical key value. Typical examples are:

- Easier enhancement, splitting or combining of existing processes/services
- Changing the execution resource (out- or in-sourcing to/from an external service provider)

• Speedy integration of merger and acquisitions into the existing system landscape

Cost reduction is the most important and frequently mentioned factor over time for implementing Shared Service. However, priorities may change over time due to legal requirements such as the effects of SOX in managing risk and compliance.

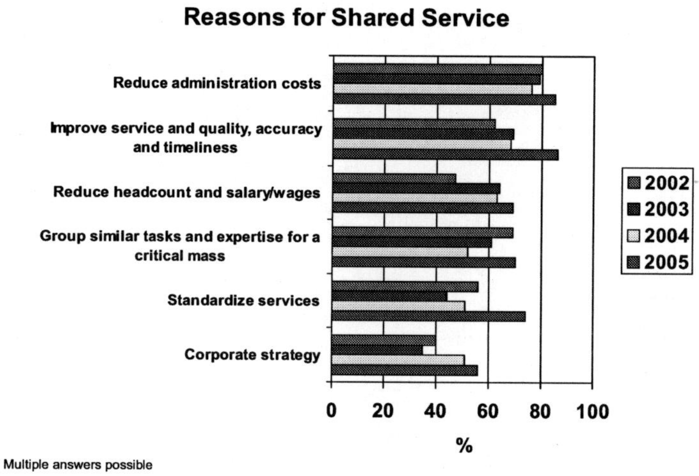

Fig. 13: Reasons for Deployment of Shared Service organizations – Empirical Study

Source: Hackett (2005a, 11)

Other studies show a primary focus on the quality aspects of tasks executed in a Shared Service hub.

The following illustrative diagram shows a qualitative guideline what kind of value can be achieved from the basic key value objectives (cost, time performance, quality, risk, flexibility) based on the different service delivery approaches.

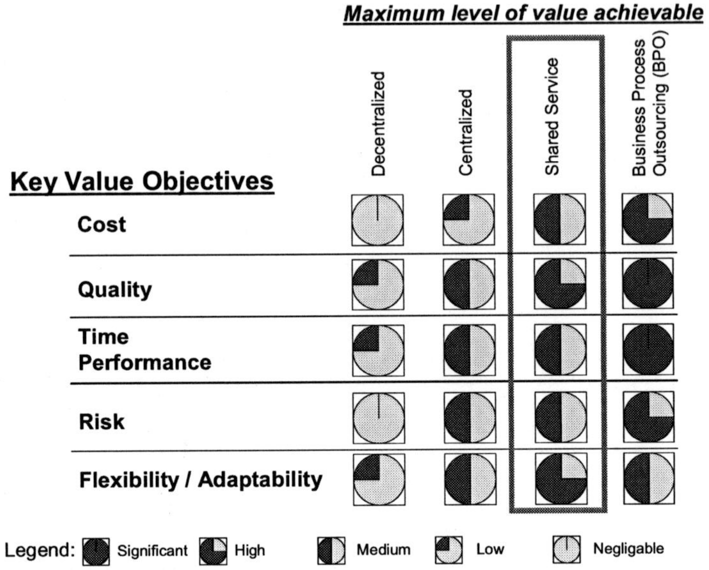

Fig. 4: Value achievable depending on service delivery model organization

The maximum value achievable is based on a typical client and provider and depends on the maturity level of both parties involved.

1.4.1.1 Benefits for Shared Services in Finance

Companies operating F&A functions as Shared Services operate at 67 % lower cost (compared to the median) of F&A. According to a recent benchmarking study by the American/SAP User Group (ASUG) in May 2006 the cost can be further broken down in the particular F&A functions.

Tab. 4: Cost of F&A breakdown per function

Cost of Finance (% of revenue)	100% Shared	Nothing Shared
Accounts Payable	0.04 %	0.07 %
Accounts Receivable	0.01 %	0.20 %
Budgeting and Forecasting	0.02 %	0.08 %
Business and Operations Analysis	0.01 %	0.11 %
Cash Management	0.00 %	0.01 %
Collections	0.01 %	0.04 %
Cost Accounting and Analysis	0.04 %	0.05 %
Credit	0.01 %	0.01 %
Customer Billing	0.01 %	0.04 %
Expense	0.02 %	0.01 %
Finance Strategy and Leadership	0.03 %	0.09 %
Fixed Assets	0.01 %	0.02 %
G/L and Financial Closing	0.05 %	0.13 %

Source: ASUG (2006), n=250 companies

1.4.1.2 Benefits for Shared Services in Human Resources

Cost reduction is a significant benefit, but Reilly (2000) notes the main quality improvement elements in some detail.
Human Resources have a desire to:

- Be more professional in the work it does,
- Achieve greater consistency and accuracy,
- Be more aware of best practice internally and externally,
- Use better processes to complete its work, and
- Deliver work on time and on budget.

This would deliver an incremental improvement in service, but Reilly goes on to note that the research uncovered a significant drive for HR to become more customer orientated. He summarized this as follows:

- Being consumer-, not producer-driven,
- Become more accessible (open more hours and ease the process of contact),
- Improve the supply of information,
- Offering better quality support in-line with customer needs, and
- Operating user-friendly services.

He also stressed the desire for continuous improvement — to offer better services on a consistent basis. By introducing this model, senior HR people were looking to affect an attitude change, a move to customer service rather than policy enforcement. Clearly, the desire and evidence point to shared service being more than just cost reduction exercise.

Shared service is here to stay, and is proven at many organizations. Nevertheless, is important to understand the risks and disadvantages of shared service. Reilly notes a number of disadvantages of shared service:

- Neglecting the importance of the knowledge and experience of those who performed administrative roles in the past. The loss of personal relationships based on knowledge and culture
- The risk of deskilling some administrative jobs to the point of tedium
- Asking too much of the business facing HR managers in concentrating on strategy and change management.
- Potential difficulties for career development because of overspecialization
- Boundary management issues – where does policy end and implementation begin
- Communication difficulties
- Absence of accountability as HR managers in the business have no control of the quality of service delivered by the shared service center
- Lack of local knowledge (esp. in heavily centralized shared service)
- Loss of face to face contact
- Large scale capital investment

It is interesting to note that technology is not seen as an inhibiting factor, and that like most large-scale projects, change and people management issues dominate. The management of change is the single greatest risk.
According to Machin and Williamson [Machin/Williamson 2001]:
"While HR professionals see themselves as guardians of change management and are happy to oversee the implementation of such programs within the organization, they may be unwilling to embrace change themselves."
Factors to be considered to minimize loss of knowledge and over specialization include job rotation and regular training. The challenges that organizations face in deploying shared service apply equally to HR.

1.4.1.3 Practice: Benefits in Shared Service

Henkel:

"So everything we were talking about in 2002 has been realized: We have lower costs with higher quality and better standards, and the company is better prepared for all eventualities, people are better able to pick up slack in the system, access data centrally and so on. That's one point where we've said that we won't be transforming Germany just yet, but the Benelux countries may come aboard somewhat sooner. They are keen to get into the SSC because they've noticed that the costs are simply lower." (Interview with Dr. Carlo Mackrodt, Henkel]

Siemens:

"... The figures have been published. Since 2003, we have reduced our cost by 40%."

"... Of course, cost is the main factor when you set up a Shared Service center. By reducing the number of locations from 90 to six, and now we have just two, we have enormous cost advantages. The transparency and economies of scale that allow me to group areas together all results in cost savings. In other words, the cost advantages always took quality and service into account. When you think about these three variables here, you have to really balance them out, so that you can reduce costs, but keep the level of service and quality the same, or even improve it." [Interview with Wolfgang Leitmanstetter, Siemens]

Surrey County Council:

"There was, there were significant savings. And some that is of course is what we would call cost avoidance. The cost of delivering local government services has year on year being going up much, much higher than the rate of inflation. And so it wasn't only just about some saving money, it was about stuff in the costs going up anymore. We had pure savings, which of course in HR alone brought in over 9 million pounds and that was mainly around resourcing. In other words, less HR staff do the work. But as well as that we have also been doing a teacher mode to reduce any future project pressure."

"It could be anywhere between 50 and 75%. What I mean, my kind of budget is about 5 million pounds, but I have been given new departments in there, so if I tick them out, just about 2 million pounds, it was 9, so whatever, it is a fraction of 11. So it is pretty impressive. By saying this we didn't just move the budget somewhere else. And we put very, very little into the organization of the shared service center. We are merely 15 or 20 people, but no real costs."

"There has. Yes, in a range of areas. The big efficiencies now are really being driven through all the employee self-service. So it's not about HR doing it quicker, it was about HR not doing it anymore. That's where the real savings are."
[Interview with Graham White, Surrey County Council]

1.4.2 Obstacles and Challenges

The obstacles and challenges to a successful HR outsourcing come from different directions. The results are often a blend of different problems. Nevertheless is it helpful to categorize them and allocate them to the appropriate phase. A phase is a time sequential group of activities which may overlap. In general there are three distinct phases (design, implement, operate) and an overall organizational and management supervision phase across the three phases. Issues come from:

- **Design/Preparation**
  - Structurally inappropriate design of the business processes
  - Poor service definition and service levels
  - Poor pricing structure and/or charging models
  - Poor business case
- **Implementation phase**
  - Poor quality of implementation management skills
  - Poor quality of resources (people, technology) or failure to close deficiencies and gaps before starting the service delivery
- **Operating phase**
  - Poor quality of resources (people, technology) to fulfill the ongoing service delivery
  - Lack of monitoring and control of ongoing operations (poor governance)
- **General organization and management**
  - Lack of support of executive management during preparation/development, implementation and operating phase of Shared Services

According to a survey from the SBPOA (Shared Service and Business Process Outsourcing Association, now: SharedXpertise Forums), the lack of executive management support is the top reason why Shared Services fails.

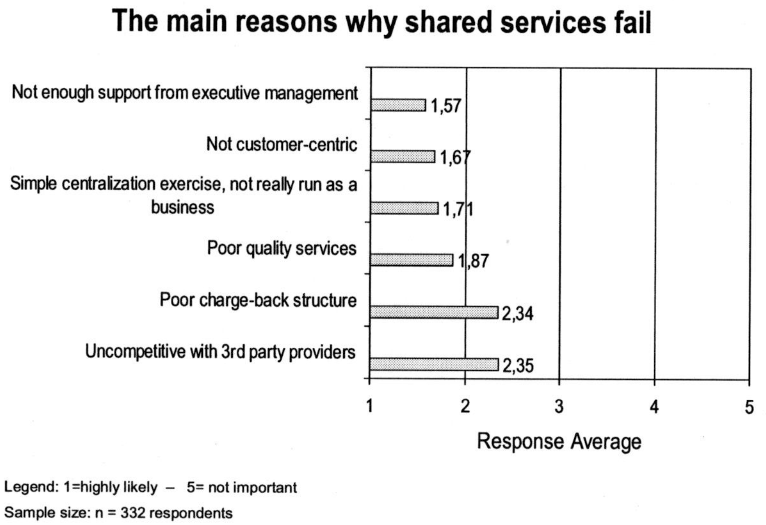

Fig. 14: Main reasons why Shared Services fail
Source: SBPOA (2002)

Companies are using a Shared Service approach as a catalyst for business process and organizational transformation. Enforcement of organizational change could be the main driver. Some people will be affected by this organizational transformation process and may try to block it by creating shadow functions in the replaced organization. The supporting ICT infrastructure has to take that into account and has to be reconfigured according to new authorizations. A complex distributed system landscape could hide the enforced organizational change. Thus an integrated IT system is a good foundation to avoid lack of transparency.

1.4.2.1 Challenges for Shared Services in Finance

According to a survey conducted by SharedXpertise in association with Hewlett Packard (December 2006) technology is still the most significant hurdle to the F&A transformation.

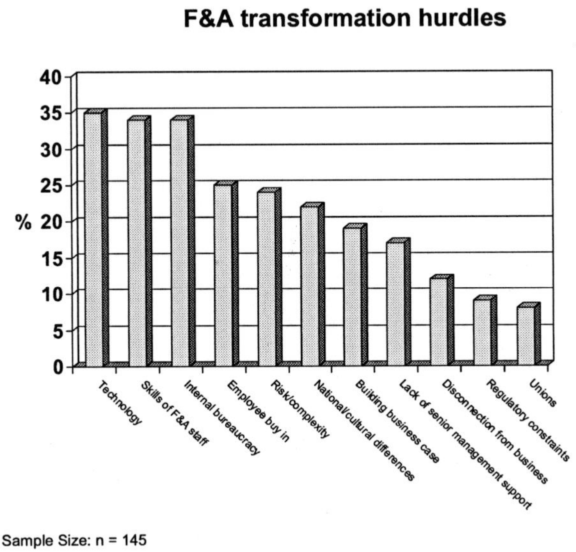

Fig. 15: F&A transformation hurdles
Source: Searle (2006)

The lack of qualified, skilled F&A staff together with internal bureaucracy are on a par with technology as major challenging factors. It is not a surprise that those three main transformation hurdles belong to the three different major components of every organizational task (process, people and technology) and should be viewed as equally important.

In the figure with general Shared Service failures (study from 2002) without differentiating Shared Service function coverage, the lack of executive support is the dominating reason. This looks different if you just concentrate on financial Shared Services. An explanation could be that both studies are published in different years (2002 vs. 2006) and meanwhile a broad acceptance of Shared Services at board level has become the rule instead of the exception.

1.4.2.2 Challenges for Shared Services in Human Resources

The challenges in HR shared service are largely people and change related. Recent studies from TPI[6] and ADP[7] show a clear dominance of

[6] TPI is the leading global advisory firm for helping organizations to optimize their business operations through the best combination of insourcing, offshoring, shared services and outsourcing.

insufficient personal skills as the most challenging factor (people resources).[8]

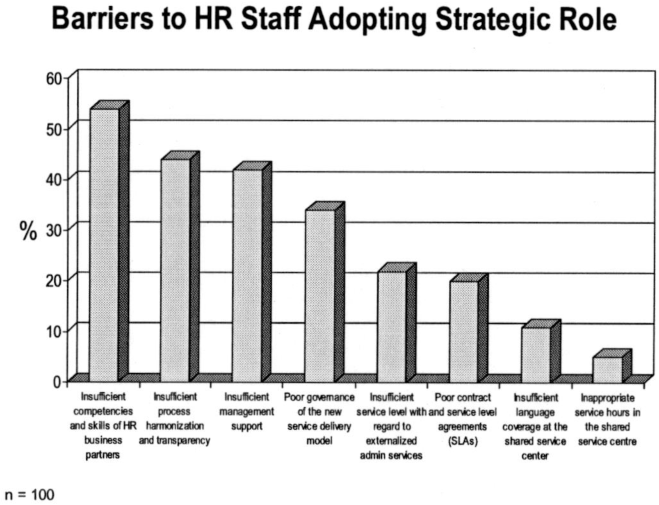

Fig. 16: Obstacles and Challenges for Shared Services in Human Resources (TPI 2007)

Source: HROA (2007, 15)

[7] ADP Employer Services is worldwide one of the leading service provider for payroll and travel and expense services.

[8] Study TPI: HR Transformation: Myth or Reality, TPI[8], Report 01/2007, p.15, with 100 HR decision makers worldwide; Study ADP: HR Transformation Survey – A global vision, ADP[8], November 2006, Survey with 195 decision makers, global organizations

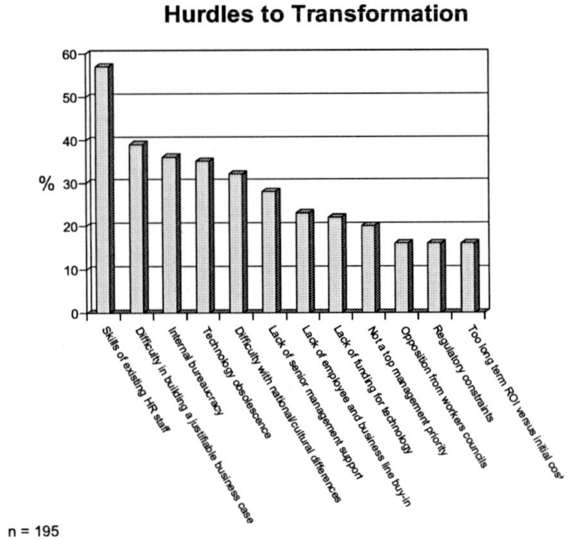

Fig. 17: Obstacles and Challenges for Shared Services in Human Resources (ADP 2006)

Source: HROA (2006, 17)

Shared service doesn't exist in a vacuum, so the success of a shared service project is largely tied up with a broader HR transformation exercise. HR executives are often not as convincing as their finance colleagues in building the business case for transformation, so the HR case may stall before it really gets moving, or not have the funding correctly estimated. The global vs. local factors are often underestimated. Labor law and Unions, as well as employee conservativism are major inhibitors.

Compared to financial shared services, HR shared services has a much broader organizational impact. It impacts every employee and manager, so the risk of public failure is far stronger. As will be explored in depth later, line managers can be a major obstacle to success, as often they have a vested interest in the current model. Keeping top management actively involved is also a challenge, as without this, the inevitable escalations are tough to manage. HR shared service tends to rely heavily on employee and manager self-service, so there is some technology risk.

Apart from the business process design, the quality of the implementation project seems to be a major contributor to a successful Shared Service operation (seven out of 12 criteria in the ADP study deal with implementation issues).

1.4.2.3 Practice: Challenges in introducing Shared Service

Marks & Spencer:

"I think the thing for me is that the experience almost dictates what makes Shared services centers successful. Having the right leadership is key. By leadership, I mean people who will use drive, who use judgment, who use influence, who use passion, who use emotional energy in the right way to make sure that things actually happen." [Interview with Dan Foley, Marks & Spencer]

Surrey County Council:

Biggest obstacles we experienced were from the line managers. The biggest challenge is to coach the organization, moving it into a culture seeing technology as an advantage, not a disadvantage.

2 Benefit Levers - How are Shared Service benefits achieved?

What kind of measures, tools, methodologies and techniques are used to achieve the desired benefits? The reasons articulated for setting up a Shared Service can be (directly or indirectly) linked to basic, fundamental benefits like cost, time/productivity performance, quality, risk and flexibility needs. Generic levers or principles to achieve the goals are organizing activities of *bundling, focusing, standardizing* and *relocating*.

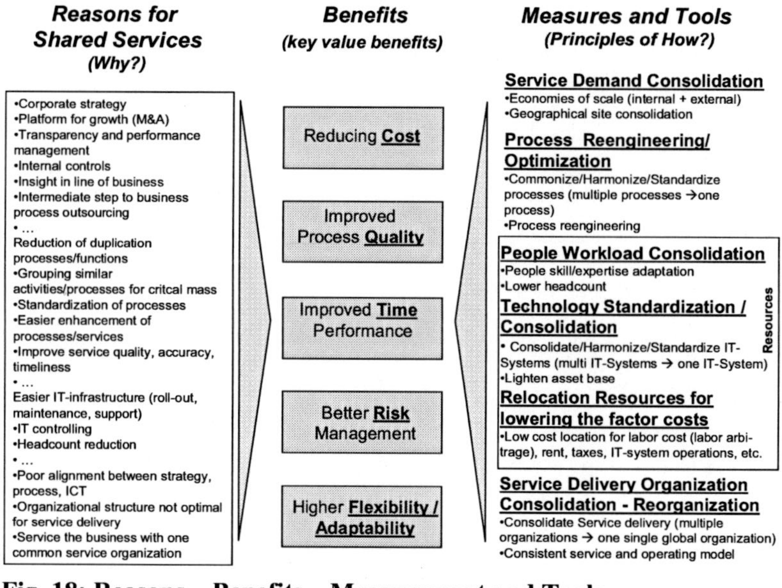

Fig. 18: Reasons – Benefits – Measurement and Tools

The achievements have their roots from the previous mentioned basic ideas or principles to achieve the desired results:

- Bundling/consolidating service demand (for economies of scale)
- Bundling/consolidating the organizational service delivery (centralized, decentralized or virtual service delivery sites; organizational settings)
- Focusing on business processes (focus for instance on core and non-core activities) leads to reengineering with simplifying (including removing process steps or entire sub-processes)
- Standardizing, harmonizing and optimizing business process activities

- Standardizing and harmonizing resources (execution resources such as ICT systems)
- Relocating decisions for lowering the factor costs (such as people workload shift to low cost locations for labor arbitrage)

The following figure provides a guideline for potential cost savings.

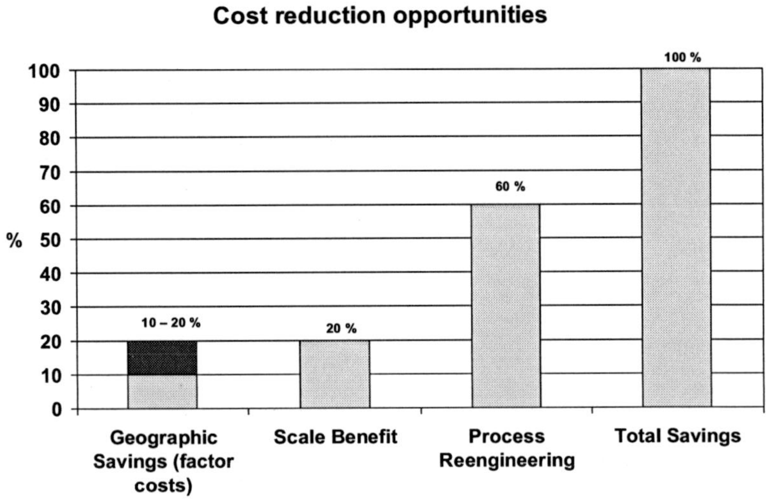

Fig. 19: Cost savings in Shared Services
Source: Bread et. al. (2004)

Geographic savings covers cost savings related to lower factor costs like rent, labor, taxes, and so on. Scale savings include people, technical (IT Systems) and organizational and managerial efficiencies. Interestingly, process reengineering of business processes leads all categories of shared service cost savings. Eliminating redundancies, simplifying business processes and applying more automation are, according to the figure above, the most beneficial.

2.1 Service Demand Consolidation

Aggregation of similar service demand is the basic business foundation of every Shared Service center. Consolidation of service demand is based on the accumulation of volumes from different geographical areas and different workload and task categorization flavors with various degrees of configurations (such as quality).

2.1.1 Economies of scale

Economies of scale can be achieved for transactional as well as for transformational activities. The primary source for driving down the cost of transactional services is the aggregation of volume. The reason for centralizing transformational (such as decision support and consulting) services is the sharing or bottleneck of skilled resources.

Contributors to the economies of scale can be distinguished as *people work effects* and *technology effects*. Both effects are based on the variation of volumes (scale of quantities). People effects are based on the *learning curve* of repetitive similar activities. Technology effects are based on experience: that, with increased company size, the expected manufacturing costs will decrease. This is heavily influenced by fix-cost-distribution[9] of technology investments with higher quantity output.

Economic benefits of transaction processing are highly affected by the amount of service volume (scale). Long-term benefits are not secured via a move to low-cost countries. The price of labor increases and the labor arbitrage effect decreases over time. Scale benefits will last longer due to better resource utilization (people, technology) which leads to higher productivity. The ability to meet the capacity demand, to take advantage of a bigger labor workforce with better skill-matching possibilities and an industrialized service delivery approach are just a few benefits to mention.

The following diagram uses an example of Human Resource Processes (Payroll and Time Attendance) to show how economies of scale can be achieved regarding cost performance. Many influences contribute to the curve. But it should be good enough to serve as a rough guideline and orientation.

[9] Fix-Cost-Distribution: Distribution (to variable) of fix (from output independent) costs over the output volume with the goal to calculate the total unit cost per unit.

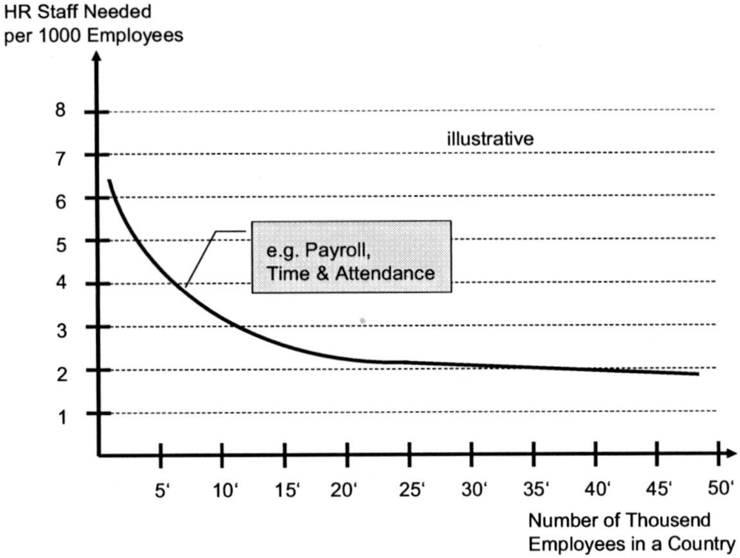

Fig. 20: Economies of scale in Human Resource processing of payroll, time and attendance

2.1.2 Geographical scope and reach

The source of service demand has a multi-dimensional view. Coverage of services is not only directed to the geographical scope or reach of a shared service hub. Multiple aspects must be considered:

- Geographical area (local, national, regional, global)
- Service (workload, task) categorization options:
  - Functional scope (F&A, HR)
  - Business processes (such as end-to-end processes like order-to-cash or purchase-to-pay)
  - Degree of value-add (transactional or transformational)
- Service (workload, task) portfolio configuration (depth and quality)

Studies regarding the geographical coverage of Shared Services show a similar result. The distribution picture looks mostly the same.

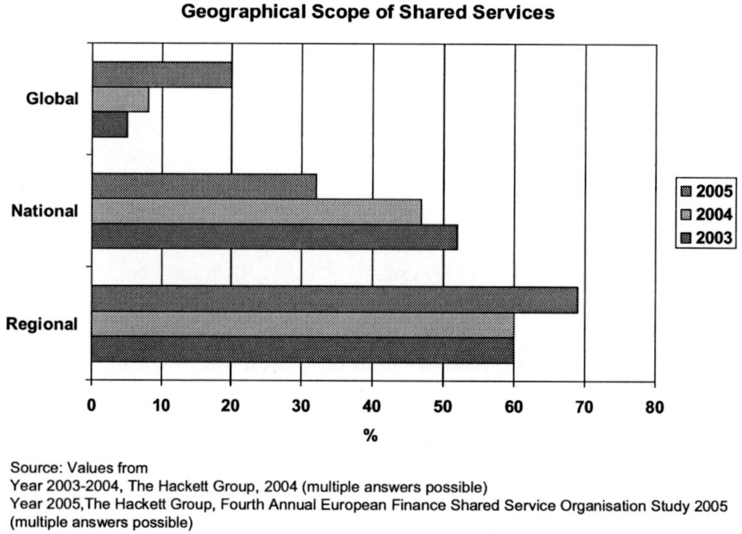

Fig. 21: Geographical scope of internal organizational Shared Services coverage

Source: Values from Hackett (2003, 2004, 2005)

There is a strong tendency to establish regional coverage of Shared Services. Global coverage is still a minority.

2.1.3 Service Portfolio Configuration

Every Shared Service Organization has to decide what kind of business services will be provided (Service Catalogue) and to what degree of depth, width and quality. Failing to document the services in such aspects will lead to potential dissatisfaction of service clients and, from the service provider perspective, the danger to under- or over-deliver services.

2.1.4 Practice: Service Demand Consolidation

Philips:

“Yes, scale is very important in this business to generate optimum savings, but also to be able to invest in technology, training and process improvements.” [Interview with Michel de Zeeuw, Philips]

2.2 Process Reengineering / Optimization

2.2.1 Harmonize/Standardize Business Processes

The dominant reason for introducing a Shared Service concept is to achieve cost benefits. Each business process has an associated risk. One of the major concerns is the fulfillment of *compliance* needs. Compliance is a summary of regulatory, safety and privacy needs. Simplification and transparency of processes help to fulfill those requirements. Ideally, there are only standardized business processes in use, but it is clear that variations of processes will be enforced by local legal requirements and cannot be avoided or controlled by the enterprise itself. But there are common business processes which can be standardized across companies, and even countries, on such a high level that they become known as *commodity services.*

Some HR processes are easy to standardize globally, others, because of compliance and cultural challenges have strong local flavors. When building a shared service centre that processes multiple countries, you need to make that you don't underestimate the national differences.

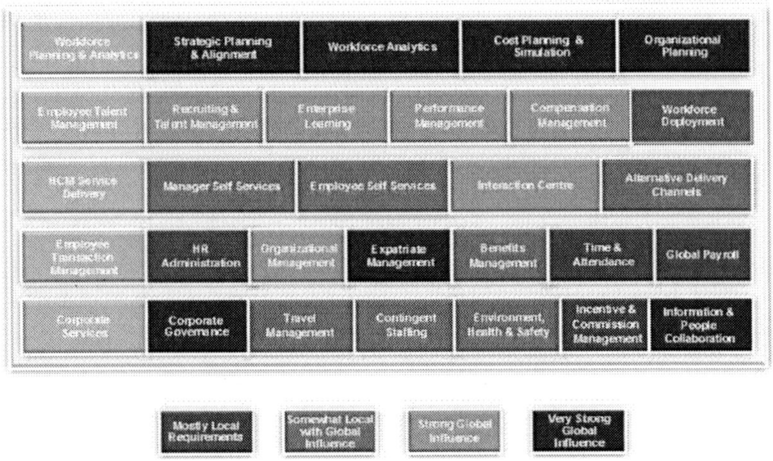

Fig. 22: Example: SAP Human Capital Management Solution Map

F&A processes have a more standardization potential then other business processes like procurement, HR or ICT processes considered for shared services. The reason is the high degree of regulation based on laws and regulations (such as General Accepted Accounting Principles, Taxation, Trading). External governance bodies are setting the rules for accepted F&A transaction processing.

2.2.2 Reengineering End-to-End Processes

One of the key differences between Shared Service and centralization is the clear split between tasks remaining in the business units and those moving to a Shared Service hub. Shared Service Organizations are supporting multiple clients (business units) of a common (or shared) business process. Splitting activities between local business entities and the central Shared Service hub has implications for the design and operating flow of the IT system landscape.

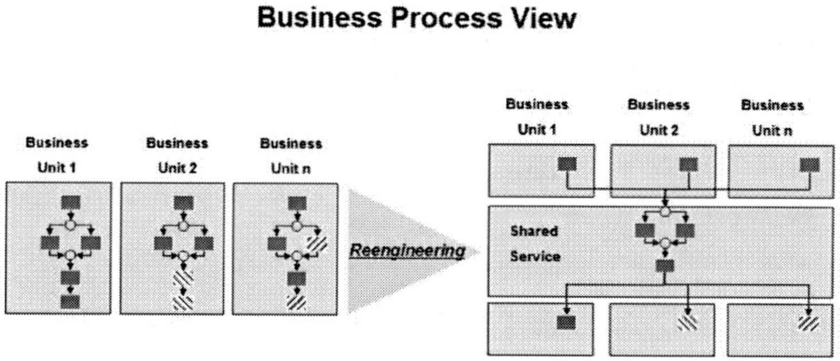

Fig. 23: Reengineering Business Processes

Reengineering the business process flow could simplify the entire end-to-end process. The following customer examples provide a good understanding of process flow changes for simplification and transparency reasons. The ultimate goal is to increase the portion of 'approved' purchase orders. This would streamline the process in the Shared Service hub because there is no additional communication necessary (such as via a workflow) with the ordering party.

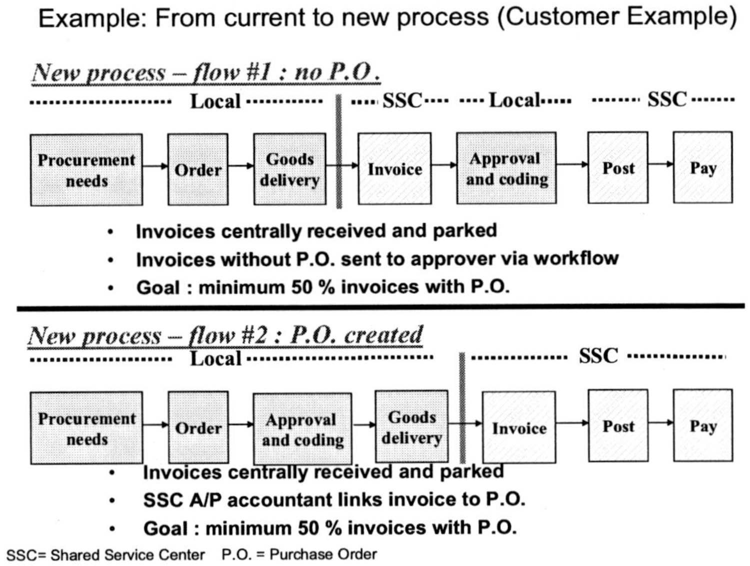

Fig. 24: Customer example of Purchase-to-Pay Process reengineering

After the reengineering of business processes, the technical IT system landscape can be designed or mapped. The process split between business and the Shared Service Organization has an impact on the design and distribution of the IT system landscape. This has implications for:

- Data management (master data, number ranges, accounting information)
- Customizing settings (parameterization of a standard application package)
- Workflow (cross application and IT systems)

2.3 Resource Consolidation

Pooling of *people and technology* resources is one of the major levers to:

- Reduce cost, because of positive effects of bigger size (economies of scale allow easier capacity leveling, sharing of personnel skills, reduction of redundant infrastructure),
- Achieve consistency in the quality of service execution, because of applying consistent corporate policies
- Increase the productivity by doing the same workload with fewer people.

- Increase the productivity by doing the same workload with fewer people. This eases the implementation and adaptation of business processes through central trigger, execution, control and governance (transparency and harmonization of processes). It is also possible to shift the workload to places with lower resource cost (such as for labor arbitrage.

2.3.1 People Workload Consolidation

HR is one pillar of execution resources. Consolidating the labor force provides potential benefits, as we have mentioned. Benefits are achieved through relocation of workload to locations with lower labor cost, lower headcount (for the same workload), and by sharing personnel skills (expertise, knowledge).

2.3.1.1 Relocation of Workload (Labor Arbitrage)

We discussed earlier how cost savings are a major driver for Shared Service adoption. Part of the cost savings come from process improvements and more efficiency, but many organizations look to labor arbitrage as a mechanism to significantly lower costs.

As Hackett noted in a recent article, "a *Fortune* 500 company can cut its HR staff by 44 percent through offshoring various HR processes."[10]

In countries where unemployment and wages vary very significantly by region, it is possible to achieve considerable savings by setting up the Shared Service Centre in lower-cost areas. This is very common in the US, and has also been popular in the UK, with many banks moving HR and Finance processing away from the expensive South East. This mirrors what happened with call centers.

Arbitrage within one country is less politically sensitive, and avoids scaremongering over issues such as data privacy. Organizations are advised to explore local arbitrage, as often regions have tax breaks and other incentives to move processing. This is often the only option open to public sector organizations. For example, the prison services in the UK are setting up their HR, Finance and Procurement Shared Service Centre in Newport, Wales.

In Germany, BASF set up its HR Shared Service Center in Berlin, where unemployment is higher than other parts of Germany. This was in part to gain a labor arbitrage advantage.

---

[10] http://www.workforce.com/section/00/article/24/59/18.html

Nearshoring and Offshoring

Many multinational organizations have set up global Shared Service models, where they service many countries from a single centre. For the last five years, there has been a explosion of Shared Service activity in major Eastern European cities such as Prague, Budapest and Cracow, with SAP, Diageo, Shell, Accenture, Phillip Morris all establishing hubs.

Labor arbitrage though, is fickle. As more and more Shared Service Centers are set up in a region, the competition for labor intensifies, and unemployment drops. This increases employee turnover, and can dramatically increase wage costs. This is already happening in some of the major Eastern European capital cities, so the next wave of Shared Service Centers are likely to be set up in tier-two cities.

A recent study[11] from the Everest Group shows that wage inflation in offshore outsourcing is over-stated:

"The labor arbitrage opportunity -- created by the significant wage gap between industrialized and developing nations -- will continue to drive offshore outsourcing for many years," said Joe Fernandes, Managing Research Director at Everest Research Institute. "Despite salary increases in key offshore markets, the idea that India and other key markets will price themselves out of the outsourcing business in the near-term is unfounded."

In the report, Sustainability of Labor Arbitrage, Everest estimates that the labor arbitrage benefit that U.S. companies can achieve by outsourcing IT Application, Development and Maintenance services, which account for a large share of offshore activity, can be sustained for: 18 to 25 years with Asian markets, such as India, China and the Philippines, 3 to 6 years with Central European markets, such as Poland and the Czech Republic, and 30+ years with Mexico.

For labor arbitrage to be really successful, it is important to standardize processes where ever possible. As Hackett note "Once processes have been centralized and standardized, they become portable, and it becomes much easier to take advantage of labor arbitrage opportunities available offshore, either through captive operations in low-cost labor markets or by outsourcing."[12]

---

[11] http://www.hroassociation.org/file/3416/wage-inflation-in-offshore-outsourcing-markets-is-over-stated-according-to-everest-report.html

[12] See: http://www.hr.com/servlets/sfs?&t=/Default/gateway&i=1116423256281&b=1116423256281&applica

2.3.1.2 Skill/Expertise Adaptation

Designing and implementing a Shared Service Center requires fundamentally different skills from managing a traditional HR or Finance department. The design and set up are by definition a project, and require strong project management skills and experience. The ability to manage change is fundamental. In this sense, a Shared Service project does not fundamentally differ from any large scale transformational exercise, in terms of skills required.

However, once a Shared Service Center is up and running, it also requires a different mindset from traditional HR and Finance departmental management. In our many interviews and discussions, we heard time and time again that Shared Service Centers need to be "Service focused and Operational".

Many HR Shared Service Centers are lead by people who have a strong operations rather than HR background. This has the advantage of bringing a more "business" focus to the centre, helping drive the KPIs, process, measurement and efficiency, not traditional HR skill sets. Nevertheless, part of the leadership team needs to have a strong grasp of the HR customer issues and demands, as being solely focused on transactional management runs the risk of misalignment.

With the maturing of Shared Services, we now see universities and technical schools building Shared Services into academic curricula. This is a welcome step.

As more processes move to Shared Services, we notice that several companies are establishing an overall head of services, who takes control of all Shared Service activities. Siemens have built a global Shared Services Organization in this way. Reporting into the head of Shared Services are both HR and Financial Shared Services. This model allows for greater synergies with Shared Services, and also helps to establish Shared Services as a career path and discipline within the organization.

---

tion=story&active=no&ParentID=1119278123280&StoryID=1168225523527&xref=http%3A//www.google.com/search%3Fq%3DHR+and+Labor+arbitrage%26hl%3Den%26

2.3.1.2.1 Management skills

By way of example, here is a job description to help illustrate the type of skills and experience profiles organizations are looking for, taken from a mix of organization type and job level.

The following is a job description for the role of the Head of HR Service Delivery for a large public sector role. (We have changed the name of the organization to XYZ.)

The Role:
Reporting to the Chief People Officer, the Director, HR Service Delivery will lead the development of a best in class HR Shared Services function, focusing initially on working with the existing management team to identify what needs to be done to drive cost from the HR and learning Shared Services business; to improve service quality; and to embed new behaviors and ways of working in the wider XYZ business community.

Responsibilities:
To work collaboratively as a member of the HR&L senior management team to:

- Lead the delivery of a range of integrated, high quality, customer-focused employee services that meet service level agreements to circa 100,000 departmental employees, including:
    1. HR transactional processing
    2. Learning and development administration
    3. HR advice services via self service, contact centers and specialist teams.
- Ensure that all staff within HR Service Delivery are motivated, developed and managed so that individual and collective performance meets the needs of customers.
- Drive continuous improvement and innovation in the delivery of HR Shared Services, benchmarking existing services against best practice in Government and the public sector; identifying action to meet best in class benchmark standards; and building up metrics of cost and resource use of the various employee services in order to support the drive to achieve best in class performance, as necessary.
- Ensure the HR service delivery is properly aligned to the achievement of Departmental policy and objectives and that all HR shared services remain compliant with relevant Departmental standards and legislative requirements.

- Work collaboratively with colleagues in other corporate service streams to develop an integrated Shared Services model, which is best in class and equipped to meet future challenges
- Identify, shape and specify HR services for provision to new customer bases, as appropriate.

Key relationships:

1. XYZ top management team
2. Chief People Officer and Chief Finance Officer
3. Senior managers and business partners of customer groups
4. Shared Services and HR&L transformation project teams
5. HR&L management team
6. HR&L Service Delivery management team.

The Person

Essential Experience:

(1) Experience of providing high quality HR shared transactional services in large-scale complex organizations with diverse stakeholder communities at a senior level

(2) Demonstrable experience of working effectively within a matrix organization

(3) Senior management experience in a customer focused organization with evidence to support a track record of delivery

(4) Experience of developing, motivating and managing individuals

(5) Experience of sharing ideas and information with others and of ensuring that innovation is applied to clear strategic purpose and demonstrably productive results.

Desirable:

Experience of service and commercial management of external suppliers would be an advantage

Skills and Knowledge:

1. Relevant professional qualification or membership of a professional body (e.g. MCIPD) is desirable
2. Knowledge of current best practice in HR Shared Services

Evidence of the ability:

1. To provide the drive and focus in the delivery of excellence in customer service
2. To communicate effectively in order to translate strategic objectives into high quality service delivery
3. To influence outcomes at a senior executive level
4. To identify and implement innovative ways to improve efficiency and effectiveness in the use of resources and assets
5. To build relationships across a wide and diverse customer base

6. To be a team player who excels in a collaborative environment

Professional Skills for Government:

As well as the qualities and skills above, the post holder will need to demonstrate to a high level the Professional Skills for Government (PSG). The PSG skills framework is at www.civilservice.gov.uk/skills. The four elements of the framework are: Leadership, Professional Expertise, Broader Experience and Core Skills. The core skills are:

1. People Management
2. Financial Management
3. Project and Program Management
4. Analysis and Use of Evidence
5. Communications and Marketing
6. Strategic Thinking

Clearly, leading a Shared Service Center is a demanding and challenging role.

2.3.1.2.2 Execution Staff skills and expertise

This is an example of a job description in a recruitment Shared Service Centre in a global professional services firm.

Job Description:

Member of the HR Shared Services Center (HRSSC) Operations team who supports the Sourcing Senior Associate in the coordination and execution of Sourcing activities housed in the Shared Services Center. In collaboration with the HRSSC Sourcing Senior Associate, the Sourcing specialist is responsible for the tactical execution of centralized HRSSC Sourcing support services to local market Lines of Service (Advisory, Assurance, Tax) and Internal Firm Services (IFS) sourcing teams. Strategic & Technical Orientation.

Job Content:

Functional understanding of HRSSC compliance and operational processes; deeper technical understanding of on-boarding protocols and related systems

Range of Impact:

Able to evaluate circumstances and, based on scope of issue and working knowledge of on-boarding processes and related systems, make independent recommendations regarding course of action to resolve issues. Consults with On-Boarding Senior Associate to address issues of a more difficult nature or which require greater skill set expertise or judgment.

Scope of Responsibility:
Member of the HRSSC Operations Compliance team who assists in the execution of department specific responsibilities and/or initiatives. No budget or direct risk management responsibilities.
Responsibilities:

- Respond/coordinate response to new hire pre-start inquires in an accurate and timely manner.
- Consult with HRSSC Senior Associate or other functional groups as necessary (Market Sourcing, Learning & Education (L&E), HRSSC Compliance, etc.)
- Working with HRSSC Senior Associate to coordinate candidate L&E start date scheduling, registration, and travel logistics related to new hire training
- Initiate background check and independence compliance processes
- Conduct related follow-up with candidates as necessary/appropriate
- Build strong working relationships with market sourcing colleagues and other relevant HR network members
- Post positions for Campus and Experienced hire needs
- Coordinate candidate interviews and related travel arrangements with market sourcing teams
- Coordinate reference checks for Campus and Experienced New Hires
- Coordinate with Compliance Group (Visa Watch) to initiate visa processing for candidates, as applicable
- Develop relationships with Campus career centers at assigned schools
- Prepare candidate/new hire correspondence (offer letters, rejection letters, information packets)
- Process candidate expense reimbursements
- Generate campus and experienced Sourcing reports for submission to Sourcing Senior Associate
- Build strong working relationships with market sourcing colleagues and HR colleagues related to Sourcing efforts
- Input candidate information into relevant Sourcing database (i.e. Career Curve and/or Recruiting Tracking System (RTS). Maintain data to ensure data quality and completeness of candidate profiles
- Respond/coordinate response to routine Sourcing-related questions from candidates.

Years Experience Required:
2+ years
Education:
Undergraduate Degree (BA, BS) or equivalent experience

Job Requirement Essential:

Minimum of two years experience, preferably in a professional services firm. Demonstrated proficiency in use of relevant technology. Proficiency in firm core competencies, with particular emphasis on contributing to team success, building and sustaining relationships, change agility and focusing on the client.

And from the SAP Shared Service Centre in Prague, here is a requirements posting for a Travel Accounting Specialist:

Role Description:

The successful candidate will be responsible for the timely and accurate performance of the full range of tasks described below.

Key responsibilities:

- Verify and approve travel expenses (accuracy, plausibility and compliance with country tax law)
- Verify and approve hourly activity records
- Reposting of hourly activity records
- Reposting of travel expenses costs
- Ensure timely payments
- Respond to relevant queries

Education:

- Certificate of Secondary Education at the minimum
- Business education
- Accounting education is a plus

Competencies:

- Timeliness
- A strong will to deliver excellent quality
- Continuous improvement of technical skills and efficiency
- Distinctive customer orientation
- Ability to work in international teams
- Good communication skills, both written and verbal
- Flexible work style and ability to work under pressure

Practical experience:

Essential	**Desirable**
Experience in international environment	Working experience within a shared service center SAP experience (Modul FI) Experience in accounting

System knowledge:

Essential	**Desirable**
Basic knowledge of MS Office (Word, Excel, Outlook)	General knowledge of SAP (or if this lacking, other Enterprise Resource Planning systems)

Language skills:
As required

2.3.1.3 Practice: People capabilities

Marks & Spencer:
Here, people's capabilities are addressed on different levels. Leadership is key to design, implement and run a successful Shared Service Center. However, the different stages in setting up Shared Services require different skills. There are three stages which Marks & Spencer distinguishes: the start-up phase, implementation phase and the maturity stage.

Solvay:
"Yes, we need different skills. I tried to meet the challenge to keep the same people. I want to do that, but I do recognize it's difficult. I believe by keeping the same people you build a real company culture.
I'm preparing a vision to keep a shared services center as an engine, an integration engine, and therefore to keep a company culture of people who are capable to promote the change. So to come back, I do believe you need different skills. I do believe that you need skills for redesign. That means you need dedicated skills on business process management first. From there you need skills in preparing the implementation and migration phase, which takes a very tough project team and change management capability. In parallel, you need entrepreneurs who are ready to build from scratch out of nowhere. So you need self-sufficient, self-motivating people.
Then for the optimization phase you need highly analytical people who are able to grow within the organization up to the certification. This is not for the pleasure of having a certification but to understand that you need to optimize every part of a process in order to have the process fully optimized. So yes, we need different skills. What Solvay did was to have another project leader besides me to take care of the redesign. He was a top financial manager too and he worked on that for three years. At the same time I was building the center here, we were reporting together to the executive committee. So in Solvay group they allocated seven people in place for two years. Very often, companies underestimate that need, or they hope to have consultants doing that part of the change management for them. You need a little bit of consultancy to give a push, but you need to do that yourself. Because that phase of knowledge capturing and knowledge transfer is essential." [Interview with Guy de Mercier, Solvay]

2.3.1.4 Practice: People workload consolidation

Philips:

"Shifting jobs is always an issue in some countries. In Europe, it was less of a problem compared to the United States. In Europe, the finance and accounting teams were already small and fragmented. Many of them found a new job within the Philips organization. In the United States it was different. We had bigger teams there and experienced a large turnover of people after we announced the change. But overall there were no major surprises due to the professionalism of our migration teams and of the retained staff." [Interview with Michel de Zeeuw, Philips]

2.3.2 Technology Standardization and Consolidation

By technology, we mean ICT technology, and specifically ICT application systems and ICT tools that support business processes. SSCs have been made possible by the rapid developments in ICT technology. Without those advances, processes could not be effectively concentrated into regional centers, the communication between people would be very hard to structure and moderate, and the vast amounts of data could not be reasonably processed. Therefore, ICT appears as a necessary mandatory condition for SSC deployment and needs to be managed accordingly.

ICT systems play an important role in business operations because of their tight alignment to the real business processes they support. Those supporting ICT systems enable or constrain the business process capabilities and (directly or indirectly) drive the efficiency of Shared Service operations. If the supported functions do not map directly to the business needs, it will be difficult to achieve a workable and successful solution. Choosing the right ICT landscape is a critical decision, because it is capable of affecting the flexibility of future business processes and controlling operational cost.

While cost reduction is the main driver behind Shared Service implementations, ICT is the enabler. According to the cost structure of transactional business processes the biggest portions of costs (about 80%) belong to the category of labor and administration costs. About 20% of the overall cost can be assigned to technology cost (hardware, communication network, software, maintenance and implementation). Choosing the right software will allow the Shared Service Organization to control and reduce the technology cost and capital expenditures. Software-enabled business process standardization and automation will improve the performance time and economies of scale and enable a high degree of labor arbitrage. The following diagram shows the impact of

ICT technology on the service delivery for business services. Regardless how the curve looks, it is mostly accepted that leveraging ICT will lead to lower cost per service unit.

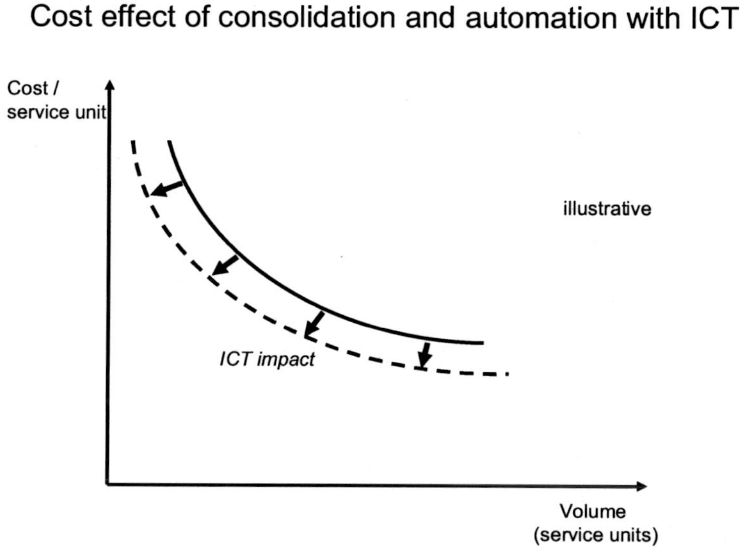

Fig. 25: Leveraging ICT resources to support Shared Service business processes

The effects are based on learning and experience, standardization and consolidation in the operational environment. Consolidation of technical resources provides the opportunity for better utilization of capacity and load balancing.

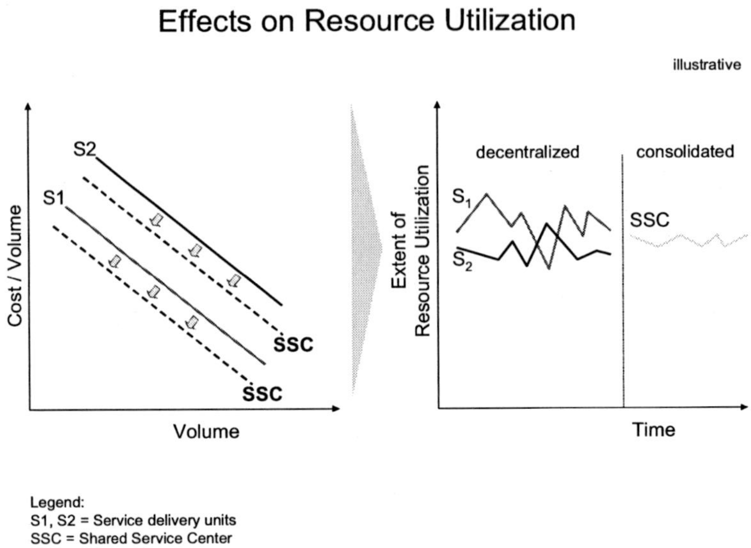

Fig. 26: Effects on resource utilization in Shared Service

According to the Shared Service concept there has to be a clear split of business process responsibilities between the Shared Service Organization and the retained process in the business clients. Thus there are a few key requirements for an ICT solution in *shared service context*:

Functionality
Built-in comprehensive functionalities are mandatory for ICT to keep costs down. Today's standard business application packages covering a broad range of business process know-how are built into the software solutions.

Communication - Integration
A Shared Service approach requires a full integration of processes into the remaining process and system landscape. ICT integrates business processes in and across enterprises. The built-in process and information flows reduce the risk of process silos and ICT interfacing cost.

Configurability
Providing flexibility and adaptability for mapping business process requirements and technical implementation in an ICT system (such as an ERP system), the underlying business application infrastructure should be

able to support process variations by setting software switches and avoiding custom code.

Scalability
Accumulated demand, scope extensions and new business processes all require a modern ICT infrastructure to support volume and the new process landscape.

In an ideal world, each core process would be supported by an application specifically developed for its purpose. Such a system can either be part of the corporate system landscape or even stand separately and communicate through interfaces. It is the core process support platform that companies want to retain in-house, even when talking about internal outsourcing. This is especially true when considering high-volume item processing like accounting systems. Interfacing and the volume of communication would mean higher costs and security risks. Companies usually overcome such risks by leveraging *one ERP system* from a trusted vendor. Such systems are already highly integrated and offer an ideal *platform for key back-office processes*.

Processes that do not involve real-time highly interactive mass-item processing can be supported either by systems within or outside of the corporate system landscape. The communication involves only limited data transfers at the beginning and at the end of processing. A good example of such a core process would be payroll processing. Clerks can be connected to an internal ERP system or use their own system as well.

Currently there are a lot of different ICT tools, ICT applications and technologies in use. The list contains a mixture of tools, technologies and business applications. Some of them are more business focused, while others are more technology related.

The most useful IT Tools Applications and Technologies

	Hackett 2003 (Range #)	Hackett 2004 (Range #)	SBPOA 2004 (Range #)	Hackett 2005 (Range #)	Hackett 2006 (Range #)
ERP	1	1	1	3	3
Workflow	2	2	3	2	2
Data warehouse	3	3	5	5	-
Automatic matching & payment allocation tools	7	4	6	4	4
Data analysis & reporting tools	4	5	2	-	-
Imaging	6	6	4	1	1
eProcurement	8	7	-	-	-
Self-service capabilities	9	8	7	6	-
CRM	11	9	-	-	-
EDI	10	-	-	-	5

Source: Ranges obtained from: The Hackett Group, 3rd Annual Financial Shared Service Organization Study 2003, 2004,2005, 2006;
SBPOA Shared Services Survey 2004

Fig. 27: Technology Enablers for Shared Services

Source: Ranges retrieved from: Hackett (2004) and SBPOA (2004)

It is hard to distinguish to which area each item should be grouped. Heavyweight line items like ERP have a different impact on an overall solution than smaller ones like imaging and scanning. The following figure shows a qualitative arrangement of ICT solutions according their primary focus to business or technology.

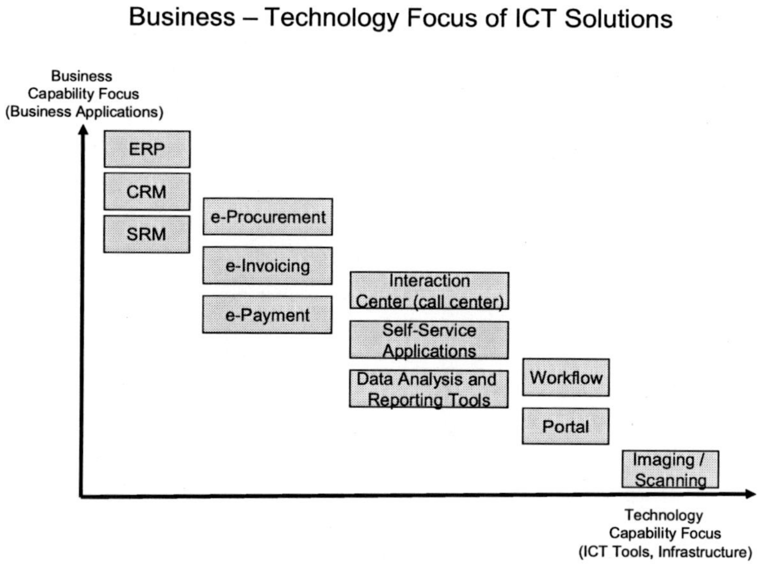

Fig. 28: Business versus Technology Focus on ICT solutions

In every study, ERP systems are the most important enabler for Shared Services. The other technology enabling measures and tools may differ in the perception of importance but ERP, workflow, imaging, data warehouse and analysis and reporting tools always predominate.

As a general result in the table of business enablers for Shared Services we see that, according to the timeline, the first wave of introducing Shared Services is over (ERP is always listed as the main priority until 2004). Most large enterprises have already implemented ERP packages within their Shared Service Organizations and are now moving to the phase of stabilizing, optimizing and streamlining the processes using additional technology like imaging and scanning tools (ERP then dropped from the primary priority to priority number 3).

2.3.2.1 Standardize and Consolidate Applications and Systems

Significant improvement exists in the standardization and consolidation of ICT systems. Standardization of business application ICT systems reduces the different types of business ICT systems. The result is one common logical business ICT system landscape but implemented on multiple (physical) ICT instances. Consolidating those physical ICT instances creates additional benefits.

Significant savings are only achievable with one or two remaining ERP systems. More ERP systems erode the savings potential of consolidation.

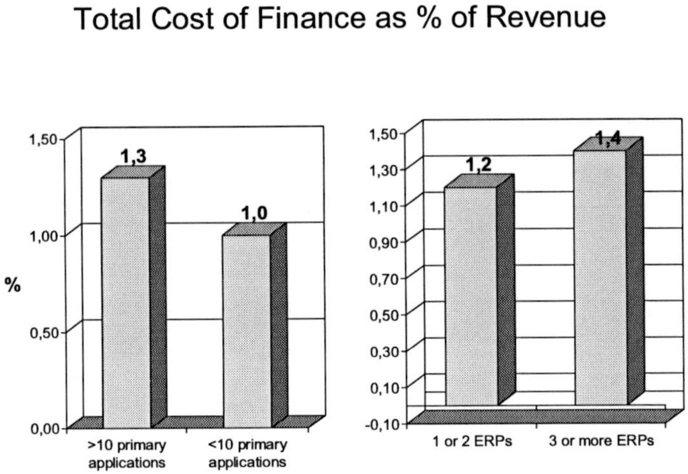

Fig. 29: Total cost of F&A as a percentage of revenue in relation to number of applications and ERP systems

Source: Hackett (2005, 43)

2.3.2.2 Summary of ICT in Shared Service

Information and Communication Technology (ICT) is an essential part of a Shared Service Organization. The foundation is and will always be an ERP system as the most important enterprise system. Most Shared Service business processes are heavily linked to back-office tasks. Centralizing resources for processing common, non-core business processes is a logical step to gain key value benefits like reduced cost, improved quality, shorter time cycles, better risk management and higher flexibility.

ICT plays an important role. On the one hand ICT costs are part of the overall processing cost and can be reduced by *standardizing and consolidating ICT* systems (infrastructure and applications). This lightens the asset base and reduces the complexity of the ICT system landscape. On the other hand there is a need for *self-service applications* which are specialized front applications that enable employees, managers, vendors, partners and customers to interact directly with the enterprise information system for common, non-core processes like administration of master data, reporting, claim processing, etc. Those front-end self-service ICT systems run in an internet infrastructure environment.

The ultimate way for technology to support business processes is the *full automation* (this is also known as lights-out processing or straight-through processing) of the entire process or parts of it. Decreasing the portion of human interaction while achieving the same results raises the necessary technical capability in the flexibility of executing business rules.

Shared Service Organizations become an *e-business hub*, especially for non-core business processes. Selecting an ICT infrastructure for a Shared Service Organization is more than selecting and/or consolidating an ERP system. It includes the selection of technology tools like workflow, web infrastructure, data base management, imaging technology, data analysis and reporting tools.

2.3.2.3 Practice: Consolidation and Simplification Technology

The most common way of consolidating is to focus on centralizing the service delivery organization, ICT system landscapes and the consolidation/harmonization/standardization of processes. Simplifying the service delivery may also include the consolidation of legal entities across a geographical area and/or countries.

BASF:
BASF currently work with seven ICT systems and want to consolidate these in the near future into three ICT systems. Their ultimate goal is to have only two ICT systems: one for Europe and one for the rest of the world.

Henkel:
Henkel has consolidated legal entities across the Nordic states. Twenty-one affiliated companies were reduced to one single legal entity. They also bundled the tasks of Ireland and UK into one entity, while in Germany they merged eight legal entities into one.

Philips:
"Improving business processes with an IT system landscape that originally had some 220 different IT systems was a difficult task. We are now down to 15-16 instances of SAP and plan on reducing further. To cope with this difficulty we have developed a very unique process harmonization methodology, which proved to be very successful."

"I hope that we can reduce down to one per business, so around four or five ERP systems." [Interview with Michel de Zeeuw, Philips]

2.4 Relocation of Service Delivery

Apart from the geographical coverage of Shared Services (which is the geographical scope/reach of providing the service) it is interesting to see how the Shared Service Organization intends to deliver the services. The most challenging Shared Service delivery approach is the centralization of the delivery sites in one global place (= global Shared Service center). While the proportion of global Shared Service Organizations is still small, it will increase in the future.

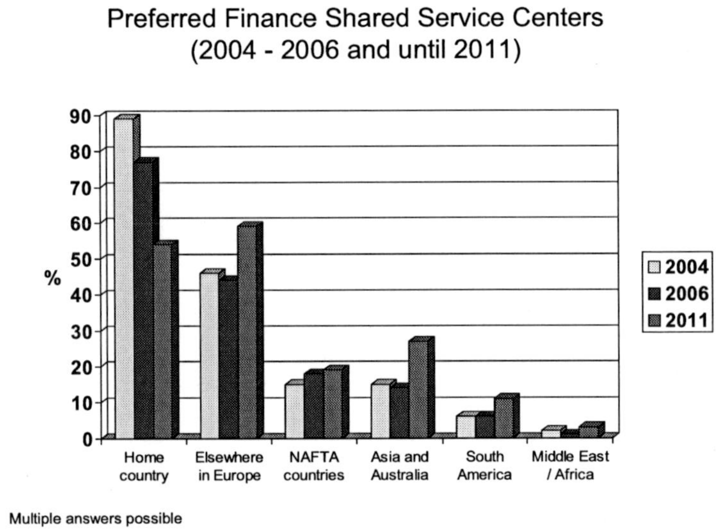

Fig. 30: Preferred F&A Shared Service Centers Location from European perspective

Source: Hackett (2007, 41)

European Shared Service Centers for F&A tend to stay in their home country or at least within the European boundary.

2.5 Service Delivery Organization and Management

Another aspect to consider is the Organizational and Management structure of the Shared Services. The organizational structures range from a centralized global Shared Service Organization (SSO) up to a decentralized approach with local Shared Service Organizations or even a virtual form of organizational design.

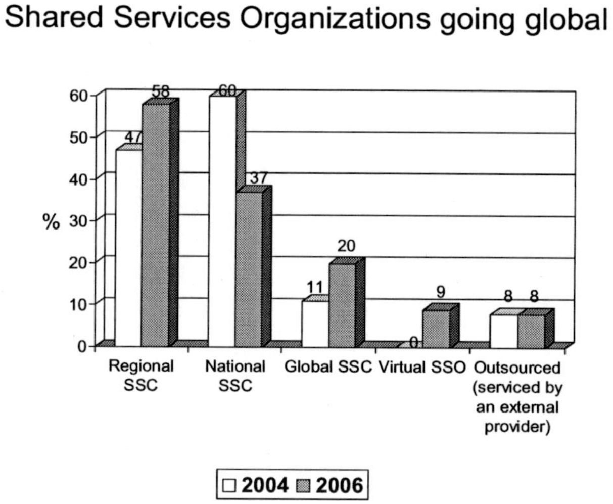

Fig. 31: Organizational Form of Shared Services
Source: Hackett (2007, ii)

The most challenging Shared Service delivery approach is the centralization of the delivery sites in one place (one global Shared Service Organization with single delivery site). Whereas the portion of global Shared Service Organizations is still in the early stage, their importance will increase in the future. Improvements in the ICT ease the adoption of virtual Shared Service Organizations with a central headquarters but with dispersed, fragmented physical service delivery locations.

2.6 Good or Best Practice

Implementing Shared Services is the first critical business decision. Achieving world class performance with the established Shared Service Organization is the second challenge. Good (or best) practice summarizes and combines selected successful approaches, components and tools which have been proved empirically to have a high correlation to high (over the average) impact to the key value benefits of cost, time/productivity performance, quality, risk and flexibility.

The overall result is a combination of effects. Effects on cost are the most mentioned and discussed factor. The following illustrative example shows the combination of consolidating volume, reengineering business processes, applying ICT technology and moving to location with lower resource cost (e.g. labor costs).

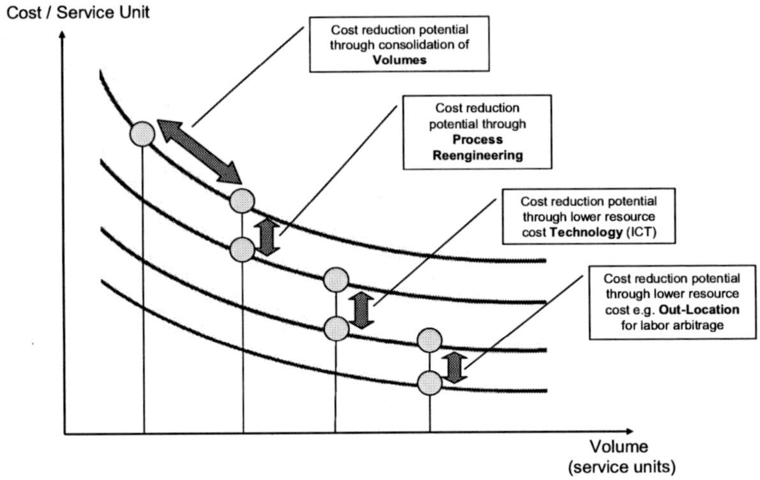

Fig. 32: Combination of effects on cost reduction per service unit

Here are some best practice examples in the areas of business processes, resource usage and utilization, organizational and managerial operational set up and strategy approaches:

Business Processes:

- End-to-end process ownership and responsibility
- Global Master Data (such as global chart of accounts in F&A or the cost center hierarchy)
- Global definition or specification of services (service catalogue, service portfolio) and associated service levels

Resources (people, technology):

- Single ERP platform
- Extensive EDI usage with business partners (such as banks)
- Implementing call center (also known as a contact or interaction center) technology
- Extensive personnel training (extending and maintaining personal skills)

- Heavy usage of self-service applications (for internal employees/managers and external business partners)
- Full automation of business processes where possible

Organizational, managerial operational set up and strategy approaches:

- Autonomous Shared Service Organization
- Heavy use of KPI (key performance indicators) measurement
- Permanently monitoring the Service Level Agreement (SLA)

3 Processes – Suitability for Shared Service

3.1 Business Functions, Processes and Services

It is very hard to determine a clear understanding and definition of functions and processes in an organizational business context. Both terms are based on *tasks* (as a piece of work or duty) which are performed towards a desired purpose or goal. Tasks can be described by a multiple range of characteristic features like the type of activity itself, time and location aspects, the tangible tools and facilities used, and so on. Among these characteristics two main elements can be used to distinguish between functions and processes. Depending on the focus of description elements we refer more to the *functional* or *process view*. The criteria are the *type of content (activity)* and the *flow of events*. Other potential additional criteria refer to internal or external view (result) on the task.

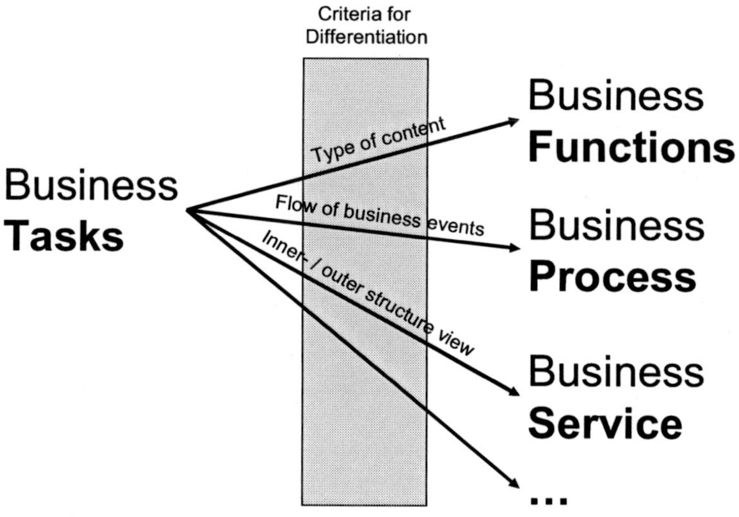

Fig. 33: Business tasks categorization

Function (Business Function)

A functional view of organizational tasks refers to a similar *type of activity* which focuses on the necessary skills, capabilities, knowledge to complete the task successfully. We assume that people have the knowledge or training to perform those (specialized) tasks. The content is in the foreground with a static view on the task. The functional view is a 'content view'.

The established industrial functional views are on F&Q, logistics, procurement, sales and distribution, production, HR, ICT, facility and real estate, and so on. More or less every industrial corporation has these tasks, regardless of how the corporation is organized. All those functions are deeply anchored in our real living environment (social, legal, business, and so on.). Thus we label them as *core industrial business functions*.

Process (Business Process)
A process view of tasks focuses, in contrast to the functional view, on the dynamic *flow and structure of events* in the task. Thus the start and end of a task plays a vital role. Functional aspects are not the primary focus. The process view is a 'performance view'.
A complex process task may contain multiple sub-tasks which include different functional types of activity. This is especially true for higher aggregated processes. Thus some authors use the term 'business process' if multi-functional activities are incorporated. Nevertheless the term business process is also used for longer and more complex functional task chains.
Unfortunately there is no commonly agreed functional grouping and naming of business tasks or activities into the major core business functions. A typical example of this is in Personnel Payroll. This is often grouped under F&A as well as in HR. For our purposes, we use the term process or business process in the broad sense even if only functional tasks are covered. Core business function is used to indicate the dedicated specialized high level business tasks categories (such as F&A or procurement).

Service (Business Service)
Regardless of whether we choose the term business functions or processes, somebody still has to deliver the results. As soon as we start identifying, specifying and packaging tasks and task-steps for execution by a resource, we address the *outer structure* (external structure) for buying and selling those task executions. The service view of tasks hides the *inner structure* or the 'how it is done'. Communicating with potential delivery partners (internal or external) should be done on *service descriptions on a supplier-customer relationship* basis. The outsourcing of business processes needs a formalized service specification.
Services are processes or functions (because they have an inner structure) but functions and process are not necessarily services. From a business perspective, it is not worth treating every tiny little function or process as a business service. We use the term service even in cases when we are talking about a *potential supplier-customer-relationship*. For example can

business processes delivered without an explicit view or description of supplier-customer-relationships. Outsourcing a business process implies buying the execution of a business service.

3.2 Process Coverage and Shared Service

The most popular business process for Shared Service Organizations is IT Services & Support followed by back-office business processing. Industrial corporate back-office business functions (such as F&A and HR) cover many processes. Not all of them are well suited for being moved to a Shared Service environment. The following figure shows the results of a survey on outsourcing company processes, but it is also applicable to Shared Service. Quite often Shared Service is called 'Internal Outsourcing' and is used as an intermediate transition to true outsourcing to a third party.

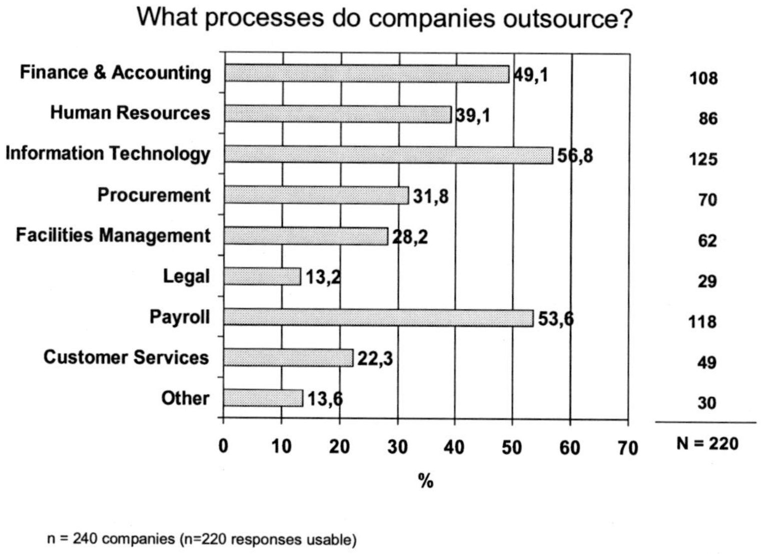

Fig. 34: Outsourcing of business processes of European Companies
Source: SBPOA (2002)

Processes evolve over time. People in organizations change processes, change resources by substituting manual work with technology work (automation) and replacing internal with external resources. One example is the change of the core purchasing process to a holistic purchase order and purchase order requisition process. Combinations of all those criteria are delivering a variety of process execution options with essentially the same outcome.

3.2.1 Determinants of process suitability for Shared Services

It is vital to analyze business processes to decide which activities should be performed in a Shared Service center and which activities should remain in the business unit.

What are the aspects to assess to determine process suitability for Shared Services?
Apart from the willingness, capabilities and availability of execution resources these aspects have to be considered:

- Separation (differentiation, isolation, identification)
- Categorization
- Standardization
- Consolidation

3.2.1.1 Separation (Differentiation, Isolation, Identification) of Processes

Sharing services and processes implies the possibility to split processes. All separated process parts have to be able to exist as independent business relevant sub-processes. It is essential to identify uniquely and then describe all business process parts. The following diagram shows on a high level the activity split for F&A functions between a Shared Service unit and the remaining business unit.

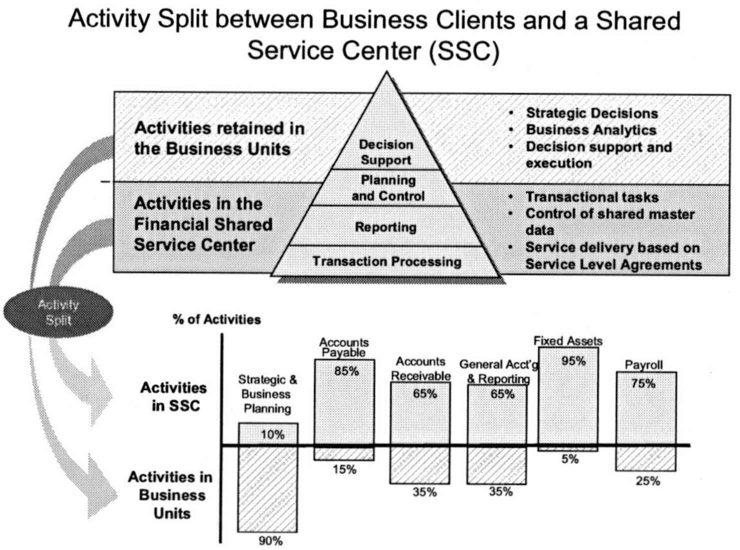

Fig. 35: Example of finance process activity separation between Shared Service Unit and Business Unit

3.2.1.2 Categorization of Processes

The previous figure shows that different portions of activities are performed by different parties. What are the criteria for selecting processes (or part of processes) to be performed in a Shared Service center?

There are multiple options to characterize a business process/function/service. Shared Services are described as a concept of centralization to provide common services for the support functions such as Finance & Accounting, Human Resources, Procurement and Information and Communication Technology. Criteria for describing the task range from:

- the degree of human intervention,
- specificity of the service delivery to the consumer and the provider,
- degree of centralization,
- degree of judgment (decisions) required,
- strategic value of the task,
- degree of formal structureness,
- degree of repetitiveness,

- risk exposure and criticality,
- complexity of task,
- time horizon of expected delivery,
- geographical dependency,
- process as competitive differentiator on the market,
- etc.

An all accepted *taxonomy* for describing business tasks does not exist.

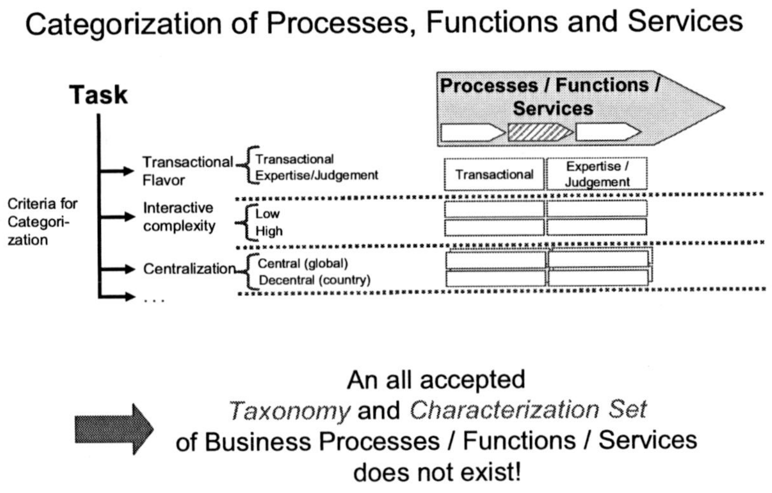

Fig. 36: Categorization of Business Processes, Functions and Services

Business processes which are homogeneous *between business units* and are not viewed as critical (from a core competencies perspective) are ideal candidates for Shared Services. Those fall into two types of processes: either transactional (or administrative) processes, or transformational processes, that require competence, expertise, judgment and knowledge.

Transactional processes are high volume processes, such as repetitive administrative similar tasks, with low strategic value and simple or structured decisions involved. Here, the interaction with the business takes place only occasionally.

Transformational processes (knowledge, expertise and judgment based processes) have a high strategic value, are less homogenous and repetitive in their process execution, require higher interaction with the business unit because of complex decision requirements and a higher required qualification profile.

Transactional as well as transformational processes are candidates for a Shared Services center or even Business Process Outsourcing (BPO). In practice, the term Shared Service center is mostly associated with transactional processes (center of scale, transaction factories), whereas the centralization of transformational tasks are labeled 'Center of Expertise', 'Competence Center', Center of Excellence' or 'Center of Skill'.

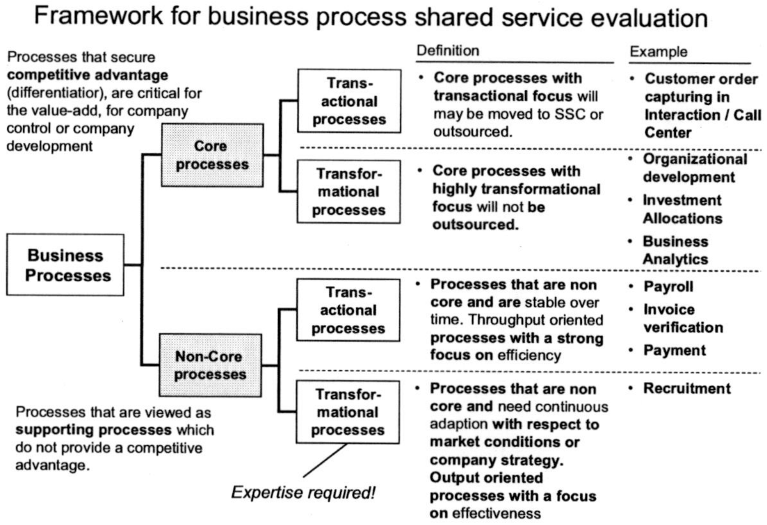

Fig. 37: Framework for business process Shared Service evaluation

Most of the business processes have a transactional *and* a transformational portion of activities to be executed. Further breakdown of the process and the increasingly sophisticated use of information and communication technology (automation) will lead to an increase of the 'transactional' portion of an overall business process. Thus more and more business processes will be considered as candidates for a transactional Shared Service center in the future.

By categorizing different types of business processes, more simplification and transparency are achieved in selecting and assigning resources for execution.

3.2.1.3 Standardization of Processes

Standardization provides homogeneity and eases the interoperability between components. In the past, standards often referred to the ICT components of hardware and software. However, standards also exist for business processes. Standards can be characterized by:

- Reach (worldwide, industry, corporate standards)
- Type (de-facto standard, de-jure standard)
- Degree of standards in composed solutions (high, low proprietary portions)

Standards are the opposite of individualization, and can be viewed from two perspectives, the vendor perspective and the consumer perspective. The consumer intends to ask for manufacturing-neutral standards to be open and flexible in the future. Proprietary vendor standards deliver potential advantages in emerging markets but bearing the risk of 'vendor-lock-in'.

3.2.1.4 Consolidation of Processes (Complexity Reduction)

The primary goal of consolidating business processes is to reduce and simplify the complexity of the overall solution from high level business process to lower levels of information and communication systems. Consolidating different versions of the same business process simplifies their execution in the underlying ICT system landscape. The execution of business processes is technically supported by ICT systems. One common business process is easier to map and maintain within ICT system solutions. The same business process may have different ICT solution options. Ideally the hierarchical ICT system (application) stack (from ICT applications to databases) is highly standardized.

Consolidation of information and technology is multi-layered[13]. (1) On the first layer, is the physical consolidation of hardware (server, ICT equipment and so on) which aims to achieve benefits in distribution and leveling of ICT capacity and reduction of physical interfaces. (2) The second layer consists of a logical consolidation of ICT application software. The primary goal is to reduce the number of redundant ICT applications for supporting one business process. Consolidating applications simplifies and reduces the software interfaces. (3) The third layer deals with data consolidation. Centralization of data from different

[13] See: von Glahn C. / Oecking C. (2006, 48)

sources within a corporation reduces the duplication of data. Effects are visible economically, provide 'one source of truth' and lower risk exposure. Data consolidation is a strong requirement for delivering consistent accounting data.

3.2.1.5 Conclusion on suitability of processes for Shared Service

Assuming that business processes can be decomposed and the elements can be separated and reengineered with the result of a new bundling and process flow orchestration, the suitability for Shared Service is heavily depended on the two criteria of *specialization* and *strategic importance* of the process.

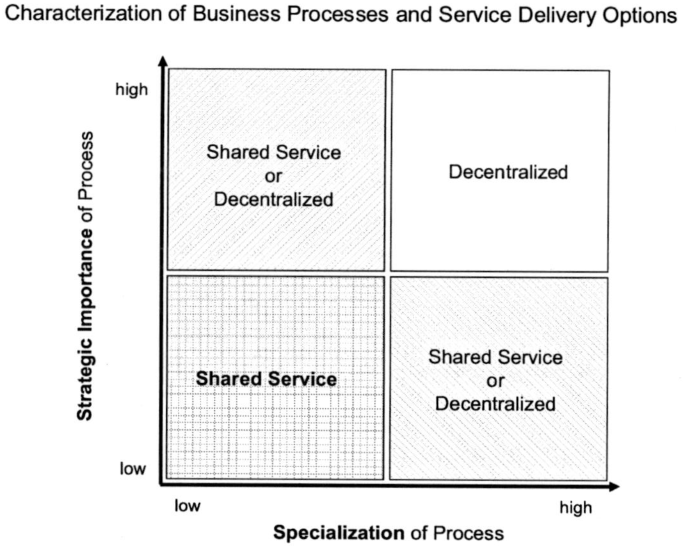

Fig. 38: Suitability of business processes for Shared Service

3.2.2 Practice: Business Process Standardization and Consolidation

Standardizing business processes is viewed as mandatory for every Shared Service Organization. Standardization provides the foundation for achieving fundamental scaling benefits to reduce costs and provide consistency and transparency for all parties involved. One major characteristic of a Shared Service Organization is that it highlights the process view of tasks and activities and not the functional view. Ultimately, responsibilities should be organized according to standardized business processes (end-to-end processes).

BASF:
Today, BASF offers transactional services for the functional categories of F&A and HR.

Henkel:
Henkel has one of the most advanced organizational structures for Shared Service tasks according to process categories like order-to-cash, procure-to-pay, record-to-report, and so on. The introduction of this concept on a regional and global level required a shift of responsibilities to the "Heads of Processes". Heads of Processes were given more responsibility than the local CFOs. While structural changes of this kind of magnitude are rarely visible in practice, the approach proved to be very successful and the concept will be deployed now worldwide.

"But the Heads of Process have been so successful that they now have responsibility worldwide. And we reached a point where we saw that they were so busy that they could no longer take care of the human resources issues, hiring and firing and so on. So we really stirred the whole organization up, changed our thought processes and stabilized our processes such that we see sine waves when the old power structures are swept away. So now we can say, we've standardized the processes, now let's let the countries get a bit stronger again and let the Heads of Process work on a cross-regional basis." [Interview with Dr. Carlo Mackrodt, Henkel].

A big benefit of standardization of processes is visible through an example from Henkel North America. "We had 19 different affiliates in the US that we were able to integrate. The financial structures were all distributed among the regions, so it wasn't standardized and everyone did things in a slightly different way. Now we've been among the leaders on the DAX for some years, and often one of the fastest companies at year-end closing. The reason is our standardized processes. In reality there are a thousand different variations, and sometimes it drives me crazy that something like that could squeak through again. I was relatively strict about one thing, and that was to be very conscientious about using only standards." [Interview with Dr. Carlo Mackrodt, Henkel].

SAP:
"… In the beginning we didn't struggle with the standard to the last mile. We rather negotiated with those countries before doing the actual migration in order to bring them as close to the standard as possible – e. g. 80%. After go live, the countries realize the effort on both sides for these last 20% and a convergence process to the 100% starts. And so they

come of their own accord, which is a better way - the SAP way. The only problem with that was that it took a bit of time and caused partly some friction. This friction led partly to increased fluctuation, which then accelerated the convergence again."
"... A clear gap analysis was done beforehand to see how far they were away from the standard and where the deviations were. And then we sat down with the CFO to discuss how to close the gaps, which were 10% or 20% – not necessarily 20%, but some proportion – and then measures were taken to decrease it and it was decided that that was it. In principle that was a question of compromising, which was the other point, "Be pragmatic"? That only works with the other side's buy-in." [Interview with Peter Rasper, SAP]

Solvay:
"For us it's very clear: I don't want at all to centralize the expertise. That's a very clear cut-off in the Solvay strategy. I'm very proud to stick to the transactional, to consolidate, to make it ISO-9002-certified, fully and only and exclusively transactional of remote processes. I do believe that it is worth centralizing the knowledge and the expertise also, but not in the same place you centralize transactions. I don't see significant synergy in that, and maybe a little more confusion." ...
"Starting from accounts payable, we are at 90%, and we have 10% remaining in order for goods received and purchase orders to be properly introduced in the system locally. We want to achieve 100% of it because we have an organization, called Strategy Purchasing and Procurement, which is a competence center, and it has the responsibility of managing the upstream procurement part.
On accounts receivable, from a pure cash-collection perspective we have 100%. That means we have credit managers in the different regions that report to one central organization. So we have roughly 30 credit managers all over the world working as a front office, but in Solvay they are considered more as a competence center to do credit risk analyses, fix credit limits, discuss with the business, and make large legal recoveries or credit insurance types of strategy and policy. But for the cash collection, going from the collection, reconciliation, and first reminder, we do it 100% from here.
Regarding closing the books, we are, let's say, split 40–45% here and 50% local. We want to grow to 60% here and 40% local, knowing that the local financial manager or controller, will remain in charge of the compliance, governance, and certification of their manage processes. We don't need here and we will never do so, even if we can. Because following the strategy of a clear split, you need on site the specific business knowledge and legal, local responsibility.

On payroll we are doing 15% here and 85% locally, and I don't want to grow more than 25–30% here. And for HR I'm pushing to leave on site a minimum of 70% of the activities. I believe you could transfer 30% to back office. We are not working in direct connection with the employee, instead we are working through a service desk through an on-site HR manager. To make it clear, we work for them, not for the employee." [Interview with Guy de Mercier, Solvay]

SAP:
"We had two months in total during which a CFO from each country affected had to come up with an acceptable standard for general accounting, P2P or C2C, for example, and sign off on it. The crucial thing was that we could not spend ages refining it: We had to have something quickly which we could start using. So speed is at the top of our list." [Interview with Peter Rasper, SAP]

3.3 Finance & Accounting Processes covered by Shared Service

Shared Service Organizations deliver a common service to multiple business units out of a centralized service hub (which is global, regional or local). Analyzing operational business processes from end-to-end shows that a big portion of sub processes or process steps are directly or indirectly related financial tasks. Those *operational financial activities* are performed with external business partners like banks, vendors and customers. Operational activities around the financial chain (dealing with the cash flow and the working capital) are the biggest costing block in the F&A function within an enterprise. The following F&A related activities are common and can be centralized in a Shared Service center:

- Display of account data with debits and credits (customer, vendor)
- Payment (e.g. via internet)
- Debit management with billing and collection (collections management)
- Customer financial issues (dispute management, customer credit management)
- Optimizing the operational financial flow (cash management, in-house cash, treasury, financial risk management)

On top of the more operationally-related F&A activities, the Shared Service center provides services which are not directly related to a single dedicated business unit. In this case, the service recipient is the enterprise headquarters. The following F&A activities are examples of such a category of tasks:

- General accounting
- Fixed asset accounting
- Inter-company settlement
- External reporting
- Tax accounting, filing and reporting
- Travel and Expense reimbursement
- Payroll (payroll accounting)

Apart from the service recipient perspective, there is also a potential qualitative perspective. Within the business function of F&A there are different types of process activities which can be grouped into the two categories, transactional and transformational.

Each of the groups can be broken down into detailed sub-groups. As mentioned previously, every task (task/process group) has transactional and transformational portions. Thus it is sometimes hard to group them clearly into one of the two categories. The transformation category can be subdivided in more "expertise based tasks" (such as business reporting and analytics, cost analysis, business performance) and more "strategy and compliance" related tasks (such as risk management, investor relations, external reporting and internal audit).

Tab. 5: Finance &Accounting Process Categories

Transaction Processes	Transformation Processes
Accounts Payable	Budgeting
Freight Payments	Forecast
Travel and Expense	Business Performance Reporting
Fixed Assets	Treasury Management
Accounts Receivable	Tax Planning
Credit Management	Internal Audit
Dispute Management	Government Compliance
Collections	Tax Regulatory
Customer Billing	Cost Analysis
General Accounting	Business Performance Analysis
External Reporting	New Business and Pricing
Project Accounting	Strategic Planning Support
Cost Accounting	Finance Function Management
Cash Management	Risk Management
Tax Accounting	Investor Relation
Tax Filling and Reporting	.....
.....	

An overall generic accepted grouping does not exist. Nevertheless it is essential to have a common terminology and distinct definitions to avoid misunderstandings.

The activity split between Shared Service center and the business unit may vary between different enterprises. The following illustrative customer example provides a rough guideline for orientation purposes.

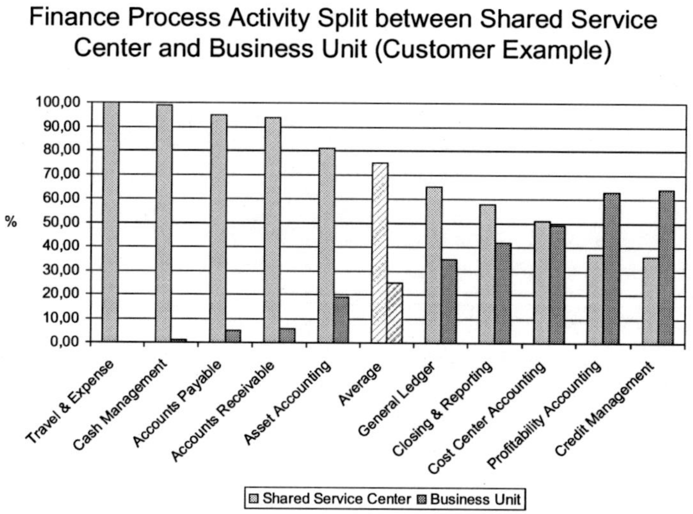

Fig. 39: Customer example F&A process activity split between Shared Service center and business

F&A processes show a different coverage in Shared Service Organizations.

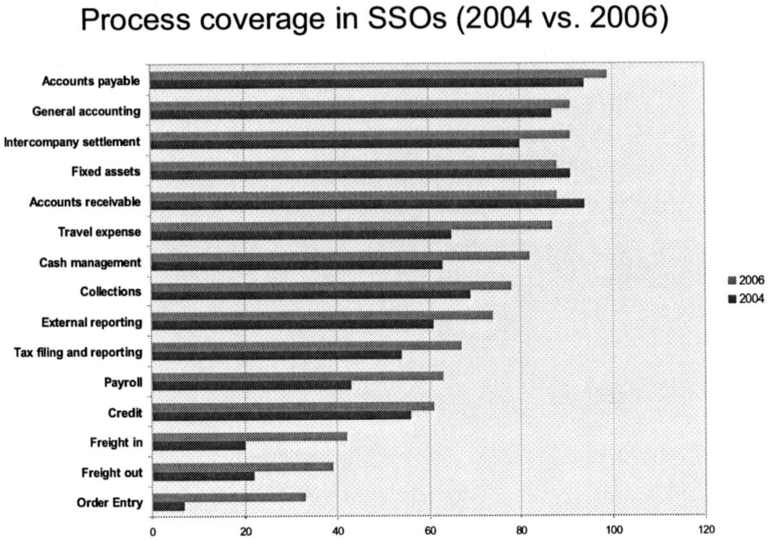

Fig. 40: Processes covered in Finance Shared Service Organizations

Source: Value retrieved from: Hackett (2007, 44).

Not all F&A processes show the same benefits (such as cost savings). The following table provides a comparison of F&A transactional processes cost savings (e.g. accounts payable, accounts receivable, fixed assets, travel and expense, freight payment) in Shared Service organizations and non-SSO in Europe.

Tab. 6: Average percentage of cost savings on F&A transaction costs between Shared Service organization and F&A organizations (non SSOs) in Europe

Finance Function	**%**
Accounts Receivable	44 %
Fixed Assets	76 %
Travel and Expense	53 %
Freight Payment	65 %
Accounts Payable	56 %

Source: Bangemann (2005, 47)

A high percentage of cost savings (e.g. fixed assets with 76 % or freight 65 %) does not necessarily correlate with a high degree of business impact. Transactional business processes that affect a small headcount (labor costs) have a low impact on the total savings figure because of missing cost volume. Cost of F&A is heavily based on personnel costs.

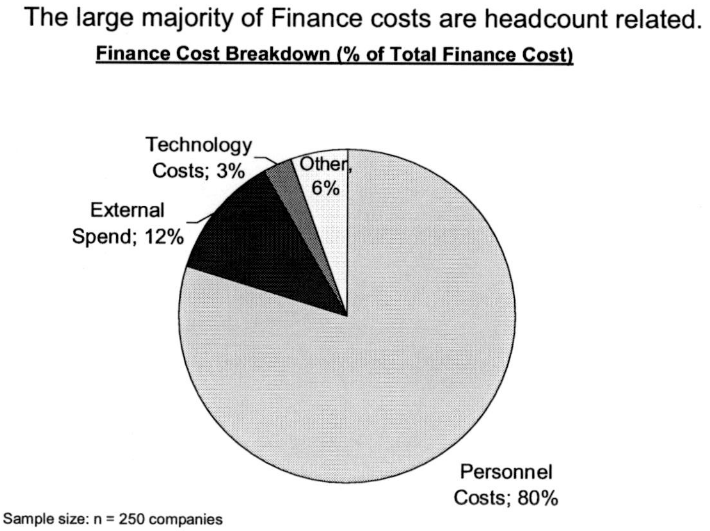

Fig. 41: F&A cost breakdown in different cost categories
Source: ASUG/SAP (2006)

Personnel costs make up 80 % of total F&A costs. It is obvious that the main lever in reducing F&A transactional costs are processes with a high headcount workforce like accounts payable, accounts receivable and travel expenses.

Shared Service centers need to adopt a customer- and market-oriented work style since, at least in the advanced SSC models, the business units can choose their service provider. The new work style helps them not to be perceived as self-centered bureaucrats, but as a value-adding factor that understands the meaning of the word "service." The SSC adds value to the whole company by letting others focus on their primary tasks. Many processes within HR, F&A and administration are well suited for moving into SSCs. We have chosen some of the most significant ones to demonstrate how the process would change, what challenges the SSC could face handling them, and what possible ICT solutions and support could be set up.

3.3.1 Accounts Payable

Accounts payable (AP) represents a transactional process with a high demand on processing large volumes of data while keeping or improving quality. As it has a direct influence on the calculation of financial results, not to mention cash flow and working capital, the whole process has to be transparent and auditable. An SSC can achieve all of this easily, which is why the majority of companies have made accounts payable their number one process in their SSCs.

Process

It is interesting to see how different companies approach their AP process. The most common method is to partially decentralize AP processing, and to allow it to develop over time. How this works is that companies keep invoices at the local subsidiaries and only the financial data gets passed over to the SSC for processing. In order to minimize the administrative effort of transferring paper invoices into electronic formats, more advanced companies have centralized the AP processing completely; so, invoices are sent to the SSC. The most desirable solution is to receiving all invoices electronically, but this is not yet fully in practice.

As a prerequisite, a purchase agreement (such as purchase order or call-off of a long term purchasing contract) needs to be issued before actual purchases are made. This system entry allows for easier tracking of incoming invoices and allows for an efficient approval process. When the goods arrive, the receiving clerk begins the process with a quality and quantity check to assure that the goods delivered match the items and quantities on the invoice. The invoice can be scanned to be available electronically in the system. If the purchase has not yet been approved according to the purchase agreement, this is handled now. The payment is then posted into accounting and released for payment by the bank.

As we can see, the AP process is not very complicated, but it can include significant effort in the communication between involved parties when anomalies occur (disputes about an improper fulfillment such as an incorrect purchase agreement, wrong delivery, delays, and so on).

Challenges

One of the challenges with moving AP to the SSC is the physical location of paper invoices. Historically, they have been stored at the individual business units for tax and audit purposes. Now that they are sent to the SSC, their location needs to be tracked somehow. A solution to this problem is having the invoices sent directly to the SSC where they are not only processed, but also stored. Otherwise, they need to be scanned and archived electronically. Communication can also be a challenge, because deliveries can be incomplete or invoice amounts needs investigation – even as an internal employee, the number of people involved and the status of the clearing process can become confusing. A solution is to carefully review the current AP process and optimize it from an organizational point of view, adding clear guidelines and authority levels. A computerized workflow can make it easier to enforce the guidelines, speed up the whole process, help keep track of proceedings via workflow, and decrease the risk of errors.

Execution Resources Considerations (People, ICT Systems)

There two major execution resources, people and ICT systems, which have to be considered in the AP process. The process execution is mostly based on the interaction between people and ICT application systems. AP is categorized as a transactional process with a high degree of administrative, well- structured information capturing and processing activities. The portion of personnel activities varies depending on the degree of automation. Automation depends on the information medium (paper, electronic), the standardized process structure, formalization of business rules (policy, decision authority levels) and connectivity to surrounding ICT systems.

The most important part of the overall AP solution is the *backbone accounting system*, which should be tightly connected to the purchasing system. As data volumes will be quite high, we suggest not underestimating how robust the solution needs to be. A company can use its current accounting system if it does not plan to outsource the SSC in the future. If such outsourcing plans exist, the system should be designed to make it easy to spin off the SSC unit later. This means a more modular approach and the demand for a robust enterprise application architecture is even higher. The AP system should be able to automatically post payments for pre-approved invoices when delivery is complete and of the expected quality. The AP clerk will then only have to deal with anomalies, leaving routine work to the system.

The second important system to consider is a combination of a *workflow* and *self-service* solution. A workflow will allow for the design and enforcement of standardized processes, eliminating many costly errors and delays. A workflow solution can be understood as a communication framework for triggering a personnel execution based business flow. Self-services are a different process sourcing option where internal people (employees, managers) or external people (vendors, customers, business partners) are enabled to perform directly their own needs (e.g. information, updates). Deployment of self-service portal scenarios can simplify the interaction for the company's employees. For example, a user is notified of a necessary action by an e-mail or through an in-box within the portal. A simple Web interface will empower the user (be it the employee placing an order or the approving manager) to quickly complete their part of the AP process in several easy steps, thus eliminating the need of one-to-one phone communication with involved parties. A communication framework like this can automate and speed up the whole process considerably.

The advances of storage devices have made *invoice scanning with or without optical character recognition (OCR)* possible on a larger scale. Before making a final decision on what document solution to use, a company should consider how closely it is integrated with the AP system and how much effort will be necessary to include the user interface into the portal solution. Solutions that come with predefined interfaces are of course preferable. This will eliminate personnel and implementation costs and significantly simplify future upgrades.

If the company already has implemented or plans to implement a *dispute management solution*, we also suggest making it part of the AP process. Disputes account for between 5 and10% of all invoices and can be very difficult to manage effectively. A dispute management solution will help you track the whole dispute history and people involved and will connect directly with your data in other systems, such as AP, purchasing, payment systems and so on.

The advantage of *shared master data* in purchasing and accounts payable (vendor, purchase order, coding block) is obvious for integrated systems.

Existing mature *ERP solutions* provide an ideal foundation for all the needs discussed above. Their AP system is closely linked with both general ledger in accounting and with purchasing within a supplier relationship management (SRM) system. Most ERP systems use a workflow backbone supported by a portal presentation layer. A *financial supply chain management (FSCM)* capability within or additional to ERP systems (e.g. *electronic bill presentment and payment*) further support the payment settlement process.

3.3.2 Accounts Receivable

Accounts receivable (AR) is the second most deployed process by Shared Service Centers. Companies generally keep AR inside since a close relationship to its customers is often considered a company's most important asset.

Process

The Shared Service Center takes over the processing of customer orders as soon as the goods or services have been delivered to the customer and the appropriate posting has been made to the AR system. The processing clerk checks that all ordered items have been delivered and then issues an invoice. Invoicing the customer can happen in various ways. However, the standard method is still sending a paper invoice. Modern technology and changes in country legislation now also allow for electronic invoicing. Electronic invoices can be sent directly to the customer or routed via a consolidator. The customer reviews the invoice for accuracy and compares the line items with the delivery. If they find any inconsistencies, they either dispute them or report them to the invoice issuer. The SSC will regularly review incoming payments and match them with outstanding invoices. If a customer pays only partially or it is not possible to reconcile the payments automatically with issued invoices, the SSC clerk contacts the customer to resolve the issue. When the invoice is past due, the SSC employee determines the best way to deal with the customer, depending on legal and cultural conditions and the customer relationship. Therefore, information on how to proceed should ideally be kept in a Customer Relationship Management (CRM) system or AR itself per customer.

Challenges

As mentioned, the tendency is to keep the customer-related processes within the corporate border. Separating accounts receivable and moving it away from the business units (e.g. moving it to a shared service hub) increases the distance between customer and invoice execution processing department. Automating the invoicing process eases the challenge. But when a dispute arises, the physical distance between the customer-serving personnel and the SSC employee has to be overcome with the help of appropriate tools. It is always important to react in a timely manner. Centralizing AR processing into one place could also mean higher costs for invoice distribution. Sending invoices abroad can prove to be too expensive and the SSC will have to look for other alternatives. One would be to retain cost-efficient administrative personnel in all countries. Electronic invoicing will be the easiest choice, when legislation allows it. An Electronic Bill Presentment and Payment (EBPP) system is a solution which is applicable for accounts payable as well as for accounts receivable.

Execution Resources Considerations (People, ICT Systems)

The ICT backbone for accounts receivable processing within a Shared Service Center is an accounting system. Companies nowadays use an integrated enterprise resource planning (ERP) solution to support their F&A function. The AR system receives all the processing data from a billing system, which is also part of the ERP system or within a CRM system. A customer can be a business customer (legal entity) or a private end-consumer. Thus the legal and taxation requirements mean that processing of invoices varies according to the legal status of the customer.

3.3.3 Travel and Expense (T&E)

Travel has become an imperative factor of doing business in a global marketplace, and video and telephone conferencing will probably not completely replace it anytime soon. Unfortunately, reporting one's travel expenses is still a major administrative effort. It is heavily dependent on a country's legislation and can involve extensive communication between the processing clerk and the traveling employee. Those two factors can make it a challenge for introduction in a SSC.

Process

Most companies have some kind of travel policy that states which group of employees can use what level of services and also defines preferred travel suppliers (for example, those offering discounted rates for its employees).

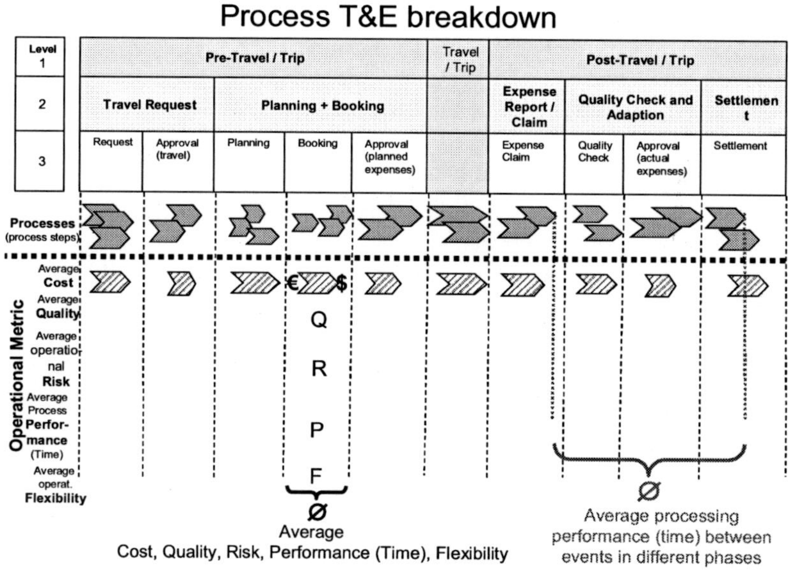

Fig. 42: T&E Process breakdown and operational key value metric categories

Each business trip starts with a travel request and subsequently with its planning. The employee chooses his or her preferred means of transportation and accommodation (according to the travel policy) and sends a travel request to his or her manager for pre-approval. Trip planning and booking can either be done on an individual basis by each employee or through a external travel agency.

Once the employee returns from the business trip, he or she needs to report the travel expenses incurred during the trip. Ideally, the employee can use the pre-approved trip file to add all receipts and calculate the total reimbursement amount. The whole trip is then routed to the travel expense clerk who checks compliance with the company travel policy and approves the reimbursement payment. If there is any discrepancy, the clerk contacts the employee and starts the problem resolution process. Reimbursement is then executed as a part of the accounts payable process or within payroll if the travel expenses are based on country specific payroll tax rules.

Challenges

Challenges with the travel expense reporting process are not much different when administered by a Shared Service hub than when each business unit manages its own operations. However, the following challenges influencing process effectiveness have been identified:

- Adherence to the corporate guidelines (travel policy)
- Filing, submitting and completion of the expense reimbursement forms
- Communication between the involved parties

We have already mentioned the *corporate travel policy (guidelines).* If travel and expense management is done in a Shared Service hub, it will be even more difficult than before to enforce paper-based travel guidelines.

An IT solution – wherever it is being used – can automatically block inappropriate bookings or expense types, or start a workflow for exception handling. Linking the system to the most up-to-date guidelines is easy. Apart from *filing and submitting claims* (which is mostly performed by the employee), any other actions (completing and enhancing the claim with additional travel claim items like company direct invoices received from airlines, credit cards, and so on) will be assigned and controlled in the Shared Service center.

The same is true for *communication.* If, for example, employees report higher expenses than allowed, they need to consult their manager to clarify the appropriateness of that particular case. Such a discussion usually takes place between all three parties involved – the employee, the manager, and the processing clerk. Moving the processing clerk away from the local office to a Shared Service hub will aggravate the situation and require extra effort in organizing a joint phone call or sending several e-mail messages. Supporting the whole process with a computerized workflow will make it easier to enforce the guidelines, speed up the whole process, and eliminate the possibility of errors.

The post trip T&E expense claim process is still highly manual. How automated the claim process needs to be depends heavily on the information and communication capabilities.

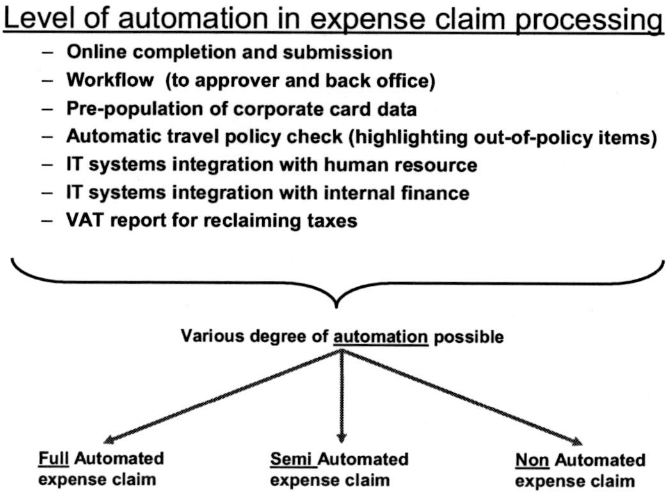

Fig. 43: Level of automation in expense claim processing

T&E expense claim personnel processing cost are still dominate the cost picture. Interestingly the portion of ICT cost between average and best performance is at approximately 8 % of total processing costs.

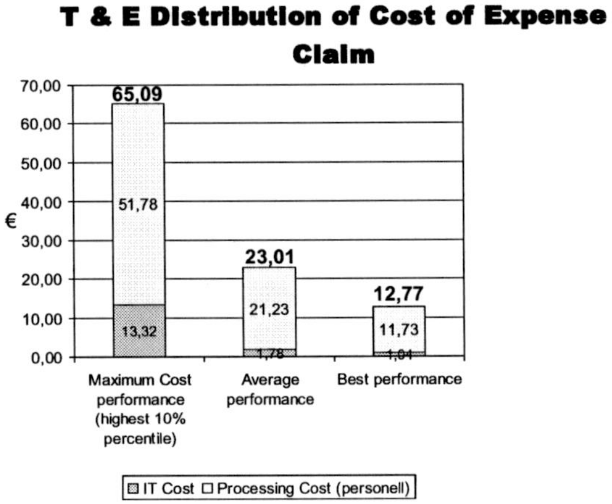

Fig. 44: T&E distribution of personnel and ICT cost of expense claims

Source: AMEX/ATKearny (2003, 31)

Once again, technology is an enabler but for an optimal performance all contributing factors to costs have to be considered and optimized.

Execution Resources Considerations

Decisions on how comprehensive the company's ICT solution for travel and expense management will be depend on the role of the Shared Service Organization. The SSO management can be responsible for travel expense processing or can also manage travel planning. The first step in taking a business trip is planning the means of travel and the accommodation. A travel planning solution should firmly lead the user and only offer choices that comply with the company's travel policy. Such a solution must be directly connected to leading travel-service brokers, the so called "global distribution systems" (GDSs), such as Amadeus, Galileo or Sabre, to obtain accurate and current information about schedules, rates, and so on. If the Shared Service hub creates a travel call center as the customer-facing interface and does all the travel planning for the employee, portal access is not necessary.

On the other hand, the company will have to think about investing in a call center solution. Another option is to introduce an employee travel portal and let the employees do the planning themselves (employee self-service). The Shared Service hub then plays a supporting role if the user becomes confused when he or she requires a complex itinerary. Exceptions from the company travel rules should be automatically routed to the manager responsible. Workflow technology is an ideal supporting framework here.

The most modern solution for expense reporting is offline reporting via mobile phone, personnel digital assistant devices (PDA), and other mobile tools. All entries will be automatically synchronized with the company travel solution the next time the employee connects to the company network. The rest of the travel expense reporting will then be completed in the office using Web access to the travel solution. The travel system should automatically match the value and type of reported expenses against the company's travel rules, and when everything is correct, it should automatically post the expenses into accounts payable. Exceptions should first be routed to the travel clerk, and when necessary, to the manager responsible for approval.

A very convenient feature is to provide information about the status of the reimbursement payment so that the employee knows whether the system has approved the trip expenses, and approximately when he or she will receive the payment. Most ERP solutions are closely linked with accounts payable in F&A or HR payroll and contain predefined interfaces to leading travel service brokers or GDSs. All systems make use of the workflow backbone supported by a portal presentation layer.

3.3.4 Financial Supply Chain Management

Existing mature *ERP solutions* provide an ideal foundation for all the needs discussed above. Their AP system is closely linked with both general ledger in accounting and with purchasing within a supplier relationship management (SRM) system. Most ERP systems use a workflow backbone supported by a portal presentation layer. A *financial supply chain management (FSCM)* capability within or additional to ERP systems (e.g. *electronic bill presentment and payment*) further supports the

- Supplier payment settlement process (FSCM inbound)
- Customer payment settlement process (FSCM outbound).

3.3.4.1 Electronic Bill Presentment and Payment (EBPP)

Billers want to reduce their cost of processing invoices and customers would like to get invoices electronically in a format that their backbone systems are able to handle automatically. EBPP systems provide the capability of the electronic processing of invoices and their associated payments but also for debit and credit advice and account statements. The entire process, including inbound and outbound invoicing processes, with reception, authorization, validation, approval, posting and payment should be fully automated. Automation results in benefits such as lower cost, faster execution with fewer corrections and errors. AP addresses the *requirements* of the *Business-to-Business (B2B)* processes. There are additional legal requirements which have to be fulfilled, such as producing an electronic, legal, taxation-valid invoice between business partners.

Invoices can be received in different medium types, such as paper, fax, PDF-formatted document attached to an email, electronically in different formats like EDI and XML, and different channels (post, email, web-access, wireless). The ultimate goal is to handle invoices electronically in a suitable format for the backbone, or ERP, system. Thus invoices in different medium types with different formats and from different channels have to be accepted, converted in an acceptable internal format, validated, approved, digitally signed (when outbound), executed and archived. Scanning paper invoices together with sophisticated optical character recognition software and channeling it for processing into the backbone system is a common approach when streamlining and fully automating the process.

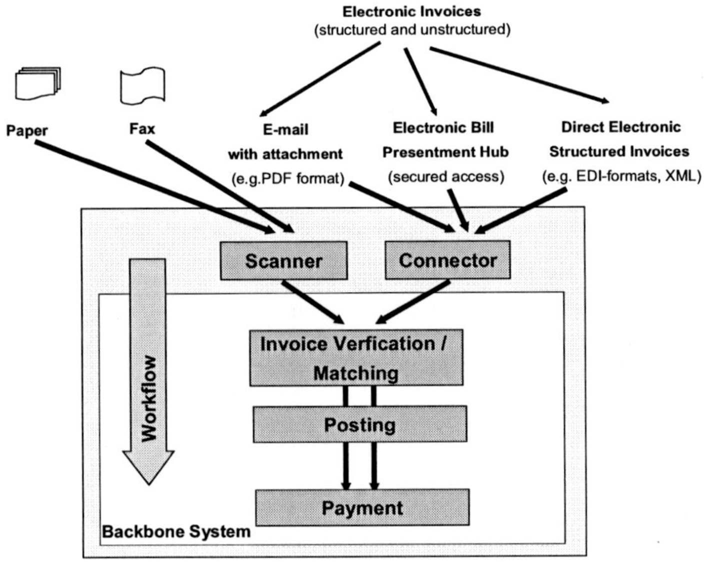

Fig. 45: Accounts Payable target invoicing execution process

There is less effort required if an *electronic invoice* (e-invoicing) can be delivered fully automated directly to the backbone system. The subsequent processing in an invoice verification/matching system and further on in an AP system should always be the same in all cases. Real-world business processes show a simultaneous existence of different invoice delivery channels. Each channel has a different cost level. The cost level between a paper-based process and a full EBPP invoicing process is roughly 10:1. Thus the total cost benefits compared to a full paper based invoicing process will vary depending on the volume portion of each invoice delivery channel.

There are two models, determined by the *structure* of electronic invoice delivery, the *Biller-Direct-Model* and the *Consolidator Model.* Both invoice processing models are applicable for debiting (customer) and crediting (vendor) invoicing processes. Thus the focus on different features and services depends whether you are looking at the biller-centric or the customer-centric view.

In a b*iller-direct-model* the biller and the customer (B2B and B2C) communicate directly without any other party involved. All biller invoices are kept on a biller-owned electronic bill presentation hub and the customer gets an email notification to access, download, accept or dispute the bill and trigger payment. The technical architecture addresses the 1: n relationship. The biller-direct-model has a great affinity to the B2C business. This model provides flexibility because customers are able to access and navigate to additional, detailed data real time (also known as hot billing). The disadvantage is the high cost for implementing and maintaining such a system and the low acceptance by the customers due to secured sign-in and authorization procedures.

A lot more synergies for electronic invoice processing are achievable if multiple billing parties are connected via a neutral, shared electronic bill presentation platform to multiple customers. This applies especially to the B2B business. In such a *consolidator-model* the biller and the customer are indirectly linked in one central system.

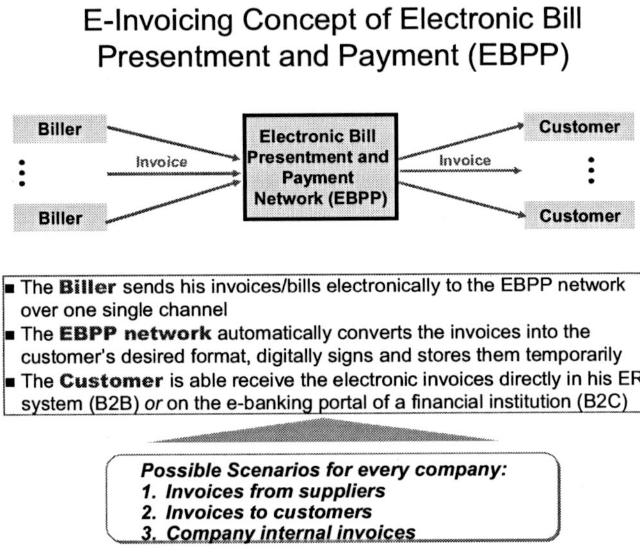

Fig. 46: E-Invoicing Concept for an electronic bill presentment and payment (EBPP)

This model allows you to have an open, scalable n:m relationship network where synergies can be achieved. For example, the converting service of invoices into different document formats can be shared among this participating community. The biggest advantage would be if the receipt of electronic invoices could be directly delivered to the underlying backbone system(ERP, for example). Whether it is used as a biller-centric or customer-centric implementation determines the importance of the supporting features. For example, dispute management, dunning of overdue items and payment reconciliation are important services in a debiting scenario. On the crediting scenario, triggering of workflows, posting the invoices and payment are the most important features. The advantage increases with the size of participating members (whether biller or customer). Services can be separated and outsourced to an external service provider. Thus the initial effort is less expansive compared with biller-direct-model. The disadvantage is that it is necessary to accept the standard formats used by the consolidator. Due to the indirect relationship between biller and customer hot billing (real time access to invoicing data) is mostly not possible.

There are two types of consolidator (or network) models: thick consolidation and thin consolidation. In the Thick Consolidation model the consolidator receives *all* invoicing data, whereas in Thin Consolidation only an *overview* gets past to the consolidator. Detail invoice data is kept still on the biller side and is electronically accessible for the customer. This basic network with biller, customer and consolidator can be enriched by additional service providers. They provide technical and business services which have to be carried out originally by the biller or customer themselves, such as:

- Archiving
- Digital signature and verification
- Electronic data interchange (EDI)
- Printing (for biller) in case of non-electronic invoice delivery
- Digitizing (scanning and optical character recognition)
- Conversion and mapping services in specific formats (e.g. different XML based formats)
- Transmission, transportation security services (e.g. HTTPS, MIME, SFTP, X.400)
- Assuring tax-compliant invoice processing
- Capturing structured data at the source
- Providing an any-to-any platform and platform-to-platform connectivity for processing invoices
- Supporting cross-enterprise workflow capabilities,
- Payment and payment reconciliation capabilities within the EBPP network
- Dunning and dispute services
- Marketing support services
- Consulting services for invoicing business processes

Electronic processing of invoices requires specialized functions and knowledge on both the biller and on the customer site. Every function necessary could be delivered by one consolidator taking over all the different biller and customer facing roles or distributed and shared among an EBPP service provider community. On the biller site there could be a Biller Service Provider (BSP), on the customer site a Customer Service Provider (CSP) and at the consolidator site a Payment Service Provider (PSP). Each service provider offers services to his clients. In practice you may find a cumulation of all different roles/functions combined as an offering of one service provider. For example a bank plays the role of a customer service provider in a B2C scenario because it has become a trusted partner for private payments. In a B2B scenario we will face additional requirements like the optimization of the entire financial supply chain and/or legal needs for the exchange of electronic documents among business partners. The benefit of the participants increases with the increase of the members of the community (network effect).

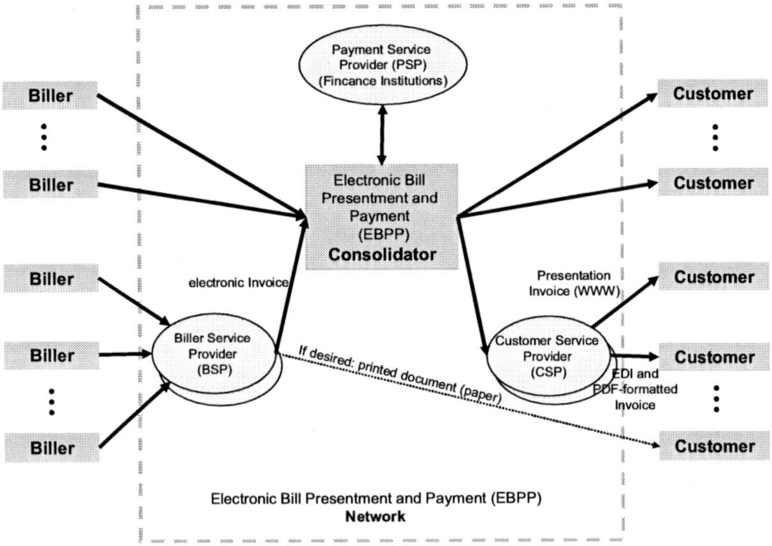

Fig. 47: Electronic Bill Presentment and Payment (EBPP) Service Provider Network

The Biller Service Provider (BSP) acts on behalf of the biller as the invoicing party. The main role here is to collect the invoicing data in different formats and make them available to the consolidator in the EBPP network. Additionally the BSP provides services like presentation of invoicing details in the Web environment, print services for non-electronic invoice delivery, archiving, and so on.

The Customer Service Provider (CSP) acts on behalf of the customer as the invoiced party. He receives the invoices from the consolidator and makes them accessible to the customer via his presentation portal or delivers the invoice electronically in the desired format of the customer's backbone system. The CSP can offer additional services like archiving, payment services and digitization if and when the customer receives invoices directly on paper.

The role of the Payment Service Provider (PSP) can only fulfilled by a finance institution (e.g. bank or credit card provider). The payment can be triggered directly out of the EBPP network.

The consolidator is the central party of the EBPP network. The role here is to cumulate invoices from different BSP providers per customer, delivers the invoices in a consolidated form to the customer or CSP and to monitor the status. The consolidator, as a mediator, is the ideal party to trigger payment orders to the associated financial institutions.

3.3.4.2 Financial Supply Chain – Inbound

Key elements of the inbound FSCM process are Invoice Management, Cash & Liquidity Management, Treasury & Risk Management, Bank Relationship Management and In-House Cash Management.

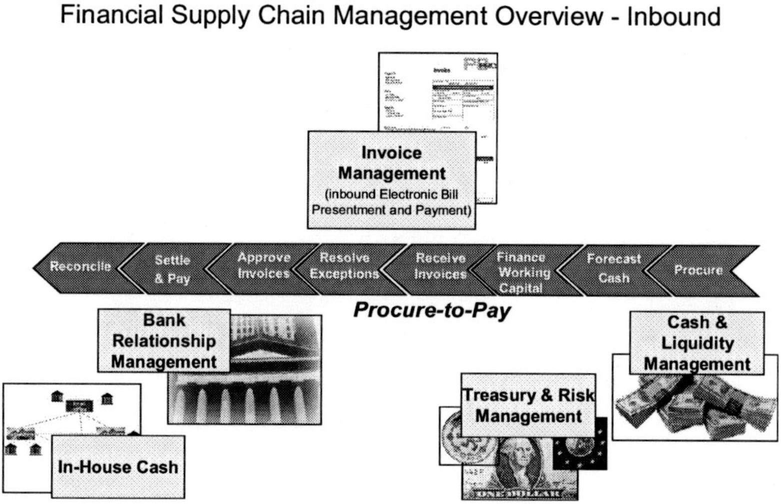

Fig. 48: Business process Financial Supply Chain inbound - Procure-to-Pay (P2P)

3.3.4.3 Financial Supply Chain – Outbound

A *financial supply chain management (FSCM)* capability within or additional to ERP systems further supports the customer payment settlement process. Key elements are Electronic Bill Presentment & Payment, Dispute Management, Collections Management and Credit Management.

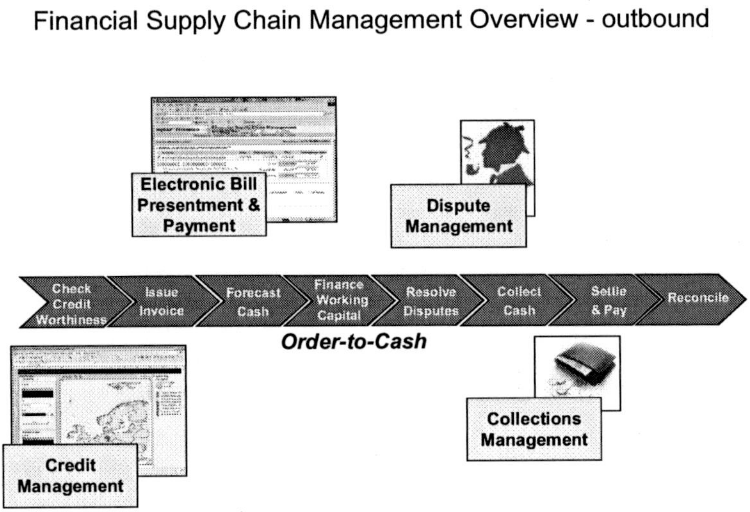

Fig. 49: Business process Financial Supply Chain outbound - Order-to-Cash (O2C)

The internet led to electronic bill presentment and payment (EBPP) as an alternative to paper or fax invoicing. The customer can access all of their invoices in an internet-based portal. Some solutions in business-to-business (B2B) scenarios even allow for the automatic transfer of electronic invoices to the customer's systems, so the customer does not have to retype all of the details.
Basic electronic billing capabilities include:

- Overview of customer account status
- Listing open or overdue items
- Listing paid invoice items
- Trigger accepted customer payment (credit card or direct debit)
- Supporting credit card processes (authorization and settlements)

Currently there are either specialized solutions that are built on top of the ERP systems or integrated solutions in the ERP packages. A dispute management tool can help the SSC track all complaints and their resolutions in a very cost- and time-efficient manner; and at the same time, collect valuable data for analysis and future improvement of the process. The payment area has also introduced a very innovative approach. Customers do not have to use only the traditional means of payment (for example, a bank transfer), but can leverage electronic payments. While the common usage of this kind of payment is still far away, there are already some communities of buyers and sellers showing its future viability. AR in ERP systems is closely linked with both the general ledger in accounting and the billing system within the CRM system. All systems make use of the workflow backbone supported by a portal presentation layer.

3.3.4.4 SAP Solution offering for the Financial Supply Chain Management

Let's have a closer look at how a state-of-the-art Shared Service leverages technology for optimizing the Financial Supply Chain. This focuses on SAP's solution offering:[14]

Financial supply chain management is the most effective approach to optimize working capital levels, streamline accounts receivable processes, and eliminate excess costs linked to payments. Analysts estimate that such efforts can improve working capital levels by 25%. Today, the best companies in a broad range of industries are implementing financial supply chain management solutions to improve business performance and free cash resources for growth and innovation.

With SAP® Financial Supply Chain Management, companies receive a single set of applications to support their entire working capital management cycle completely. These applications, which companies can tailor to their specific needs, work in harmony with their sales, inventory, and accounting systems. SAP Financial Supply Chain Management (SAP FSCM) is a set of applications that can address virtually every process of the entire cash-to-cash cycle. These applications include:

- **SAP Biller Direct:** for handling Web-based payments and account and bill display
- **SAP Dispute Management:** for processing customer invoice complaints
- **SAP Collections Management:** for proactively collecting outstanding receivables
- **SAP Credit Management:** for managing customer credit lines
- **SAP Cash and Liquidity Management:** for efficiently managing and optimizing liquidity
- **SAP In-House Cash:** for centralizing intra- and inter-company payments

[14] The description of the SAP FSCM solution is based on the SAP White Paper SAP ERP: Financial Supply Chain Management with SAP.

- **SAP Treasury and Risk Management:** for managing financial transactions and risks

These applications are modular in design, allowing companies to configure and deploy individual components according to their particular business needs. In this way, SAP FSCM helps companies map their ICT implementation strategies to their business strategies – greatly improving their return on investment. SAP Financial Supply Chain Management is now delivered as a set of applications in SAP ERP. As a result, companies have the power and flexibility to link their financial supply chain management strategies to broader objectives that improve order-to-cash, customer support, procure-to-pay, supplier enablement, and treasury management functions. Using SAP FSCM with other financial management applications in SAP ERP, companies can improve both their financial and their operational processes.

3.3.4.4.1 SAP Biller Direct

SAP Biller Direct helps companies manage account, billing, and payment information. Business partners can display account balances from their finance and accounting departments – as well as data from their billing systems, such as information from the sales and distribution applications in SAP ERP. That means customers can access both their open items and any available credits via the Internet and compare these against outstanding receivables. Suppliers can also view the status of invoices and payments via the Internet.

The business benefits of SAP Biller Direct include:

- Considerably lower transaction costs for bill processing
- Improved liquidity planning
- Simplified payment, settlement, and reconciliation processes
- Reduced errors
- Increased customer loyalty
- High potential for cross-selling and up-selling
- Improved customer management

SAP Biller Direct fills the existing integration gap of companies current e-business solutions for financial management. It is suitable for all companies that want to exchange bills and account information directly with their business partners. As with traditional electronic data interchange connections, vendors can maintain an electronic connection with multiple customers.

Close integration between SAP Biller Direct and SAP Dispute Management allows collaboration among business partners via the

Internet. It also lets customers view the status of their disputes, thereby improving customer relationships and increasing employee productivity.
Integration between SAP Biller Direct and SAP Cash and Liquidity Management enables real-time visibility of bills and invoices for liquidity management, which can improve liquidity forecasting and certainty of cash flow. Companies can combine SAP Biller Direct with SAP Cash and Liquidity Management to account for open or disputed invoices when monitoring cash positions, for example. The system adjusts the cash forecast when there is a change in the status of open or disputed items, giving companies the most accurate statement of liquidity.
Bill recipients are informed by e-mail about changes to an account balance (due to new bills or credits) and can then access the Web page or portal of the biller to view bill and account data. Recipients can also download bills in various formats and import data into their accounts payable systems. They do not need SAP software to access this information – only a Web browser that will operate and interact with SAP Biller Direct.
SAP helps companies in many industries deploy an intelligent solution for electronic and Web-based invoicing and payments. Companies can integrate SAP Biller Direct with their existing customer-service portal to deliver additional accounting capabilities and support for invoice inquiries from customers.

3.3.4.4.2 SAP Dispute Management

SAP Dispute Management supports the processing of receivables-related disputes. Because customers typically do not notify their suppliers in advance about payment reductions or nonpayment, many vendors must deal with huge numbers of payment deductions or delays. The result is declining cash-collection percentages and eroding day sales outstanding (DSO) averages.
Without an enterprise software solution, suppliers must spend a great deal of time manually processing disputes. Estimates show that the average cost of an invoice dispute can range from $128 to $640 per invoice. Because the vast majority of these disputes can be settled with a simple credit memo, companies often waste significant resources to fix rudimentary invoicing issues. SAP Dispute Management is designed to eliminate this inefficiency.
SAP Dispute Management is an industry-leading solution for integrating dispute resolution into the order-to-cash cycle. By helping companies resolve disputes earlier in the settlement process, SAP Dispute Management can significantly reduce collection costs. It can also facilitate cooperation across department boundaries, considerably increasing operational efficiency.

Customer disputes arise for many reasons, including damaged goods or incorrect bills. SAP Dispute Management lets you process these disputes using a different reason code for each type of business transaction that may cause a complaint. These reason codes could include differences in price, quantity, quality, or delivery time. The system logs the status of a dispute as either open or completed. The status, along with the reason codes, controls subsequent actions on the dispute – such as notifying employees via workflow processes or generating an e-mail to the customer.

With SAP Dispute Management, all information related to a dispute is summarized in one central business object: the dispute case. This new SAP object is like an electronic folder for bundling all the information related to a customer dispute. In a single view, companies can see the reason code, processor, disputed amount, and amount paid. Companies can also see all actions that have been taken to resolve the dispute, as well as all customer correspondence.

SAP Dispute Management allows finance departments to analyze a dispute case and examine the invoices, notes, and accounting records that are linked to a particular customer. The drill-down capabilities of this application allow users to view information from other SAP FSCM applications – such as SAP Biller Direct, SAP Credit Management, and SAP Collections Management.

3.3.4.4.3 SAP Collections Management

SAP Collections Management can help companies handle receivables proactively and prioritize accounts by risk. Efficient receivables management has become critical for many companies in a difficult economic environment, where classic dunning notices may no longer be effective with customers. Analysts estimate that efficient receivables management can help companies reduce DSO by 10% to 20%.

With SAP Collections Management, collections agents and accounts receivable analysts have account sort-and-search tools for organizing and prioritizing their work. The agents and analysts can identify accounts that require the most attention based on receivable value, name of customer, or DSO.

SAP Collections Management allows companies to navigate customer accounts directly through a collections work list. The work list provides an overview of all the information companies might need when contacting customers. The customer collection view shows all open invoices, including their current status, as well all open promises to pay and dispute cases. Users can also display a history of each invoice, along with any related promises to pay or dispute cases.

In addition, the application allows collections agents to document the results of customer contacts. An agent can, for example, create a promise to pay and trace it later at the invoice level. Promises to pay that customers do not fulfill automatically receive a status of "broken" or, if the payment received does not correspond to the amount indicated, "partially kept." Agents can also create dispute cases or provide information about the status of existing cases.

SAP Collections Management can help companies:

- Proactively collect outstanding receivables
- Identify and prioritize customer accounts
- Establish a customer-specific receivables-management process to improve customer relationships
- Reduce DSO
- Improve cash flows
- Increase the efficiency of collection agents

3.3.4.4.4 SAP Credit Management

SAP Credit Management helps companies manage their customer's credit lines. Using a centralized system to process and check customer credit lines is especially important for companies with large customer bases. By integrating the financial and non-financial aspects of companies' customer bases, SAP Credit Management can reduce credit risk and optimize credit terms for each customer. SAP Credit Management is a standardized credit-control solution that can integrate data from multiple systems – an advantage for vendors that need to distribute accurate customer credit information in real time. With this capacity, accounts receivable personnel can proactively reduce credit risks and eliminate losses on uncollected receivables. Sales personnel can use credit-limit information to manage individual accounts. SAP Credit Management makes it easier to issue credit to the best-paying customers. If companies rely on external credit standards, SAP Credit Management can integrate credit-scoring information from third-party services. Combining external scoring standards with internal credit rules can improve decision-making and reduce credit risk.

A centralized credit-rules engine lets companies' segment customers according to their creditworthiness and payment reliability. This gives them a powerful decision-support capability for sales, marketing, and other customer-relationship functions. With the credit-rules engine, companies can define their own rules for decision- making and automate a large proportion of their routine credit decisions. Such automation

makes it easier for the credit management department to concentrate on processing the more difficult credit accounts.
With SAP Credit Management, companies create a credit case for processing credit-limit applications. Using the credit case, different parties in the company can request new credit limits for a customer. The credit case is routed to the work list of the corresponding credit manager, who can handle the application or send it to other parties for further review. Through this process, companies can track any credit-limit decision in the system, identify which manager accepted or rejected a credit limit, and determine the reasons behind that decision.
Through integration with a powerful set of preconfigured reports in SAP Business Intelligence, companies can identify high-risk customers and plan special activities to reduce the risk of loss from those customers. Tools for credit portfolio analysis can help companies compare their overall credit exposure company with its strategic goals. With this information, companies can plan special marketing activities for profitable customer groups and adjust their pricing for high-risk customers.

When making a liquidity forecast, the cash manager can use integration between SAP Credit Management and SAP Cash and Liquidity Management to distinguish new and confirmed orders from orders that the system has blocked.
Using these and other capabilities in SAP Credit Management, companies can:

- Control credit risk via real-time credit allocation and ongoing monitoring
- Speed up credit checks for faster decision making
- Reduce effective DSO by reducing payment delays and bad debt
- Increase revenue with risk-free accounts
- Reduce transaction costs by automating the credit application process
- Link dunning and dispute information to the credit-decision process
- Improve customer relations by concentrating on your more profitable customers

3.3.4.4.5 SAP Cash and Liquidity Management

SAP Cash and Liquidity Management, a key application for financial supply chain management, helps companies monitor how their strategic planning affects cash flow – from both a macro and a micro perspective. The application's pre-built data integration capability links with other SAP FSCM applications. As a result, companies can depict activities from operational areas such as F&A, treasury, logistics, and sales and distribution.

SAP Cash and Liquidity Management also lets companies integrate data from third-party or legacy applications and link the systems from different subsidiaries or countries – eliminating the need for duplicate data collection or retention. With SAP Cash and Liquidity Management, cash managers can focus on the most critical figures, make key liquidity decisions, and implement those decisions more effectively.

In addition, SAP Cash and Liquidity Management lets companies:

- Determine and optimize liquidity by individual departments, subsidiaries, business subunits, or organizations
- Support various internationally recognized formats for electronic banking
- Choose between centralized or decentralized cash management
- Identify reserves held in foreign currencies
- Automate data aggregation with real-time integration of different source systems
- Choose between short- and medium-term cash-flow analyses
- Generate short-, medium-, and long-term cash-flow forecasts

Through a range of key functions, SAP Cash and Liquidity Management makes it easy to transfer inbound data, handle liquidity analysis and decision making, and effectively process outbound data. Companies can transfer liquidity information quickly and reliably – from both internal and external sources – including transfers of account statements for the previous day, intraday account statements, lockbox statements, data from the operational systems, and budgeted financial commitments.

The application also delivers accurate results from reports and analyses – results that are essential for effective cash management decisions. Companies can access central treasury information, then structure and process this information according to their needs. In addition, SAP Cash and Liquidity Management provides powerful tools for liquidity analyses, drill downs to line items and documents, standard operational reports, and flexible drill-down reporting. It offers a variety of comparison and control functions – such as cashed check control, value date comparison, and list of balances. Through links to SAP Business Intelligence, SAP Cash and Liquidity Management supports reporting across applications and allows companies to create customer-specific reports.

In processing outbound data, SAP Cash and Liquidity Management supports many standard formats for bank communications. It assigns various statuses to outgoing payments before they are completed – from the initial entry in the payment program, through the dispatch of the payment order, to confirmation of the payment via the account statement. Companies can identify outgoing payments by their particular statuses and display them in a variety of ways. There are several options for payment methods, cash concentration and bank transfers, recurring bank transfers, and free bank transfers – as well as for creating and processing standard formats for electronic bank communication.

3.3.4.4.6 SAP In-House Cash

Multinational organizations often manage a complex network of international business units and banking relationships. An increase in affiliates has led to a significant rise in internal and external payments for international organizations, as well as an increase in bank accounts. SAP In-House Cash can help reduce the substantial costs associated with both cross-border payments and global, intra-company transactions.

With SAP In-House Cash, international companies can centrally process the payments of their subunits by netting and consolidating internal accounts. This provides considerable savings in the administration of various bank accounts, as well as internal and cross-national payments. Through a central payment function, SAP In-House Cash helps companies settle subunit debts with external business partners and transfer the payments to their affiliates. Local payment scenarios are also possible, as companies can include the external bank accounts of subsidiaries.. As payments are made, the system immediately updates cash-position data within SAP Cash and Liquidity Management. This gives the cash manager a global view of the company's incoming and outgoing cash flows.

Additional SAP In-House Cash functions – such as those for cross-bank area postings – allow companies to set up several in-house cash centers (for example, one per region) and enable automatic or manual currency exchange. The in-house cash center lets companies monitor and aggregate various current account balances and plan incoming and outgoing payments for group companies over the medium term. This makes the process of controlling payment flows far more efficient.

SAP In-House Cash also provides many account-management functions – such as calculating and debiting interest and charges, granting current account overdrafts, and generating bank statements for subsidiaries. Companies can configure the features and conditions of each account to meet their needs.

3.3.4.4.7 SAP Treasury and Risk Management

SAP Treasury and Risk Management offer a comprehensive set of functions for managing financial transactions and risk. These functions enable straight-through processing for all conventional types of instruments used for investment, debt, and foreign-exchange management – from trading to the back office – with postings that go directly into financial accounting. In addition, companies can automate and link their financial processes with treasury functions on an enterprise-wide scale. With SAP Treasury and Risk Management, companies can run a centralized treasury and reap the benefits of economies of scale – without the cost of creating and maintaining separate interfaces.

Integration between SAP Treasury and Risk Management and the system's cash- and liquidity-management functions lets companies base trading decisions on data from current global liquidity and risk analyses that reflect cash flows from their operational business.

With the risk-management application, companies get more than the traditional, isolated view of individual sections or specific risks. It includes all the information needed in a single, fully integrated solution – including data on operative cash flows and financial transactions. To measure foreign-exchange and inter state exposures a calculation of the value of the positions and simulation what would happen to future values should interest rates change. Exploring possible hedging transactions to reduce interest rate risk is possible as well. Traditional corporate treasury management transactions are less susceptible to error because the application is completely integrated, in real time, with the SAP accounting and financial reporting solution.

The application can also help companies measure and control their credit and settlement risk. Companies have significant freedom in defining and structuring the levels for default risk. Flexible reporting and evaluation tools – which include key customary figures such as net present value, duration, and value-at-risk – allow companies to analyze financial transactions, positions, and portfolios.

Tab. 7: Key features of SAP Financial Supply Chain Management

Feature	Advantage
Web-based invoicing and payments	Through SAP Biller Direct, customers and suppliers can access invoicing and payment information via a company's own business portal. Seamless integration with the accounting system lets companies handle electronic payment and settlement processes with customers or suppliers.
In-house banking	Using SAP In-House Cash, companies can net accounts, pool cash and payments on a regional basis, and reduce transaction costs for intra company payments.
Online credit evaluation	SAP Credit Management accelerates the ability of your credit managers to extend or deny customer credit limits. Your credit scoring system for each customer is greatly improved through the real-time aggregation of your own credit data and information from third-party credit scoring agencies.
Financial risk management	With SAP Treasury and Risk Management, your trading decisions are based on real-time liquidity positions and operational data. The ability to run scenarios that test the impact of fluctuations in exchange or interest rates can greatly improve risk analyses.
Collection case management	SAP Collections Management helps companies improve the productivity of their collections or agents. By making it easy for agents to identify problem accounts or issues, companies can greatly increase collection rates.
Dispute case management	SAP Dispute Management gives their accounts receivable department 100% transparency for customer invoicing and billing issues. Comments, open items, credits, and resolutions are all visible via a single access point – accelerating invoice settlement.
Advanced cash and liquidity reporting	SAP Cash and Liquidity Management greatly improves companies' ability to forecast and react to cash and liquidity positions. All components are preconfigured for real-time reporting and analysis of their liquidity position.
Portal integration	SAP FSCM applications integrate seamlessly with SAP Enterprise Portal, as well as with existing customer- or supplier-facing portals.

Source: SAP (2004) White Paper – Financial Supply Chain Management with SAP

SAP FSCM can greatly simplify financial supply chain management in an organization. With this set of applications companies can more easily address the multifaceted challenges of managing cash flow and optimizing working capital – two critical elements for successful financial performance today.

The move to Shared Services with the disruptive change of existing processes in accounts payable and accounts receivable is often taken as an opportunity to enroll also new processes in the Financial Supply Chain and gain additional potential to optimize working capital.

3.4 Human Resource Processes covered by Shared Service

In the same way as financial processes can be divided into different categories the the HR processes can be separated too.

Fig. 50: Human Resource process grouping and cost saving potential
Source: Mercer (2002, 8)

All activities with a high potential of centralization (upper two quadrants) are candidates for Shared Services. According to the skill profile we have to distinguish between Transactional tasks (Center of Scale) and Transformational tasks (Center of Expertise).

HR processes typically managed through shared Services:

- Payroll processing
- General policy enquires
- HR administrative data management
- Time and Attendance processing
- Benefits and Pensions
- Organization Management
- Compensation

- Training and Learning administration
- Expatriate and Global Assignment management
- Recruitment
- HR procurement management
- Management and executive reporting

3.4.1 Payroll processing

Payroll is the most common shared service process in HR. It is well suited to centralization, and payroll administration resources can be scaled relatively easily.

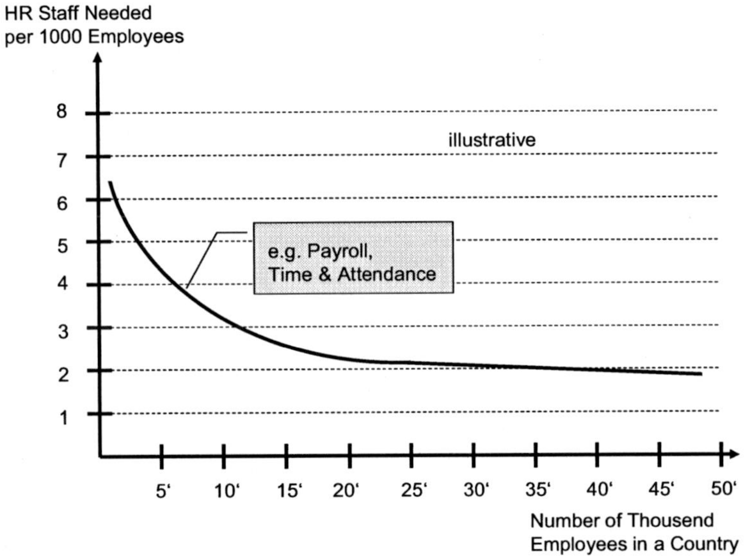

Fig. 51: Scaling capabilities for payroll processing

For payroll to function effectively it has two major requisites.

- A legally and policy *compliant configuration*
- An accurate set of *employee master data*

Compliant configuration

Payroll is unlike any other process, in that government changes are very common, and often unpredictable. Centralizing payroll processing allows an organization to better control system, policy and process updates that are driven by government changes. Close collaboration with both the payroll vendor and the authorities is essential.

Managing multi-country and multi-company payrolls does place significant demand on the system architecture.
Complexities:

- Sheer number of tax and legislative changes
- Competing year ends, makes it difficult to find a "quiet period"
- Conflicting rules (privacy vs. Retention, for instance)

Payroll also requires integration with the financial systems, both the General Ledger and the costing system. Any complexity in these systems adds to payroll complexity and risk. Payroll remains a batch process, in that it needs to run a large number of complex calculations to produce a pay slip. This means the payroll needs to be closed sometime prior to month end in order to be processed. The more efficient the payroll system and processes, the longer the payroll can remain open for entry. There has been a significant trend a way from weekly and bi-weekly payrolls. Monthly payrolls now dominate. This is more efficient and less costly, both in terms of processing and bank costs.

3.4.2 Policy inquiries

A large portion of HR shared services is inquiry based. In larger organizations, policies tend to be complex, and often issues such as Grandfathering complicate matters further. Grandfathering is when a company has old policies still in operation. Often HR policies are negotiated with unions or other employer representatives, and to change them is usually very difficult. Examples include pensions, where the policy may have been set up decades ago. A real example from a railway is the uphill vs. downhill pay scales. All the train routes are described according to their elevation differences, and train drivers are paid more for uphill legs. This is a legacy from the days of steam, where the driver and stoker would have to work harder on uphill.
It is not as easy to rationalize HR policies as is imagined, the realities of labor law and negotiations means that many different rule impact employees, based on factors such as union, length of service, pay scale and so on. Many of the queries for HR are about helping managers and employees navigate the policy legacy. A major transformation project such as shared services deployment offers an organization a great opportunity to renegotiate legacy rule and procedures, but it is not always possible to reengineer policies. Typically these old policies are poorly documented, and the rules and procedures lurk in the memories and informal practices of local HR generalists. As part of the move to shared services it is vital to document these into a formal knowledge base to enable effective query handling.

Vital to a successful HR shared service center, policy and process documentation! Much of the complexity is driven by law. Take for example, maternity pay and absence. Almost ever country has different rules, so advising employees either requires an expensive expert in the shared service centre, or a very well designed and maintained policy database and scripts. Any attempt at labor arbitrage will fail without significant focus on policy and process documentation. Despite large process complexity, Siemens has broken all the HR processes down into simple, manageable, measurable components. Each step is clearly documented. This is at the core of their success.

3.4.3 HR administrative processes

Payroll acts as a calculation engine, processing HR administrative data. If the administrative data is of poor quality, then the payroll and other processes tend to suffer. Organizations are moving as much administrative data input into self services as possible. This move to capturing data at source does improve data quality, but the process changes involved need to be managed carefully.

Administrative processes include:

- Name change
- Adding Dependents
- Changing Address
- Changing Marital status
- Change in grade or pay scale
- Change in working time
- company asset register
- Car scheme management
- One time payments and deductions.
- Regular deductions and additional payments
- Transfers
- Terminations

Organizations running shared services try to drive as many as these through electronic self services as possible, using both employee and manager self service.

3.4.4 Time and attendance processing

This area can be very complex, especially in heavily unionized production environments. Complex rules for overtime and shift work mean that the demands on both technology and staff are significant.

Systems and processes need to be flexible in order to adapt to changing rules and business demands.

Self services are extensively used to enter time related information, and more companies are deploying kiosk systems. Integration with clocking systems is now common, and the shared service centre tends to spend time handling queries, and resolving issues such as missing time pairs. Many organizations have now automated leave processing, using self services to enter and approve holiday. The shared service organization should ideally only get involved in complex cases such as extended sick leave or maternity/paternity calculations and advice.

3.4.5 Benefits processing

In some countries, for instance the US, Australia, and UK, employees often have complex options with regards to healthcare, pension, holiday and other benefits. These processes tend to be highly automated, with extensive use of self services. The shared service centre should be set up to handle queries, and this often requires significant specialist support. In countries with strong state systems, benefits processing tends to be subsumed into payroll processing, given that many of the processes are passed via the payroll interface to government.

3.4.6 Organization management

Keeping the organization structures up to date is an ongoing battle in most organizations. Constant reorganizations and changes are commonplace. Many shared service centers provide a service to HR and line managers to maintain these structures. Often these structures drive workflow and self service processes, so it is vital to keep them in order. Sometimes they are integrated with cost structures so as to help drive better cost distribution.
Organization data is also used to produce reporting charts. Much of this work has now been automated through the use of web based charting tools, but the work in maintaining the structure when it is wrong often falls to the shared service center.

3.4.7 Compensation and performance appraisals

The process of managing pay and bonus distribution is also complex, and can be fraught with problems. The shared service centre can play a vital role in making sure that the managers submit increase and bonus recommendations on time. The shared service centre will typically receive high levels of calls relating to compensation and performance appraisals in a very tight window, just before the round closes. The service center will often be responsible for calling up managers who are late with data.

3.4.8 Training and learning administration

The service center will often maintain course materials and catalogues in e-learning systems, and sometimes be responsible for the procurement of training courses and materials. Classroom based training may also be administered from the shared service center. Employee training records have largely moved online, but the training and learning process still generates a significant amount of administrative work.

3.4.9 Expatriate and Global assignment management

Managing expatriates and their assignments is often done by experts in a shared service center. It scales well. There is a mix of administrative work, such as arranging visas, work permits, accommodation, travel, schools and so on, but there is also a significant amount of more complex advisory work, especially in areas of tax and cost of living adjustment. The shared service centre helps to ensure global consistency and fairness. It also enables more centralized buying of services such as removals and temporary accommodation.

3.4.10 Recruitment

Recruitment has tended to be a local process, but we have seen large portions of the administrative components of recruitment being centralized via shared services. Agency agreements are becoming more global. Shared service centers now process applications, such as CVs and covering letters, arrange interviews, arrange references, and even perform telephonic interviews. The shared service center can be heavily involved in processing the paperwork, such as offer letters, draft employment contracts.

3.4.11 Procurement

With the move to shared services, many HR buying decisions and processes have also been centralized. Examples include training providers, pension providers and recruitment services. Sometimes this procurement is part of HR, often working closely with centralized procurement.

3.4.12 HR, Line and Management reporting

The shared service centre is often responsible for delivering management information such as headcount reports, shared service performance, and more complex trend and benchmarking data. More companies are adding statistical experts into a centre of expertise to produce reports and advise line, HR and executives what they should do with the data. The drive to shared services tends to make both internal and external benchmarking more likely to work, as the data is typically more standardized and consistent.

3.5 SAP Solution offering for Human Resources

For some time SAP has provided the core application process functionality that HR Shared Services typically process: HR Administration, Payroll, Benefits, Compensation, Recruitment, Global Employee Management, Time and Attendance Management.

The figure below highlights the SAP payroll and localization coverage:

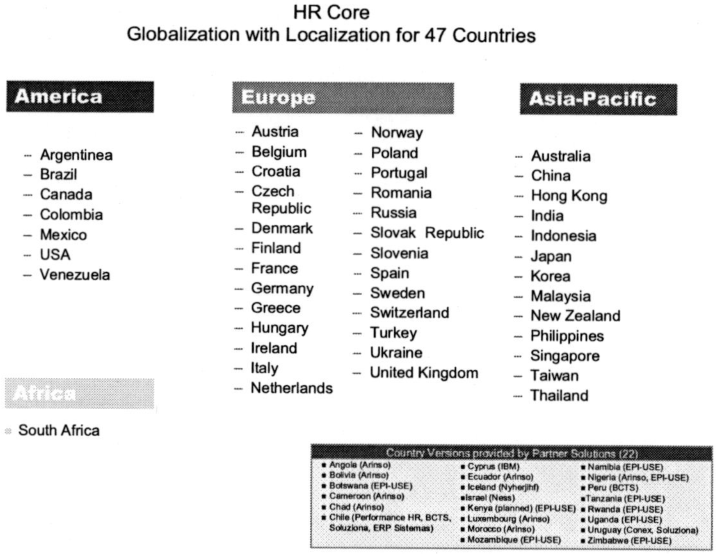

Fig. 52: HR Core – Globalization with Localization

A significant change with the most recent release of SAP ERP, (ERP 6.0) has been the rearchitecting of the core HR process engine for more optimized Shared Service usage.

This journey began with the success of employee and manager self service, but with customers such as Siemens using SAP CRM to manage the HR call center, SAP realized that it needed to rethink how HR processes were managed in the application.

SAP also worked closely with Adobe to build an interactive form solution, improving the flexibility of the manager driven "personnel change request" process and form handling.

By bringing the CRM concepts of ticketing, multichannel contact management together with more flexible forms handling, SAP has rearchitected the HR processes to fit with a Shared Services model.

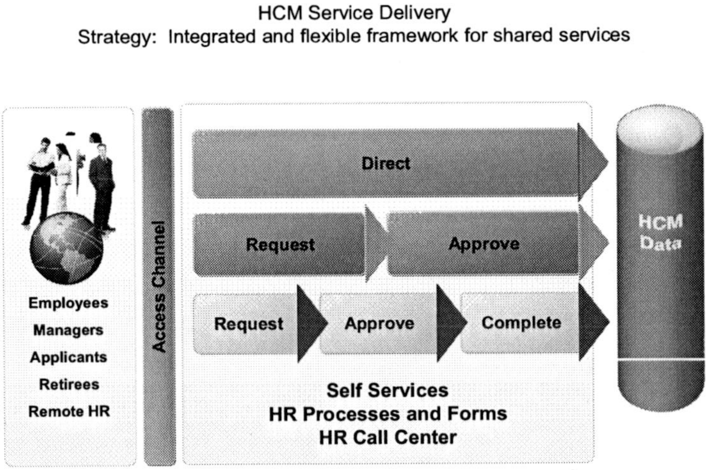

Fig. 53: Human Resource Access Channels and framework for Shared Service delivery

Process integration into HR Portal Roles for support of collaborative processes in HR include Manager, Employee and HR Administrator.

Flexible Definition now includes:

- Forms (Adobe Interactive Form Designer)
- Process (Configuration and Workflow)
- Integration into Digital Personnel File

The Standard SAP delivery contains example, processes, a workflow task repository and back-end services for HR Master Data. SAP has also created a new role in ERP, known as the HR Administrator, with these features:

- Decentralized execution of HR tasks
- Worklist-based work style

- Integration into HCM Processes and Forms
- Data Access Box for direct data maintenance
- Tight integration
- Reporting
- Integrated Digital Personnel File

All the tasks are pushed directly to the worklist, enabling the admistrator or pool of administrators to process the transactions quickly. Let's break this down into a little more detail:

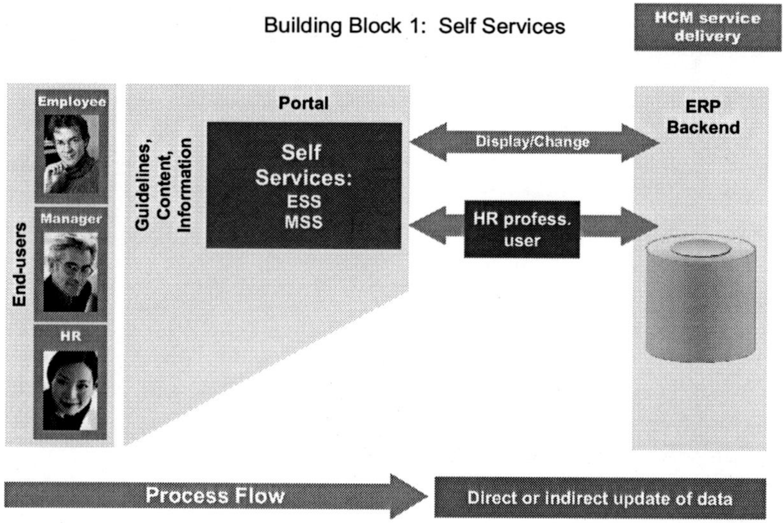

Some simple transactions are performed directly via self services, such as booking a holiday.

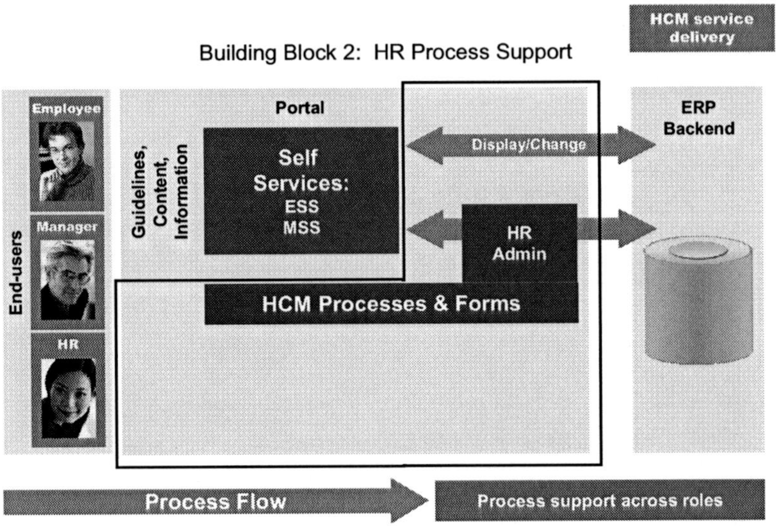

Fig. 54: HR Process Support

Some of the more complex processes are better handled with a form, such as employee transfer. SAP makes use of the Adobe Forms tool to make this process as user-friendly as possible.

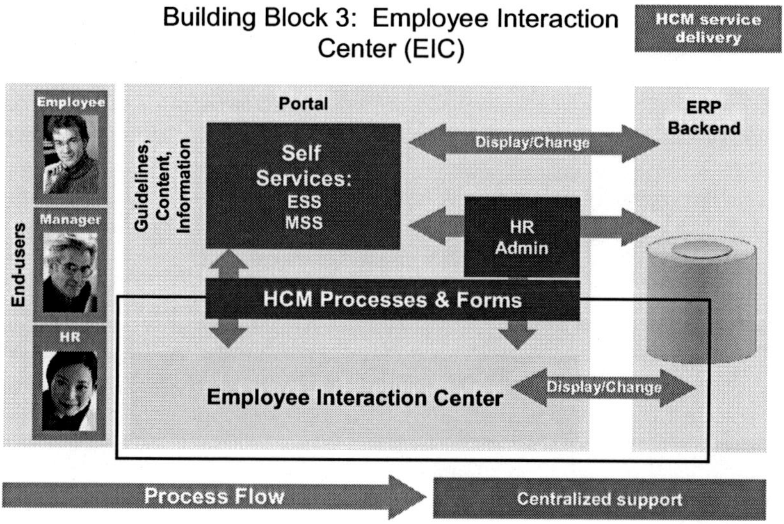

Fig. 55: Employee Interaction Center

The employee interaction center (EIC) provides the tool to manage and track the complete process. The HR administrator would drive much of their work from the EIC .There has also been significant development of EIC analytics, enabling Shared Service leaders to monitor service level agreements and performance.

Key Figures would be,

- Number of created activities
- Number of completed activities
- Average completion time
- SLA Target completion time
- Average (overall) customer satisfaction rating
- Number/rate of activities with a violated SLA
- Number/rate of activities escalated from Tier 1
- Number/rate of activities forwarded to an external contact
- Number of activities completed by an external contact
- Number of activities completed by Tier 1
- Number of activities completed by Tier 2
- Distribution rate (channel usage percentage)

Shared Service delivery has moved to the centre stage in the SAP ERP architecture. This enables organizations to put in place the framework for successful Shared Services delivery.

3.6 Practice: Business Function coverage of Shared Service

F&A and HR business functions are the most frequently used functions that run in Shared Service mode. Procurement functions are catching up and earning an increasing focus. It very seldom happens that ICT support functions are discussed as Shared Services.

Philips:
"We handle finance and accounting, purchasing with requisition handling, catalog management, and supplier negotiations for indirect goods. In finance and accounting, we centrally execute accounts payable, general ledger, fixed assets, travel and expenses, administration tasks, company cards processing, and cash applications.
More directly customer-related processes such as payment collection and relationship management are handled by Shared Services on country level. This is because of language and local regulatory needs. Additionally, we perform some reporting and analytics as well as compliance management tasks. The share of expertise and knowledge-based tasks is a lot lower compared to transactional activities."
"… We will have a split of governance and responsibilities. Philips keeps a front office in charge of internal customer relationship management, vendor relationship management, and specific sensitive customer-facing activities."
"The percentage varies greatly per process. For example, accounts payable has 10% of work remaining onshore. For accounts receivable and collections, we have retained roughly 75 % locally, and general ledger has a percentage of approximately 40 % that is still kept locally." Interview with Michel De Zeeuw]

SAP:
"… These were general accounting, consulting-billing, education-billing, procure-to-pay and customer-to-cash."
Regarding Process split between Business - Shared Service – Outsourcing:
"… At the moment we're at about 30:70, but I think that will change again. " … "As I said, 70:30. So 70% are in, 30% are still out, and these 30% are still out because of the defined process cut, which leaves work within the local subsidiaries." "… it will probably change in the direction of 20:70:10 or so. And it just keeps moving in that direction. It is also the case, as I said, that we have these transactional services at the moment,

but of course it could be other services such as reporting, cost accounting, or whatever." [Interview with Peter Rasper, SAP]

Siemens:
Regarding the national German Shared Service Center:
"It was all pure HR – I'm only talking about HR topics here. That means all the administrative processes, including, of course, payroll, recruiting administration, travel expenses administration, and so on. At the same time, we implemented what is normally only done in the second step – we integrated social processes. That means healthcare management, doctors' processes, company social welfare. These were also the two areas we built up with the Global Shared Service Center."
"The results from our base-line year of 2003 enabled us to find out which services or tasks we could centralize or in other words, incorporate in the service. We found out that 60% of the HR organization's tasks can be integrated."
"Siemens AG decided to integrate a global Shared Service here – a place where different faculties can be grouped together. But we have already spoken about HR, and we have already touched on the German delivery. We have a second business area or cluster, as we call them internally, with A&F, a third one with IT, and a fourth with global procurement, mobility services, and all the purchasing topics. These four business areas all belong under the global Shared Service Organization and are going global in late 2007. They offer all the services and products in this area for Siemens internally."

Regarding the process split between Business and the Shared Service Center:
"The results from our base-line year of 2003 enabled us to find out which services or tasks we could centralize or in other words, incorporate in the service. We found out that 60% of the HR Organization's tasks can be integrated. ... But the ratio then was 60 to 40, 60% was with us, 40% remained with the business partner. And gradually we built up the SSCs, as I said, always keeping this idea of a factory in mind."

Regarding offshoring processes:
"We tried one isolated process – a travel expense process – where we tried to build up knowledge. We have offshored this on a nearshore basis to Bratislava. ... The whole process, therefore, takes place in Slovakia. Whether or not this process remains a one-off, or whether more will follow, remains to be seen, but I believe there will be more."

Regarding value-add services:
"The topic is a difficult one, but I will say yes to start with. How we will do that is another question. At the moment, for example, we are testing a pilot project in the UK to also offer advisory services for top processes such as for severance pay, semi-retirement, and so on."
[Interview with Wolfgang Leitmanstetter, Siemens]

4 Resources – Execution Resources

When making the decision to share services, companies need to both assess and source their business processes. *Business process sourcing* (BPS) is one of the most difficult and challenging tasks. It refers to *who* and *where* the business processes are performed. The triangle of process, people and technology is the basic foundation of every organizing task. The original business processes are always accompanied by a matching information process, so the triangle also applies to information processing.

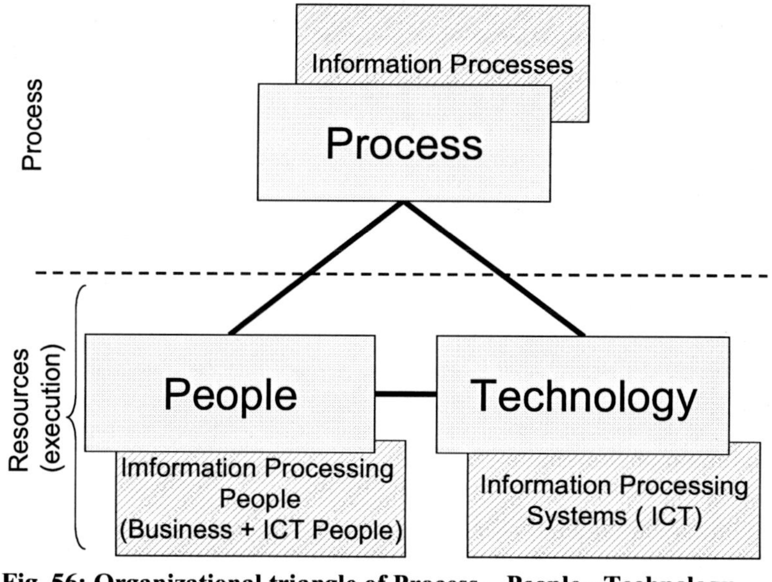

Fig. 56: Organizational triangle of Process – People - Technology

For reasons of simplification, we refer to the business process and the associated information process at the same time. For the purpose of Shared Services we focus on the resource categories of people and technology, especially ICT.

The primary goal of Shared Services is to deliver services that are cost efficient, timely, of acceptable quality, conscious of exposure to risk and with the ability to respond to dynamic changes. Thus the resource based view (RBV) is the dominating view when it comes to resource category decisions, in- and outsourcing considerations (make-or-buy) and dedicated product and service offering selection. The components are inter-related, and made more complex by the people and technology decisions.

When considering people and technology resources, two major aspects are important:

- Capability (competencies, knowledge to deliver the service)
- Availability of process execution resources
  - Location of resources (especially with regard to the delivery cost)
  - Time availability of resources

The capability and availability of people and technology are crucial in supporting the business process. As tangible assets they are bound to a physical location. Digitized information and communication technology services impact less on location issues from the technology perspective. Nevertheless most ICT services in the arena of people and technology are interactive activities. Access to ICT technology is available anytime and anywhere. In contrast, people are location-dependent. Personnel costs form the major part of the total processing cost. The differences between personnel costs at different locations will have a great impact on the overall Shared Service cost structure. Besides assessing the capability and availability of both people and technology, deciding on location also has an important effect on cost.

Unfortunately, this is not straightforward. Companies need to identify and specify their business processes, and assign relevant resources. They also need to make decisions about whether to make or buy, and then to select the appropriate products, services and suppliers. We limit our discussion to the needs of ICT support for genuine business processes. A genuine process will contain a physical, or value-based, supply flow and an information flow for documenting the action in business IT systems. Those IT systems form the basis for business documentation, internal and external reporting requirements, analytical work, decision support, planning and disposition, and so on. Like any other business process, the information processing tasks have to be performed by a resource. Information processing is a combination of manual work and systems work, with full manual or full automation as the two extremes. Most of the information processing is interactive. Both resource categories can be delivered by internal sources, external sources, or a combination of the two (make-or-buy decision). Building proprietary IT systems from scratch becomes a costly and time consuming exercise that later requires upgrades, development and support. ERP systems that package enterprise business applications are the first choice.

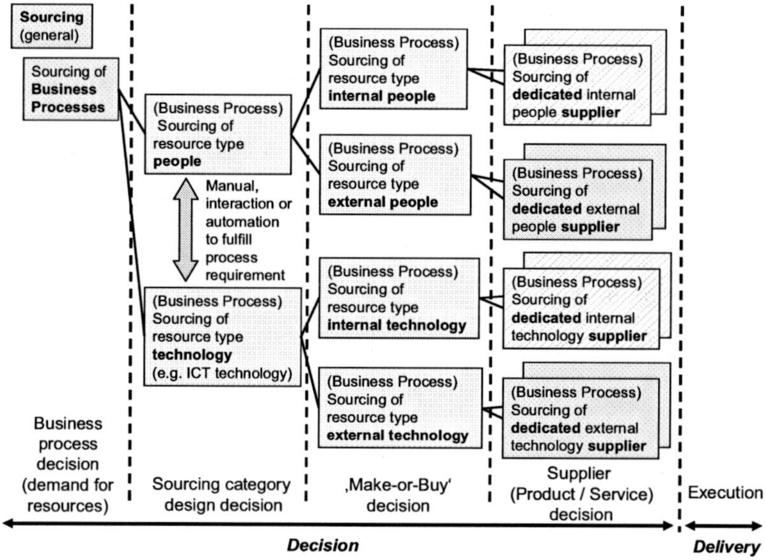

Fig. 57: Business process sourcing decision path

Selecting the appropriate enterprise business applications and resource assignment for handling a project is a critical decision for every corporate unit. Assessing the capabilities of execution resources to fulfill current and future needs is an ongoing and essential task. The decisions have long-term impact and so must be strategic. Unfortunately, the decisions are not independent, which complicates the entire task. Supplier ICT solution offerings for products and services may not match the desired process split landscape, costs and risks may be high. All this complicates the decision-making process. Over time, business requirements and technology capabilities will change, thus affecting the decisions made.

There are different types of *business process sourcing,* depending on the different arrangements of business process, people and technology. It ranges from full internal sourcing (own process governance, own employees, own ICT systems with software owned and operated by the enterprise) and 'true' business process outsourcing (external process governance with dedicated interface specification, external people, external ICT systems).

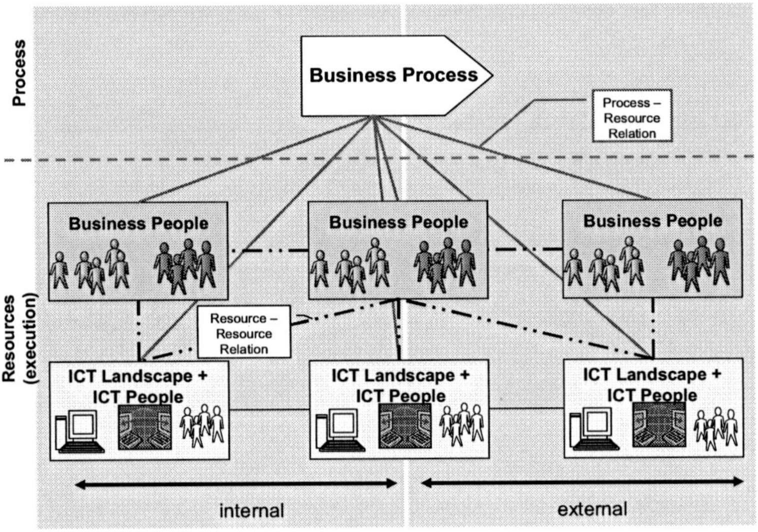

Fig. 58: Process – Resource – Relation

Between the two extremes (internal versus external delivery via BPO provider) there are many variations such as application service providing (ASP), application hosting (AHP), Software as a service (SaaS), Software-on-Demand (SOD) and so on.

Splitting business processes and assigning them to different resources for execution does not necessarily imply a split of the ICT system landscape as well. People with the correct authorizations are technically able to *access* different ICT systems regardless of whether they belong to those systems. Additionally, business ICT application systems can communicate automatically without any human intervention (using application-to-application integration).

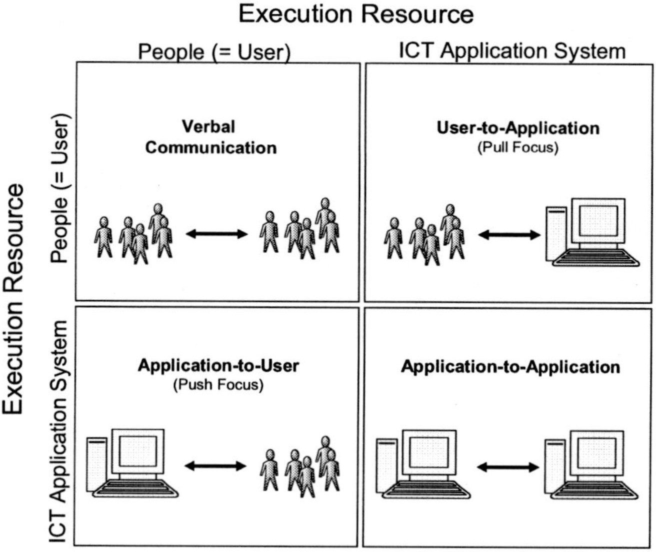

Fig. 59: Communication scenarios of people (users) and ICT systems

In a Shared Service environment there is a communication pattern visible in the above figure. Apart from the direct verbal communication between people, there are communication flows between people and the underlying ICT system landscape. There is also interactive people/user communication (user-to-application, application-to-user) as well as ICT system communication (application-to-application).
Certain business processes may only be assigned to information systems for execution, but an ideal allocation of resources applies to both people and information systems.

A Shared Service environment has two major borders. On the one hand there is the link to the business client (Shared Service buyer) and on the other hand there is a link to the potential outsourcing partner. From ICT system landscape perspective, the Shared Service Organization uses its own independent Shared Service platform or can use the corporate central enterprise system (such as the backbone ERP system). Having just one single corporate enterprise system simplifies the ICT system landscape. No system interfaces have to be considered in shifting work to other internal business people. People and ICT system accessibility is theoretically possible in every sourcing scenario. Seamless interfaces should hide the access complexity between an ICT system landscape.

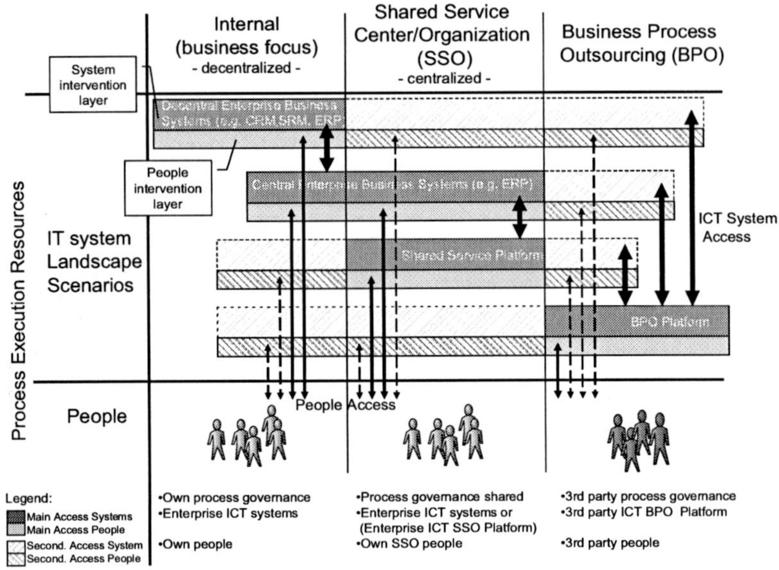

Fig. 60: Business process execution resources assignment scenario

Collaborating with the outside world on an ICT system level is not limited to a third party service provider, such as BPO. The essential difference between the BPO provider and other internal sourcing scenarios is that with BPO, a single major process or set of processes is transferred, with the provider being responsible for the results and for execution resources, such as people and ICT systems. The BPO provider is the full owner of the process governance. The provider synergizes processes, people and technology with existing infrastructure. This requires a well defined data model and process clarity, since both impacts ease of transfer. Coordination is achieved not via the organizational hierarchy as in internal processing (business clients, shared service center) but with a contractual agreement. The dedicated process interfaces become the points of contact in such a scenario.

A Shared Service solution (based on an in-house Shared Service ICT platform) is the most demanding scenario, given the fact that it will outsource certain business processes or sub-processes to external outsourcing partners as well.

The Shared Service approach needs a highly flexible and adaptable ICT platform, which can communicate with the remaining ICT system landscape on one hand, and with the outsourcing partner ICT system environment on the other. Flexibility is needed to cover all the emerging business needs like flexible process change management, faster integration of mergers and acquisitions, faster carving-out of sold business units or companies, automation possibilities, lights-out processing, changing resource assignments to processes, and so on.

The capability and availability of execution resources plays an important role in any process sourcing task. This applies especially to the distribution of work among different resources. Shared Service is characterized by shifting work from multiple business places to a central Shared Service processing unit with or without standardizing business processes. In principle it is shifting the workload of business and people to a central hub. The ICT systems that enable Shared Services remain under company control but may require consolidation. The underlying ICT systems can enable or constrain business process cost, performance, quality, risk and flexibility. To make a sound decision about Shared Service process sourcing, companies require a good understanding of the current and potential capabilities of their ICT systems and workforce. There are other elements that also affect a Shared Service solution decision, such as strategy, process definitions, operational locations and operating models.

4.1 People

People, as one category of execution resources, can be subdivided into two groups: those who support the business and those who support ICT (by maintaining and updating the system landscapes). Shifting the same work from one place to another place requires the same set of skills. Splitting processes along *functional* lines into more granular elements changes the required skills profile. For example, if business processes can be broken down into more administrative transactional tasks, separate from the more transformational, expertise-, experience- and knowledge-dependent activities, then people with a different skills profile can be assigned to those tasks. Allocating resources with a *lower skills profile* (with the assumption of lower labor cost) and/or sourcing from location with a lower *labor cost level* will lead to lower overall processing cost.

4.1.1 Introduction

Throughout the literature and the various interviews, people issues emerge time and time again as a major factor in the success or failure of Shared Service. This section will explore this in more detail. The move to Shared Service involves significant transformation that impacts people in these ways:

- Locational: Shared Service Centers are often located away from where people previously worked. Moving people involves significant cost and personal stress.
- The nature of the work: Shared Services tend to create specialization, and sometimes the work is more repetitive than in traditional HR models. People that are used to face to face interaction may find Shared Service delivery alienating.
- Reporting lines: Often in non-shared service organizations, HR and Finance staff report into the local organization. With shared services, new reporting lines into a central Shared Service can create significant organization politics. Old loyalties often die slowly.
- More formalized KPI and MBOs: Shared Service Centre work tends to revolve around meeting KPIs and SLAs. These in turn, influence reward models. Compensation and other rewards need to be adapted to cope with the demands of Shared Services.
- Cultural differences with the traditional organization.

The change is not only for the people moving to the Shared Service Centre, but for those remaining behind. Managers and employees who were used to calling up their friendly HR guy will still do so, unless the process is carefully managed.
In both HR and Finance, there is a move to the business partner concept, namely Business Partners being advisors to the line. This role requires careful definition, not only in terms of what they do, but also what they don't do. This is especially true if the business partner was previously an HR or Finance Generalist under the former model. It requires significant support and discipline for the HR or Finance Business Partner to tell their colleagues to "contact the service center".

Shared Services creates new career models and organizational demands. It is vital to build a model that enables employees to build a career; otherwise the shared service center becomes a revolving door. This may be adequate if only menial tasks are processed in the centre, but a high turnover will damage the credibility of the centre, and create significant hiring costs. Many mature Service Centers offer Job Rotation, and deploy the principle that spending some time in Shared Services is a good career move.
Shared Services are by their nature process driven. This move to standardization requires training and a significant shift in mindset.
According to Machin and Williamson (2001),
"While HR professionals see themselves as guardians of change management and are happy to oversee the implementation of such

programs within the organization, they may be unwilling to embrace change themselves." [Machin/Williamson 2001]

HR and Finance generalists are typically skilled in the legal and policy issues of one country or one division, but by moving these people into Shared Service Centers they are often expected to service more than one country or organization. This complexity is not to be underestimated. There is more to this than just language.
Some people find the shift to shared services difficult, others adapt to the new way of working. Several organizations suggest that it is often better to start fresh, with new people, especially if there is a strong first level support based model with scripted policy support. This is especially so if you are also doing a locational move.

The flexibility to "exchange" the workforce will also depend on the labor law of the countries in which you operate, and your union climate. It makes sound business sense to engage with Unions or Works Councils at an early stage in the project. In many countries there is a legal obligation to do so.

Shared service has been a great success in the US. The homogeneous language and legal system allow significant economies of scale. Downsizing and redundancy are far cheaper and socially acceptable than in Europe. Multinationals should not underestimate the complexity and differences between European countries. There is often a business case for shared service on a pan-European basis, so it is vital to avoid dropping in American business case and expect it to work. US assumptions need to be tested against local labor law and organizational reality.

4.1.2 Works councils and employee representation

Typically, and this varies from country to country employees in Europe have a much stronger say in reorganizations and disposals than in the US:

In Germany this is known as "Mitbestimmung" (deciding together).
In the space of this article it is not possible to provide an explanation of European labor regulations and the industrial relations framework, but the key points to be aware of are:

- The union movement, although somewhat weaker than in the past, is still strong, especially in traditional industries in continental Europe
- Supervisory boards in Germany consist of 50% employee representatives. (The supervisory board is the highest level of corporate governance and approves major decisions made by the

executive board). Many other continental countries have similar models

- Much is much stronger state involvement in corporate redundancy actions.[15]

The works councils need to be involved early and any headcount reductions will need careful justification and negotiation.[16] I'll rely on a rather lengthy quote from the European Foundation for the Improvement of Living and Working Conditions to illustrate the issues of a significant organizational change: *BETRIEBSÄNDERUNG* or substantial alteration to the establishment is a:[17]
Concept which relates to an instance of co-determination within the works constitution (Works Constitution Act §§ 111 ff.). It covers major decisions on the closure, reduction of operations or relocation of the establishment or of important parts of it, amalgamation with other establishments, fundamental changes in the establishment's organization, objectives or equipment, and the introduction of radically different work methods and production processes. Rationalization programmes and the introduction of new technologies are examples falling under this heading. The assumption is, for the cases listed, that the changes may result in serious disadvantages for the workforce or for large sections of it. Consequently, in establishments regularly employing more than 20 employees eligible to take part in works council elections the works council must be given prompt and full information on any such proposed changes. In practice, substantial alterations to the establishment constitute the main area of use of the participation, information and co-determination rights of the works council in economic matters, and entitle the works council to a reconcilement of interests and a "social plan".

In France for instance,
Companies with a workforce of 50 employees or more are required to develop a redundancy programme (plan social) when they intend to make redundant more than nine employees within a 30-day period. A redundancy program is a series of measures designed to avoid

---

[15] October 2002, the French government appointed Claude Viet to the new position of impact of company restructuring and its effect on employees.
http://www.eiro.eurofound.eu.int/2002/11/InBrief/FR0211103N.html
[16] http://www.eiro.eurofound.eu.int/2003/06/InBrief/FR0306101N.html An example of a works council dispute
[17] See:
http://www.eurofound.ie/emire/GERMANY/SUBSTANTIALALTERATIONTOTHEESTABLISHMENT-DE.html Makes a useful introduction to works councils and other European concepts.

redundancies or curtail their number and to facilitate the redeployment of those made redundant.[18]

The United Kingdom (UK) labor market is considerably more flexible than the German or French markets, but there is still a significantly stronger set of worker rights than in the United States (US).

Any ROI study will need to take into account the cost of redundancy programs and other labor law related matters. The earlier negotiations and discussions begin with works councils and other representative bodies, the better. It sounds obvious but Europe is not a country, but lots of countries. Most administration law differs greatly from country to country although European Directives have gradually begun to harmonize legislation; there are considerable country level variations. (Data protection is an example of this, where there is a Directive, but differing national interpretations thereof). There is little correlation between country size and administrative complexity. A relatively small country, Belgium has an equivalent compliance burden to France, for instance. The centralization benefit needs to be assessed carefully against the cost of redundancy and the political fallout.

The Mercer report goes on to note:
Whilst the various national cultures, languages, and legal frameworks across Europe mean that set-up issues are more complex than in the US, the business case is nevertheless very strong. Many companies continue to duplicate HR activities across Europe and overlook opportunities to standardize policy and practice. Specifically, the high salaries and workforces employed by multinationals in Europe enable economies of scale that deliver substantial ROI, and the consistency that is being introduced by the EU regulations means that centres of expertise are an effective option for ensuring consistency and quality of service across Europe.[19]

A significant number of senior HR professionals in Germany have trained as lawyers, such is the complexity of legislation and its impact on HR processes. However: successes at PWC, Gillette, IBM; Du Pont, Ericsson and others prove that shared services work in Europe. It is more complex, not impossible.

---

[18] See: http://www.eiro.eurofound.eu.int/2003/04/Feature/FR0304105F.html
[19] Mercer ibid.

4.1.3 Cultural and psychological aspects of change

Even beyond the legal issues related to people, it is the cultural and psychological issues of change that create the biggest challenge- for instance one of the major stumbling blocks for effective Shared Service Adoption is Line Manager behavior in the client organization.

From the Siemens interview:
"Then we have the issue of additional effort: The Shared Service is seen as creating more work – shifting it from the Shared Service to the individual areas – which is of course not true at all. If I used to have to write something down, and today I have to enter it electronically, that does not require any more effort. But our culture presents a problem here: Trying to convince older managers or secretaries that they now have to work on a PC and use the new tools. They get their tasks from the universal worklist. Trying to convince them of the benefits of these changes cost us many sleepless nights in Germany."

And from Surrey CC:
"Biggest obstacles we experienced from the line managers. The biggest challenge is to coach the organization, moving it into a culture seeing technology as an advantage, not a disadvantage."

As Henkel noted-
"You need very, very strict governance of change order management if you really want to change something. We repeatedly missed opportunities when someone insisted that something was a legal requirement, where we later found out that we'd been misled."

It is important to recruit your leaders early on. Make them accountable for the ramp up and build up of the center. They will need to build alliances and bridges with the client organizations to drive through change, and they will be critical in setting the culture of the Shared Service Center, establishing benchmarks and early KPIs.

It is often tempting to simply move existing HR people into the service center, especially if this makes sense from a locational perspective. Although easier, this can cause significant challenges.

Graham White from Surrey explains.
"The service team we started out with was to do a twin track approach to recruit externally or new to the organization and at the same time to move across original staff, who have been with us for some time. I mean, with hindsight I'm not sure that was the best solution. I think there were some

real stars came across from the organization, but we also inadvertently transferred a lot of old culture and old traditions, which we spent a lot of time trying to fix, which wasn't a good idea. And realistically, I think if I was planning it again, I would far more circumspect how many people I would bring from the old regime into the new. That said, there were still some great jumping's came across, but proportionally I think I would have taken less."

"I think in terms of the people that you bring in from outside, it's a whole new skill set. No matter how much you think it's the old way done differently, it's not. It's a completely new skill set and one in which you do need to spend as much time as possible analyzing what it is you're going to be doing and making sure you bring in the sort of people, who will adapt to that role quickly."

Mix policy experience and a fresh approach. The Shared Service Center will create new processes and policies, so having a team staffed completely with people used to doing things the "old" way will be challenging, as the desire to change will be limited.
Where possible inject some new blood. Building a completely new organization and team enables you to build a new service and process focused organization, but it will be politically naïve. A balance is vital.

In the Solvay case, they took senior managers who knew the business well to lead the team, but hired the team from scratch. This is an excellent strategy for a greenfields site:
"We started from scratch. But for the building phase I took with me six expatriate directors. That means six senior top experts knowledgeable about every process. That was my agreement with the executive committee that I could choose my people. I've been working with them now for three years – 2005, 2006 and 2007 – and I want to keep them until the optimization phase. They are very senior and well recognized as people who know their jobs. For example, a finance manager who is managing 150 financial operators here was the financial director of the biggest Solvay plant; he was on site operating cost accounting in the biggest Solvay plant in France, 2,000 people. So he knows exactly how to close the books and how to do everything. He is a professional.

So I took with me six professionals. And from there I hired all the rest here locally, and I took about three to five people hired through headhunters, who already had a little bit of Shared services experience."

The BASF story makes for interesting reading. It provides an alternative to the typical Eastern Europe greenfield move. BASF set up the Shared Service Center in Berlin. There are several important lessons to be learnt from this case:

- Early union involvement and negotiation.
- Detailed demographic analysis of the potential workforce.
- A well developed diversity strategy.

This has paid off for BASF.
"Berlin came into it quite late. Of course, the savings that can be made in Eastern Europe are far larger than in Berlin. However, one contributing factor in the decision was the positive response from unions towards negotiating a separate labor contract for the East German region. We were faced with a decision about concluding a labor agreement that would have had a major effect on whether we chose Bratislava or East Berlin. The unions did the right thing. This meant we were able to stay in Germany and, together with the innate attractiveness of Berlin, the availability of employees with good knowledge, good rail connections and infrastructure, the decision was made considerably easier. The prospect of lower start-up costs gave us a cost level that is lower than is standard in Eastern Europe."

Seeger also noted.
"Our advantage is our very low employee turnover, for example. It was 3.4% last year. Sure, we're still expanding and we have highly motivated people on board. Absence is at 1.3%, which is very low. I think there's a lot of motivation there. Our employees enjoyed coming here."

He continued, commenting on BASF's strategy not only to target young graduates, a typical Shared Service employee, but also to focus on women returning to the workplace.

"..we're also trying to make the pool of employees not overly dependent on university graduates. University graduates are under a lot of pressure to go away and develop themselves further after one or two years. Our aim is to have a pool of 1/3 university graduates, 1/3 technical college graduates and 1/3 trained and apprenticed. The average age of our employees is 35. That's relatively high for a Shared Service center but it gives us the opportunity to keep employee turnover under control And for graduates from universities, I have to say we have a good chance of hanging on to them for a long time because there are still lots of management positions open and process experts that can work their way up the service chain, as it were."

As Shared Services take on more high-level, value-add processes, the importance of career planning grows. High turnover is especially detrimental in knowledge worker roles, so providing career opportunities for growth both within and beyond the Shared Service Center. If the Shared Service Center is perceived as just a call center, it will difficult to attract the right employees. If organizations don't build career models that enable employees to grow and move, then the Shared Service center will not attract the people required to do more value-added work.

When building the Shared Service Center as a separate company is vital not to create a perception of second class citizenship.

As BASF notes.
"Our company is a full component, an equal component of the BASF group. We don't have first and second class group companies."

Siemens has been aware of this danger, and has built job rotation into their model from the beginning. Employees don't spend all the time answering calls on just one type of issue.

At Surrey CC, for instance:
"We do a lot of career success and planning and talent spotting to make sure that people who show a forte and an opportunity to develop a move within the organization."

"We had some of the traditional concerns about turnover. I have to say that it hasn't become intolerable for us. We worked very much on the cultural side of working in the shared service center and build very strong team working, so that people actually enjoy the experience. And we've taken advantage of the fact that some staff like the flexibility and the coming and going within that type of environment. So, on that basis we haven't had any real problems. And to be honest, we should have done, because you know, we built a shared service center, which has virtually zero unemployment."

"I wouldn't say it was easy, but we've not had some of the horrendous problems that we've heard from other shared service centers. But I put some of that down to the cultural work we do at the same time as the technical work."

An Accenture white paper (2002) stresses the importance of collaborating with stakeholders to drive change:

"The clients in the business units also have a responsibility for their end of a shared transaction. Many new processes and systems will be implemented, business functions will be relocated, positions will be eliminated, some new jobs may be created.

In fact, the organizational changes at the business unit will be considered by the clients to be much more dramatic and important than the creation of the shared services organization. The Shared Services Organization Design must therefore have a holistic view of the complete Shared Services operation, including the linkage among centers in a networked environment."

This is sound advice. Getting the service center functioning electively is a major challenge, but the larger challenge is to drive the change in people behavior in the customer of the service center.

This change management requires active senior management support. As Graham White from Surrey noted:

"I think number one, stakeholders. You cannot engage enough with stakeholders. No matter how much you think you have engaged, it won't be enough. This is absolutely critical. You've got to do it much, much earlier than you think you should and you've got to keep it going for much longer than you thought you'd have to. I think secondly, in an organization, which is changing from one model to the other, start communicating with staff as early as possible. For them it is a meteoric change and very challenging for them, and the biggest concerns they always have is, they're not getting enough information.

I think, number three is top level buy in, and not just agreement. They've got to actually become champions of the new model. Because the fourth is really just be on your guard, because the big problem will always be line managers. It's a Machiavellian philosophy. They've been successful under the old regime and they don't actually want to change to a new one."

The supervisory level in the SSC is key, especially if the first level work is highly transactional and low level. The supervisors will need to handle a broad span of people control, and be sensitive to both the client organization demands and the Shared Services culture. In cases of highly repetitive transactional work, they should be comfortable in managing a higher employee turnover than is typical in traditional HR or Finance roles.

The people challenges in shared service should not be underestimated. All the interviews stress the need to manage both the Shared Service Center and the cultural and organizational changes in the client organization. The success or failure of the center will largely depend on this.

4.1.4 Practice: Career Opportunities for Shared Service Employees

Shared Service Centers are separate organizational units operating mostly remotely from the operational business. There are two ways to operate a Shared Service Center. Either it is loosely coupled to the company or it is viewed as part of the entire enterprise, sharing long-term vision and goals.

BASF:
The company BASF chose a solution with an overarching "BASF Logo". This shows their commitment to making Shared Service employees an integral part of the BASF community with the same career opportunities.

Marks & Spencer (M&S):
"I have always found that the talent pool in Finance has to go through all the elements of Finance itself. ... What I have always found is that the top companies have Shared Service as part of their road to success and Finance. It's part of the job ladder for career success in that case. At Marks & Spencer we started that by transferring people from London into our senior management positions. We want to continue that going forward."
"One of the things we're about to roll out at Marks & Spencer is a revised approach to development. I would like to mention what John F. Kennedy said in 1963. He said, "All of us do not have equal talent, but all of us should have an equal opportunity to develop those talents." That's very, very important. We're all at different levels of understanding the talent, but we should provide everybody with an equal opportunity to develop what they have within themselves. And that's we're doing at Marks & Spencer, because we're setting up four key structures for development. The first two are basics that everybody should have: customer service and finance and accounting knowledge. And then you have a role capability, which we'll work with, and then you have a personal challenge as well. And they will become your four development opportunities for the year.
I always say that if I had one thing to rank first in the budget, it would be training and development because I think that's the key. If we want to drive efficiencies when you see you've no budget for efficiencies, you won't drive efficiencies by investing in travel. You'll get it by investing in people and training and development and culture." [Interview with Mr. Foley, M&S].

SAP:
"This issue of fluctuation will remain to a certain degree the same, I think. In order to mitigate the risk you have to invest in people. We offer them functional and management career path within the Shared Service and outside and/or develop or certify them over a two year time period as professionals – which helps to improve their market value. Very important is to have a very sound, easy accessible knowledge management with training curriculums and learning tools, which are always up-to-date. The continuous drive for more standardization is another brick , which helps to solve this issue, as is easier to transfer knowledge and people."
"We are investing heavily in training, not only within the finance subjects or processes but as well in order to develop the colleagues personally. We offer them career paths, in principle via the different organizational divisions within our Shared Service Center, but also in the Shared Service Center HR. It is important that the strategy is understood and the SSC is part of this. Therefore we conduct multiple sessions to convey this content to our employees." [Interview with Peter Rasper, SAP]

4.2 Technology

When referring to technology, we mean Information and Communication Technology (ICT) and ICT application systems, ICT infrastructure or IT tools that support business processes. Most of the business activities in large enterprises related to back-office functions run through a Shared Service Organization. This applies especially to payment in F&A, cash disbursement and cash collection in business end-to-end processes like Order-to-Cash, Procurement-to-Pay, Travel & Expense and Freight payment. These are typical examples of Shared Service business processes. ICT is the foundation on which those business processes are designed, built and implemented. Selecting the right ICT platform becomes a critical decision. Selecting the right IT applications (ERP, CRM, SRM, as well as e-applications like e-payment, e-invoicing, e-procurement) is another. Companies will also need to choose other enabling tools like workflow, imaging tools, web access equipment, database management, specialized additional applications for matching and optimization of payments, electronic data interchange (EDI), and so on.

Managing dedicated business processes within a Shared Service hub is the core target for every Shared Service Organization. Success depends largely on the fit between the business processes and ICT. Process design must be included in the ICT design mapping. Standard ERP packages provide a lot of parameterization (customization) capabilities to support the intended business process. Carving out the best solution for an enterprise in a unique situation is a sophisticated and challenging task. Customizing is not the same as programming missing functionalities. Standard packages provide a framework of parameter settings to adapt the IT system behavior to the desired business process. Nevertheless there are gaps within in the parameter setting framework which can only be closed with additional programming. The capability and adaptability of the ICT, both now and in the future, have a major impact on the efficiency and effectiveness of the Shared Service solution.

In general there are no doubts that the appropriate use of ICT will lead to a reduction of costs per service unit. The following illustrative diagram shows the impact of leveraging IT and cost reduction.

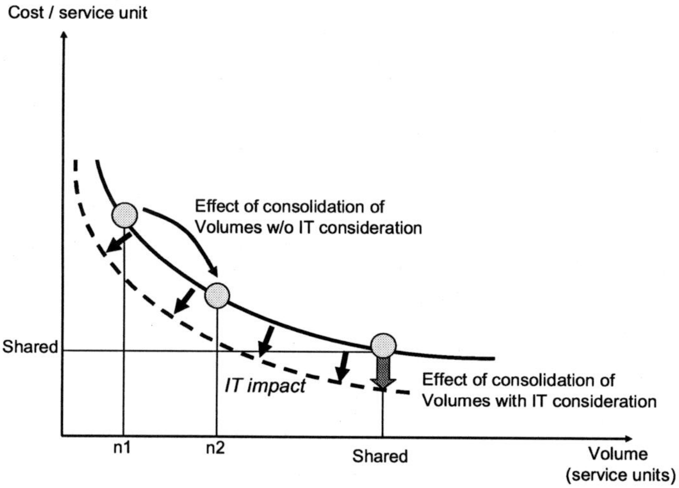

Fig. 61: Leveraging IT resources

There are so many buzzwords around sourcing business processes by ICT such as 'Right Sourcing', 'Best Sourcing', 'Intelligent Sourcing', 'Multi Sourcing', and so on. All of them have a common intention, the optimal supply of services, particularly ICT services. Sourcing business processes by ICT has a multi-faceted view. [Ortwein 2006, 8]

- Degree of partnership (vendor, system supplier, strategic partner, joint venture)

- Magnitude of sourcing a single activity type (total sourcing, partial sourcing)
- Time period agreed for service (limited contractual time period, long term, indefinitely)
- Resource transition (execution people transiting to service provider, ICT system transfer to service provider)
- Dimension of compensation (usage based, fix price, pay per use, pay by success, on-demand)
- Number of service providers (single sourcing, multi-sourcing)
- Reality of service unit (dedicated organizational unit, virtual sourcing)
- Objective (reducing cost, improving quality, acquiring know-how, increasing flexibility, better risk control)
- Distance of software experience of the service client (ICT infrastructure, ICT applications)
- Service type (consulting, development, maintenance, operation)
- Business criticality (core competence, complementary)
- Geographical dimension (local versus regional, international or global; onsite versus offsite).
- Geographical distance (a shored service center in one country could serve locally as on-shore, as well as remotely (off-shore)

All these facets are inter-dependent and create a multi-*dimensional profile.*

In the past there was little awareness of the difference between ICT *sourcing decisions* and ICT *sourcing delivery*. Today it is still common that the internal ICT department covers both functions. Together they form the ICT *sourcing strategy*. According to recent studies on the future competencies of ICT, it is clear that there is a strong trend to question the current role and to distinguish between the sourcing of ICT services and the supply decision and delivery part. [Ortwein (2006, 8)]

ICT service delivery can be offered by internal or external enterprise ICT resources. It is still common practice to source business processes with internal ICT resources. There is a perception that certain tasks would be better executed by internal resources. Below we list the pro and cons of using either internal or external resources.

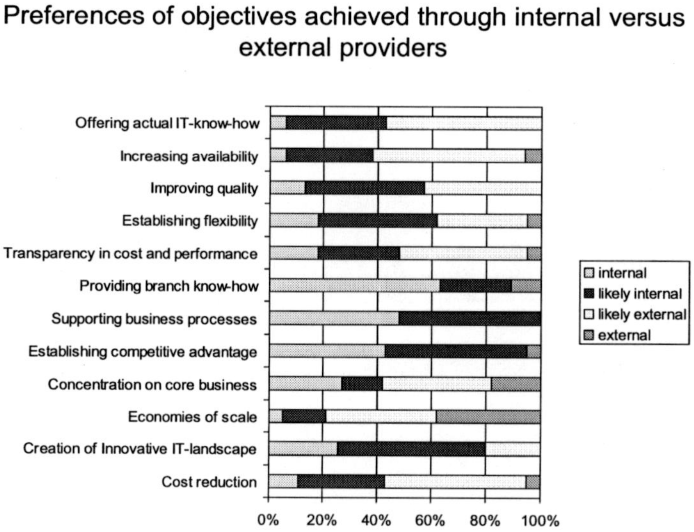

Fig. 62: Preferences of objectives achieved through internal versus external providers

Source: Ortwein (2006, 9) own translation

There is obviously a strong common understanding that economies of scale can only achieved with external providers. Items like access to know-how, availability, concentration on core business and cost reduction opportunities still rank second.

4.2.1 Technology Solutions in Shared Services

There is a wide range of technology solutions for Shared Services. Some of them could be grouped into business-oriented solutions like ERP systems and e-applications. Others are more generic, such as workflow, imaging and scanning. It is sometimes hard to distinguish what is more important - the business aspect or the technological capability (such as a call, contact or interaction center).

Empirical surveys show a similar picture. The foundation of Shared Service is mostly an ERP system and workflow.

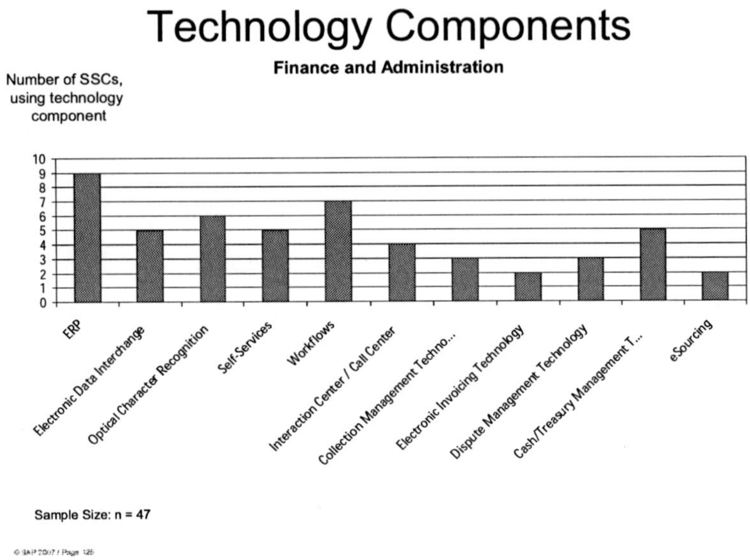

Fig. 63: Technology Components
Source: SAP survey (2007)

The focus and priority may change over time. In the first initial phase of implementing Shared Service is the focus on building a solid ICT foundation such as an ERP system. This foundation will be augmented by additional automation tools like imaging, optical character recognition (OCR) and digitizing the communication (such as Electronic Data Interchange, EDI).

4.2.1.1 Enterprise Resource Planning Systems (ERP)

Technology is an enabler for Shared Services. This applies especially to ICT Application Systems. Enterprise Resource Planning (ERP) systems are the foundation for Shared Services today as the main application information system infrastructure. ERP systems support the shift from departmental, siloed applications to an integrated, cross business corporation. No wonder that ERP systems are considered the most useful and important technology. Without them, Shared Services would not be possible. The success of a Shared Service implementation and its sustainability over time depends on a strong and integrated ICT platform.

Integration has so many aspects that it is worth clarifying the term from the point of view of business software applications. From the ICT perspective, the term refers to data and process integration. *Data integration* deals with the size and structure of data fields (data model, data format) required in business application systems. This data can be understood by dedicated business applications within the borders of a certain application or even within a given ICT system landscape. Data formats and structures are stored in a central data repository. Storing captured data in one central place provides "one version of truth" and avoids redundancy. Sharing data among a defined ICT system environment is not enough. Processing the data (preferably in real time) is required as well. *Process integration* ensures the consistent processing flow of data (in a processing integration hub). The advantage of packaged business applications (such as ERP) systems is the common, consistent data model and predefined end-to-end integrated business process flows based on predefined *business events*. To a certain degree, application processes can be tailored to corporate processing needs. Triggering non-predefined activities can be achieved via an additional business workflow.

The implementation of ERP systems brings many benefits to the corporation such as internal standardization, simplification of system landscapes, lower cost, higher productivity with lower headcount, faster business process execution, higher data quality, process transparency, and so on. Unfortunately the world is constantly changing. Previously, stable business processes would have had to quickly adapt to new requirements like internal organizational repositioning to the market, increased merger and acquisitions or divestitures, regulatory requirements and new ICT capabilities (such as the Internet) of networking with business partners and customers. This has had an impact on the increased demand of ICT support for business processes. Solving *data and process standards* with associated connectivity is still a major issue in ICT organizations today.

4.2.1.2 Self-Service Applications

Self-services are characterized by a decentralized service enablement for geographically remote users like employees, managers or even external business partners and consumers. While the point of engagement is decentralized in self-services, and thus viewed as an opposite approach to Shared Services, the enabling IT system application is centralized. The definition of Shared Service is a narrow concept covering only the centralization of workload execution to Shared Service people. A wider definition includes centralizing resources regardless of whether they are manpower or technology. This may include the centralization of technology in the Shared Service concept, in which case self-service applications could be considered part of the general Shared Service approach as well.

Additionally, self-service concepts have a major impact on the processing split between local and central processing execution and responsibilities. Self-service ICT applications usually require a higher level of performance, availability, security and general operating requirements. Self-services are usually the well-known HR processes. The most common examples are the change of personnel master data like bank account, postal address, travel and expenses, information on policies, time and absence reporting, and so on. In the background the self-service application can feed multiple ICT systems.

Self-services are emerging as a trend in F&A for business partners (vendors) and consumers as well. Master data changes, viewing the status of payments and billing and payment disputes are examples of F&A Self-services. Self-service applications have to validate and feed the back-office applications just as a standard ERP system does.

4.2.1.3 Contact - Interaction – Call Center

A Shared Service Center acts as an autonomous organizational unit with a clear separation of tasks. Communication between the Shared Service Center and the clients as internal customers becomes critical. Like any other external customer communication there are many different communication channels (phone, email, fax, letter) in use. Thus it is advisable to use the same solutions for supporting internal Shared Service customers. Usually those technologies and tools are assigned to Customer Relationship Management (CRM) software solutions. Those solutions include contact/interaction/call center functionality. Based on a generic technology foundation the content of implementation is context specific. Therefore there are different kinds of interaction centers, such as the accounting interaction center (AIC) or the employee interaction center (EIC) for HR resource related processes.

The interaction center is an agent desktop which enables Shared Service center employees to manage in- and/or outbound contacts on a single business platform. The interaction center is the tool that links front and back-end is, and unifies them. Every contact can be logged and this ticketing mechanism tracks and triggers execution.

4.2.1.4 Workflow

Resistance to change is often a major issue with the implementation of Shared Services. Employees fear the loss of direct contact once they suddenly become clients. They were used to talking directly to the processing clerk in the office around the corner and valued such a personal approach. Workflow brings a personal touch back into the

process, but not on the previous scale. Clients of the SSC will be able to see who is processing their items and will be regularly informed about the processing status. When the number of clients is limited, it is highly recommended that the SSC processing clerk spend some time with them at the beginning. This means that employees in the SSC will not be just names where the items are sent for processing. Workflow should run across all the IT systems to deliver a seamless integration. Only then will the whole SSC process be manageable.
Workflow capabilities are a necessary tool to get a workable Shared Service solution over geographically dispersed sites. It becomes the most important communication tool between Shared Service centers and clients. Approval and dispute processes are unthinkable without workflow. Nevertheless only 58% of the Hackett Benchmarking Study from 2004 shows the use of workflow. Obviously there are a lot of unstructured and informal communication tools (such as telephone and email) still in use.

4.2.1.5 Data Analysis and Reporting Tools

A vital piece of feedback that has been identified is closing the loop in the management processes. The same is valid for SSC management. All aspects of core processes, such as SSC employee performance, benchmarking with external SSC vendors and so on, should be continuously evaluated. Such analytical feedback will function as an early warning system, giving the SSC management enough time for corrective reaction. Data warehouses have proven themselves as an ideal solution for multidimensional analysis. Users can gather information from various sources and then view it from different perspectives. Vendors have just started coming out with the next generation of data warehouses offering the first useful applications of automated data structure recognition, allowing users to find patterns and insights in otherwise unworkable data. Some vendors have gone even further and developed specialized applications on top of the data warehouse. Such applications help manage performance, they structure strategy direction and make it executable, or offer analysis of specific parts of the operational processes. Those applications are evolving more and more into whole suites copying the same evolution pattern as ERP. We could therefore view them as "analytical ERP" suites. Analytical platforms for SSCs are deployable either as part of the corporate system landscape or as an SSC-specific application. Deciding which route to choose depends on the long-term strategy for the SSC evolution. When the company thinks an SSC could be outsourced sometime in the future (we mean a complete spin-off here, not just personnel outsourcing), it would be a smart move to design the analytical platform separately from the corporate landscape right from the start.

4.2.1.6 Portal

The Shared Services concept makes increased demands on structured communication and information sharing. Traditionally, information was sent and received using many communication channels – telephone, fax, paper, e-mail, and so on. Merging the majority of those channels into one brings significant advantages. Users (SSC clients and SSC employees) have one place to find everything in a structured form. Every user obtains only the data sets relevant for their daily work, and these are incorporated into the individual portal structure. This way, an employee sees information on the status of their travel expense reimbursement and, at the same time, personnel from the travel SSC have all the information needed for expense processing at their fingertips. A portal always represents two views: one, a way of displaying all relevant information on the employee's workplace, and two, as a way to roll out company policies (such as travel guidelines for hotel and flight categories or planning and budgeting procedures for managers). By using a portal, companies can filter offers individually, and guide the employee's behavior according to company rules. Using portals is convenient not only for its ease of customization and personalization, but also for its positive impact on costs. Portal deployment drives down the IT maintenance cost significantly, contributing to an overall lower Total Cost of Ownership (TCO).

4.2.2 Summary of Technology Solutions in use

In the past, ERP systems were always on top of the ICT technology usage list, but recent trends show a growing focus on ICT tools and applications (e.g. imaging, scanning, EDI, e-applications) that complement the ERP application package.

Harmonizing business processes benefits from the capabilities of ICT applications on a homogeneous ICT system platform. SAP leads the list of ERP systems in use.

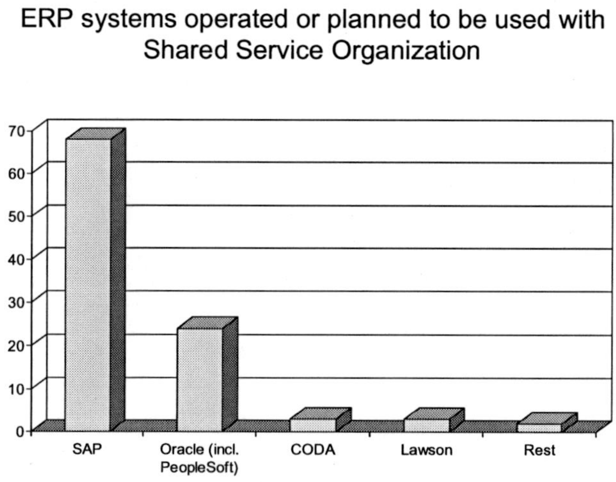

Fig. 64: ERP systems operated or planned to be used within a Shared Service Organization

Source: Hackett (2005a, 24) (own diagram)

From Shared Service perspective, the following requirements are vital to an IT solution:

- Functionality: ERP systems or more specialized applications like customer relationship management (CRM), supplier relationship management (SRM) and e-application (e-Procurement, e-Invoicing, e-Payment) systems provide built-in business functionalities. Access to these functions can be designed for an experienced user or in as self-services (such as a HR employee interaction center).
- Integration of communication: Predefined connection points in ERP package systems together with workflow provide the communication capability to integrate with the remaining processes. Portals are a common interaction tool which enables access to business functionalities for internal and external parties.
- Configurability: There are different styles of doing the same business process. Mapping those styles by setting switches, without having to perform extra programming, eases the ICT systems adaptation and configuration tasks.
- Scalability: Centralization of processes cumulates business transaction volumes and collects a portfolio of supporting processes. Shared

Service systems therefore require a high degree of adaptability to supporting volume and different processes.

The impact of the consolidation of multiple ICT application instances is clearly visible in the following diagram.

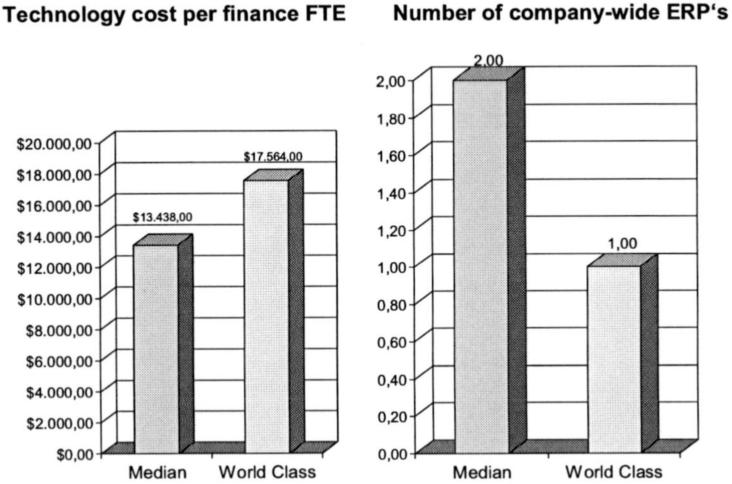

Fig. 65: Technology cost per finance FTE and number of company-wide ERPs

Source: Bangemann (2005a)

Highly successful or world class companies are investing more in technology with the goal of having one single ERP application system.

Another important aspect is the degree of integration of applications. In F&A, world class companies have a higher integration ratio than the rest. This percentage seems to increase over time. An example of integrated applications between Accounts Payable and Purchasing illustrates the trend.

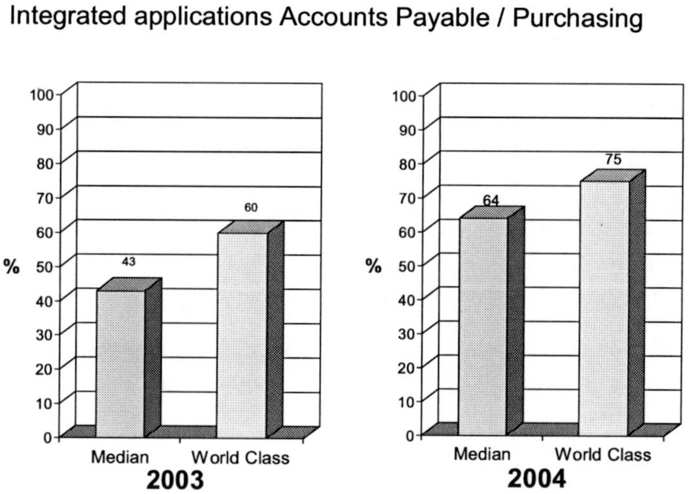

Fig. 66: Integrated applications accounts payable and purchasing
Source: Bangemann (2005 a) (own adapted diagram)

4.2.3 SAP Solutions as a technical and business foundation

Interview with: Bernhard Fischer, SAP Vice President Solution Management Shared Services

Introduction: Shared Services have become a common optimization strategy for cost, quality and risk in Finance, Human Resources and Procurement. Leading analysts confirm that top performing companies frequently operate Shared Services. Let us take a closer look at the optimization levers the Shared Service approach presents.

Shared Service owners have mastered the transition of teams and functions into their Shared Service Centers. Shared Services Centers have routinely off-shored and successfully unlocked labor arbitrage effects. What will be the next big trend in Shared Services?
Bernhard Fischer:
To summarize the findings of many analysts as well as feedback from Shared Services events in recent months, the answer is surprisingly clear: Automation via technology; becoming a 'professional service provider' who can stand against external (BPO) competition.

Looking at the Shared Services factor cost - which changes and trends are visible now compared to the early Shared Services wave?
Bernhard Fischer:
Labor availability in offshore locations is increasingly problematic as wage levels increase by 10 to 15% annually. Technology being a small component (between 2 and 5%, depend on process and decreasing) of the cost model with a big effect on total cost through automation of previously manual tasks. For example the introduction of an Employee Interaction Center at a large global electronics manufacturer reaped HR cost improvements of 30% with the platform cost being a single digit fraction.

Is BPO the ultimate goal? In other words, is Shared Services just a transition stage for the organization to prepare itself for BPO?
Bernhard Fischer:
Shared Services and BPO are two types of service centralization. Both follow similar principles (in that they need clear interfaces, need governance of the provider-consumer relationship, and that the platform is very important).

Our observation is that BPO and Shared Services are no longer treated as opposites. Depending on company size and company culture, Shared Services can be a definite alternative to outsourcing. Companies make selective use of both strategies. For simple transactional services (payroll or invoice management), specifically for those processes with local variations of language and legal rules, using BPO offerings can be easier than building the same expertise in captive mode.

Companies using Shared Services are - by design of the internal service provider-service consumer relationship - well prepared to make use of selective outsourced offerings. I would go as far as to recommend to Shared Services owners to consider employing selective BPO services to optimize their service portfolio and cost. The Shared Services Center can thus become the integrator and facilitator of the two sourcing alternatives (captive and outsourced).

What principles should be considered for Shared Services automation?
Bernhard Fischer:
Companies should identify incremental services that can be 'bolted-on' to the business processes used at the internal clients. These 'bolt-on services' will be similar or even the same for all internal clients establishing a natural realm of the Shared Services Center. Examples for bolt-ons are

the automation of invoice reception (scan/OCR/text extraction) or Interaction Center.
Designing automation demands means handling exceptions. Exceptions (such as customers disputing invoices) need defined mechanisms to be detected early and processed efficiently. For example, the receipt of the respective payment of a disputed invoice would automatically close the dispute.
When designing process automation do not forget that the separation of service provision and service consumption intrinsic to Shared Service induces extra communication. This additional communication - if left unattended - will easily destroy the savings achieved by automating the 'local' Shared Services Center processes. Remember to consider the periodic exchange of items-to-be-processed, results, master data changes, service reports, approval workflows, amongst others.
Obviously the more previously decentralized business processes the Shared Services Center can attract and centralize, the bigger the scale effects will become. When changing the previously decentralized processes, Shared Services owners need to balance the cost and resistance to change against the incremental benefits of Shared Services centralization. The combination of process harmonization and system consolidation achieves maximum savings.

Why should Shared Services Centers strive to own the services platform?

Bernhard Fischer:
Today many (if not most) Shared Services Centers operate on whatever system landscape has been in place before incubation of the Shared Services concept. This leads to situations in which the Shared Services Center staff has to login to numerous different backend systems depending on the internal client they are serving. These backend systems are often not 'in control' of the Shared Services Center, neither on a day-to-day basis nor in terms of longer-term investment and optimization. The delivery platform however is key for any service provider to ensure deliver-against-promise (SLAs) and to decide autonomously about investments into efficiency improvements.
If the Shared Services Center wants to withstand competition from external (BPO) providers it should employ the same principles. Platform ownership and authority to take business-driven decisions is one of these principles.

Why should Shared Services Centers consider SAP as their Shared Services platform?

Bernhard Fischer:

As a high-volume operation a Shared Services Center's first-and-foremost need is to ensure a stable transaction platform. SAP's architecture has proven itself in some of the world's largest companies as a stable and reliable backbone. SAP's bespoke benchmarks as well as customer references prove scalability in supporting the Shared Services Center to take on more and more business.
SAP's renowned multi-client architecture supports true multi-tenancy for functions which require separation of data or require a certain extension of process specifics while still leveraging scale effects.
The long-term viability of the SAP-based service platform will protect the investment necessary in platform requirements and skills training for the Shared Services Center's staff. Viability stems from SAP's predictable roadmap and maintenance strategy as much as from SAP's 35-year stability and organic growth as a company.
The ease of SAP-to-SAP integration counts when considering that SAP is in use in more than 70% of all companies operating Shared Services (according to Hackett). A SAP Shared Services platform is open to communication with non-SAP applications as well.

Shared Services are a consideration at SAP in the design of forthcoming versions of the software, such as in the design of the Enterprise Service enabled Business Platform. Enterprise Service Architecture brings the deployment flexibility desirable in a service-provider-to-service-consumer process mapping. The Enterprise Services reflect natural units of process execution while also defining the process interface between the Shared Service Center and its internal customers.

Finally SAP nurtures a comprehensive ecosystem of software partners - leading solution providers in their respective area - to round-off SAP's portfolio with capabilities like Service Level Management or paper invoice automation.

How does SAP support Shared Services and Shared Services Automation?

Bernhard Fischer:
Let's start with SAPs support in the most prominent Shared Services areas, HR and Finance.
SAPs HR solution has been designed for a scenario in which the HR department sees itself as a service provider to the employees and managers. The communication mechanisms (SAP HCM ESS/MSS Employee and Manager Self-services, SAP CRM-based Employee Interaction Center, HR Processes and Forms) are designed to ensure that the employee receives service when needed and with minimum effort for

both the employee and service provider. Automation in SAP's HR solution does not mean avoiding communication - it makes communication more efficient and helps to avoid ambiguity. For example, an employee can notify the company about the birth of a child via Employee Self Service and – if there is a question not addressed by the self service - contact HR with a single click. When addressing the employee's concern. The HR business partner receiving the request will already have the employee's data immediately available. The Employee Self Service interface leverages Interactive Forms based on Adobe technology with an intuitive look and feel appropriate to tasks required only a few times during an employee's life cycle. The HR Shared Services Center on the other end of the service delivery chain has the support of Processes and Forms mechanisms to manage the employees' contacts and communication in a cohesive way, and thus is able to provide answers and contextual help. SAP's HR Payroll module is designed to provide payroll services to multiple customers, the HR benefits module complements the aggregator role a Shared Services Center can play for a company's healthcare and pension plans aggregation volume towards external plan providers. The HR Shared Services Centers will conquer Talent Management in the years to come starting with recruiting support, extending into facilitation of training services and more. SAP's HR solution in conjunction with the SAP CRM Interaction Center will support the Shared Services Centers in this direction.

In F&A SAP supports the current Top Ten of Shared Services starting with the SAP ERP modules Invoice Management, Receivables Management, Inter-company consolidation and Financial Reporting. Recognizing the trend to manage Finance as a supply chain, SAP offers a set of Financial Supply Chain solutions: SAP Collections Management., SAP Credit Management, SAP Cash Management, SAP Dispute Management, SAP Biller Direct and SAP Bank Reconciliation.

Looking at Receivables Management more closely, SAP provides the platform for the Shared Services Center to bill clients in various industry contexts, act as a collection agency and to manage disputes related to the outstanding payments. Account Receivables Management automates follow-up to events like payment due date passed, payment received, dispute created, partial payment received and implements the desired level of automation. All this is configurable via rules.

Invoice Management is routinely shared in Shared Services Centers and also seen as a function with high automation potential. SAP - together with partners - automates the paper-invoice-to-pay process to the extent that only exceptions need human intervention. These exceptions are brought to the attention of the accountants through automated workflow. The media by which the invoices are received should receive close attention. Paper invoice reception can be automated by OCR solutions from a broad selection of SAP Solution Partners whose solutions ensure minimum human involvement in turning paper into digital invoice information available in SAP. However, it's important to question why the invoices are received on paper in the first place. Companies should consider enabling their suppliers to send their invoices electronically to make the process dramatically faster, avoid duplicate work and save both sender and recipient money. SAP’s response to electronic supplier enabling is SAP Biller Direct. SAP Biller Consolidator applies the same concept to buyers.

When invoices are received, they need to be stored and archived. SAP’s Archive Link interface together with archive solutions from SAP partners establishes a integrated and powerful Shared Services platform. The paper management infrastructure built for managing invoices in the first place can later be leveraged to manage the communication around HR, which are often forms oriented.

In Finance, as in HR, Shared Services manages communications, such as questions from suppliers and requisitioners, in a Shared Services set-up in which service consumption and service provision are separated is key to not lose the gains obtained through automation of the transaction itself. The SAP Accounting Interaction Center (a variant of SAP CRM-IC) together with workflow addresses communication along the same principles as described for HR.

Travel Expense Management is another service frequently shared today for which SAP has an elaborate solution following the same principles of automation - self service- and which is workflow-oriented, rules-based with minimum human intervention

For Procurement, SAP provides automation of the procurement process itself by (again) enabling the requisitioner to procure goods and services with minimum human intervention. Approvals are requested via workflow. The electronic enabling of suppliers (SAP SRM-SUS) and category and catalog management lend them selves to Shared Services Centers. Companies can extend the Shared Services Center's scope in procurement, by implementing spend aggregation via business analytics and supplier rating, as these promise significant savings.

The SAP Interaction Center together with the SAP Business Workflow and the SAP Enterprise Portal provides a single communication front-end to the Shared Services Center for its internal customers, spanning all lines of service.

What else should Shared Services owners consider when deciding on their business automation platform?
Bernhard Fischer:
The business automation platform should be specifically designed for and supportive to integration with multiple back-ends of varying vendors and releases. This support should include workflow, master data synchronization and homogenization.

With SAP's NetWeaver Integration Platform, the Shared Service Center can cater for all levels of business process integration – from communication interfaces to information syndication to orchestration of process chains operated between internal client and the Shared Services Center. These process chains include SAP Exchange Infrastructure (widely known as 'XI') for communication, SAP Master Data Management for data harmonization and catalog syndication, Business Process Management and SAP's Business Workflow to facilitate the desired process orchestration between the Shared Service Center and the business processes at the serviced organizations.

The world is moving to Service Oriented Architectures. How is this relevant for Shared Services?
Bernhard Fischer:
The Enterprise Service model will be to Shared Services as the name suggests – the platform reflection of the Service-Provider / Service-Consumer model. The Shared Service Center should envision itself as a provider of Enterprise Services in a technical sense while its in-house clients consume these services via their backend systems. The granularity of the Enterprise Services will provide support in designing process chains. These chains flexibly allow decisions on execution authority that is whether certain process steps are executed in the Shared Service Center while other process steps remain in the execution of the in-house client. In that sense SOA is the ideal vision for a Shared Services platform.
SAP has put SOA firmly on its roadmap with many Shared Services-relevant Enterprise Services already available in ERP 2005.

Beyond the transactional service platform, what other automation aspects should be considered important for the top performance of Shared Services?

Bernhard Fischer:
First and foremost, the Shared Services Center is a mass processing unit that ensures stability of throughput, transparency of workload and bottlenecks, performance and cost per unit transacted. The platform response is a cockpit function allowing companies to analyze the health of the operation at any moment.

SAP applications deliver a comprehensive set of reports which can be executed in SAP's Business Intelligence data warehouse. The Visual Composer toolkit supports configuring cockpits to the needs of any Shared Services operation – large or small. The BI data warehouse supports extension of business analytics or for performance metrics leveraging the wealth of intelligence gathered during the Shared Services Center's day-to-day operation.

Governance of the relationship with the internal consumer is key to assure acceptance. This is an area where Shared Services Centers today make compromises in order 'to avoid overhead'. Agreeing expectations with internal customers along KPIs and Service Level Agreements is the most efficient way forward as it avoids endless disputes and justifications. Special mention goes to the critical incubation phase in which the internal resistance is usually biggest. Being able to test the Shared Services achievement can make the difference between failure and acceptance of a Shared Services Center approach.

Inefficient tracking of delivery performance can indeed cause cost in the high single-digit percentage range of total cost of operation. KPI reporting can be automated through a Service Level Management solution for which SAP cooperates with a solution partner (Digital Fuel Technologies).
Charging mechanisms finally support transparency of value versus cost and support autonomy of the Shared Services Center in budget and investment decisions. Here SAPs industry solution for Professional Service Providers should be considered.

What should Shared Services Center owners consider in terms of platform to make their Shared Services operation move up the value chain?
Bernhard Fischer:
With the wealth of transaction intelligence gathered from serving several units of the company in several business processes, the Shared Services Center is in a unique position to provide the company with information to support better business decisions. For example, the Shared Services

Center 'sees' the aggregate purchasing volume of one client and sees the client's payment behavior at the same time. This information brought to the sales department through convenient business analytics tools like SAP BI can help to serve good customers more effectively and reduce the cost of capital.

Another point to consider is the synergies between different business activities, for example the automation of invoice handling can be cross-leveraged into handling HR forms received by the HR department, the Interaction Center can be leveraged across HR, Finance, Procurement and so on. It's important to recognize that this cross-fertilization of best practices in service provision and automation does not stop with platform technology but extends to people skills as well.

4.2.4 Practice: Technology an enabler of Shared Services

Organizing Shared Service tasks implies a split of execution and assignment of resources to different process execution resources. Shared Service Organizations may use one or multiple heterogeneous ICT systems. Working collaboratively in such a fragmented ICT system landscape is a challenge.

BASF:

Regarding Contact Center:

"We use contact center functions for both the HR area and for the financial area. For example, we offer a language-dependent answer service in the accounting interaction center, depending on how the caller's number is identified. The question is always, do I have a one-to-one relationship? Lots of companies want a single contact person for their company for all questions. This of course means that one person takes the questions and then runs backwards and forwards between departments to find the answers. I mean, if one contact person is responsible for general ledger issues, for AP and cash management, that person can't answer every question competently. The question is whether you couldn't channel these requests through a type of CRM tool as well, because then you could at least answer questions in people's native language. Then I tell the caller, in a friendly voice of course, that I can't answer the question immediately; there might even be the possibility of answering simple questions straight away. Most answers are noted and stored in CRM. Then you can statistically evaluate them in the standard way and generate FAQs with the corresponding answers. This is why I advocate following a two-fold strategy. A one-to-one relationship exists more in the general ledger and management accounting areas, and the rest is more anonymous.

To start with, we were all very skeptical about whether they would be able to provide answers there. At the beginning they weren't able to answer questions, but they built up knowledge. We now answer HR questions for all of Western Europe. This means that someone calls up and says that they haven't got their wages. Why is that? Or that they have travel expenses and some amounts are missing. Could we check it? Our people can switch into the systems and have access to a knowledge database that was fed by the local HR departments. In other words, they have all the information in once place and can give an answer to these questions really quickly. If not, the question is noted down and the customer is contacted later.
We also have to make sure that we don't become too brittle for our own organization. Because then the following happens: yes, I spoke to Mr. X, he doesn't have a clue, but Mr. Y, he's good. And if I call, I always ask for Mr. Y. Then poor Mr. Y gets all the calls and Mr. X doesn't get any anymore. So it's best keep it anonymous and to create a customer interaction center."
"It's important that the questions don't get lost. That happens frequently if there is a one-to-one relationship to a contact person. It's really important and I'll get round to that, I'm sure. If we provide a service for more than 100 companies, then it's not possible to build up and maintain a one-to-one contact person relationship to each and every one of them. If the answer is not immediate, the customer can be contacted by e-mail. Not all of our staff has e-mail access, but there is what we call the kiosk in a lounge where people can log on. It works fine."
[Interview with Hans-Jürgen Seeger, BASF]

Regarding ICT system landscape:
"We're currently working with seven IT systems and want to consolidate these into three IT systems as the core systems here in Europe. Worldwide, we'll be working with four IT systems. If we consolidated even further, I can imagine using only two IT systems: one for Europe and one for the rest of the world."
"If you roll out this type of project, there are a lot of things linked in to it. Business trip accounting systems in Europe are all very different. We're trying to implement SAP. In the meantime, we're in a bit of a gray area. Additionally, we have a variety of different archiving systems that we want to get rid of. And let's not forget the different paycard systems in the AP area that we have to deal with. So there are all sorts of different solutions on the purchasing side, where the local companies have set up all kinds of subsystems. Understandably, we're not particularly happy about this situation. Then there's also the banking area, where we use different banking tools.

This is not really good for a Shared Service Center because we have to try and limit the variety down to one standard."
[Interview with Hans-Jürgen Seeger, BASF]

SAP:
"We use it very intensively – that's a significant point – to make the whole thing more efficient. Especially e-billing and OCR to avoid as much input as possible. Because the less input I have, the less I need to do during the process. Pre-configuring things so that I only need to deal with the exceptions in the Shared Service Center is the decisive moment. That's the basic idea. Other tools are the Duplicate Analyzer, which helps us to make sure that things are not entered twice – or the AIC or Accounting Interaction Center. The AIC is a call center functionality adopted for finance processes and is used for the interaction with our external and internal customers. This tool is essential to organize the helpdesk work and to monitor and optimize issues in all areas."
[Interview with Peter Rasper, SAP]

Siemens:
"What initiated the whole process was the implementation of a national, comprehensive HCM system in Germany. We used to have, I think, 70 proprietary systems and we merged them using SAP software. That was the impetus behind it all – this common data storage."

Regarding the usage of a contact/interaction center:
"… From the very beginning, we had a vision or a concept in mind. We wanted this Shared Service Center to be a factory. That was the concept behind it. We looked to the manufacturing industry for inspiration. They had done it all before with their industrial processes. We asked ourselves: What are they doing and how can we do it too? We were quick to use the EIC as more than just a call center. We envisioned a complete order management system. … We were one of the first to use EIC in that way, and ultimately all these features like management, ticketing, roll outs, cataloging the individual products, tracking, and all the topics we manage from the EIC came out of it."
"We didn't stop with the Employee Interaction Center (EIC) order tool. We optimized the workflow systems. It was a long, hard struggle to find the right approach. We have built a type of process engine, …". You need to imagine it lies between a portal, between EIC and the Human Capital Management (HCM) systems, which allows us to map processes even at multiple levels. … The machine takes care of all the manual work. Today, we do 18 processes like that.
[Interview with Wolfgang Leitmanstetter, Siemens]

Solvay:
Solvay was in the lucky position to start its Shared Service with one single ICT system.
"... Yes, and that's thanks to our Head of Information and Communication Technology of the Solvay Group, who has invested a lot of effort and money to push SAP for the last 10 years. And now we get the value, sorry to say this, of having suffered that much of SAP; now we know why we had to suffer. The single shared services center was the final touch in a long-term strategy to integrate everybody into an integrated system." ... "That's the reason Solvay is a little bit late in the game. It's because, as I told you, we not only wanted the process to be redesigned but also stabilized. Stabilized means being run through the same single enterprise resource planning (ERP) platform. We are running everything on SAP R/3 4.6 at the moment. So that's the condition before migrating the shared services center. We are running just one single ERP platform for finance; we are running another one for HR, SAP; and we are running Arinso outsourcing for SAP payroll. We have a dedicated cash management system, CICC, but which is totally integrated in SAP software also. So we enjoy a very stable and harmonized IT environment. My 250 operators here have SAP profiles dedicated to their job descriptions." [Interview with Guy de Mercier, Solvay]

Surrey County Council:
Regarding Self-Services: "Yes, and where we couldn't, because not everybody has a computer, we also put assisted services. That's where they are able to telephone and someone else would do it for them. The saving isn't as great, but you still get some of the economy scale."
"Yes, we have all of them and workflow has been the backbone of the success of our SAP system." [Interview with Graham White, Surrey County Council]

SAP:
"It's the nuts and bolts of the whole thing. The fact that we're all in the same boat is the basic requirement for being able to work so quickly and not to have to worry about system consolidation or similar problems. We're all in the same boat, as I said. Once a workflow has been defined, it is rolled out worldwide into the various company codes and that's that." [Interview with Peter Rasper, SAP]

5 Organization – Process-People-Technology Integration

Business processes and resources are two major pillars in every organizational construction framework. The organizational task provides two challenges:

- Master the start-up problem: which organizing phase sequence (strategy, process, structure and systems) is the most likely to be successful? Should the business process determine the resource (people, systems) requirements or does the capability of the ICT system landscape determine possible types of business processes?
- Determine and optimize the structures and task flows with dedicated selected execution resources in a way to fulfill the needs of given strategic and operational goals.

5.1 Organizing Task - Foundations

5.1.1 Organizing Task Sequence Challenge

With a given set of goals the ultimate organizing challenge is to determine where to start. Is the first step the logical business process, followed by organizational structures of assigned people resources and then the requirements for an ICT system landscape? Or is it the other way around: that the ICT system capabilities (with their implicit built-in business process support application limits) guide the organizing task in supporting the process and subsequently the people and resource requirements.

In the past, the problem was talked via the common categories of strategy, process, structure and systems. We assume that every activity has to be aligned to an existing strategy. The term structure stood for organizational hierarchy of people with assigned types of tasks. The enforcement of execution and coordination assumed a hierarchical structure. With the emerging trend in distributing the workload to external parties (outsourcing) a networking type of arrangement has to be found. The type of coordination therefore also has an impact on the ICT system landscape requirements. For our purpose the term structure covers the coordination form as well as the organizational set up of people execution resources regardless if they are kept internally or externally.

There are a variety of options available. They all have their own pros and cons.

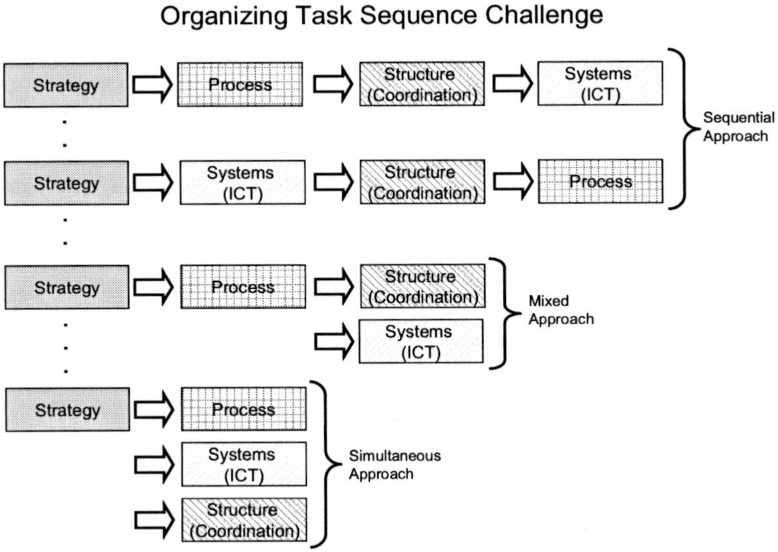

Fig. 67: Organizing Task Sequence Challenge

There is no silver bullet to solve the conflict of how to start organizing. Preferences may change over time. Organizational activities have to consider the strategy and the given or expected:

- *Capabilities* of resources (people and information and communication technology)
- *Availability* of resources (time and location; scalability of resources),
- *Coordination model* (organizational hierarchy, network arrangements, market)
- Internal and external economic, social, legal, political *environment*

A *scorecard* contains the key basic measures : cost, performance/ productivity, quality, risk, flexibility. It provides the foundation to assess the options for a *business case*. The *transition plan* should be based on the Shared Service scope, governance structure, the process split between business and the Shared Service Organization, the Shared Service organizational model and coordination model for all the affected areas (processes, people and technology).

5.1.2 Organizing Task Landscape

Organizing and managing the Shared Service delivery requires an overall decision about how business processes and resources, particularly ICT, are aligned to the business strategy. Thus, defining dedicated *tasks* (functions, processes, and services) and assigning them to *internal and external execution resources* (people, technology) becomes a critical decision. Freedom of choice is limited by internal and external factors. Business targets, future expectations, resource capabilities and availabilities, and the legal and economic environment are susceptible to dynamic change. They are also important guiding the decision-making process of *how* everything fits together.

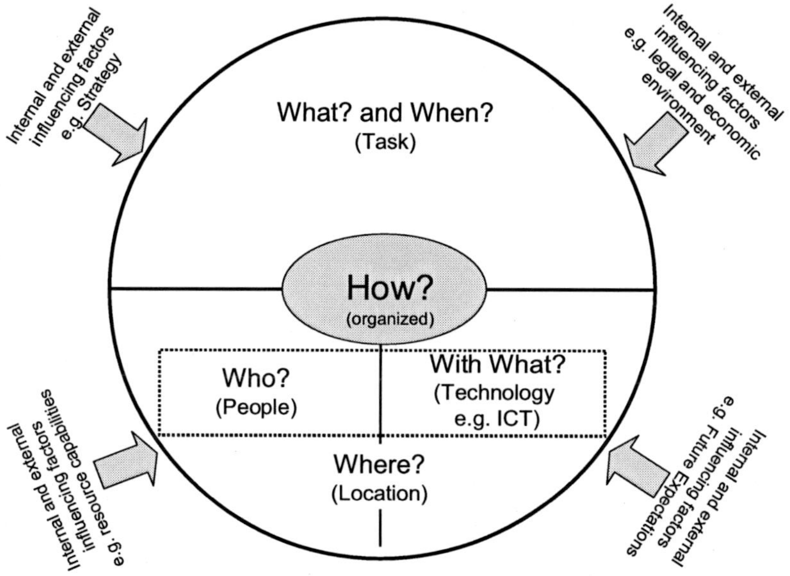

Fig. 68: Organizational challenge of how to align tasks, people and technology

Shared Service solutions are strongly influenced by the impact of associated costs for a given selected solution. There are two main cost categories to consider:

- *Production costs* (sourcing the execution of the task)
- *Coordination costs* (additional cost due to the distribution of work; known in the science community as the transaction cost. These deal with the searching, negotiating, monitoring, adapting and enforcing of the distributed tasks)

Production costs are determined by the volume, structural profile (people or machine work) and values (price, cost rates) of execution resources. Transaction costs are the same as coordination costs in this context. They depend on the coordination model, which is determined by the organizational hierarchy, network arrangements and market. The transaction costs are selected for executing distributed tasks. Both of these cost categories are discussed in the following chapters.

5.2 Business Process Sourcing

It is not easy to come up with an exact definition of the different types of *business process sourcing*. Most of the terms used overlap each other. Nevertheless, it is possible to distinguish between two types. In the traditional one, a corporation owns its business processes and its execution resources. In the other type, a corporation may fully outsource processes, including the execution of the business process up to a minimum limit of remaining governance activities, coordination and interface descriptions. The vast majority of ICT service delivery solutions lie somewhere between these two poles.

Shared Services are a *form of service delivery* where the:

- Business process is *fully owned* and controlled internally (end-to-end)
- Corporation's own business people are executing the activities in a *centralized* approach (cumulating identical or similar tasks which are previously executed in multiple places; Shared Service tasks are assigned to a dedicated organizational unit)
- Underlying entire or partial ICT landscape (applications and infrastructure, with associated design, development, operations, maintenance and support) is *mostly owned* but can also be outsourced

Looking at the description of Shared Services it is clear that the characterization is based on the following characteristics:

- Business process (centralization, full owned responsibility, governance, coordination, process control)
- Execution resources (resource categories people and ICT, type of resource ownership/control like internal versus external)

Those two groups represent the basic layers of a *business process sourcing stack*. The business process sourcing stack consists of the resource allocation, independent business process on the top and the execution resources ranging from business execution people and enabling ICT resources (ICT system landscape, ICT assets).

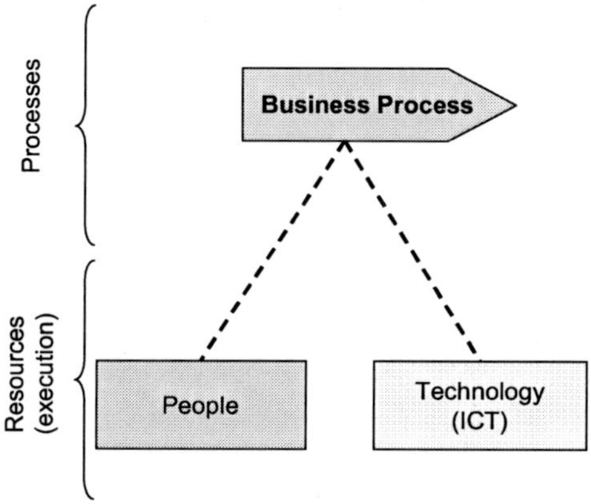

Fig. 69: Business Process and Execution Resources

The most common view contains just the process layer and the ICT layer. In contrast, we are explicitly adding the business people to the picture and creating a more comprehensive *execution resource layer*. This creates an explicit separation of process and enabling resources and the various degrees of ICT support for business processes. In an extreme case, the business processes can be fully and manually executed without any ICT. Equally, they can be fully automated without any human intervention.

The Shared Service Organization has to deal with multiple organizational decisions such as: What should be kept internal? What should be outsourced in all areas like business processes and resource categories (people and technology)? Also, the execution resources of people and technology (in our case ICT) must be further differentiated.
From a business process perspective, the people resources can be subdivided into *business people* (the same as business process execution people) and the people resources allocated to design, develop, operate technically, and those that maintain and support the ICT landscape (ICT applications, ICT infrastructure). The ICT infrastructure incorporates the operating systems, middleware, servers, hardware and networks.

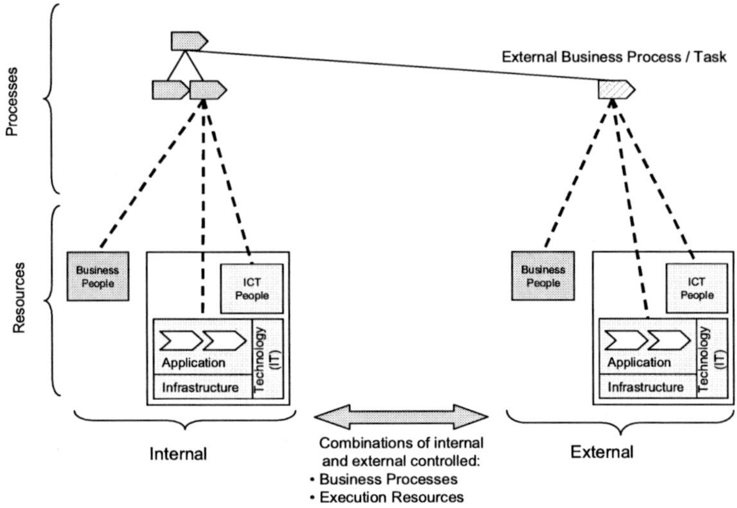

Fig. 70: Business process and resource allocation options

Assessing the potential of different service delivery models requires a methodology. The business process organizational characteristics must contain the delivery model characteristics (centralization) as well as the execution *resource allocation* of people and ICT landscape. The latter is the main contributor to the different types of process sourcing.

A common approach to visualize the solution frame for certain delivery models is to characterize the service delivery models according to selected criteria. The number of dimensions (criteria) will limit a visual presentation of a potential delivery solution to a combination of two or three characteristics. The following figure provides an example of two selected criteria (time horizon and volume/number of processes) and their potential service delivery model (SSC versus BPO) options.

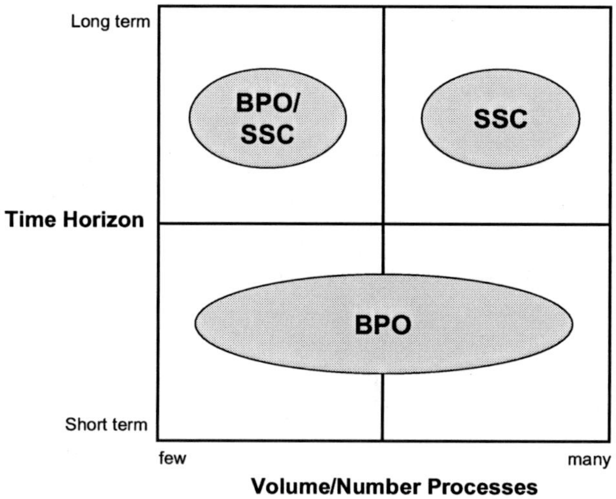

Fig. 71: Shared Service/Business Process Outsourcing Analysis based on two selected criteria

Source: Dressler (2007, 108)

The limit of such a visual approach is obvious. On the one hand there is a limit to two criteria (including their measuring challenge) and on the other hand it is difficult to position the service delivery models in the matrix. Nevertheless is it an acceptable method to indicate a tendency [Dressler (2007, 108)]. More sophisticated approaches combining multiple criteria and profiling single business processes (or even process steps).

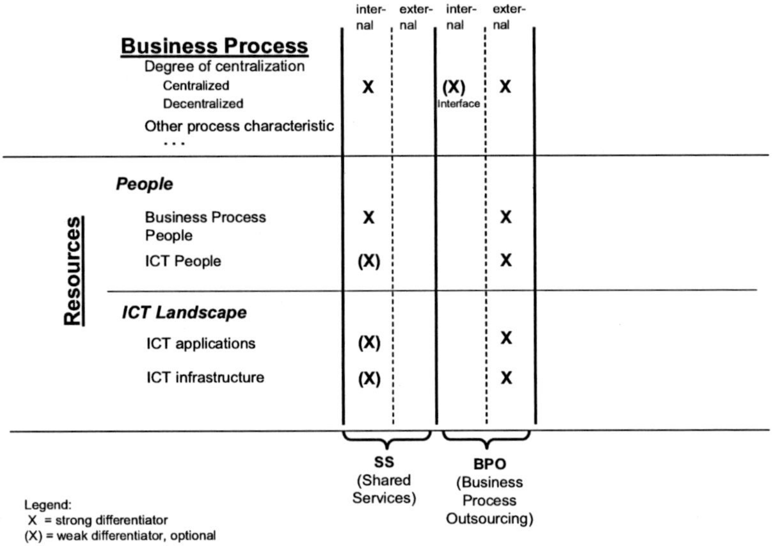

Fig. 72: Differentiation Shared Service from Business Process Outsourcing according process sourcing options.

A service delivery concept, or service deployment model, is not only characterized by business process and execution resource characteristics. Additional features are possible further differentiators, such as pricing and settlement of services and the degree of formal contractual relationship.

There is, of course, no black and white ("x" or blank in the above diagram) in determining the profile structure. The "x" represents an important *differentiating characteristic*. In the best case, it is a mandatory characteristic and an important constituent for a profile. The most important difference between Shared Service and Business Process Outsourcing is the execution of major parts of a business process by *internal (in case of Shared Services) or external business people*.

Even in a Shared Service environment, there are single tasks within a larger business process that can be outsourced. Keep in mind that complex real world business processes are *mix of different sourcing profiles*. We can label Shared Services as long as the entire business process is under own responsibility, governance and organized for central execution with internally owned or controlled executing business people.

How the enabling ICT system landscape is organized is not viewed as a major terminology differentiator.

5.2.1 Fragmentation/Breakdown of Processes and Resources

The *fragmentation/breakdown/decomposition*[20] according the horizontal ICT layers, vertical fragmentation or any mix of approaches, plus the optional distribution to single or multiple execution resources lead to additional different organizational sourcing settings (terminologies like selective sourcing, multi sourcing, best-of-breed sourcing).

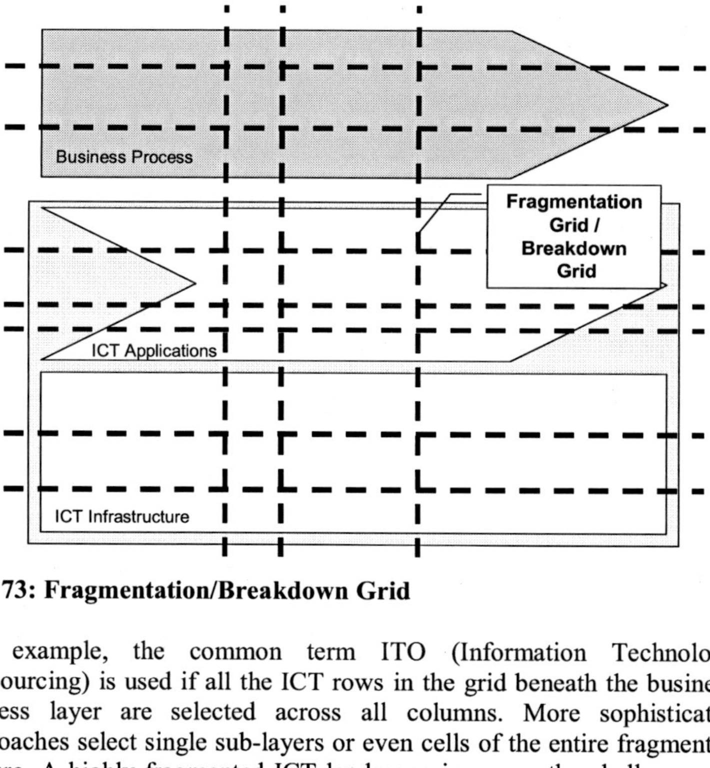

Fig. 73: Fragmentation/Breakdown Grid

For example, the common term ITO (Information Technology Outsourcing) is used if all the ICT rows in the grid beneath the business process layer are selected across all columns. More sophisticated approaches select single sub-layers or even cells of the entire fragmented picture. A highly fragmented ICT landscape increases the challenges on ICT service integration.

[20] The terms breakdown or decomposition are mostly used in conjunction with the splitting and categorizing of processes/functions and less in discussions about the distribution of ICT hardware environment. Fragmentation is mostly used in a negative sense of a non-integrated distributed ICT landscape regardless of software or hardware.

5.2.2 Common Terminology for Sourcing Profiles

Shared Service and Business Process Outsourcing (BPO) are *business service delivery* concepts. Both of them rely on resources like the ICT landscape to enable and support business processes. How the ICT landscape services (especially the ICT application services) are designed, implemented, used (delivered) and are paid for (settlement, charging) leads to further differentiation characteristics. Differentiation of sourcing may use the following characteristics:

- Ownership/ control (internal - external)
- Business process magnitude (complete process/function – selected subset of tasks - single task)
- Resource categories (people - technology)
- Resource categories subtypes (business people – ICT people, ICT applications – ICT infrastructure)
- Distance to the business (onshore - nearshore - offshore)
- Other differentiation characteristics like software license ownership, hardware sharing options, data storage location, settlement and charging models

Any combination of the selected major differentiation characteristics, characterizes a business *process sourcing profile* (deployment models). The naming of service delivery models (such as SSC, BPO) are a *summarization term* for a bundle of characteristics on processes, resources and operational settings (such as charging concept).

We focus on ICT application centric profiles. Business ICT applications are closest to the technology independent business process. To distinguish the different profiles a memorable short name is assigned to the profiles. The following figure provides a rough guideline to categorizing the different terms using a selected set of dimensional characteristics.

Profile Name						SS		ITO		APH		ASP		SaaS		. . .		BPO	
						I	E	I	E	I	E	I	E	I	E	I	E	I	E
Process	Degree of Centralization	Centralized				X		X		X		X		X				(X)	X
		Decentralized																	
	. . . (other)																		
Resources (execution)	People	Business People				X		X		X		X		X					X
		ICT People				(X)			X		X		X		X				X
	ICT Landscape	ICT Applications	ICT Apps. License ownership			X		X		X			X		X				(X)
			ICT Apps. Payment	on-demand											X				
				... (other)															
			ICT Apps. Operations	Maintenance /Support		(X)			X		X		X		X				X
				Upgrades	control (trigger)	(X)		X		X		X			X				X
					executing	(X)			X		X		X		X				X
				ICT Apps. Sharing											X				
				... (other)															
			... (other)																
		ICT Infrastructure	ICT Infrastruc. Licenses ownership																
			ICT Infrastruc. Payment																
			ICT Infrastruc. Operations	ICT Infrastruc. HW sharing	Multi-tenant										X				
					Multi-instance										(X)				
				... (other)															
			... (other)																

Fig. 74: Process - Resource allocation characteristic profiles and associated profile names (service requester view)

Legend: X=strong differentiator, (X)=weak differentiator, optional; I=internal, E=external

To ease the understanding of the characteristic profiles, this is a list of short descriptions of the major differentiators:

SS (Shared Services):

Processes and Resources are centralized. Internal business people execute the process. ICT Application license ownership is kept internal. ICT landscape technical operations, maintenance and support are not considered major differentiators. Still, business process and enabling ICT application are strongly linked. Thus, ICT application upgrades are triggered by internal decisions in case of selective or complete ICT landscape outsourcing.

ITO (IT Outsourcing):

Internal business people execute the process. ICT landscape (applications and infrastructure) operating, maintenance and support are outsourced to a single or to multiple ITO service providers. There is still a close link between the business process and the underlying ICT landscape. Service requestor (customer) triggers upgrades, but execution will be performed by the ITO provider.

APH (Application Hosting):
Internal business people execute the process. Application licenses are kept internally. Licenses are paid up front with a monthly maintenance fee. ICT applications are operated, maintained and upgraded by the APH service provider. The APH clients controls customizing and upgrades.

ASP (Application Service Providing):
Internal business people execute the process. The ASP provider keeps the application licenses. Thus, the ICT applications can be often used on a subscription basis.

SaaS (Software-as-a-Service):
Internal business people execute the process. Enabling applications are not controlled and maintained internally. Multiple SaaS customers share the same ICT application from a software provider. Modifying software program code is not possible. The software provider and service provider may differ. The ICT applications and the ICT infrastructure layers share clients in a multi-tenancy architecture. Configuration settings are per SaaS client/customer (company), role-specific and kept in a metadata layer. The SaaS service provider keeps the application licenses. The charging model for software is moving to a subscription ('pay-as-you-go') model or is based on user and/or time period.

BPO (Business Process Outsourcing):
External business people execute the process mainly on their own ICT system landscape. Process, people and ICT systems are outsourced. The intended goal is the decoupling of the business process and the execution resources.

AAS (Applied Application Services, Application Appliance):
The primary goal of this service delivery model is to reduce the complexity of installation, configuration, maintenance and operation for the business client. One way of achieving more simplicity is "ready-to-run" bundling. Delivering services via an appliance application approach is often labeled as an internal SaaS delivery model. There are two kind of delivery model:
(1) The more traditional pre-configured, pre-installed bundle of hardware and software. In some cases local legislation forces the business client to store data physically in local accessible IT equipment. Thus the location of hardware data storage plays an important role. Another reason is that a big client community prefers to have the data under their physical control. Instead of moving everything to the service provider (people and systems) the pre-configured, self-installing ICT systems will be kept on

the premise but managed remotely. Except for local hardware changes (new installations, enhancements, component exchange) there is no local ICT expertise required. Those ICT systems operate behind (from service provider point of view) the firewall of an enterprise. The term *sealed systems* is used to describe such an ICT landscape scenario.
(2) On the other hand companies would like to outsource their entire ICT landscape. Pre-configured, software bundles (appliance-based application bundles) with self-installation running in a virtual environment are an emerging alternative.
In both scenarios, the business client receives all the service and support for the application from the appliance vendor eliminating the hassle of license management, service contracts, hosting and operating the application, maintenance and upgrade issues. The same pre-configured "ready-to-run" application software operates with virtual separated business client data. A subscription based charging model ("pay-as-you-go" as an option) makes this form of service delivery highly attractive for the business client.

AAS (Applied Application Services):
In some cases, for example because of legislation needs, data must be stored physically on locally accessible IT equipment. Thus the location of hardware storage of data plays an important role. On the other hand, some companies would like to fully outsource their ICT landscape management. Instead of moving everything to the service provider (people and systems) the ICT systems will be kept on the premises but managed remotely. Except for local hardware changes (new installations, enhancements, component exchange, etc.) there is no local ICT expertise required. Those ICT systems operate behind (from service provider point of view) the firewall of an enterprise. The term *sealed systems* is used to describe such an ICT landscape scenario.

According to our previous Shared Service characteristic profile of process sourcing options Shared Service is just a subset of mandatory "X"-es. Selected characteristic features are not limited to internal versus external ownership, or different types, or granularity of resource categories. Further differentiation with additional characteristics is possible. It leads to new *differentiation of profiles*. Each profile has its own prerequisites, benefits and challenges, business drivers and risks.

Looking at the different process sourcing profiles there are the following major groups. Each group may have a different focus, but may overlap each other as well:

- Business people focused (internal, external) based on sourcing decisions (SS versus BPO)
- Independence of business process from the enabling ICT landscape (SaaS or BPO versus APH, ASP)
- Different ways of managing the enabling ICT landscape (this includes developing, operating, maintaining, supporting ICT applications and infrastructure).

Additionally every execution resource can be allocated to a different *physical geographical location* (local-regional-global). From the business process perspective, the assignment of execution resources is often grouped into Onshore-Nearshore-Offshore[21] aspects. They are additionally categorized as Captive versus Non-captive[22] service delivery options.

5.2.3 Customization of Business Process and ICT technology

The majority of today's business process sourcing solutions is streamlined to the needs of corporations. Each component of a process sourcing solution has various individual capabilities on various layers. For example, there are layers like business process, ICT application and ICT infrastructure. Thus, the degree of individualization (1:1) and standardization (1: n) has to be viewed in its layer context.

[21] Onshore - Nearshore - Offshore: These terms indicating the distance of the business to the executing shared service unit with respect to the country borders. A move of an onshore business to near or far countries for execution is mostly triggered by lower cost opportunities.

[22] Captive: In the context of business processes is the term captive used to characterize processes which are owned and executed by the process owner itself (may be dispersed), rather then an external provider.

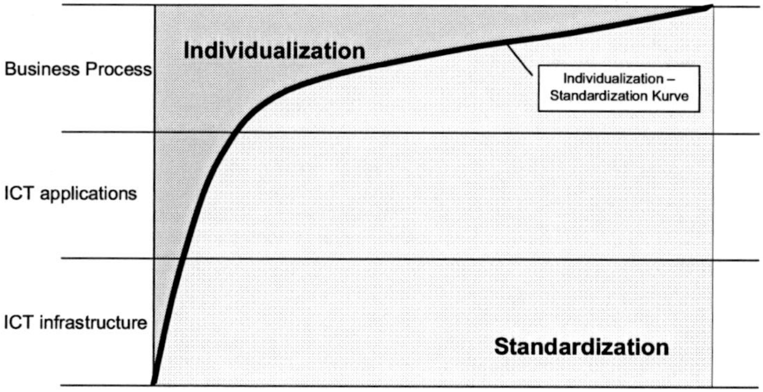

Fig. 75: Individualization and Standardization in its layer context

5.2.3.1 Customization of the Business Process Sourcing Layer

Looking at the evolution of enterprise systems and their networking capabilities standardization plays an important role. Standardizing components of any form, like hardware or software in ICT, is a prerequisite for cost efficiency amongst a community. They benefit from sharing common components.

Decades ago, the dominant model of providing ICT support was purely on customized application code on business unit level and rarely on an entire enterprise level. Collected best practices led to tailorable, standardized packaged enterprise application solutions. Individualization was achieved by taking the packaged applications as a starting template and modifying it on the program code level.

An alternative means of adaptation depends on how well parameters can be set in ICT systems without any code changes. The degree of individualization is limited to a set of predefined scenarios, with settings envisioned by the programmer and then consolidated and articulated as business requirements. The degree of individualization and standardization changes over time with the ongoing maturity of involved components. Traditionally, the stack is divided into various major categories or layers, like the business process layer and the technical (ICT) layer. These can be further subdivided into the two subgroups of ICT application and ICT infrastructure. All these layers have their own standardization history.

The ICT infrastructure stack is driven by technical innovations, which create or improve the capabilities of hardware, networks, application developing tools, and operating systems. The above-mentioned layer represents the ICT application stack. ICT applications are implemented software that support or anticipate business processes. Their efficiency and effectiveness depends on the sophistication of the ICT application or application framework.

The top layer is always the business process layer. The business processes are standardized across multiple enterprises, industries, geographies, and functions. This is a prerequisite for sourcing the business process as a *service* from the market. Individualization is limited to the business interface parameter settings. Sourcing processes with ICT applications from the market requires a *commoditization* of the business process/service. Commoditized business services are a well-known accepted standard among multiple business players and not a just one-to-one solution. A commoditized business process does not necessarily imply a commoditized ICT landscape. The opposite of commoditization is *differentiation*. Differentiating business processes, applications or infrastructure provides advantages to competitors. The degree of individualization and standardization can be presented for each layer as a commodity (Type A) or a differentiation approach (Type B). The preferences for individualization and standardization may change over time.

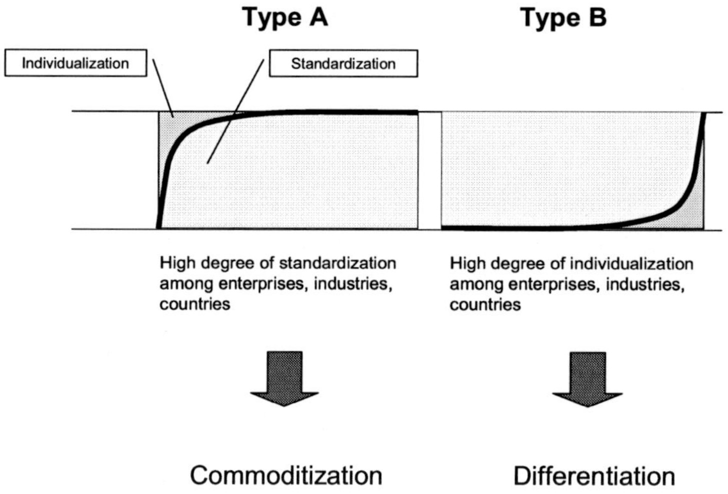

Fig. 76: Commoditization versus Differentiation

5.2.3.1.1 Customization of the Business Process Layer

Certain business processes are common among different corporations. For example payroll services have a clear structure and well-defined result. Another example is dunning services, where there is a commonly accepted procedure based on overdue items. The degree of business process standardization is very high. Individualization is limited to providing the individual data input. The processing follow-up is straightforward (standardized) and not individualized. Both examples fit into the business process type A shown in the following figure.

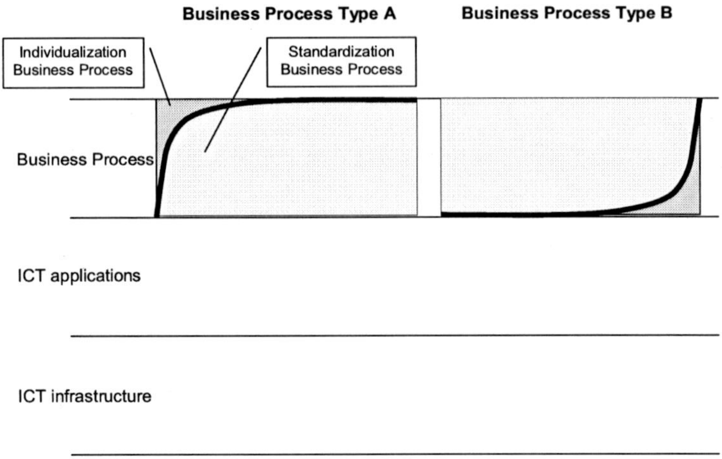

Fig. 77: Individualization and Standardization of Business Processes

The other extreme is the high degree of individualization of business processes. Unique processes don't allow any comparison, or the sharing of process structures and flow. This makes the outsourcing of these processes, or part of them, more difficult. A one-to-one individualization of an outsourcing solution for business processes is inevitable.

A high degree of individualization of business processes doesn't necessarily imply a high degree of individualization of the ICT technology layers beneath the business process layer. In the best case, it is possible to use standard package application software with associated parameterization without any program coding enhancements or changes.

5.2.3.1.2 Customization of the ICT Applications Layer

ICT applications enable and support business processes in an interactive or fully automated mode. Those applications can be designed, built and managed by their own internal controlled ICT environment. The same internal IT service can be acquired and managed by an external service provider. Customizing applications ranges from simple parameterization without any code or data structure changes, to modifying and extending the existing code basis, or modifying or enhancing the persistent data layer. Developing and/or modifying program code or developing or modifying data structures are the strongest individualization actions from the business perspective.

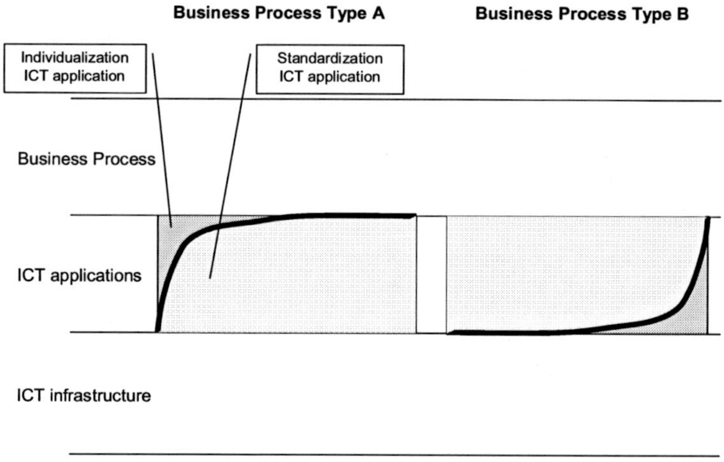

Fig. 78: Individualization and Standardization of ICT applications

Non-differentiating business processes like corporate accounting, HR administration services and indirect procurement evolve to become commodity business processes.

5.2.3.1.3 Customization of the ICT Infrastructure Layer

ICT infrastructures provide the foundation for ICT applications with internal and external connectivity capabilities. Individualization of ICT infrastructure reduces the sharing capabilities.

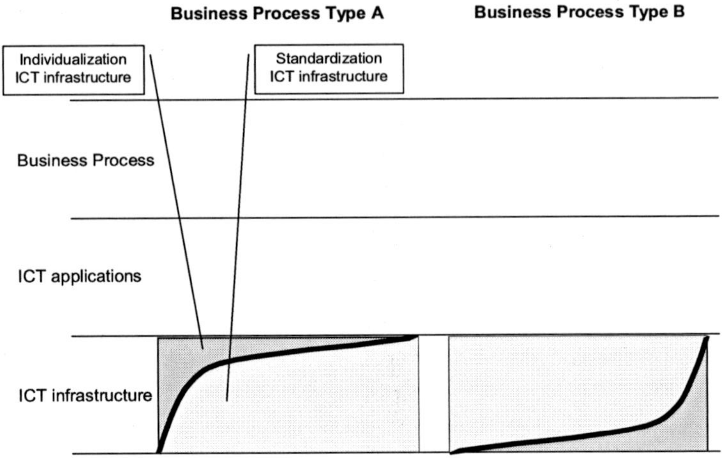

Fig. 79: Individualization and Standardization of ICT infrastructure applications

5.2.3.2 Conclusions to Customization

Making this into a composite puzzle provides a picture close to the composite individualization/standardization curve.

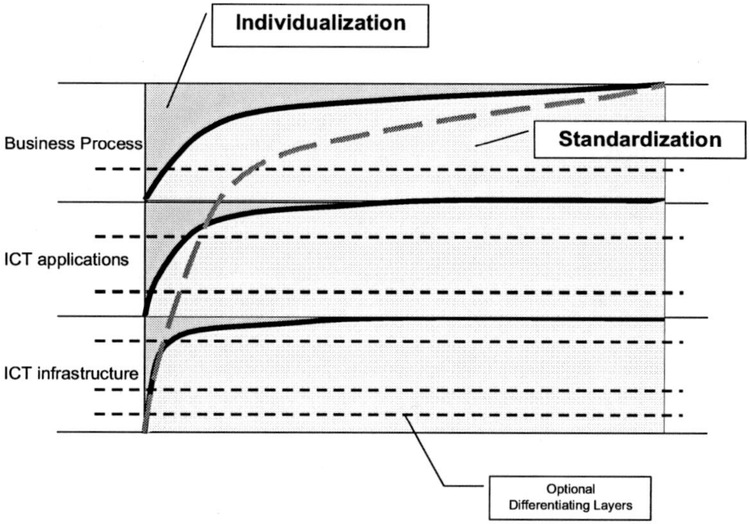

Fig. 80: Composite Individualization – Standardization - Curve

Looking at this figure from the Shared Service perspective demonstrates two opposing views. The service provider would like to standardize everything, from the business process up to the ICT infrastructure. The Shared Service consumer would like to set up business processes according to their needs. From their perspective, they wish to operate in a customized (individualized) business process environment. To achieve this, the supporting ICT applications have to be very flexible to avoid any complexity and costly enhancements like program code modifications. A common approach to provide customization capabilities without code modification is to *parameterize* ICT applications. Parameterization of ICT applications is a *predefined* set of switches for flexible adaptation to business process requirements. A more sophisticated approach is to support a business process evolving from a set of dedicated ICT application services. The *service oriented architecture framework* (SOA framework) provides the framework for invoking internal or external sourced services. For Shared Services, the worst case is if the entire business process is based on a single, unique coded ICT application to support the needs of one single Shared Service client. Thus standardization and consolidation across all the sourcing stack layers is mandatory for Shared Services.

5.2.4 Communication Channels

The business process sourcing decisions are rooted back to business process structures and flows and to sourcing capabilities through people and technology. The service provided by a Shared Service Organization is a portfolio of interactive and fully automated tasks that flow between service provider and service requester. Most of the enterprises accommodate a layered approach.

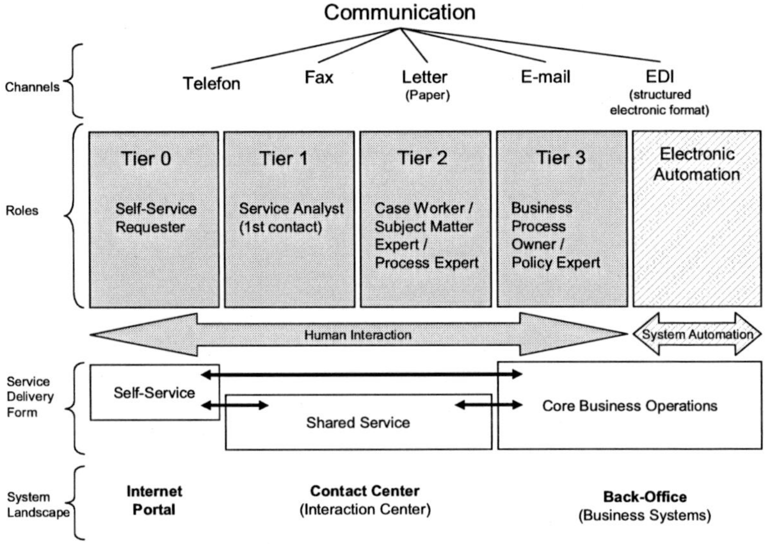

Fig. 81: Communication Channels – Service Delivery Form – System Landscape

Tier 0: *Self services* are grouped into the first layer. The service requester is able to extract or maintain desired information or alone. It is able to pull real-time data from application systems, or maintain and update data without complex access routines to the data/information store. A prerequisite for this mode of operation is a predefined set of (routine, common) services and their access parameterization.

Tier 1: Not every piece of information needed by a service requester is well structured. Also, retrieval might not be straightforward, well known or easily supported by ICT systems because of complex decisions. Thus, a well-trained experienced user must assess the requirements and steer the requester to the right application needed to support the request.

Call/Contact center is the type of service that is allocated to this layer. In such a call/contact center it is possible to handle transactional (customer order collection) as well as transformational tasks (consulting).

Upper Tiers: Complex business processes with a high degree of business decisions and business events require *specialized and trained people* with access to dedicated ICT system support. Those people require deep knowledge in business policies and are subject matter experts. Analytical tasks with structured or unstructured processes are allocated to this layer. The information/data retrieval is from multiple internal and external sources (ICT systems). The results are fed back into the same information/data sources.

5.2.5 Governance – Risk - Compliance

5.2.5.1 GRC - Introduction

In the recent history the business world has undergone a series of severe company scandals rooted back to poor corporate governance, risk assessment and lack of compliance control. To reestablish trust in our business world government and other institutional bodies released new regulations to improve the situation. Those regulations require documenting the business processes, identifying risks and defining the controls to mitigate them. Regular mandatory demonstration of the effectiveness of those controls should assure a high quality of the process. The increased number of regulations, rules and best practice proposals from different legislation bodies led to a complex set of interrelated risk and compliance issues.

Governance is part of the highest level of management and leadership process. Governance is the establishment of an organizational framework of *steering and control* in the sense of structures (static and dynamic) of a political social organizational unit regardless if privately or publicly held. *Corporate governance* deals with the control and steering framework within and beyond legal rules of a corporation.

Risk (and its counterpart, opportunity) deals with the *identification, evaluation and monitoring* of potential damages to assure that objectives are achieved. Identification, documenting the risk in a catalog, establishing the control measurements and analysis of the risks are key parts of comprehensive risk management. Risks can be categorized according multiple dimensions:

- Geographical reach (such as global risk)
- Market direction (such as demand, supply risks)

- Size and time horizon of impact (strategic versus operational risks)
- etc.

Compliance deals with *acting* in accordance to defined rules. Those rules can be derived from legislation (compliance to law), rules of de-facto standards (e.g. ISO-Norm), rules of the business eco-system of collaboration (e.g. RFID acceptance), rules of best-practice standards (e.g. corporate governance codex) and internal rules (e.g. corporate code of business conduct).

Achieving compliance becomes a costly task. The following figure provides a rough estimate of compliance cost (without the cost for risk and governance).

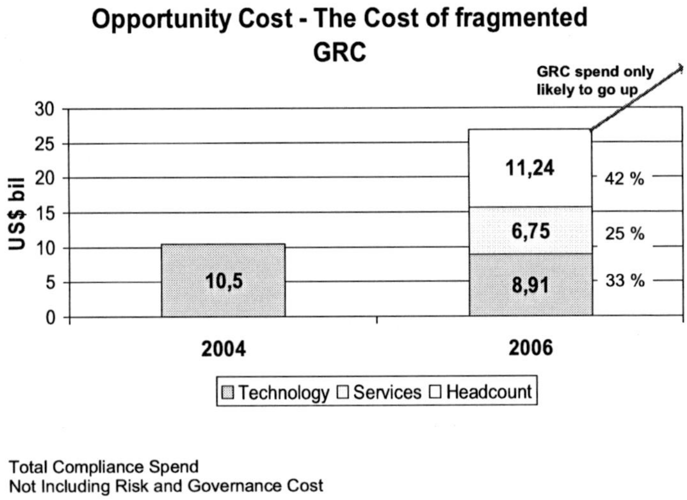

Fig. 82: Compliance Spend (not including Risk and Governance Cost)

Source: SAP research (2006)

Businesses responded to the emerging requirements by implementing fragmented solutions to address the needs of governance, risk and compliance (GRC). Each of the fragmented GRC solutions defined, implemented and monitored their own set of controls. The efforts led to duplicated activities, high costs, wasted time and resources and limited GRC effectiveness. Thus a more promising approach to comply with multiple fragmented GRC requirements is to build a comprehensive GRC system by reusing existing controls. To assure that the controls are in place, documented and operate as designed a supporting technology becomes mandatory.

5.2.5.2 Practice: Governance – Risk – Compliance

Surrey County Council:

"We form a strategic alliance, where we have a committee or a group that meets once a month to review the working relationships. And there is an escalation process built in around that. Escalations are very rare." [Interview with Graham White, Surrey County Council]

5.3 Globalization

Globalization is a term which has a bad reputation in western industrialized countries. The reason is the association with the shift of human workload abroad to nearshore or offshore locations. Keep in mind that offshore is not the same as outsourcing. Outsourcing relates to the allocation of work to an external provider regardless of location. Globalization is much more then just the economic aspects of this trend which affects entire societies and countries. The following characteristics describe roughly the term globalization:

- Globalization is in general the *increasing international inter-connectness* in: economic, political, social, cultural and environmental areas.
- *Economic globalization* is only one dimension of (general) globalization and depends on the free flow of: international trade of goods and services, human migration, technology diffusion and utilization (especially information and communication technology) and financial capital.
- *Globalization impact* manifests on: individuals, institutions, societies and countries.
- *Globalization reasons* can be rooted back to: *technical progress* (e.g. information and communication technology, transportation technique) and *political decisions* (deregulation, liberation)

Globalization has an impact on organizational decisions. Sourcing the information processing of real business processes becomes a global challenge. This applies to both sourcing categories of people and technology. Progress in the Information and Communication Technology (ICT) are enabling solutions which were viewed a couple of years ago as visionary. A reasonable portion of information processing work can be *delivered and consumed independent of location* of the consumer and the provider. In the ultimate form could an identified task (or task step) separated from the retained task (process), remotely executed and results seamless reintegrated in the remaining business process frame.

Location decision of the execution resources is mostly driven by differential factor cost and especially labor cost. Although the delivery side of business processes play a dominant role in sourcing the process the demand side on the business process requirements (such as language and cultural skills, local expertise) has to be considered as well.

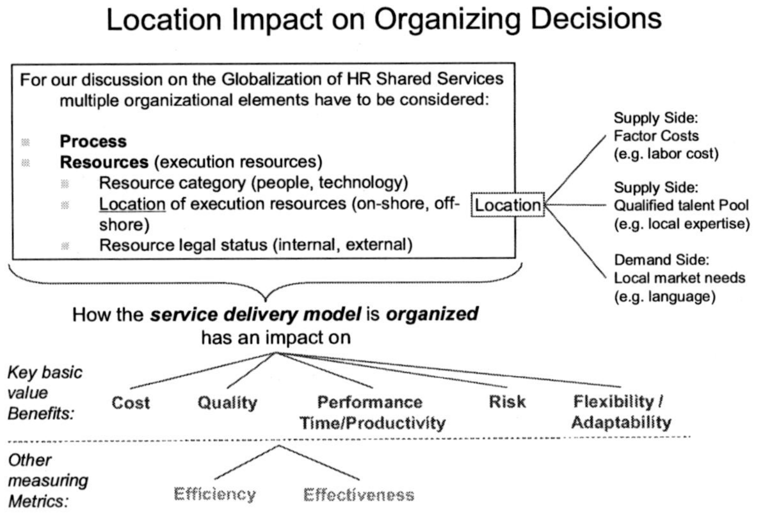

Fig. 83: Globalization and organizing decisions

Decisions of the location of execution resources have an impact on the measuring metrics of sourcing decisions. Like any other organizational decision is cost just one aspect of the multi variable decision frame.

Pros and Cons regarding the localization impact on Shared Services are summarized in the following figure.

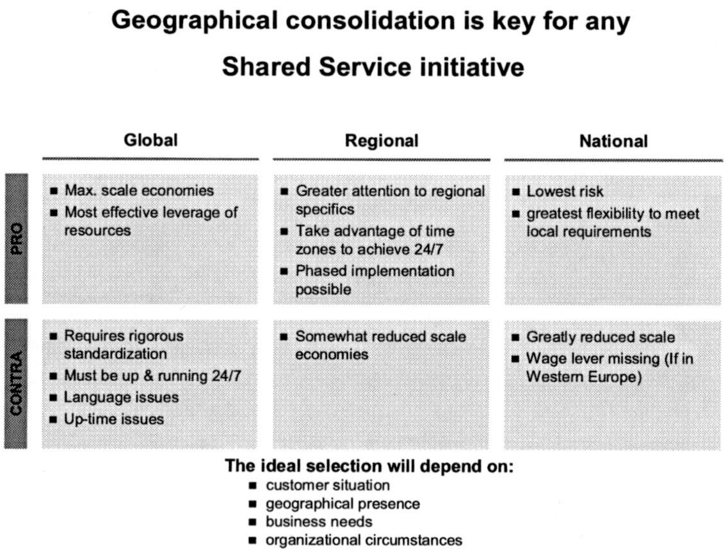

Fig. 84: Location consideration in Shared Service

5.4 Coordination Concepts

The distribution of work requires task *coordination* (for function, process and service). Shared Service breaks down and distributes the work between the Shared Service Organization and the business clients. Both parties are internal partners within the corporation boundaries. The complexity increases if parts of the business process activities are outsourced to an external service provider. A business and a technical ICT system interface exist between the process internal and/or external execution partners.

Back in 1937, Coase R. H. [Coase, 1937, pp 386] argued that firms and markets create two alternative organizational forms for organizing transactions. But what are the criteria for choosing one or the other? Are the two pure forms applicable for every goods and service production? There are obviously some aspects which have to be considered in sourcing decisions. The possible answer can be found in the "Transaction Cost Approach" developed by Coase.

Sourcing the same goods or services via an internal organization (hierarchical coordination), or externally via markets has different economic implications. Sourcing via markets and using market mechanisms leads to additional costs for searching, negotiation, specification, monitoring, adaptation and enforcing of desired goods or services. The goal of the transaction cost theory is the selection of the most appropriate organizational institutional agreements of delivery depending on the specificity of the goods and services and within given production costs. Transaction costs rise with the specificity of the good or service. Thus sourcing via markets is considered for low specificity goods or services whereas the coordination through hierarchies is the preferred means of coordination for highly specific goods or services (from economic perspective).

Pure coordination forms of hierarchy versus market are not the only ones visible in our real economic world. For instance, there are hybrid forms like cooperations, alliances, joint ventures, franchising and collaborations. These are established forms of coordination among business partners and are either a tight or a loose network relation. These hybrid coordination forms are known as network-type coordination forms. They try to leverage the benefits of hierarchies and markets.

In summary, there are three major coordination forms or coordination:

- Hierarchy (organizational hierarchy)
- Market
- Hybrid coordination form between market and hierarchy (networks)

The transaction costs of coordination are dependent on such coordination forms and the degree of specialization or uncertainty of the execution of the work. A decision point (S1 and S2 in the following figure) is reached when the cost curves have the same transactional costing level.

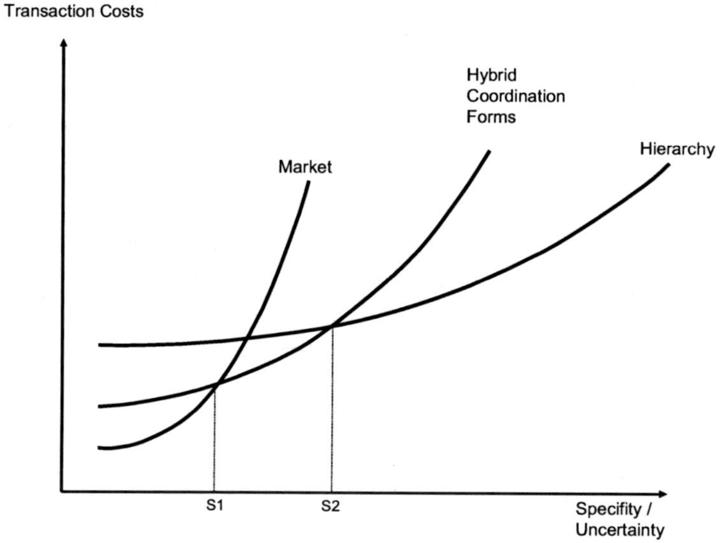

Fig. 85: Transaction cost depending on coordination forms
Source: Reichwald / Piller (2006, 36) (own translation)

According to the transaction cost theory, the market coordination form ensures the lowest transaction cost. A pre-requisite is unfortunately an assumed low specificity or uncertainty of tasks. On the other hand, organizational hierarchies are the coordination form of choice for highly specific or uncertain tasks. Decreasing the specificity of tasks means standardizing and creating commodity tasks which are commonly defined and accepted. Potentially this will lower the coordination costs if an established sourcing market for executing those tasks is available.

Network and market coordination forms are highly dependent on communication standards. Emerging modern communication standards reduce the coordination complexity with other market participants. Network effects can be achieved if there is a high penetration (adoption and support) of a common network-based communication standard among business partners.

It is the intention of Shared Service Organizations to standardize activities among business clients within their own internal organizational boundaries. Leveraging the standardization of tasks could be further increased if the tasks can be commoditized. This encourages standardization across enterprises with potential usage of external service providers and market mechanisms. Looking at the current practice the organizational hierarchy is the dominating coordination form. Internal and external standardization are prerequisites to reducing transaction cost and implementing coordination forms by means of networks or, in the most desirable form, markets.

What are the consequences with respect to Shared Services?
Standardizing Shared Services, which is a reduction of specificity and uncertainty, provides the potential to move to other coordination forms like networks or markets. Networks and particularly markets are coordination forms with lower transaction costs. Standardization eases the searching, uncertainty, assessment/evaluation of services and reduces the informational gap between the demanding client and Shared Service provider.

Emerging ICT communication standards support more work distribution in a network without higher interaction and transaction costs. This leads to a shift in the decision points of organizational coordination forms (see diagram). A shift from the hierarchy to network type arrangements can be expected. An increase in market and network coordination will erode the hierarchy (enterprise centric) coordination form. From the Shared Service client perspective, a higher transparency and price competition can be achieved.

5.5 Shared Service Organization

The Shared Service Organization is a distinct organizational entity within the central corporate boundary. It is sometimes even implemented as a separate legal entity. Shared Service hubs provide common services to business clients. They are primarily accountable to business units and not to headquarters.

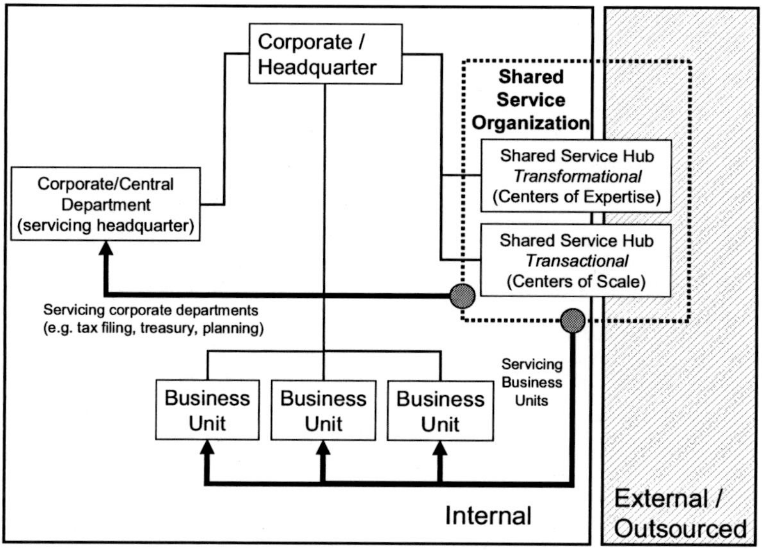

Fig. 86: Organizational structure of Shared Services

Business processes will be partly or fully assigned and executed by one of the multiple service providers:

- Business unit
- Shared Service Organization
- Central/Corporate service departments
- External (outsourced) business partner

It is highly likely that during an end-to-end process flow, some of the parties are involved in execution. Instead of assigning an end-to-end business process to one execution party, the process actually has an organizational profile of different service providers.

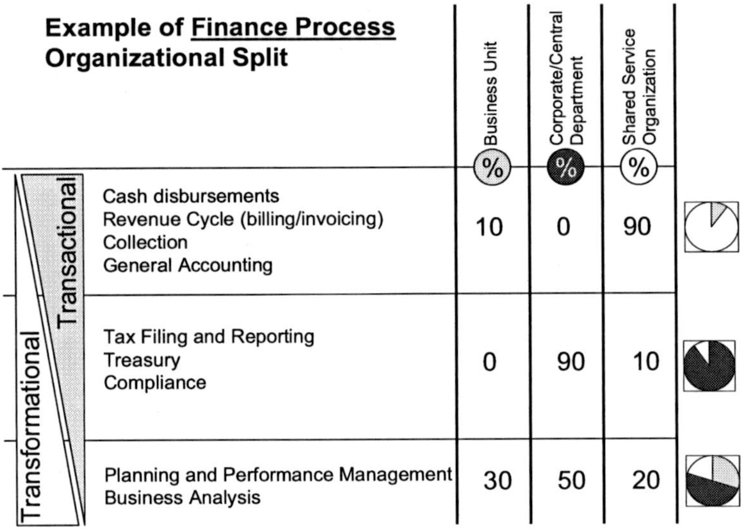

Fig. 87: Example of Finance Process organizational split

The figure illustrates very clearly that business processes have a sourcing profile and are not easily grouped in one category. Even the grouping may change over time as a result of the automation of process steps. Thus the interpretation of empirical survey results must be carried out very carefully.

5.5.1 Shared Service Delivery Locations

5.5.1.1 Delivery Locations - Foundation

Shared Services can be delivered from multiple physical sites known as Shared Service centers. Physical delivery sites can be spread around the globe. A delivery site may serve geographical areas (local, regional or global) with the full range of the Shared Service portfolio or just a subset of services. Criteria for selecting a service delivery site include:

- Existing infrastructure (buildings, facilities, water and energy supply)
- Communication networks (information and communication infrastructure)
- Travel and commuting conditions
- Skilled labor force available (language, local expertise)
- Political conditions (risk)
- Cultural conditions (cultural fit)

- Economic conditions (cost level)
- Existing company operations at site

The *cost level* is a dominant factor in deciding on a location, beside individual preferences of the Shared Service management or client needs. Labor cost are the highest portion of overall costs for Shared Services. Thus the difference in labor rates at different sites is a major contributor to lower the service costing level.

Determining the decision figures at the start is one thing, but keeping an eye on the ongoing Shared Service operations is another. Experience shows a substantial increase of cost (especially of labor cost) after a couple of years of operation. This is due to the general increase in standards of living at the site, increased dificulty in hiring skilled people from competing Shared Service centers and higher infrastructure costs. Monitoring trends (especially costing trends) may lead to selections of new low-cost locations.

Supporting business operations out of one Shared Service center with global delivery is a challenge. Processes that interact with people (customers, vendors, employees and partners) may require substantial language skills. Providing those language skills or other local expertise out of a central global delivery site is difficult. Regional or local (country) sub-Shared Service delivery centers are a way to overcome the bottleneck.

5.5.1.2 Practice: Shared Service Delivery Locations

Selecting a Shared Service location is a difficult organizational task. Regional Shared Service operations of our interview partners are mostly in low labor cost, nearshore countries.

BASF:

The exception in our comparison study is the company BASF. BASF decided to set up their Shared Service Center in Berlin. Germany is not known as a low labor cost country. Thus there were other reasons overweighing the low labor cost benefit of the eastern European countries. For BASF there were two essential criteria: (1) Suitable employees with financial and business know-how and (2) language skills. With a catchment area of more than three million people, the capital city provided a reservoir of people speaking many languages. A skilled workforce and an immediately available good infrastructure (traveling, communication, facilities) lowered the start-up costs. Moving to an already established Shared Service location, the labor costs were relatively high compared to the first Shared Service Center at the same location. The accumulation of Shared Service Centers is creating competition for skills and salaries are rising every year. The final boost to the location selection was the open discussion with the unions and their positive response to signing a special labor contract for the labor workforce. This agreement, with its lower labor rates, made Berlin as competitive as eastern European locations like Bratislava.

Henkel:
The company realized that further cost savings were only achievable with lower labor cost rates after standardizing processes, optimizing them on local and regional level and extensive use of ICT system consolidation. They selected Bratislava in 2005.

Philips:
"We now have more than four and a half years of operational experience in off-shoring and Shared Services." [Interview with Michel de Zeeuw, Philips]

Siemens:
Regarding the use and location of contact/interaction centers in the national Shared Service Center Organization:
"At the beginning, we weren't using it. We had a total of 90 locations in Germany and the first step involved reducing them to six. That was a matter of philosophy for us too – do we choose one, two, three, or more locations? And six was the most sensible approach for us, in terms of reorganization costs that are incurred. But also, and this is very important, it was about keeping the know-how. We always considered that if we just chose one location, which is feasible, it would be a risk. We would have lost too much expertise and competence. That's why we went for six locations.
These six locations are responsible for the one-to-one relationship of HR employee to service recipient. Service recipient is the name we give our employees out there, which would be about 170,000 in Germany." [Interview with Wolfgang Leitmanstetter, Siemens]

5.5.2 Shared Service Organizations Service Delivery Model

5.5.2.1 Service Delivery Model - Foundation

Physical Shared Service delivery locations should not be confused with the organizational structure for Shared Services. The most appropriate term is Shared Service Organization (SSO) which is responsible for leadership, governance and process sourcing execution. The service delivery can performed out of one or many dedicated physical service hubs or virtually from any physical location. One central global Shared Service Organization with global governance and process control would be called the Global Shared Service Organization. It would have one or more Shared Service delivery sites. However, if local service delivery sites own the governance of Shared Service processes, they are called Local or Regional Shared Service Organizations. Looking at the evolution of the Shared Service operations model over time, it is clear that corporates are starting to globalize their Shared Service Organizations.

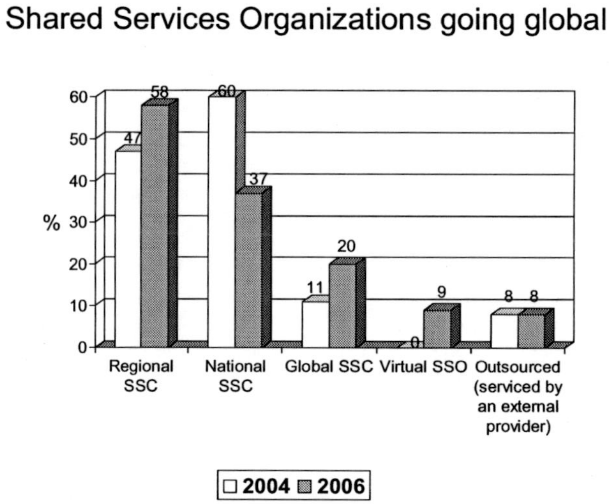

Fig. 88: Operational delivery mode of Shared Service Organizations
Source: Hackett (2007, ii)

Most corporations are aiming to operate with one global Shared Service Organization with one global management structure.

5.5.2.2 Practice: Shared Service Organization Operations

All the companies interviewed operate or have introduced regional Shared Service Centers. One key question is how they manage the size of working groups and responsibilities.

BASF:
BASF decided to introduce large groups with a large breadth of control. They talk about group sizes of more than 50 to 100 people. “If you can save on managers and trigger the whole structure down to a lower level, you make significant savings.” [Interview with Mr. Seeger, BASF].

Henkel:
Henkel has a sophisticated organizational structure for Shared Service tasks, such as order-to-cash, procure-to-pay and record-to-report. When they introduced the concept on a regional and global level they shifted responsibilities to the “Heads of Processes”, who have more. responsibility than the local CFOs. This approach proved to be very successful and the concept will now be deployed worldwide.

Marks & Spencer (M&S):
M&S sees their priority as training and developing people. Investing in people and training is viewed as strategic initiative in a Shared Service Organization. They believe that managing the talent pool and providing better education and training is a crucial factor for successful Shared Service centers.

SAP:
“Responsibility for F&A and HR Shared Services are divided in the Business Center. We have two separate divisions, but we work closely together. In fact, that is an SAP principle: You don’t have to centralize all organizations; you merely need to create networks between them. It’s the same principle which we already share with the existing Shared Service Centers.
We have a network of Shared Services which are not part of one organization, but which work very closely together and ensure that processes are aligned. Aligned, indeed, with the knowledge that this will help us to reach the IT spending level and that we could send people here and there with it. That is the principle we are working with at the moment, as well as cooperating with the existing Shared Service Centers in Asia Pacific, Latin America and partly in the USA.”
“ ... It is the balance between diversity gains of decentral units and central governance - we use this gap as a momentum to allow creativity and innovation in order to have a convergence of best practices. Ideally we would not need a line organization, but we would align along the process chain and create federations of small units, with clear in and output, which optimize themselves and the whole chain.” [Interview with Peter Rasper, SAP]

Siemens:
Regarding the service delivery approach for HR in the national German Shared Service Center:
"… From the start, we tried to avoid setting up a call center. In other words, we also answer questions. And the number of questions we answer first time round is high. We currently answer approximately 80% of the queries at the first point of contact."

Regarding the organizational set up of the Shared Service Center:
"No, there is no separate company. We have taken tasks from the HR department and an HR service has been set up in Germany, that's what we still call it today. This 60% of employees I mentioned before has been integrated in the Shared Service area."
[Interview with Wolfgang Leitmanstetter, Siemens]

6 Shared Service Operating Model

Describing a Shared Service operating model requires a set of characteristics:

- Type of customers (internal business units, central departments, external clients)
- Legal status (internal versus external)
- Organizational Status (e.g. cost center, revenue center, profit center, investment center)
- Governance (hierarchical, network relationship)
- Service/Process Types (transactional, transformational/expertise/judgment based)
- Service/Process (service description and *optional* service level agreements offerings)
- Service Agreement with specified Service Level Agreement (SLA)
- Pricing/Charge Back approach
- Mandation of service (internal mandatory or optional, external market)
- etc.

The commercial aspect of Shared Service characteristics starts with the dedicated description of service offerings, client specific service level agreements with specified service levels, pricing/charge back structure and degree of mandating the services. The combination of shared service characteristics delivers different profiles of Shared Service operating usage models.

6.1 Shared Service Operations Usage Model

Successful SSCs are designed according to company culture, strategy and goals, and the structure of business units. Over time the industry has recognized four major usage models, which sometimes are steps in the evolution of a SSC. Barbara Quinn, Robert Cooke and Andrew Kris (Quinn et. al. (1999) distinguish between four major groups:

- Basic model
- Marketplace model
- Advanced marketplace model
- Independent business model

These vary in attributes, such as what kinds of processes are being handled by the user (transactional versus transformation with professional and advisory services); and if services are compulsory for the business units or not. Most companies' SSCs will probably be a mixture of the attributes.

The following table uses a similar classification approach with an extended list of differentiation attributes.

Tab. 8: Shared Service operational models

Model →	**Cost oriented Model (Basic Model)**	**Customer/ Quality oriented Model**	**Market oriented Model**	**Market model (Competition Model)**
Objective	Cost reduction, stable quality	Cost reduction, improved quality	Cost reduction, high quality, additional profit generation with external clients	Profit / revenue generation, independent business responsibility
Customers / Clients	Internal clients	Internal clients	Internal + external (low number) clients	External (low number internal clients) clients
Legal status (service provider)	Internal	Internal	Internal / External (potential joint venture)	External independent enterprise
Organizational status (service provider)	Internal organizational unit (as a cost center)	Internal organizational unit (as a cost center)	Internal / (potentially external) organizational unit (as a profit/ investment center)	External enterprise
Governance (process responsibility, decision competence)	Hierarchy	Hierarchy	Hierarchy, building relationship	Contract, building relationship (Network)
Service Process Type	Transactional	Transactional (potentially transformational)	Transactional, transformational	Transactional, transformational
Service-description *with* optional service level specification offering	Potential service/ process described in a catalogue	Service catalogue, Optional formal/informal Service level agreement (SLA) offering	Service catalogue, formal Service Level Agreement (SLA),	Service catalogue, formal Service Level Agreement (SLA),
Service agreement (client specific)	Agreement (loose)	Formal agreement (internal client determines the service level agreement (SLA))	Legal binding agreement, contract for external clients	Legal binding agreement, contract
Pricing / Charge back	Cost (full cost shared, distributed)	Cost (market oriented rate)	Market oriented price, profit will be shared	Market price, profit remains in the SSC
Mandation of service	Mandatory	Mandatory	Optional service provider selection	Free external service provider selection

The Basic Model

The main objective of this type of SSC is to reduce costs and to keep quality levels stable while standardizing business processes. Examples of the most common SSC processes are AP/AR, general ledger, and payroll processing. The SSC provides its services solely to internal departments and business unit costs are simply allocated and shared across the business units. Hence, the SSC is not under a lot of pressure to be efficient, as its services are mandatory to the business units. Often, the SSC is also responsible for the adherence to company rules (that is, there is no separation of governance function). An example is travel expense processing, where the SSC employee would not only check the documents provided and process them, but would also check if the right means of transportation (such as economy versus business class) or a preferred provider of services (such as hotel chains) was chosen.

The Customer/Quality-oriented Model

This model builds on the basic model and extends its reach. The main objective is still cost reduction but with an improved level of service quality. Often, the SSC also broadens its processes' scope and offers professional and advisory services (transformational services) beyond pure transaction processing. Pricing is as in the basic model and the SSCs services are still compulsory to the business units; however, line managers oversee the governance function.

The Market-oriented Model

This model is very close to what a company would receive from an external service provider in an outsourcing agreement. The objective is to let the business units choose the most efficient service provider, so the SSC must compete with external service providers. Usually, the SSC has the advantage because of the necessity for the business units to supply sufficient, qualified reasoning for going external. The SSC may also provide its services externally, but only with surplus capacity. Prices have to cover the costs of the whole process. If the SSC makes a profit, it is allocated and distributed to the business units.

The Market or Competition Model

Here, SSCs are completely independent businesses and thus organized as separate entities. Actually it is a true outsourcing model with internal customers as well on their customer base. Their objective is to generate revenue and profits by delivering services under competitive conditions. There is a regular market price charged, with profits retained by the SSC.

6.2 Shared Service Management and Governance

Shared Service clients ask for daily ongoing service delivery as well as for organizational procedures to channel upcoming changing business requirements. Lack of proper Shared Service management and governance is among the top reasons for Shared service implementation failures. Managing Shared Services requires:

- Service Portfolio Management (service offerings, service catalogues, customization possibilities)
- Commercial Management (service agreement, agreement on service levels (SLA's), measuring and benchmarking processes, settlement/charge back)
- Service Quality Management (performance/productivity, accuracy and timeliness, client satisfaction)
- Compliance Management (legal, regulatory, safety, privacy, audits)
- Change Management (process improvement, innovation, changing business requirement)
- Operations Management (monitoring, performance dashboards, issue handling, incidents and problem handling, escalation)

6.3 Service – Agreement – Service Level

A Shared Service Organization provides common corporate business services to multiple clients (business units). The range of sourcing the business process starts with self-service applications with little personal support from central Shared Service employees over full service execution by internal Shared Service employees to external service providers (outsourced operations). As a consequence there is a different type of relationships and agreements between service delivering party (or the service provider) and the end-user service recipient.

From the operational perspective, the Shared Service Organization acts as the responsible service vendor. The service vendor has to guarantee a certain service level. The degree of formalization of agreements between the two parties may vary. Between two internal partners a more informal agreement, known as a Operation Level Agreement (OLA), is the foundation for the business operations. Between an internal and an external partner a more formalized agreement such as a legally binding service contract becomes mandatory. The services provided will be explicitly listed with their according agreed service level. From operational perspective the service level agreement (SLA) is the most important part of the service contract.

6.3.1 Service Catalog

An SSC has to choose the means of presenting the range of services to its clients: either through the business units or external companies. A product catalog lists all the possible services and levels and states the prices. Process Business units either choose required services in defined intervals (on a yearly or quarterly basis) or in special situations (on needs basis). Streamlining of service orders will make the internal planning of necessary resources and their utilization easier and therefore will drive down the costs. Choosing from a catalog is often directly connected with an order system. This is especially convenient for larger SSCs. Centers servicing only a handful of clients can use a scaled-down version and take orders by e-mail or phone.

Challenges

Fixed pricing per unit or volume means higher risk for the SSC. Prices and structure of the main services should stay constant for an agreed period, usually one year. Such a requirement is not always possible to fulfill; therefore, there should be a clear procedure defined for changes to the catalog when the market environment changes considerably. When first creating a service catalog, many managers are tempted to design a complicated structure distinguishing services and prices for different audiences. The general recommendation here is once again simplicity. Highly differentiated offerings are technically possible to manage, but will require extra effort and costs. In addition, increased complexity usually leads to unperceived complications.

Possible ICT Solutions

A suggestion for a reasonable level of IT support depends mainly on the size of the client base and the range of services offered. Generally, a sufficient solution is a document-based product catalog for when there is a limited number of clients using a standard portfolio of services. The catalog can be posted on a web site and orders can be taken via e-mail or an externally created purchase order. However, if there are be many clients ordering services (the best example would be an IT SSC in a large corporation), we would suggest introducing an electronic procurement solution. Such a solution will let companies dynamically maintain their service catalog in an electronic form and, at the same time, manage all of the clients' orders.

6.3.2 Service Agreement - Contract for Services

An SSC fulfills not only the core process for which it has been created. Imagine an SSC as a company within a company. In order for it to function properly, it also needs proper handling of its supporting administrative processes. Before the people in the SSC can start with their daily work, the SSC and its customers have to sign an agreement/contract. Such a contract defines general conditions, under which the SSC will deliver services to the business units and external clients. A service catalog will have detailed specification of the services offered, different service levels, and the respective prices. Service *levels* are sometimes specified in a separate agreement called Service Level Agreement (SLA).

All incoming service orders then have to be administered the same way as a company itself would for its customers. Once the SSC delivers the service, they will issue an invoice and track the payment process. Administrative processes are an important part of the SSCs processes. The proper management of these will assure that the SSC is able to concentrate fully on its core tasks.

6.3.3 Service Level Agreement

A service level agreement (SLA) is an agreement between the Shared Service center and the service clients (such as business units) and defines the service (quality level) relationship. Quite often there is no distinction between the content of a Service Agreement (e. g. as a legal binding contract) and the Service *Level* Agreement. Thus the content of a SLA varies a lot. There is no common understanding what should be kept on the Service Agreement and what should be part of a Service Level Agreement. The following figure provides a blurred picture on the content of a SLA.

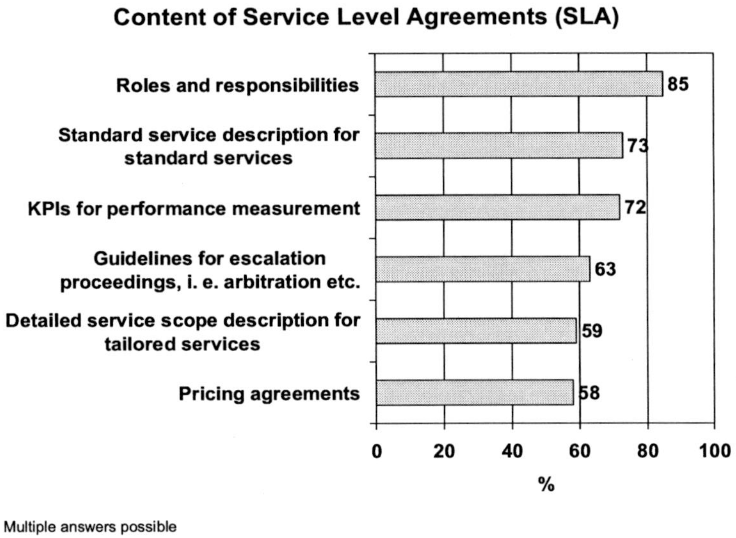

Fig. 89: Content of Service Level Agreements (SLA)
Source: Hackett (2005a, 21)

A SLA document should be kept as simple as possible to avoid a voluminous publication that lists every possible situation. The more complex the SLA agreement is, the more it costs to maintain on all levels (for example, project, legal, IT, and so forth).

Major chapters of an SLA include a definition of the client's expectations with associated roles and responsibilities, what is going to be part of the service delivery, documented process flows and in what frequency, to what quality standard, how the performance will be measured, escalation procedures, operational hours and so on. It is vital to the obligations of both sides – to know what happens when the SSC does not deliver according to the agreement or when the client does not meet their obligations. Recourse actions should be added as a closing statement.

Another important aspect to consider is whether the SLA is legally binding or not. An internal SSC with no external sales will most likely create only an internal document and escalate potential issues through corporate hierarchy. In the case of external sales, the SLA should be handled as legally binding for both sides. A survey of the largest European companies using SSCs shows that 50% of the SLAs are exclusively internal, 38% are legally binding, and 12% of companies do not use SLAs at all. The preparation and then signing of such a document is a clear signal to both parties that something has changed significantly. There is no longer this centralized group that was not responsive and employed the push model for all activities. The client will now order only those services that are of value to their organization. So, Shared Services may be an excellent means for organizational development as part of a corporate strategy.

Challenges
The concepts of centralization and Shared Services are often confused. An SLA can be the first clear sign of how serious the company management wants to be about an SSC implementation. When the SLA does not contain a clear definition of the business units being in the customer role that chooses the services and their levels based on their needs, the SSC will probably shift into a centralized model. Motivation to provide a businesslike environment will not be as strong and the main benefit will reside in the consolidation and potential reduction of people. It is the client–service center's relationship that makes the SSC offer the best services possible.

Possible ICT Solutions
Economic rationale for IT automation of the SLA is only marginal. The SLA is a document that can be posted on an internal web site so that it is accessible for everybody.

6.3.4 Practice: Shared Service Operations- Services and Agreements

Shared Service Organizations are semi-autonomous units which can be legally independent. The formality of the agreements varies a lot.

BASF:
"We have a precise description of the processes and then another precise description of who does what. There are different aggregation levels that we use to design the process and desktop procedures about who is responsible for it, as well." [Interview with Mr. Seeger, BASF].

Henkel:
Henkel did not set up a formal service contract at the beginning when they rolled-in the local processes. "There were no contracts because they were legal entities. The processes were simply rolled-in. So that wasn't an issue." " … when a process is transferred from A to B, we basically have an internal agreement. They were not officially signed contracts, but in essence we had made agreements."

"… , when we go to Bratislava we'll have service levels. We're working on a Management Cockpit where we can do quarterly KPIs for every legal entity, every process, down to whatever depth you want."
"When I recently left the Shared Service Center, fixed price agreements were under discussion. These were not legally binding agreements, mind you. For tax purposes, of course, we always have to do that. There are rules for this that covers what service is rendered for whom, and that fulfills our tax requirements." [Interview with Mr. Dr. Mackrodt, Henkel].

Philips:
"We established regional service level agreements (SLAs) with the business units. With our new outsourcing deal with Infosys, we are now also creating a formal SLA between the retained Shared Service Organization and Infosys. Overall Philips remains the owner of the end-to-end processes, and delegates the execution of transactional and rules based tasks to Infosys."
"Roles are very well documented in detailed working instructions available for each instance of SAP. We measure the compliance to these working instructions, and have reached a level of 89%. When we started with the centralization process the compliance level was only around 35%, so centralizing has enabled us to harmonize very quickly." [Interview with Michel de Zeeuw, Philips]

SAP:
"Service level agreements are the basis of the whole thing. At the same time, we also have target agreements jointly set, both in the Shared Service area here in Prague as well as on site. This makes it clear that it is a common issue."
"… the important thing is that it is transparent, and we achieve this transparency by means of KPIs. These KPIs are held in service level agreements in relative detail. They are also in the service item lists, SILs, as we call them, so that they can be tracked precisely. We discuss this every month with the relevant CFOs or F&As on site: They all get a report and have access to a dashboard where they can see the process status. That's important. Then you have a basis for discussion and you can say that we need to do something here and there." [Interview with Peter Rasper, SAP]

Siemens:
"… We have service level agreements for certain products and processes and work packages, they are discussed with and agreed on by the customer."

Regarding usage of tools to manage service level agreements:
"No, we don't do that yet. Our service levels are defined with our customers and stored in the EIC for controlling purposes. In this way we can see if we have infringed these agreements and where we stand at the moment. The EIC is also the basis for the reporting. Apart from that, we have no background system."
[Interview with Wolfgang Leitmanstetter, Siemens]

Solvay:
Solvay chooses an operating model with legally binding service contracts. "It is very, very simple. The agreement is no more than five pages, the same general service agreement. Legally, it's prepared with the legal department. So we have legally binding general service agreements. We have dedicated service level agreements by process, which describe the standard way to deliver optimal services. And we have descriptions of all the exceptions that are accepted by the customer business entity and run the processes for a limited period of time.
When I said "legally," that's my intention. Today I'm still very quiet on that, but we have 160 contracts signed; I have a lawyer in Portugal doing that." [Interview with Guy de Mercier, Solvay]

Surrey County Council:
"I mean there are some, what we called subjective service standards as well, but at the heart of it, it had to be objective, analytical measures, everything has to have a number behind to make it viable. But as well as that, we also as an organization are developing new values of how we deal which each of our customers, so that was there as well. But the base measure for the effectiveness in the shared service center has always been the KPIs and how we are measuring against that."

"Yes, as much as we can, we're both part of the same organization, but yes, it is a formal service level, operating level agreement, which outlines the expectations. I have to say, by definition it is an agreement, so it is not only what they must do for me, but it is also what the others must do for them. And that's quite important because, that was a big challenge at the beginning, because everybody wanted to get perfection from the shared service center, but didn't have to want to deliver anything to them in the first place. So, by making an operating level agreement, it is of both sides an operating level." [Interview with Graham White, Surrey County Council]

6.4 Pricing – Charge Back

The final step in the administrative process is invoicing the clients and getting paid for delivered services. The complexity of the whole process very much depends on the clients (sometimes legally independent companies) and method for setting up the prices. Dealing with internal clients will be more informal when the business units are in a different organizational unit (such as a subsidiary in other country) or when it can be managed only through internal communication (such as a business unit within the corporation). The type of pricing will have an impact on how the payments are processed. Allocations based on cost-center postings will not require a formal document (such as an invoice); on the other hand, profit-based pricing strengthens the customer service culture in the SSC. Companies usually start with a definition of their service portfolio and its corresponding prices. Pricing can be well leveraged as a market driver that will help distinguish a purely centralized unit from an SSC. There are many ways to price services and we will look at some possibilities. By means of pricing of the services the shared service center may influence their customers to change their processes towards optimized processes (for example,. mandatory purchase order usage).

As mentioned before, it is difficult to set prices. Management at many companies is not certain of the feasibility of the fully loaded costs model, so they often decide to go only with cost allocation. Cost allocation creates a distortion in the Shared Services model and makes it very hard or even impossible to benchmark the service unit with external suppliers. There is no direct push or incentive to constantly optimize the cost structure. Services might seem cheaper for the business units, because they do not include all of the costs incurred. The company as a whole, however, still has to pay those costs.

Cost-based pricing or charge back is used by a very large group of companies in Europe (~ 70 %). It is possible to infer that those SSCs are still in their basic form in the majority of these organizations. Most of the companies just allocate costs (~45 %). A further step is the transfer price concept. In their simplest form, transfer prices can include only direct costs with a profit margin (~ 25 %). The most sophisticated approach to pricing is market pricing (~ 15 – 20 %). Such pricing includes all costs incurred by the service unit, and profit, and is still competitive when benchmarked with the external providers. The complexity of creating such a model can be seen given the small share of companies that have already mastered this pricing method.

6.4.1 Process

Transactional processes are usually highly standardized and lead to economies of scale. Shared Service has to decide what is going to be the *base for charging* for the transactions. It can either choose a unit price per transaction or charge certain volume of transactions for a fixed price. If different levels of service are desirable, transaction prices should reflect it. There could be, for example, a standard price per transaction, a higher price for fulfilling the transaction in a shorter time, and an even higher price for immediate action. Just remember one simple rule: the more complex the pricing is, the more complex the supporting structure to track the whole process will be. Project-based pricing is also possible and would be used for activities that occur on a regular basis (for example, period-end close). This being said, we have to admit that it is more of an academic approach to pricing transactional services than reality.

The majority of companies do not set any pricing model and simply allocate the costs back to the business units based on a chosen key (for example, proportion of revenues brought in by the business unit). This means that the business units are still viewed more as a cost center than as a client. Professional services usually involve a mix of daily rate charges and a fixed fee for the project. The design of the daily rates is up to the SSC, but here the complexity rule also applies. You can design different rates for different time periods (a one-day or a half-day rate is usual; an hourly rate is not recommended), but be aware that you will have to provide a reliable infrastructure to track them.

One question still remains unanswered – how should the SSC determine the price? Determining an agreeable price that would be acceptable for the business units and would also cover all the costs and possibly profit is a complex process that depends largely on the corporate environment.

A *stable environment* gives the SSC a very good basis to plan the future service quantities. Actual quantities delivered in the past can be extrapolated and form an acceptable prediction for the first draft of the price scheme. The service group can then offer the prices in the planning cycle and check whether the response from the business units will meet the expected demand. Several iterations will make it possible to arrive at an acceptable price for the service. In general, this approach is recommended for transactional services.

A *dynamic environment* poses a challenge for the pricing exercise. First of all, there is a constraint in the form of external vendor prices. If the price offered by the SSC is too high, it will be very hard to defend it. If it is too low, it will not cover all the costs. Probably the best start is to ask the business units what quantity of services would be ideally needed. Gathered quantity requirements will provide a basis for the preparation of the first draft's price scheme. The rest of the iterative process is then the same as previously described. This approach is best suited for professional services within SSCs.

In the end, it all comes down to measuring costs and revenues. Making the service self-supporting (covering all costs or even making profit) should be included in the design concept of each SSC. The main decision is probably which *controlling concept* should be used. We can see a great challenge for the companies here. The concept of fully loaded costs suggests that we have to know the price of the whole process, not what was budgeted for respective departments that are part of this process. *Activity based costing* would be the preferred solution; however, most of the companies still stick to the cost center model. A probable explanation is that it is easier to implement, because they already use the cost center concept for the business units.

The complexity of the controlling processes depends on what services the group offers and how differentiated the portfolio is. The easiest is the processing of unified transactions that have only limited variations. There is usually a unit price for one transaction or a volume price for a set. The service center records the number of transactions and multiplies them by the final price. It is a bit more complicated when the transactions have different prices depending on the priority of the service (the higher the priority, the higher the price). Professional services bring more factors into play. The service group has to account for a service it is offering plus it has to keep a time sheet for all employees. Time sheets should not be very complicated, otherwise the infrastructure costs would rise and the time spent on recording them would become a real burden. Ideally, a client should be billed on a daily rate basis. The half-day rate is also acceptable, but hourly is too detailed.

The issues described above deal primarily with direct costs. It is essential that the price for the client also involves indirect and administration costs. In case there is only a cost allocation back to the business units, such costs should be transferred on the service usage ratio (whichever business unit uses the services the most should also pay for most of these costs). If the price is set, controlling has to constantly monitor whether the indirect and administration costs are covered at all times. There should be an agreement about price adjustments in place between the service unit and the business units in case unexpected situations occur.

As you can see, there are many factors to watch for. The best advice is to keep the service conditions as flexible as possible and to limit the number of possible differentiations – at least in the beginning, before the new structure establishes itself and the SSC gathers some knowledge about its costs structures. Revenues should be handled the same way in order to allow for an easy comparison. After some time, it will automatically be obvious which services are the profitable ones and which ones need to be changed or abandoned. The market environment changes with dizzying speed, which also has a high impact on the relevance of the pricing. Calculated prices should be regularly checked so that they still cover the fully loaded costs, but are compared to other SSCs at the same time using equivalent levels. Such an analysis should be performed at regular intervals at least once a year. Depending on the agreements within the SLA, prices can also be adjusted during the year; but we would suggest doing that only in exceptional cases. This way the SSC is forced to plan better by solving the market changes in the beginning by optimizing its processes.

Before describing the regular invoicing and payment settlement process, let's mention a simpler option that is being used by most companies in Europe. These companies decided to stay closer to the centralization model and did not focus as much on the motivational factor of pricing. Costs incurred while providing the service to the business units were allocated back based on a defined allocation key. One example of the allocation key could be the number of people processing the transactions for the respective business unit as a percentage of the total number of people in the SSC. However, companies that are thinking about spinning off their SSC in the future will be better off setting up an invoicing and payment settlement process. The SSC starts with an evaluation of the amount of actual delivered services and matches it with the agreed prices. Then they issue an invoice referencing the purchase order and send it to the business unit. Payment conditions are automatically tracked and the administrative staff is alerted in case of late payment. Payments will then be matched with the invoices and the whole service contract will be closed. In case the business unit does not agree with the invoice, a regular dispute process is started to resolve the issue.

6.4.2 Challenges

The second type of invoicing and payment settlement process will pose a challenge with the invoice medium. If the SSC sends regular paper invoices and resolves issues using the mail or over the phone, there will be additional personnel costs for the administrative personnel. One way to address this issue is to transform the whole process into an electronic form (of course, this is possible only in countries where digital signatures are a recognized and accepted form of signing the invoice).

6.4.3 Possible ICT Solutions

The main supporting tool that can help with price calculations is a controlling module usually delivered together with F&A by all major ERP vendors. It must be linked closely to all other IT systems within an enterprise to be able to obtain information about employees, processes, costs, and revenues. There has been a growth in analytical tools using multidimensional analysis and data warehousing. Data from operational controlling systems is transferred to the data warehouse to take advantage of more flexible analysis and simulation. At the end of the 1980s activity-based costing (ABC) was introduced as another approach to dealing with costs, which is especially well suited for service industries. ABC allows for a more exact allocation of costs to processes and therefore provides a better answer to the question, "How much does the whole process of delivering this service cost us?" With this said, we have to note here that ABC has not experienced a wide adoption. Even though this concept would be well suited for SSCs, only a minority of the current practitioners use it. ABC is either available as a separate tool that can connect to ERP systems or it is offered by the ERP vendor. Analysis of the outcome of the selected pricing level can be well performed within the data warehouse leveraging its multidimensional nature. Results can be connected directly with prior calculations and can serve as a basis for simulations. Therefore, introducing a data warehouse should be a high priority for an SSC. An ERP solution provides an ideal set of the tools mentioned. Prices can be calculated by the controlling module using both the traditional and ABC approaches. Most ERP packages delivering a Business Information Warehouse component with out-of-the-box interfaces to the operational system and contains a predefined set of data structures that the customer can quickly customize to its particular situation. All systems make use of the workflow backbone supported by a portal presentation layer.

Cost allocation between the cost centers will be done only within the *corporate accounting system* and will not require any new investment. The AR system can be fully leveraged as long as the SSC is part of the company (not a separate unit). Purchase order entry will be automatically matched with the invoice details and the system will also track the status of the payment. A valuable extension of the AR system is using a web-based portal to present the invoices and matching them with payments in a self-service scenario for the client. Potential issues with the invoices are then handled through a dispute management system with a predefined escalation workflow. Previous descriptions of possible uses of IT solutions should be understood as an ideal scenario. An SSC will most likely not invest in such solutions alone; rather, they may use the parts of the solution currently implemented by the corporation. One other possibility is to use the SSC unit as a pilot for new software implementations within the corporation. The ERP solution provides an ideal fit for the IT infrastructure. Its AR system is closely linked with both the general ledger in accounting and with the purchasing and CRM systems. All systems make use of the workflow backbone supported by a portal presentation layer.

6.4.4 Practice: Setting the Price for Services

There are many different ways to charge back and price Shared Services. It is hard to pick out a model to nominate for its best practice.

BASF:

The BASF Shared Service Center charges its customers on a model which passes the average percentage savings to all of its clients throughout Europe. This means that companies that make minimal savings also receive a correspondingly higher saving as per average. High wage countries, where savings are significantly higher than average, receive correspondingly lower savings.

"We have a charging model that applies to everything. And since we naturally have higher costs here in Berlin than in Eastern Europe, for example, we decided that we'd have to make sure we make savings on average throughout Europe and this saving, this percentage, is then passed on to all the companies. This also means that companies that make minimal savings also receive a correspondingly higher saving as per the average. High wage countries, where savings are significantly higher than average, receive correspondingly lower savings.
Take Antwerp or Paris, where salaries are high and costs are also high, making fewer savings. So we all have the same percentage saving, but measured against potential savings, these go to the countries with higher costs and lower savings. We balanced this out using the user pay factor. That means that we have either 1.1 %, 1.2 %, 0.8 % or 0.9 %, depending on the costs in the country in question and the company in that country. On average, it has to balance out to 1 again."

"We start off with a charging model for the run-up stage. We have to calculate our costs plus 5 % profit margin. But this is of course directed towards the planned costs. What were your costs? We'll give you a price per FTE that is lower by amount X than it was previously. That's our way of ensuring that we stick to the costs we calculate here."

"Yes, once it's running we'll move over to process costs. That is, we'll charge per transaction and transaction characteristic. An invoice with an order costs 3 € or 5 €, an invoice without an order is more expensive because our expenses are higher with all the sending backwards and forwards. Sure, that's our goal, but we've not got round to it yet. We've not been using market prices either, which would be another possibility. If you have 25 countries and are working in 5 main areas but then have another 5 or 6 companies within each application area – so let's say you have 30 companies times 25 countries – then you would have to hire a few people who do nothing other than keep track of market prices. You have no idea what a fuss there would be if you debated market prices with the local units. Bearing that in mind, we said that we would use a simple charging model, to start with at least, and then we could consider a process cost-oriented charging model once we're up and running." [Interview with Hans-Jürgen Seeger, BASF]

Henkel:
"Another step we've taken is to introduce a single price for the same services. No matter where the service is used, it costs the same. But that's also something that, to some degree, we do to soften the blow to Germany, because otherwise no one would buy services from Germany. We wanted to avoid that because we are committed to Germany. That's part of the Henkel culture, very employee-oriented. That may seem a bit old-fashioned compared to some other companies. But I think it's a great strength that we at Henkel are so employee-oriented." [Interview with Dr. Carlo Mackrodt, Henkel]

6.5 Planning and Controlling Process of a Shared Service Organization

So far, we have covered reasons why SSCs exist, what their major focus is, and how they administer their business. What we have yet to describe is how an SSC can – and should be – managed. The next step after pricing of Shared Services is the planning of future requirements for resources and capital, together with forecasting the revenues. A selected approach to planning and forecasting will determine the accuracy of the estimation. Closed-loop management requires not only on-time decision making on the direction in which the SSC is going. Even more important is an ongoing evaluation of the performance and its subsequent adjustments.

Overall, managing an SSC does not differ much from managing a small company. The fact that the clients are primarily internal may simplify some of the processes; however, the staff still has to follow them.

6.5.1 Planning, Budgeting and Forecasting

The SSC in our examples has already agreed to a certain commitment stated in the SLA and issued prices that it will charge for the services (or even different levels of services). It should now plan future activities throughout the year to make sure it is able to meet the obligations.

6.5.1.1 Process

Planning can be instituted on different levels; ideally it should contain both top-down and bottom-up approaches. Service units have a great advantage in their position within a company. Their services are usually mandated, so their clients are already
known. The planning group should try to contact the business units and agree on the types of services demanded, its volume, and distribution of demand in time. Such information will help the SSC tremendously in planning the output levels. With the information about output levels, the SSC can plan all the remaining resources and activities to be able to meet the time and quality expectations. We also highly recommend introducing a risk-rating factor into the planning process to better reflect the changing market environment. The yearly budgeting process is usually enough for most of the SSCs. A major prerequisite is an environment with low to medium level dynamics. This is the case at SSCs that provide transactional services. SSCs in highly dynamic environments would quickly find out that the budget is not an accurate basis for the planning and evaluation of future activities, and should employ forecasting instead. Professional services will most likely require this type of planning.

6.5.1.2 Challenges and Possible ICT Solutions

The size of the service unit, the differentiation of the service levels, and the volume of processed transactions and projects are key decision factors for planning support tools. Management has to choose how sophisticated the planning framework should be. One extreme is having only a simple planning spreadsheet; the other could be a highly sophisticated and complex set of planning tools. The reasonable solution is usually somewhere in the middle.

Cost controlling systems can be used as a support for cost planning; however, they do not offer acceptable flexibility. Planning is viewed in general as an extension of actual tracking; therefore, a change of the planning structures is almost impossible. The same statement about flexibility is true for the levels of detail used in cost controlling, because it leads to exaggerated levels of planning detail. The whole system is built on a centralized model, where every dependency has to be predefined before the start of the planning cycle. Therefore, a sophisticated planning process is very problematic with such tools. Spreadsheet calculations probably exist in every company. They were first introduced to help with simple ad hoc models, but have grown into sophisticated planning models over time. A major issue with such growth was the initial approach. Starting small also meant a relatively unstructured approach. Steady growth of the content led to exponential growth in its overall complexity and became a major roadblock at some companies. The possibility of decentralized processing was also an attribute valued by every controller. Different departments processed their particular sheets and returned them back to controlling for consolidation. Lack of a centralized component in the planning framework led to a serious number of errors during consolidation of the different sheets and made a lot of manual work necessary. Planning objects are generally multidimensional; therefore, the use of data warehouses is the current best approach. Simpler planning frameworks can be developed directly on top of a data warehouse. A more sophisticated and dynamic approach is to use specialized planning, budgeting, and forecasting software. It focuses not only on the framework itself, but also on the reconciliation of all levels and on support of versioning.

6.5.2 Performance Measurement

Customer service is the single most important factor in the SSCs activities. Therefore, there should be an effective system in place for monitoring and evaluation of performance in this area. Performance means not only delivering the service, but also delivering it on time, in a desired quality and quantity, and to the full satisfaction of the client.

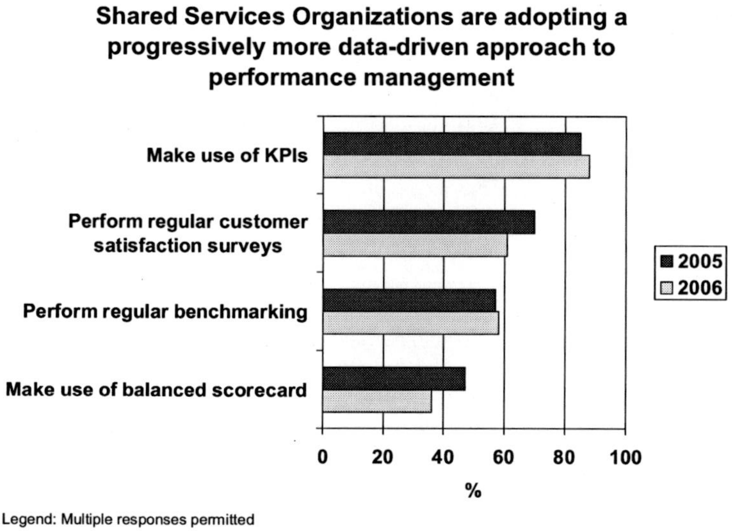

Fig. 90: Methods used for measuring Shared Service performance
Source: Hackett (2005a, 20) and Hackett (2007, 53)

Process

All of the companies employ at least a basic level of performance measurement. From the financial point of view, management usually tracks how the group and its team members stick to the budgeted numbers. This can work quite well in a stable environment. Some include a comparison of the internal performance with a benchmark of other companies. Benchmarking is a suggested approach if the organization considers the independent business model for its SSC. One step further would also be to employ non-financial measures or key performance indicators (KPIs) to measure the performance. Financial measures are a good indicator of results that the group reached in the past. Non-financial indicators can help track information relating to the possible future performance. Examples of such indicators can be customer satisfaction, level of expert knowledge among the members of the team, or the average time for processing a transaction. Management consulting firms offer service centers many methodologies for performance measurement. The Balanced Scorecard concept developed originally by Norton and Kaplan is the most popular one. Balanced Scorecards can be structured into hierarchies and offer each management level in the organization the right granularity of information. An even more innovative approach is to use the scorecard as a "strategy communication" medium to execute relevant parts of corporate strategy within the SSC.

Challenges

Challenges with performance measurement are more business than technological in nature. Management has to make a clear decision on how to evaluate the performance of the employees, regardless of whether they are within corporate, the business unit, or the SSC.

Budgets have been used as a tool to track and evaluate performance for decades. So employees are most often evaluated according to how they meet their planned financial targets.

Some companies tried to extend the performance tracking to non-financial measures and introduced a Balanced Scorecard in addition to the budget. This caused serious confusion within the workforce. Two tools now evaluated them, but only one had direct influence on the remuneration. The result of such a decision was clear: Balanced Scorecard KPIs became "nice to have" measures, but nobody paid much attention to them afterwards. There must be a clear decision up-front. Either people should be evaluated by how they conform to a budget or on reaching the set KPIs within the Balanced Scorecard. Budget numbers are absolute numbers; Balanced Scorecards are mostly relative numbers. Mixing those two performance evaluation tools together has not yielded satisfactory results. If a corporation still uses budgets, but would like to test the Balanced Scorecard mechanism as a pilot, an SSC is a very good opportunity to do so.

Possible ICT Solutions

The ideal approach is to closely tie the planning process with the performance measurement process. The number of chosen indicators, management levels at which they will be tracked, and the size of the service center are all major factors when deciding on proper application support. The simplest way to analyze performance is using a spreadsheet. The same way as for planning, it has some advantages and many disadvantages. It is a very flexible tool for very small implementations. Increasing the scope of performance measurement, either by adding people or KPIs, increases the complexity exponentially. Regional or global use will require a more sophisticated solution. Some companies start building their performance measurement solutions from scratch using an analytical environment of data warehouses. Such a solution will be able to satisfy all system performance and scalability requirements; however, it will be very costly to implement and maintain. Only in the last several years have companies gained one more possibility to address all previous issues. Specialized solutions for performance measurement emerged as parts of "business performance management" suites from leading software vendors. These should be built on a data warehouse platform, should be closely linked to other parts of the suite, and offer tools such as Balanced Scorecard or a KPI dashboard. Some vendors are going even further by offering specific predefined content for selected industries. Such a solution can and will drive down the total cost of ownership (TCO) dramatically.

Benchmarking has become a vital source of comparison with other companies in the industry. Several benchmarking suppliers offer the data in a structured electronic form, which is perfectly suited for automated import into a customer's performance measurement system. ERP solutions provide an ideal set of all the mentioned tools. Performance measurement is part of the strategic enterprise management capability. It comes with tools supporting all leading methodologies (for example, shareholder value management, Balanced Scorecard, management cockpit, and so on). A customer obtains a set of best practices content specifically selected for their industry to minimize the time of design and implementation. Benchmarking data can be automatically exchanged with external providers via the Extensible Markup Language (XML) standard. All systems make use of the workflow backbone supported by a portal.

6.5.2.1 Practice: Performance Measurement SSO

Measuring performance of a Shared Service Organization includes the measuring of internal performance compared to own targets and comparison by means of benchmarks with external enterprises.

Henkel:
"Every two years we set benchmarks, at the end there's even a comprehensive benchmark done by Hackett which includes everything, procurement, IT and HR. We've set benchmarks for everything. It's been a great success. That's one part, but I've also always told my people that I want to know it internally, too. So I've always had my costs. In the Management Cockpit we have KPIs for every process, such as OTC Controlling, GA Intercompany and CPM, Central Payment Management." [Interview with Dr. Carlo Mackrodt, Henkel]

Marks & Spencer (M&S):
"I think there are three types of success. The first one is, have we delivered what we promised? Did we promise to build the best-of-breed shared services? Are we on the right track for that?" [Interview with Mr. Foley, M&S].

Siemens:
"What will probably cause us a lot of headache is the topic of benchmarking. Siemens AG wants to benchmark. We want to benchmark ourselves here in Germany first. We want to see where our Shared Service stands in Germany, and of course on a global structure. ... If you read benchmarking studies, regardless of whether they have come from, they very often compare apples with pears, as far as I am concerned. You can interpret how you want, and everyone does well, but you don't get any real concrete information. We want to change this. At least in my area of responsibility in Europe, I want to know where I stand. But I want to compare apples with apples."
"Benchmarking companies can give you an initial overview. But I believe, and I'll say this bluntly, it's often not worth the paper it's written on. You can use it as a wake-up call, but it's of no help when it comes to making, when I want to know where I stand now. What we are doing now, and it is a very interesting approach, we want to go down to the level of individual services to be able to compare and to create the basis for benchmarking. But we are still in the very early days. What we are looking for are allied companies that want to do this with us." [Interview with Wolfgang Leitmanstetter, Siemens]

7 Implementation, Transformation, Transition and Change Management

7.1 Transition into Shared Services

Centralizing the execution of processes and tasks in Shared Service hubs provides the foundation to achieve better economies of scale. Consolidation of resources (people and technology like ICT systems) as well as the consolidation, harmonization, standardization and simplification of business processes are the roots for cost reduction, better time performance, improved quality and better risk management. The magnitude of deploying the Shared Service concept varies widely in geographical coverage and type of business process scope (functional and transactional or transformational).

Each transition into a new organization (structure and process flow) has an impact on the business process (process governance and process execution) as well as the resources usage. Business processes are documented and supported by ICT systems. Splitting business processes between the Shared Service Organization and the remaining business clients is heavily affected by the capability of the underlying ICT system landscape, especially the ICT application systems. Business processes have a longer life cycle and are normally defined independently from any assignment of resources or resource categories. Specific assignment of resources to business processes by means of ICT technology and/or people is an instantiation of an implementation.

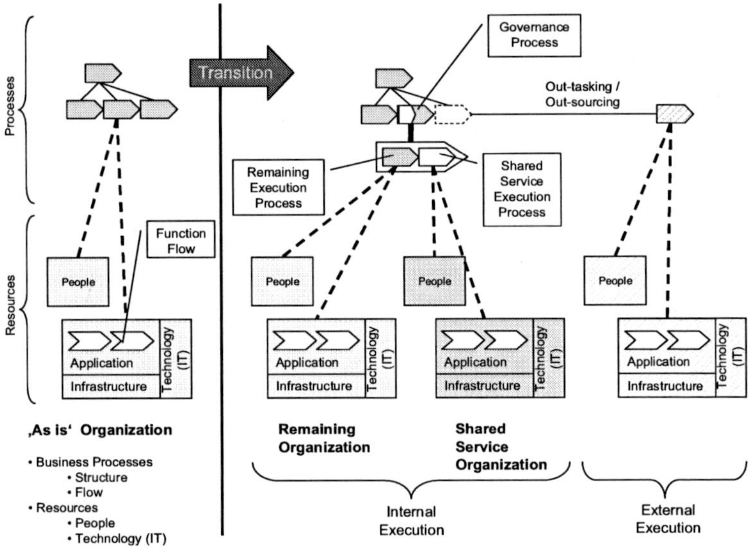

Fig. 91: Organizational transition into shared services

These are the essential aspects from the diagram:

- Splitting the original process has an *impact on the information process flow*
- There is a need for dedicated *process governance*. Splitting business processes and assigning the process chains to different execution resources requires an orchestration governance task (design and runtime).
- Process execution resources can be *internal or external resources* regardless of the resource category like *people or technology*.
- Business processes can be executed completely *manually, interactive* with ICT systems or fully *automated*.
- Business process structures (process level structure) and business process flows are ideally *independent of the underlying ICT application systems* (functional process steps and flows).

Organizing a solution means dealing with various combinations of business process modeling, capability of resources of people and technology and their location. In very rare cases, these solutions are developed from scratch. ICT systems capabilities (especially ICT application systems) are a crucial decision. Existing ICT application packages are mostly the foundation for *reference processes* and available ICT instantiation solutions.

To assess the different options a score card with the profile of the key values is advisable.

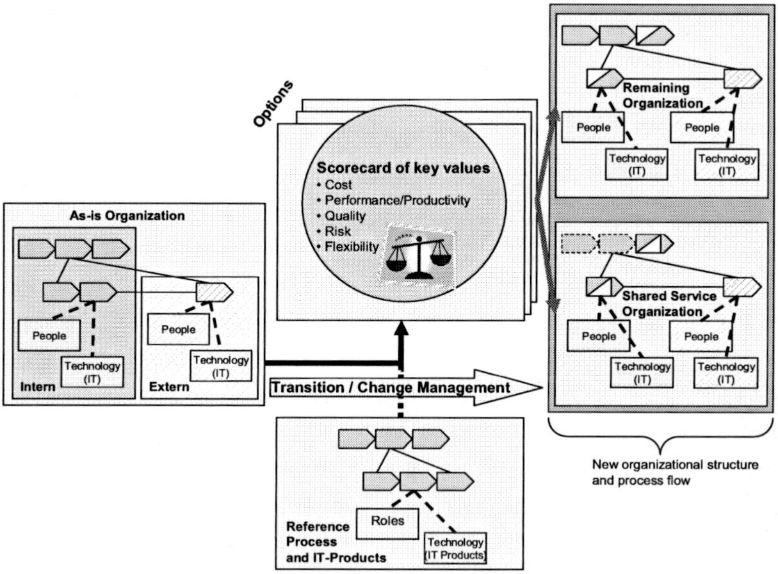

Fig. 92: Assessing organizational options with a Scorecard of key values

Different business process types, a scattered heterogeneous landscape of supporting ICT systems and different execution people on different locations create enormous complexity. Thus simplification and standardization (such as ICT system consolidation) are rated as essential in a Shared Service environment.

7.2 Implementation considerations

7.2.1 Lift-and-Shift versus Transform-and-Shift

One of the first questions to ask is which *business processes* (or portion of business processes) should be targeted for the initial implementation. If a Shared Service Center is already up and running the question has to be extended to which additional business processes can be added. Process coverage is just one aspect of the decision frame. Selecting a *service delivery location* and choosing an internal or external *process sourcing* approach are also vital.

The goal of implementing an economically successful Shared Service Organization can be achieved in two ways:

- Lift-and-Shift
- Transform-and-Shift

The *Lift-and-Shift* approach takes the existing business processes (without reengineering and optimizing them), centralizing them (which is a sort of simplification) and selecting a cheaper sourcing delivery location. Originally, sourcing was purely a shift to a place with cheaper personnel costs. The main driver of this approach is to gaining fast economic benefits from the labor arbitrage between the different salary and wages level. After shifting the existing business process to a new location the transformation of captive processes may lead to additional savings.

The *Transform-and-Shift* approach is different. The first step is a business process transformation (simplification-standardization-optimization) before deciding on the sourcing delivery location.

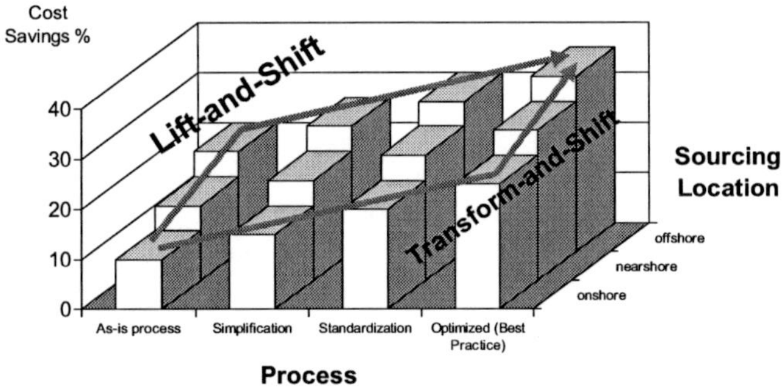

Fig. 93: Process sourcing potential cost savings – Transformation and Sourcing Location

The cost of process sourcing is not driven just by the labor cost of the executing business people at a certain location. For example, a shift of the sourcing delivery category (service delivery category) is also possible (full-automation of previously manual processes; sourcing out the business process to external providers; moving from decentralized processing of local internal business people to self-services as a different service delivery category). Combining the different sourcing delivery categories with a cheaper sourcing delivery location would present a more holistic view of business process sourcing options.

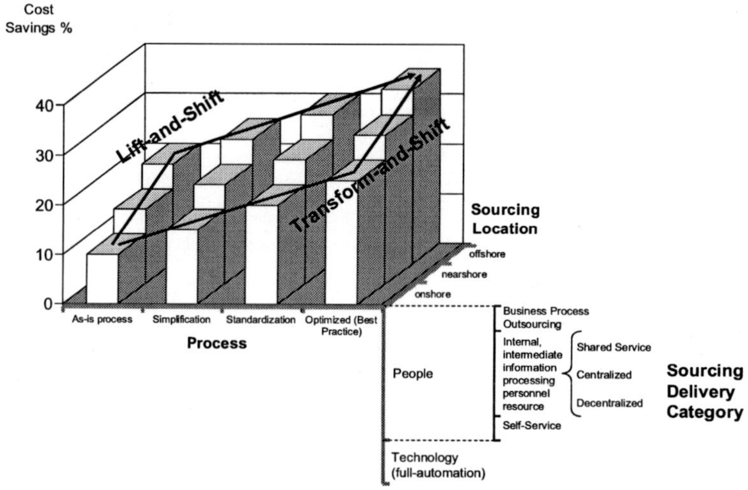

Fig. 94: Process sourcing potential cost savings – Process, Sourcing Location and Sourcing Delivery Category

The diagram shows the potential approaches and their impact on the perceived economic (cost) savings. Keep in mind that *cost* is just one key value benefit which companies would like to improve through a Shared Service implementation.

Transformation of processes is a multidimensional view of the:

- Process itself (simplification, standardization, optimization of the process)
- Sourcing framework (simplification, standardization, optimization of the executing resource framework with various degrees of people and technology involvement on different locations)
  - Sourcing categories (high level: people, technology):
    - People:

    - Internal intermediate information processing people (an internal or personnel resource performs information processing work with or without enabling ICT; operating deployment concepts range from a centralized Shared Service approach to the decentralized work of local business people; coordination within enterprise boundaries is necessary)
    - External service provider (external personnel resource performs information processing work with or without enabling ICT; collaboration and coordination across enterprise boundaries is necessary)
    - Self-services (internal - employees - or external -. customer, vendor, partner - performing information work by themselves with enabling ICT; collaboration and coordination within and across enterprise boundaries are necessary)
  - Technology:
    - Automation (fully automated execution of business processes; for partial automation of a defined process we still require a personnel resource for remaining information processing work)
- Sourcing locations (onshore, nearshore, offshore)

The outcome of a process transformation is driven by the availability and capability of execution resources, additional organizational preferences (centralization, decentralization) and environmental constraints (such as economical, political, cultural and social influences). Reducing the variations of processes (simplification, standardization) and a variation of associated enabling execution resources with ongoing optimization of process requirements (for example, adaptation to dynamic changes of technological, economic and political conditions) is a permanent goal.

In practice, companies choose a combination of the ideal approaches of process sourcing with a tendency in one or other direction. Process reengineering and sourcing options (people, technology) and service delivery locations are interdependent. The capabilities of the process resources, especially of ICT, either enable or constrain the potential Shared Service solutions.

Empirical Results on Cost Savings of Lift-and-Shift versus Transform-and-Shift.

The question is now: What is the economic impact on the two pure implementation approaches of lift-and-shift versus transform-and-shift? A recent study across General & Administrative functions, carried out by Janssen M./ Ramirez J./Dorr Erik (Janssen et. al. 2007), for a typical Fortune 500 company shows the economic impact on those different approaches. General & Administrative functions are the enabling information technology (IT) and the direct business functions Finance, Human Resources and Procurement. Each of the core business functions covers the transactional and non-transactional activities for a potential transition.

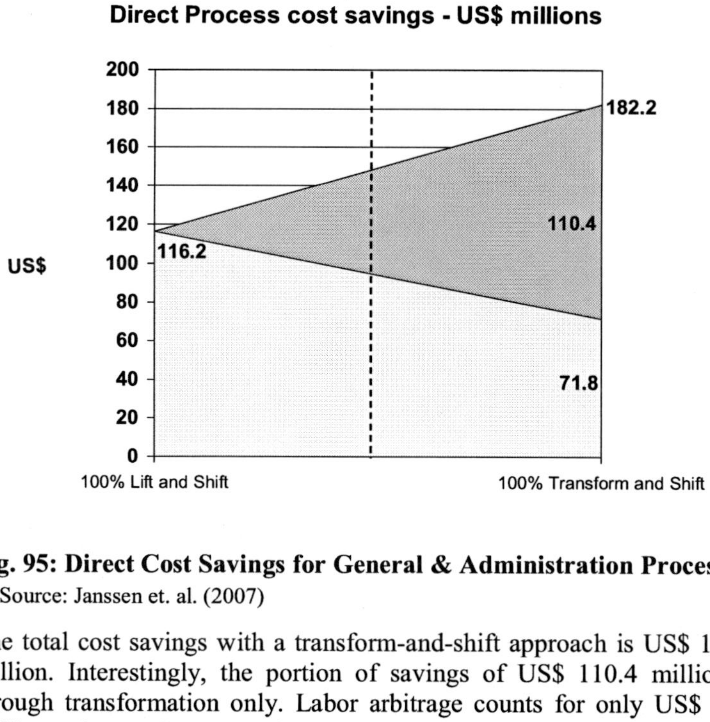

Fig. 95: Direct Cost Savings for General & Administration Processes

Source: Janssen et. al. (2007)

The total cost savings with a transform-and-shift approach is US$ 182.2 million. Interestingly, the portion of savings of US$ 110.4 million is through transformation only. Labor arbitrage counts for only US$ 71.8 million after a best practice approach was applied during process transformation. Transformation means simplification, process re-engineering, a higher degree of automation, centralization and consolidation. But higher amounts of cost savings do not necessary have a higher net present value (NPV). Transformation processes require a higher investment effort. Those investments have to be depreciated over a time period. Thus the benefit of cost savings will be achieved later. Monetary figures are just one key value benefit measurement category. Other key value benefits, like quality, risk, performance, productivity and flexibility, have to be considered in order to gain a holistic picture.

How much cost savings are achieved by F&A and human resources? Both business functions show a higher total cost saving potential when used with a transform-and-shift approach.

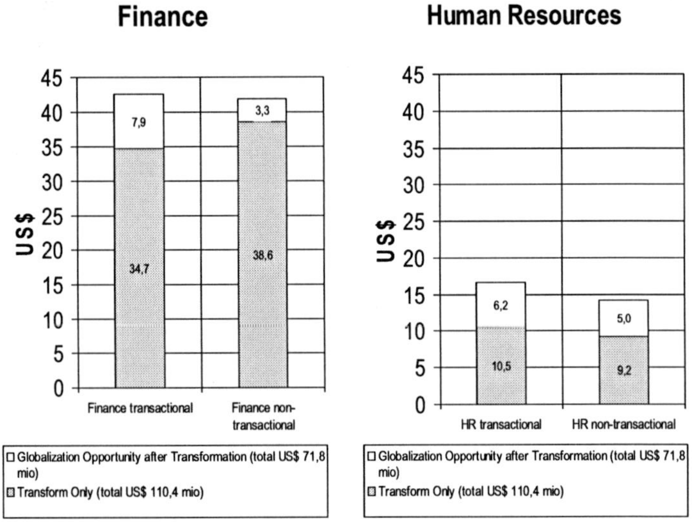

Fig. 96: Transform and Shift total benefits for business functions finance and human resources of a typical Fortune 500 company

Source: Janssen et. al. (2007)

How this picture will change in case of defining highly commoditized transactional processes which will be externally sourced, is a still open question. Commodity services are mostly processes transformed according to best practices. Thus a lift-and-shift approach should show higher cost savings. In this case, costs are mainly driven by the labor arbitrage. Costs are one process metric measurement. There are other non-monetary process metrics (e.g. quality, risk) which have to be considered as well.

7.2.2 Greenfield-Brownfield-Headquarter Location

Another decision is the physical *geographical* location of Shared Service operations. A central approach from the headquarter site is still the preferred service delivery location. If Shared Services explicitly select an geographical location away from headquarters the Brownfield approach tends to dominate the Greenfield approach.

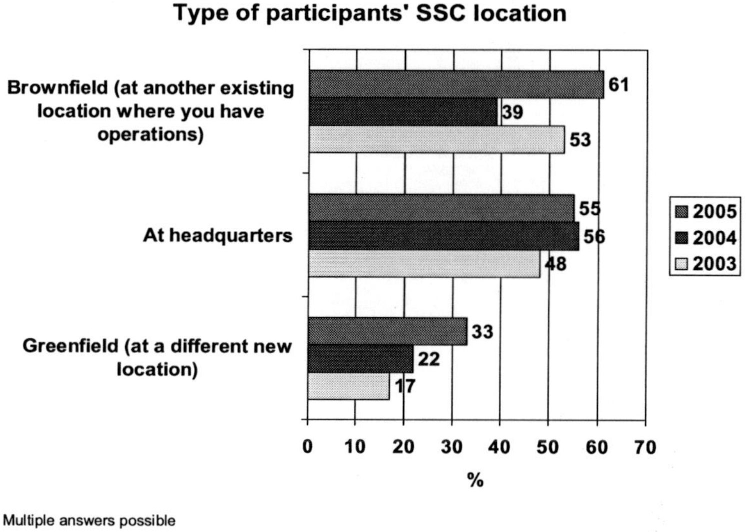

Fig. 97: Implementation approaches - Greenfield–Brownfield-Headquarter

Source: Hackett (2005a, 14)

All approaches have their pros and cons. Brownfield location (which means co-located with existing company operations) decisions take advantage of the use of existing infrastructure. Through the co-location with other business operations, there are better career opportunities for Shared Service staff.

Greenfield location decisions are explicitly made mostly to visualize the separation of Shared Services from headquarters and business locations. Increasing the distance prevents the people picking up or falling back in undesired corporate habits.

7.2.3 Advantages through Scaling

Cumulating a critical mass is one of the fundamental requirements to achieving cost benefits in Shared Services. The degree of potential cost savings depends on the volume. This volume can be reached by a single large enterprise where all the businesses are serviced out of a big Shared service center. As the cost savings depend on the size of the volume it is obvious that cumulating service volumes across customers would provide bigger potential savings. At a given cost degression curve the cost advantages decreases because of lower incremental margins.

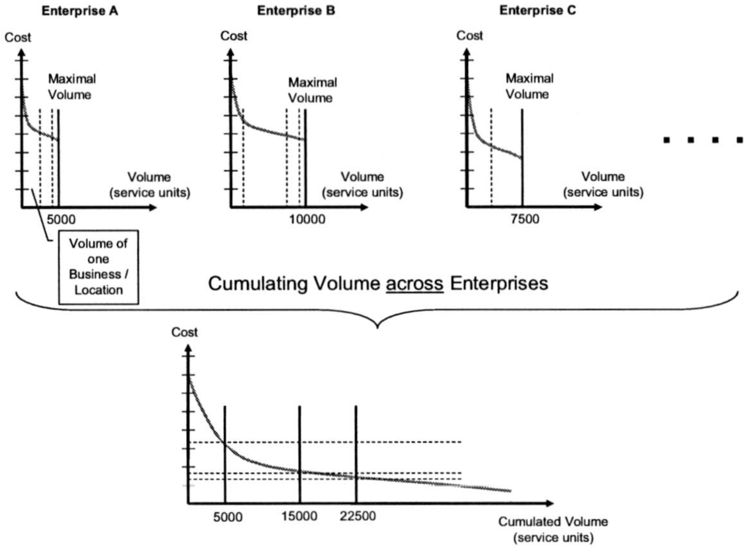

Fig. 98: Shared Service scaling potential across enterprises

By assuming a given costing curve for all participants, the consolidation of volume provides a cost advantage. The cost advantage for a given enterprise is limited by the maximum potential volume per enterprise. Further cost savings are only achievable via cumulating volumes across enterprises.

With the assumption that an external service provider is capable and willing to deliver the service, the advantages of a single enterprise depends on its own volume and the aggregated volume of the service provider at the time of operation.

7.3 Implementation Best Practices

In the previous chapter on empirical studies of obstacles and challenges in Shared Service the criteria relating to the implementation of Shared Service (such as "Not enough support from executive management") was ranked as the number one challenge. We can extract further success factors that influence the implementation of Shared Service. An empirical survey among the SAP user group in America (ASUG) shows a clear picture of the most important implementation success factors.

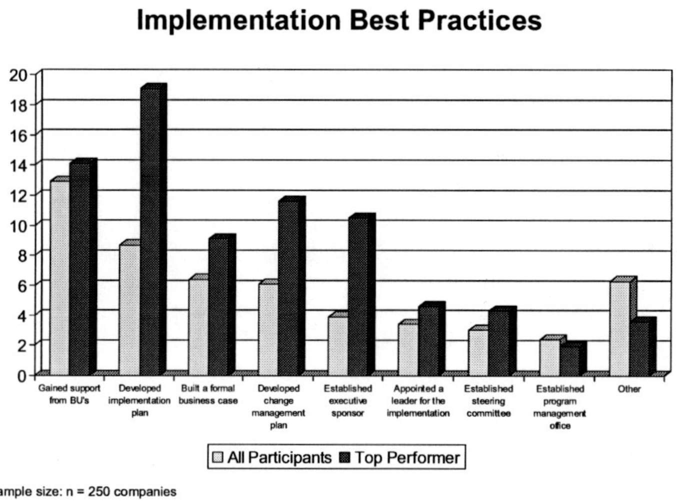

Fig. 99: Implementation Best Practice Success Factors

Source: ASUG/SAP (2006)

Top performers in shared services invest significantly more in implementation planning (+ 119%), prepared change management (+90%) and securing executive commitment (+172%). These organizations recognize the important of a careful preparation, the crucial role of the executive support during the roll out as well as conscious risk management associated with the lag of communication and end user adoption.

7.4 Practice: Implementation Approaches

In general there are different approaches, although there are no implementations of one of the pure approaches.

BASF:

"With hindsight, it was a very ambitious task. It could certainly have been implemented quicker and better, but in principle it was all very orderly and easier than I had originally thought." "We had good support from the board but we could have been quicker and lost less time." [Interview with Mr. Seeger, BASF].

Henkel:
"First we transformed the processes and then we shifted them. …
We started with standardization and then proceeded with the centralization of all the countries. " [Interview with Mr. Dr. Mackrodt, Henkel].
Standardizing processes was one of the preconditions in process reengineering. They started with process standardization and then proceeded with the centralization of all countries. In 2003 they established the first cross-regional Shared Service Center.

Marks & Spencer (M&S):
M&S distinguishes three different stages in setting up Shared Services. "As a strategic approach, you go to your first phase: "I'm going to do that, and I want to implement it." Your second phase occurs when you've implemented it and you get business in. Your third phase occurs when it's moving up the value chain and possibly to BPO, outsourcing, and so on." [Interview with Mr. Foley, M&S]. For all of the different stages you need different people with different skills.
"However, within the phases you have different tactics. So for example, in the first phase if you decide to do Shared Services, the tactic is which market do you start with? Do you start with a small market and pilot it, or do you start with the biggest market because the biggest market will set up the global process? If your biggest market is Great Britain or Germany, you wouldn't expect Portugal to change the process as much, because it wouldn't have as much focus." "It's also about your risk management. If you start with a small market, you build your processes for that; if you go to a medium market, you have to change your processes. If you then go to a large market, you've got to change your processes as well." [Interview with Mr. Foley, M&S]. At the end you have to make a trade-off decision.

Philips:
"Implementation speed was a crucial factor for us. Of course we did some harmonization work but in general I would say the lift-and-shift approach was our preferred approach."
Finance and Accounting took a functional approach (such as accounts payable, accounts receivable). "Human resources has taken until now a country per country approach." [Interview with Michel de Zeeuw, Philips]

SAP:
"Our building principle was quite simple, in fact. As I always put it, "Be brave, be quick, be pragmatic." That is to say, we put together a Shared

Service Center pretty quickly there and … we were able to achieve this because we made sure that the stakeholders were brought along with us. We considered the change management issue to be very important, and we included employees, stakeholders, CFOs and MDs in every phase of the project."

"The alignment was achieved with steering committee meetings, advisory council meetings and other measures which we used to inform the stakeholders and include them in decision-making. We started with a small country, which was the milestone as you know, a small willing country, namely Switzerland. Then we quite simply had a proof of concept for Europe. And then we said to ourselves, let's do it on a larger scale, and then essentially included the whole company. It was important to note that critical mass is key. You have to see quickly that you get as much in as possible, so that you can leverage better later."

"… We did it country-for-country with the F&A processes, HR started out service-for-service in Europe. We learnt from each other in doing this, and then HR switched to country-for-country too. We co-locate, which is very advantageous as we can move people from one area to another in accordance with their career plans. We can take advantage of the leverage effect from the training measures for other infrastructure issues, or we learn from each other – through the customer surveys, for example – how to approach things, or from customer-facing activities such as the Accounting Interaction Center or HR Interaction Center. This simply makes a great deal of activities easier."

"… Our approach was to tackle larger countries after a small, willing pilot country. The situation today is that we have the large countries all in. At the moment we're working on bringing in small countries, where the cost effect is not so great, but the compliance and quality effects are a factor." [Interview with Peter Rasper, SAP]

Solvay:

"We were relatively late to the game of the shared services center. Officially we started in 2005, but we started to study it in 2003. The reason it took a little bit longer is that Solvay decided to follow a strategy of BPM, business process management. That means the first priority was put on "redesign first and transform after." We saw many, many experiences of existing shared services centers in which they tried to fully centralize or delocalize, and when the process was done, the centers were hoping to be able to optimize. But they didn't have anymore local resources – sometimes not even energy – to do the optimization after the centralization. So at Solvay we followed a strategy of BPM: the first phases, the as-is and the should-be; the implementation of that gap; and then the transfer to the shared services center." [Interview with Guy de Mercier, Solvay]

Surrey County Council:
Regarding the preferred approach of Transform-and-Shift or Lift-and-Shift.
"We did the first one. But we did it in a laboratory, when it moved, it was already fixed. But we didn't change it and so the instance has moved. We would have blue printed the new solution, but we wouldn't actually have used it outside of shared service center. But in shared service, where we did move it and the technology wasn't ready, the shared service center would have operated in a sort of invisible manual basis."
"We did it as a big bang, but we did it some - not right across the as a big bang. We introduced it to the organization service by service. It was a total package each time." [Interview with Graham White, Surrey County Council]

7.5 Practice: Implementation Challenges

Henkel:
"You need very, very strict governance of change order management if you really want to change something. We repeatedly missed opportunities when someone insisted that something was a legal requirement, where we later found out that we'd been misled. But ultimately the process was up and running, we went live and the customers got their products approved. Currently we're doing a retrofit." [Interview with Dr. Carlo Mackrodt, Henkel]

Philips:
"I have to admit that it was quite easy for Philips. Of course we experienced some obstacles in convincing stakeholders, especially when it came to onshore-offshore discussions for North America, but everything flowed without disruptions within a normal decision-making process." [Interview Michel de Zeeuw, Philips]

SAP:
"... For the first year, a Shared Service Center runs in kind of crisis mode, because the organization and the employees of the different organizations and of the Shared Service Center are not yet used to working in this virtual environment. To achieve this, you need completely new skills – in the Shared Service Center, too. You need somebody battle-proven there, as a manager, for example, especially in the initial phase. Somebody who is very accepted in the organization who has both the specific know-how and the potential to push the thing through. But

that changes over time, when after two or three years you see that the Shared Service Center has arrived in the organization and conflicts are back on a normal level. From that point of view, then, the level of acceptance is quite different."
"Now you need a salesperson more, someone who will see to it that more services are added and that the organization is controlled differently. It's ultimately an evolution of the skills which are needed there. It's important to remember throughout the whole process that the organizations have to be taken on board. We have noticed that it's important not only to look after the F&A organizations during change management, but the organization as a whole must understand that things are now going to be done differently. This change management aspect is a very important one for the organization. For this reason, you can't check often enough that somebody, maybe even a CEO, is paying attention and gives his views on this and similar issues."

"In principle, the problem was that neither the people who had stayed "at home" in the locations, nor the Shared Service Center employees had ever worked in such an environment. That is to say, virtually, with a lot of cultural differences and now with a new division of labor. The issue of conflict management is a very important one, as is cultural diversity. People have to accept that others are different, react differently and address others differently." [Interview with Peter Rasper, SAP]

Solvay:
Regarding the implementation challenges Solvay has its own experience on this topic.
"I do believe the cultural problem is not helping, but the main reason is that the upstream process part, which was the procurement, was not yet in SAP software. They didn't use the workflow in SAP software. So when you are not using the normal procedure for connecting properly to your shared services center, and therefore when you rely on verbal communication, then you are facing significant challenges, because I believe that a shared services center is not a tool created for verbal communication. We developed an interaction tool which is very successful, because instead of a call center I put in place an expert contact center, which is charged with solving the problem, not just hitting the contact." [Interview with Guy de Mercier, Solvay]

Surrey County Council:
"The service team we started out with was to do a twin track approach to recruit externally or new to the organization and at the same time to move across original staff, who have been with us for some time. I mean, with

hindsight I'm not sure that was the best solution. I think there were some real stars came across from the organization, but we also inadvertently transferred a lot of old culture and old traditions, which we spent a lot of time trying to fix, which wasn't a good idea. And realistically, I think if I was planning it again, I would far more circumspect how many people I would bring from the old regime into the new. That said, there were still some great people came across, but proportionally I think I would have taken less."
I think in terms of the people that you bring in from outside, it's a whole new skill set. No matter how much you think it's the old way done differently, it's not. It's a completely new skill set and one in which you do need to spend as much time as possible analyzing what it is you're going to be doing and making sure you bring in the sort of people, who will adapt to that role quickly.

"We had some of the traditional concerns about turnover. I have to say that it hasn't become intolerable for us. We worked very much on the cultural side of working in the shared service center and build very strong team working, so that people actually enjoy the experience. And we've taken advantage of the fact that some staff like the flexibility and the coming and going within that type of environment. So, on that basis we haven't had any real problems. And to be honest, we should have done, because you know, we built a shared service center, which has virtually zero unemployment.

I wouldn't say it was easy, but we've not had some of the horrendous problems that we've heard from other shared service centers. But I put some of that down to the cultural work we do at the same time as the technical work." [Interview with Graham White, Surrey County Council]

8 Shared Service in Practice

8.1 Interview: BASF

Interview with Hans-Jürgen Seeger, Head of BASF Business Services, Berlin.

Introduction:
BASF, the world's largest chemical company, has a Shared Service Center for the European BASF group, which covers 25 countries, approximately 150 companies and more than 25,000 employees. The Shared Service Center, headed by Mr. Hans-Jürgen Seeger, a long-serving BASF employee and former CFO of BASF China, has been up and running since early 2006.

Mr. Seeger, BASF made an unusual move in its choice of location for its new Business Service Center. Could you tell us what criteria you weighed up when selecting Berlin?
Hans-Jürgen Seeger:
The list of selection criteria was very short. The two essential criteria were suitable employees with financial and business accounting know-how and, of course, language skills. There are 180,000 students in Berlin with a catchment area of 3 ½ million people in the immediate vicinity. Berlin is also attractive for people from Frankfurt/Oder, which provides an enormous number of potential employees. The city offers specialist knowledge, good language skills and an international community thanks to the embassies here in the capital. In addition to this, there was an unemployment rate of 18 % in 2000 (when we made our decision), even amongst graduates.

Did you take a large number of locations into consideration back then, or was the international make-up of the staff and the high unemployment rate the real background for coming to Berlin?
Hans-Jürgen Seeger:
There was nothing background about it. We did, of course, also ask ourselves where we could save the most money. We also discussed using shared tools that we could introduce for all our companies. This would mean savings in investment, making use of scale and thereby saving costs. But to get back to your question, we looked at Eastern Europe, we looked at Dublin, we looked at Manchester, we went to Hungary and even looked at smaller cities there like Szeged and Pecs. That would have made an ideal location for IT. The university there educates far more people than are needed in the region. Unfortunately the city is not

particularly well connected to the rest of Europe. We went to the Baltic, to Tallinn, and to Barcelona in Spain.

When did Berlin come into the question then?
Hans-Jürgen Seeger:
Berlin came into it quite late. Of course, the savings that can be made in Eastern Europe are far larger than in Berlin. However, one contributing factor in the decision was the positive response from unions towards negotiating a separate labor contract for the East German region. We were faced with a decision about concluding a labor agreement that would have had a major effect on whether we chose Bratislava or East Berlin. The unions did the right thing. This meant we were able to stay in Germany and, together with the innate attractiveness of Berlin, the availability of employees with good knowledge, good rail connections and infrastructure, the decision was made considerably easier. The prospect of lower start-up costs gave us a cost level that is lower than is standard in Eastern Europe.

Does that mean that you would make the same decision again today?
Hans-Jürgen Seeger:
I was a little skeptical to start with, to be honest with you, but I see know that it was a very good decision. To be completely honest, I wouldn't have looked at the capital cities; not Prague, not Budapest and not Warsaw either. Definitely not. Krakow was a good tip. It's a very beautiful city with lots of young people, several universities with a large number of students. Krakow is not all that small, either. Of course, it always depends on being one of the first to arrive in a place. If the competition heads the same way, then costs start to explode. Bratislava as a possible location offered relatively low costs and it's well situated: not far from Budapest and not far from Vienna either. But we could already see that the prices were going up. Each provider that comes along uses up the reservoir of employees. If Slovaks get a job in Vienna, then they're also lost to the local job market. This means that they're under a lot of pressure.

So if I understand you correctly, you also bore long-term considerations in mind when choosing Berlin. Many Shared Service centers work for seven or eight years before the cost level gets very high and they move on. I don't think that's the case here, is it?
Hans-Jürgen Seeger:
We haven't felt any pressure yet and I don't see any coming in the foreseeable future. Our advantage is our very low employee turnover, for example. It was 3.4% last year. Sure, we're still expanding and we have

highly motivated people on board. Absence is at 1.3%, which is very low. I think there's a lot of motivation there. Our employees enjoyed coming here.

It looks like you're following a strategy of bringing women who have been out of work for a long time back into employment?
Hans-Jürgen Seeger:
Yes, and with a lot of success as far as motivation and loyalty to BASF as an employer – building up a sustainable working relationship – are concerned.
Besides this, we're also trying to make the pool of employees not overly dependent on university graduates. University graduates are under a lot of pressure to go away and develop them further after one or two years. Our aim is to have a pool of 1/3 university graduates, 1/3 technical college graduates and 1/3 trained and apprenticed. The average age of our employees is 35. That's relatively high for a Shared Service center but it gives us the opportunity to keep employee turnover under control And for graduates from universities, I have to say we have a good chance of hanging on to them for a long time because there are still lots of management positions open and process experts that can work their way up the service chain, as it were.

Do you see this as part of a BASF career in general?
Hans-Jürgen Seeger:
We have been deliberate about this. In Asia, we saw competitors with a low-end solution. For this reason, we don't want to advertise our company's image: a service center should be more neutral. BASF made a conscious decision, both here and in Asia, that the logo would be on the roof, it would say BASF. The people who are employed here also have the opportunity of a career in BASF, of course. Naturally, that depends on certain conditions. They have to be very good, they also have to be flexible. Working in Ludwigshafen or somewhere else in the world is not everyone's cup of tea.
Lots of Berliners are willing to pay a small premium in return for not having to leave Berlin, and some accept lower wages. These arguments should be enough to confirm our expectations that employee turnover in Berlin will not increase. Our company is a full component, an equal component of the BASF group. We don't have first and second class group companies. By the way, our board of directors regularly invites our new employees to newcomer meetings in Ludwigshafen. They have the opportunity to present themselves to the board. The directors also come here at regular intervals to see what kind of people we're employing, whether we're up to standard, that we're not only employing people with

limited knowledge and that there's a good potential for development. And the answer is, we've got great people. Companies who entrust their service to us tell us time and again: your experience may not be as extensive as we would like, but your people are better qualified as a rule than our own employees.

Is there an attempt to switch employees from the companies whose functions or services you take over to Berlin?
Hans-Jürgen Seeger:
That's the exception rather than the rule. Unfortunately, they're frequently not flexible. We're only really interested in process experts with many years' experience.

What does your management structure look like? Do you tend to have large or smaller groups?
Hans-Jürgen Seeger:
One of the fundamental decisions we made was to specify the span of control and authority to issue instructions. Instead of small teams with 10, 20, 30 people, we built up really large teams. Our manager for Shared Service processes in the financial area is responsible for over 100 people. There are no managers for smaller groups. If you can save on managers and trigger the whole structure down to a lower level, you make significant savings.

Let's take a look at the processes that take place in the business service center. How far are you trying to provide qualitatively higher value services besides the administrative and supporting processes, such as management and accounting processes?
Hans-Jürgen Seeger:
We would very much like to provide these services, and it is one of our main objectives. We're training up a large number of people here and we need a good number of people who are already experts. These could then train and support new people. This is precisely the area where we need real experts. They can't just go about things in a conventional way. They have to know how to merge data for reporting, for example. General ledger and reporting is an area where people do, of course, need some prior knowledge, but that's working fine. We have a lot of accountants with experience that we can train relatively quickly. They are on site for three to four months and are then able to say, OK, I understand what the guidelines are. IFRS is not something that only exists at BASF, after all. There might be a slight BASF tinge to things, but in general, a good accountant won't have any trouble with it. This makes it possible to keep

down training costs. What's more, many accountants are familiar with SAP as a tool and there's no need to train them specially.

How do you actually measure success? Do you have any cost targets?
Hans-Jürgen Seeger:
We do, of course, have budgets of how much we can spend on the project as a whole. We have separate budgets for HR and finance and accounting. The budget for HR is relatively large because we decided to introduce a pan-European payroll. This decision also meant that we deliberately installed a new SAP payroll system. That takes a while, needless to say, and costs money. And in financial and business accounting, we use the modules and all we did is to stabilize them, so to speak. We also introduced a range of technologies such as scanning, character recognition and call center functions from CRM.

In other words, you would also carry out the customer-focused processes from the business service center? Do you provide first and second level support?
Hans-Jürgen Seeger:
We use contact center functions for both the HR area and for the financial area. For example, we offer a language-dependent answer service in the accounting interaction center, depending on how the caller's number is identified. The question is always, do I have a one-to-one relationship? Lots of companies want a single contact person for their company for all questions. This of course means that one person takes the questions and then runs backwards and forwards between departments to find the answers. I mean, if one contact person is responsible for general ledger issues, for AP and cash management, that person can't answer every question competently. The question is whether you couldn't channel these requests through a type of CRM tool as well, because then you could at least answer questions in people's native language. Then I tell the caller, in a friendly voice of course, that I can't answer the question immediately; there might even be the possibility of answering simple questions straight away. Most answers are noted and stored in CRM. Then you can statistically evaluate them in the standard way and generate FAQs with the corresponding answers. This is why I advocate following a two-fold strategy. A one-to-one relationship exists more in the general ledger and management accounting areas and the rest is more anonymous. To start with, we were all very skeptical about whether they would be able to provide answers there. At the beginning they weren't able to answer questions, but they built up knowledge. We now answer HR questions for all of Western Europe. This means that someone calls up and says that they haven't got their wages. Why is that? Or that they have

travel expenses and some amounts are missing. Could we check it? Our people can switch into the systems and have access to a knowledge database that was fed by the local HR departments. In other words, they have all the information in once place and can give an answer to these questions really quickly. If not, the question is noted down and the customer is contacted later.

We also have to make sure that we don't become too brittle for our own organization. Because then the following happens: yes, I spoke to Mr. X, he doesn't have a clue, but Mr. Y, he's good. And if I call, I always ask for Mr. Y. Then poor Mr. Y gets all the calls and Mr. X doesn't get any anymore. So it's best keep it anonymous and to create a customer interaction center.

The examples you've given so far apply for a typical call center, which is also oriented towards verbal telecommunication. SAP has an enhanced approach that is intended to link in all channels of communication, from e-mail, through the telephone, into a centralized ticketing system. Are you thinking of using the Interaction Center for more channels of communication, because, after all, saving the queries is important?

Hans-Jürgen Seeger:

Exactly. It's important that the questions don't get lost. That happens frequently if there is a one-to-one relationship to a contact person. It's really important and I'll get round to that, I'm sure. If we provide a service for more than 100 companies, then it's not possible to build up and maintain a one-to-one contact person relationship to each and every one of them. If the answer is not immediate, the customer can be contacted by e-mail. Not all of our staff has e-mail access, but there is what we call the kiosk in a lounge where people can log on. It works fine.

The call center or interaction center is a typical area where queries from different functional areas, such as HR and finance, can come together. Will the individual functional HR and finance processes blur into each other here as cross-functional business service processes?

Hans-Jürgen Seeger:

It's all a matter of interfaces. We're also trying to do a lot in this area with the local specialist department managers. That means that if you have master data about employees in the HR area, you can also use this master data to carry out a lot of checks. In other words, things like organizational and IT system authorization checks. A typical example of this would be signature authorizations. If an employee is transferred to another department, his or her old authorizations are removed.

Do you mean that you carry out centralized authorization checks here in the business server center?
Hans-Jürgen Seeger:
We have a massive problem with authorizations. And it's not easy, I realize that. Our employees work in various company codes and to start with, they were authorized for all company codes. We've now changed that.
It was probably really just the IT department making things easy for themselves by not introducing any differentiation. Well, then sometimes there's a deadlock situation that has to be solved. The IT mentality is then to handle the authorizations more generously.

We're still not entirely satisfied because we're still being charged high costs in this area. We have specific standard profiles for employees in the AP area for when new companies are added and the profile has to be authorized for more companies. It should in theory be very easy to simply open this profile for this group of staff only.

Relocating business processes to a business center or Shared service Center also involves shifting responsibilities and process controls. How did you approach this topic, particularly with regards to the Sarbanes-Oxley Act?
Hans-Jürgen Seeger:
BASF is not listed in New York. However, we still have to deal with this issue. We have the following task: BASF has a range of companies that are defined as A companies, B companies and C companies. This means that some companies are affected by the full scope and others aren't. The interesting thing here is that we've been an A company since January. In addition to this, we will take over a series of A companies. Because there will be so many companies, we'll also become a bucket A company and then we'll have to meet these requirements.
We've started up a small project with a consulting company in this area. The only things we still have to incorporate are the control steps. We're on the way, but the implementation is not yet complete. We have to be fully compliant by the end of the year.
On the question of transferring responsibility for execution, there is a contract that precisely sets out what is processed locally and what centrally. This defines that we're accountable for the process.

Remunerating, settling and pricing services in a shared service center is always a delicate and difficult subject. What does your model look like?

Hans-Jürgen Seeger:

We have a charging model that applies to everything. And since we naturally have higher costs here in Berlin than in Eastern Europe, for example, we decided that we'd have to make sure we make savings on average throughout Europe and this saving, this percentage, is then passed on to all the companies. This also means that companies that make minimal savings also receive a correspondingly higher saving as per the average. High wage countries, where savings are significantly higher than average, receive correspondingly lower savings.

Take Antwerp or Paris, where salaries are high and costs are also high, making fewer savings. So we all have the same percentage saving, but measured against potential savings, these go to the countries with higher costs and lower savings. We balanced this out using the user pay factor. That means that we have either 1.1 %, 1.2 %, 0.8 % or 0.9 %, depending on the costs in the country in question and the company in that country. On average, it has to balance out to 1 again.

Your charging model only uses costs that were averaged using a procedure. What about the costs-by-cause principle? For example, the large site in Antwerp, with its large number of intra-enterprise service flows and fewer external customers, has fewer manual invoices than a company in the end-customer area.

Hans-Jürgen Seeger:

We start off with a charging model for the run-up stage. We have to calculate our costs plus 5 % profit margin. But this is of course directed towards the planned costs. What were your costs? We'll give you a price per FTE that is lower by amount X than it was previously. That's our way of ensuring that we stick to the costs we calculate here.

Are you planning to maybe transfer to another model once the current one is up and running?

Hans-Jürgen Seeger:

Yes, once it's running we'll move over to process costs. That is, we'll charge per transaction and transaction characteristic. An invoice with an order costs €3 or €5, an invoice without an order is more expensive because our expenses are higher with all the sending backwards and forwards. Sure, that's our goal, but we've not got round to it yet. We've not been using market prices either, which would be another possibility. If you have 25 countries and are working in five main areas but then have another five or six companies within each application area – so let's say you have 30 companies times 25 countries – then you would have to hire a few people who do nothing other than keep track of market prices. You have no idea what a fuss there would be if you debated market prices with the local units. Bearing that in mind, we said that we would use a simple charging model, to start with at least, and then we could consider a process cost-oriented charging model once we're up and running.

You've been operational for a year now. A year ago, did you think that you would get to where you are today, or were you more ambitious?
Hans-Jürgen Seeger:
To be honest, I thought it would all be much harder. I joined the company in 2004 and I presented our plan at the end of 2004 or the start of 2005. The reaction was pretty hostile in some quarters. Despite a decision by the board of managers, the companies had a hesitant, negative attitude. We had good support from the board but we could have been quicker and lost less time.

Did the board have to intervene in the initial reluctance?
Hans-Jürgen Seeger:
The culture at BASF is driven by consensus. A Shared Service center will fundamentally change the culture at BASF. Perhaps we have a hand in that. Yes, in certain tough cases, where there were very heated discussions, the board intervened. Mistakes will always be made, but the mistakes that happen in the Shared service center could just as easily have occurred locally. With hindsight, it was a very ambitious task. It could certainly have been implemented quicker and better, but in principle it was all very orderly and easier than I had originally thought.

We've talked about people; let's take a look at the technical side now. One of the most exciting questions is consolidating the IT systems. What does the IT system landscape look like for the BASF business services of the future? How many IT systems do you want to merge?
Hans-Jürgen Seeger:
We're currently working with seven IT systems and want to consolidate these into three IT systems as the core systems here in Europe. Worldwide, we'll be working with four IT systems. If we consolidated even further, I can imagine using only two IT systems: one for Europe and one for the rest of the world.

The aim is naturally to get by with fewer IT systems. You mentioned core systems; are there also additional IT systems upstream or downstream?

Hans-Jürgen Seeger:
If you roll out this type of project, there are a lot of things linked in to it. Business trip accounting systems in Europe are all very different. We're trying to implement SAP. In the meantime, we're in a bit of a gray area. Additionally, we have a variety of different archiving systems that we want to get rid of. And let's not forget the different paycard systems in the AP area that we have to deal with. So there are all sorts of different solutions on the purchasing side, where the local companies have set up all kinds of subsystems. Understandably, we're not particularly happy about this situation. Then there's also the banking area, where we use different banking tools.
This is not really good for a Shared Service Center because we have to try and limit the variety down to one standard.

What about further development of the services you offer? Are you planning additional services beyond HR and finances?
Hans-Jürgen Seeger:
We can see all sorts of opportunities; we've already received requests in this area. In Berlin, there are good and cost-effective employees with good knowledge. We would, for example, already be able to carry out part processes in the area of entering customer orders. Normally, many customer orders still come by paper fax. Converting to digital fax would save us the laborious task of scanning paper faxes in, analyzing them, interpreting them and processing them further in an intelligent way. If you bear in mind that many faxes are created automatically – in other words, they're already coming out of an ERP system – a simple and pragmatic solution would be to access the print stream and forward them in digital form. Using relatively intelligent software, it would be possible for orders to be processed automatically in many standard cases. However, we've put the project on hold for the moment because we're going to be fully occupied for the next year or two.

What level are the processes that you have in your contracts at the moment defined at, so to speak? Is the service description called accounts payable, for example, or does the description go a few process steps further?
Hans-Jürgen Seeger:
We have a precise description of the processes and then another precise description of who does what. There are different aggregation levels that we use to design the process and desktop procedures about who is responsible for it, as well.

Looking back ayear, and looking forward from today, where do you think you'll be in three to five years?

Hans-Jürgen Seeger:

I think we'll be serving all the companies through the business service center. The challenge we'll then face is optimization. I would really like to work on optimizing the procedure, the method itself. In the future, we'll be experiencing more mergers and acquisitions, or even company sales. To do this, we'll need a standardized procedure for how to integrate new companies that are acquired in the future into the BASF business services. A template would enable us to add new companies in the shortest time. This would have to be a relatively fixed procedure. I assume, therefore, that we'll have to build up the relevant expertise for this. These are important points as are, of course, ongoing optimization projects in all areas.

Shared Services are often seen as a stopover on the way to business process outsourcing. Do you see any opportunities for outsourcing some processes that you still handle today to external service suppliers?

Hans-Jürgen Seeger:

I could well imagine that we will outsource parts of certain areas, for example the AP area. I'm thinking about sorting the mail; we're already trying to offload certain things.

Do you still do your own pretax declaration or do you see potential to hand this over to third parties as well?

Hans-Jürgen Seeger:

The pretax declaration simply involves filling out a form, handing it in to the local authorities and taking out money. This is no problem because we have our local companies. We're represented throughout Europe and have on-site companies that do it for us. We don't need anyone internally. But, sorting out the documents, there's no third party that would do that for you. You have to do that yourself. It's exactly like if you travel somewhere; there's a company at Frankfurt airport that does this already: you hand over your invoice to the company and they do the rest for you. You only have to hand over your documents, provide your name and address, show a copy of your passport and the company does it for you. But you have to sort out the documents first, and someone with expert knowledge has to do it.

In the AP process, a nice example is reverse charging. From the suppliers' point of view, the tax-free principle applies, but it's possible that the recipient of the service still has to pay 16% or whatever first and can then reclaim it from the tax authorities. Then it's not so clear. I can think of one area we've had a rough time with: VAT code harmonization in Europe. The usual story, master data growing up uncontrollably. Regardless of the number of different forms, dynamizing the tax code is an issue. When tax rates change, the old tax code is retained because it's still in some orders.

I have one last, obligatory, question for you: what part of your daily work keeps you up at night? Or what's the worst case scenario that could happen? Would it be a breakdown, a failure of the computer center?

Hans-Jürgen Seeger:

The good thing is that I don't think we could actually impede business in any way. Not like logistics, where orders wouldn't be able to go in and invoices couldn't go out: we're at the end of the process chain. So business will carry on. What could, of course, happen is a problem in the cash area: that's where the biggest risks are. What already has happened – we ran a few tests, a series of tests – is that people have sent in their invoices to us thinking that the Shared Service center will just pay out. But what they didn't realize is that we look first to see what the facts are, which tax office they are registered with, which company it is that is registered with the district court, etc. If a standard has to be created, then you make inquiries. And then we have to ask, is this really a supplier, has anyone heard of them? We've received invoices without any factual background to them. Just thinking it's worth a try. We therefore need web tools that enable traceability. So that you can be sure that there's an authorized transaction behind it. The cash area is where the biggest problems can occur.

Thank you very much for the very valuable interview. We wish you all the best in establishing a successful Shared Service Organization. It proves that it is worth considering many option in the location selection process .

8.2 Interview: Henkel

Interview with Dr. Carlo Mackrodt, Head of Henkel Shared Services.

Introduction:

Henkel, headquartered in Düsseldorf / Germany, has about 52,000 employees worldwide. The company operates in approximately 125 countries around the world. In 2000, Henkel launched its ambitious "Best Practice in Finance" project aimed at creating a cross-country, process-oriented Shared Service Organization. The main objective was

sustainable improvements in the efficiency and effectiveness of financial processes (F&A) combined with the development of a service culture in the F&A area. One of the core issues was the introduction of regional and global process ownership, focusing on the bundling of competencies from the local organizations and their restructuring.
Dr. Carlo Mackrodt, Vice President of Financial Services until late 2006, had been in charge of the extensive transformation project in the financial services area since 2003. Since 2007, Dr. Mackrodt holds the position of the Vice President of Supply Chain Management EMEA in Henkel's technology business unit.

Mr. Mackrodt, if you look at Shared Services at Henkel today, can you tell me what the essential driving factors were that led you to introduce Shared Services at Henkel?
Dr. Carlo Mackrodt:
When I joined the process in 2002, we thought about how we could improve financial accounting at the company. We noticed two things, a) we didn't know how expensive we were. We were hearing in the markets, and from Hackett, that companies with Shared Services had roughly 35% lower financial costs than companies without them. And b), that a paradigm had collapsed, the idea of lower costs with higher quality through standardization, simplification and optimization.

So the development at Henkel resulted from a strategy aimed at setting business standards on the European level?
Dr. Carlo Mackrodt:
Around the end of the nineties, the leadership decided that the businesses should no longer be run at the country level but rather globally, and in that context it became clear that financial accounting would be done on a global level as well. That meant that financial accounting would be under central control, which in turn raised questions about what kinds of internet and e-technology functionality we would be able to support by internet or extranet.

How much progress have you been able to make in that process? When exactly did you establish the Shared Service Center; it was relatively late, 2005 or 2006, was it not?
Dr. Carlo Mackrodt:
That depends on how you define Shared Services. Remember, in the north, in the four Nordic states, we had 21 affiliated companies. If you look at that number, a lot of those affiliations go back to the end of the nineties. And so we looked at that and said, 'let's put it all together and form a single legal entity'. And we had financial operations - and that's a

fair description - in four countries. So we said, 'let's centralize financial accounting for these four countries'. When I came in 2002, we got the process started and looked at which operations are not done in Denmark, not in Norway, but all in Stockholm, and so on.

Those were the first steps in which we officially, though on a modest scale, began to introduce Shared Service Centers and bundle tasks on a regional level. In the UK and in Ireland, for example, we went in with the objective of bringing everything together in Headfield, near London. And in Germany, for example, we took eight operations and legally merged them. We did that merger, with the help of SAP solutions, at the end of 2005. And with that we had integrated practically all the entities and achieved significant cost reductions.

Did you then pursue process integration, instituting unified processes for all of these legal entities?

Dr. Carlo Mackrodt:

Exactly. First we transformed the processes and then we shifted them. We had our Best Practice Blueprint as set out by my predecessor. Starting in 2002, when I came in, we simply went a lot further in standardizing and expanding it. Defining the standard process was a huge task because when you asked three people about a process, they all came up with different structures. To standardize them and develop a common language, in the awareness that we wanted just one single version which would people would really internalize, was difficult. That was one of the preconditions to continuing with the process and coming up with something we could implement.

We started with standardization and then proceeded with the centralization of all the countries. We centralized Spain and Portugal, for example. In France we had five operations, and we're not even quite done there yet, but we've brought everything together. And the biggest step was at the beginning of 2003 when we opened a Shared Service Center in the Asia Pacific region, which includes, I think, 17 countries. There's a lot of water, a lot of big mountains, between them, and we just started to build it. We didn't do any big analyses; we just proceeded pragmatically, looking at who settled where in India, Manila or wherever else. Manila is home to some big companies, so it made sense, looking at the local factor costs, to go to Manila.

We started in 2003 and at the end of 2003 we had the first cross-regional Shared Service Center for very simple tasks. It didn't include invoice verification; it was just a question of getting the invoices posted. We had written documents being faxed back and forth and the invoice was ultimately posted to some cost center. They were very simple tasks. And we rolled them out for the order-to-cash process (OTC); they were essentially incoming invoices which were then posted there. We then successively added more and more countries, and by 2005 we had 30 employees in the Shared Service Center.

At the same time we were standardizing the cost processes, we began using SAP more and more to eliminate certain positions as we harmonized our processes and organizational structure as a whole. Then we worked for a year. At the end of 2005, we committed ourselves to expanding the Shared Service Centers, without which we would not have been able to achieve further savings. Remember, Henkel is a family-run company, and this step had to be well-considered. At that point, despite some layoffs, we had over 1000 employees.

Were those savings the result of process optimization?
Dr. Carlo Mackrodt:
Yes, process optimization and optimization locally on the country level. We've taken it a step further and are going ahead with a Shared Service Center in Bratislava. That's when it really started with all the localization scenarios, which kept us busy day and night. Scenarios involving Düsseldorf, or the other bank of the Rhine, were discussed as possible sites in Germany, and weighed against the advantages and drawbacks of Bratislava. In the end we decided to leave Düsseldorf as is for the time being, we're not pro-actively laying off any workers in Düsseldorf.

If someone goes, we think about where we want to have those people. I think it's a great achievement that over the years we've been able to avoid any negative press because of our pro-active information policy and the cooperation of the works council. Slowly but surely in one direction, I think that was the greatest success.

In the end we'd looked at all the scenarios and changes, such as employees being willing to give up the 37.5 hour workweek in favor of a 40 hour week, and weighed our options. We went through all the options, but Bratislava clearly offered the most favorable conditions. If you look at the local factor costs at that time, they were 25% of our current costs. Even if wages there rose by 10% a year, it would still take 15 years for them to reach our level. By then we may well be somewhere else with another SSC. We just set up shop there and we now employee about 50 people.

That was my next question, in what kind of timeframe are you able to do a roll-in like that?
Dr. Carlo Mackrodt:
Our plan was to have 60 employees by the end of 2007. That's been agreed with the works council. We actually have to slow down to make sure we don't go over 60. The feedback from all the countries is that everyone wants to join the SSC because it's been running so smoothly and has boosted quality. So everything we were talking about in 2002 has been realized: We have lower costs with higher quality and better standards, and the company is better prepared for all eventualities, people are better able to pick up slack in the system, access data centrally and so on. That's one point where we've said that we won't be transforming Germany just yet, but the Benelux countries may come aboard somewhat sooner. They are keen to get into the SSC because they've noticed that the costs are simply lower.

Another step we've taken is to introduce a single price for the same services. No matter where the service is used, it costs the same. But that's also something that, to some degree, we do to soften the blow to Germany, because otherwise no one would buy services from Germany. We wanted to avoid that because we are committed to Germany. That's part of the Henkel culture, very employee-oriented. That may seem a bit old-fashioned compared to some other companies. But I think it's a great strength that we at Henkel are so employee-oriented.

How have the process optimization measures affected the daily work of your employees?
Dr. Carlo Mackrodt:
The scope of some employees' work has changed. For example, the Heads of Process have been given more responsibility than the local CFOs. That extended all the way to personnel decisions in the respective countries. We discussed it in countless workshops and made the decision. And the local CFOs said 'no, that's the worse option, we'll give the Head of Process the lead. And I can tell you that blew me away; I'd never encountered something like that before.

The change management was phenomenal and I have to say, we always look at what you showed in your earlier presentations, this change from country organizations to process ownership. It's seen as exemplary, a lot of companies want to do what you've done, yet few of them - very few - have done it as resolutely as you.
Dr. Carlo Mackrodt:

We had a western European organization and then we extended it to Eastern Europe. But the Heads of Process have been so successful that they now have responsibility worldwide. And we reached a point where we saw that they were so busy that they could no longer take care of the human resources issues, hiring and firing and so on. So we really stirred the whole organization up, changed our thought processes and stabilized our processes such that we see sine waves when the old power structures are swept away. So now we can say, we've standardized the processes, now let's let the countries get a bit stronger again and let the Heads of Process work on a cross-regional basis.

They've now progressed to the point where we have decided to start looking for a solution for North America. After a long search - my most recent initiative - in collaboration with our consulting partners, we made the decision to go to Manila. Currently we're in the process of transferring tasks to Manila. This inevitably led to some reorganization in North America. That it's been so successful was beyond even my expectations. My original thought was that we would go to Latin America, to Puerto Rico or somewhere else where we have production locations. Instead we opted for the best location, and that was Manila.

Did that make it easier to integrate Dial?

Dr. Carlo Mackrodt:

No, I think the main thing was that we introduced SAP. We had 19 different affiliates in the US that we were able to integrate. The financial structures were all distributed among the regions, so it wasn't standardized and everyone did things in a slightly different way. Now we've been among the leaders on the DAX for some years, and often one of the fastest companies at year-end closing. The reason is our standardized processes. In reality there are a thousand different variations, and sometimes it drives me crazy that something like that could squeak through again. I was relatively strict about one thing, and that was to be very conscientious about using only standards.

A strict governance process to promote change?

Dr. Carlo Mackrodt:

Yes, and also as regards local preferences. You need very, very strict governance of change order management if you really want to change something. We repeatedly missed opportunities when someone insisted that something was a legal requirement, where we later found out that we'd been misled. But ultimately the process was up and running, we went live and the customers got their products approved. Currently we're doing a retrofit. In Germany, for example, we went live in 2002. Over the course of the roll-out, we continually introduced improvements so that, in the end, the system we launched in 2002 was no longer the standard. At present we're retrofitting the functional enhancements.

The roll-out at Henkel seems to have been a great success. But let's move on to my question: How would you describe the formal relationship between your Shared Service customer and the Shared Service Center? Do you have contracts with service level agreements or just how formally do you handle it?
Dr. Carlo Mackrodt:
To begin with, in our own country it was the case that we took the employees on. There were no contracts because they were legal entities. The processes were simply rolled-in. So that wasn't an issue. What we did is simple.

Point A, for example Germany, initially we had 330 people, whereas now we're below 200, perhaps 120. I don't know the exact figure. So we were able to make radical reductions in capacity while maintaining the same or even better quality.
Point B, when we go to Bratislava we'll have service levels. We're working on a Management Cockpit where we can do quarterly KPIs for every legal entity, every process, down to whatever depth you want. At the same time we've introduced a base lining process. How many people are working on all these sub-processes and the like? That allows us to work with certain baselines like: An order without a requirement coverage request costs us 10 times as much as one that runs automatically.

It was only after we introduced the process optimizations, for instance increasing the proportion of supplier invoices with orders that we began to discuss the capacity reductions.

At the beginning, the departments tried to argue that they needed all the same people even though they had fewer tasks. But my argument was always, 'we originally budgeted 23 million and now we're at 100 million'. But there's always a price to be paid. And that price, in terms of administration, is the headcount or IT.

Do you have internal benchmarks? Now that you've pushed through the use of modern methods, how do the countries deal with the comparison of best practices?
Dr. Carlo Mackrodt:

Every two years we set benchmarks, at the end there's even a comprehensive benchmark done by Hackett which includes everything, procurement, IT and HR. We've set benchmarks for everything. It's been a great success. That's one part, but I've also always told my people that I want to know it internally, too. So I've always had my costs. In the Management Cockpit we have KPIs for every process, such as OTC Controlling, GA Inter-company and CPM, Central Payment Management. We've continued to improve them along the way.

Functionally speaking, we're just talking about finance, or do you draw a distinction?
Dr. Carlo Mackrodt:
Functionally speaking we're just talking about finance, and we were just addressing the point because you asked how we did things with invoicing, whether we did it locally etc., and were just arriving at the question: What is the real cost driver? We had 12 cost drivers, 4 per process, or 3 per process with PTP. In this case they would be Invoices without PO, Invoices with PO and Electronic Payment. People were working on that and had been assigned to that, and then we said 'OK, when a process is transferred from A to B, we basically have an internal agreement'. They were not officially signed contracts, but in essence we had made agreements.

When I recently left the Shared Service Center, fixed price agreements were under discussion. These were not legally binding agreements, mind you. For tax purposes, of course, we always have to do that. There are rules for this that cover which service is rendered for whom, and that fulfills our tax requirements.

What percent, say in terms of turnover or by users, of your activities have been transferred to the Shared Service Center?
Dr. Carlo Mackrodt:
It's not too much as yet because, as I mentioned, of the 913 employees we have in eastern and Western Europe, only 50 are based there. So it's not exactly dominant at the moment. But even in the next step - and this is the positive message for companies that are a bit more progressive - we were able to win the employees over very quickly and in unconventional ways. That would be no problem. That's an important issue for us, and that's what we agreed with the works council. We are employee-oriented and we don't go faster than our employees are able to go or for which we can find some sort of solution. But as you can imagine, we're not sleeping and we do have to stay competitive, so we obviously have a number of things

to keep in mind. As I said, we work very closely with the works council on these matters.

That fits well with your whole logic, your procedure. Has the high degree of automation of your processes enabled you to achieve the kind of optimization you wanted?
Dr. Carlo Mackrodt:
Well, as I've said, we had reduced the workforce from 1234 to 913 by the end of 2006, in a space of four years. I think that's fairly good. As a consultant, it didn't surprise me. The real challenge is sustainable reduction.

Dr. Mackrodt, thank you very much for taking the time to talk with us and give us some insight into Henkel's Shared Service Center.

8.3 Interview: Marks & Spencer

Interview with Dan Foley, Head of Finance and Accounting Shared Services, Marks & Spencer, UK

Introduction:
Marks & Spencer is one of the leading retailers in the United Kingdom. In early 2003, the organization began using Shared Services in Manchester in the areas of finance and accounting. In 2006 Dan Foley joined Marks & Spencer with his broad experiences in shared services acquired at Diageo, a beverage company with a shared services center in Budapest.

Establishing a Shared Services center is an important decision within a company. From your point of view, what makes a shared services center successful?
Dan Foley:
I think the thing for me is that the experience almost dictates what makes Shared services centers successful. Having the right leadership is key. By leadership, I mean people who will use drive, who use judgment, who use influence, who use passion, who use emotional energy in the right way to make sure that things actually happen.

And what you've got to say to yourself is that somebody who has a stuck-up face is not the right person for somebody down the line. There are almost three stages to what I find: There is the start-up phase that takes you from thinking to the business case, to the budget, and to the implementation. There is then the next stage when you implement; that's the go-live, and after the go-live, there is bringing it into the business. And then there is the maturity piece.

It takes different people going through different stages through it all. Based on the maturity phase, the workload will move to business process outsourcing (BPO) with fewer people in the services center, and many more Shared Service activities will move up the value chain. The role of the services centers transforms into the management of the BPO organization at that stage. And I think that's very key.

Is it correct to say that leadership also means not only one person who is the leader of the Shared Services center, but also having the next level with you?
Dan Foley:
Correct. It's almost as if leaders come up in different sizes and different molds, and there is no magic dust. But if you look back, all you are applying here does affect the leader's general management skills in particular. All you're saying is: Who is the person who can actually take this idea and make it happen? But you have to make it happen in a way that you basically bring the team with you and leave nobody behind. You use the skills for what we talked about, and you have to know your limitations. That is, world class is not something in Shared Services, whatever you want to be in. We want to be world-class in the creation of suits and foods and in our retail and our general merchandise. Shared Services is best in breed, but we don't have a big budget.

Costs are a very key focus in that, but what we have is basically the ability to get right what we do have. That's always making sure that there is enough information out there. So coming to this sort of environment means that I get ideas, and I go back and say, "What did it cost us?" It cost us airfare and the ability to contribute to this. And that's nothing for the ideas you walk away with. Being in that environment means you're learning all the time. You've got the right captains of industry here. It's like when I said that the GEs of this world, the Procter & Gambles of this world, are the top guys up there who've done this. And then you come down to the Diagios of this world, which are less experienced but have caught up very quickly. In the Diagio case, it was really strong leadership, belief, and ability, but external recognition is as important as internal recognition. It's good to be recognized by our customers; it's probably more to be recognized by our peer group. So when Diageo won the reward in 2004 in Manchester, that said to people, wow, they've got the external recognition; therefore, they must be doing something good – we need to look at them again.

I think any services center needs to look for two things. You have to have something internally, but you want to delight your customer base over a period of time. And then you have to get peer recognition externally. Peer recognition can mean anything from being invited to these events, to speaking, to sharing, to saying to others that we're getting an award or that we've been nominated for awards along the way.

Internal recognition really comes when people see you as part of the team; they look in the mirror and see you on their shoulder because you are a virtual part of that team. You're joined by common systems, common data, common software and common platforms. If you want to do something separate, you can't, because your shared services isn't with you. It's very different from embedded finance, because embedded finance thinks that the services center is more of a rubbing through the service level agreement.

Certainly, what you mentioned is the first phase-in period in which you bring or transfer functions from the lines of business to the shared services center, and then you optimize them and have this under your control at the end. Then there is the as-usual business, in which you have to transfer it, as you mentioned, to a different type of leader. I could imagine that regarding this engaged leader, there must be someone who does the execution of operations afterwards, a shared business provider. Is this what you mean?
Dan Foley:
Exactly. As a strategic approach, you go to your first phase: "I'm going to do that, and I want to implement it." Your second phase occurs when you've implemented it and you get business in. Your third phase occurs when it's moving up the value chain and possibly to BPO, outsourcing, and so on.

However, within the phases you have different tactics. So for example, in the first phase if you decide to do Shared Services, the tactic is which market do you start with? Do you start with a small market and pilot it, or do you start with the biggest market because the biggest market will set up the global process? If your biggest market is Great Britain or Germany, you wouldn't expect Portugal to change the process as much, because it wouldn't have as much focus.

Is it not beneficial for a Shared Services center to have a small market, which is more easily feasible, before going with a big bang?
Dan Foley:

It's also about your risk management. If you start with a small market, you build your processes for that; if you go to a medium market, you have to change your processes. If you then go to a large market, you've got to change your processes as well. If you start with a large market, you can say to the medium market: Sorry, I have a big market box there, why shouldn't I work for you. I don't want to impose it, but that's what could actually happen. If you start with a large market, you probably start to have a global approach and a common process that's a lot closer rather than building up the chain. It depends on your risk profile.

Is it a bit of a trade-off decision that you have to make?
Dan Foley:
Correct. It also depends on the people you use. If you're starting off, how do you set up your team? Do you use a large number of consultants? Do you use people for project purposes internally? Is it a development opportunity for somebody in the team? Or do you get mercenaries? You know, people very much like mercenaries – people who have done it before, have the scars on their backs, and show you what to do very quickly. And that's a big, big question because I think what you basically find is that most people not only tend to get external consultants in, but lots of them on the project. What they do is that they actually look at people internally to do it, and then they go out and get one or two contractors. To me, if you went out and got more contractors early on, they will add more to the party because they will "go native." That is a big difference there in those.

We have spoken with the leader of Shared Services and also with the line management level. We're also discussing this within SAP. There are some people who stay for a maximum of two or three years because they then expect to take the next step in their career path. Do you think that working in the Shared Services center is part of the career path within the finances function? Do you expect this will happen with Marks & Spencer?
Dan Foley:
We have started that already because one of the things that I believe is that finance has a talent pool. I have always found that the talent pool in finance has to go through all the elements of finance itself. So perhaps they have to do a bit in the supply chain in finance, and they have to do a bit operationally. One thing Shared services does is that it rounds you in terms of your actual people management capability, development, and understanding of operational key performance indicators, and you become quite a good operator. And an operational general management

function would be an analyst, based more on financial planning and recording.

What I have always found is that the top companies have Shared Service as part of their road to success and finance. Its part of the job ladder for career success in that case. At Marks & Spencer we started that by transferring people from London into our senior management positions. We want to continue that going forward. We've just finished our succession planning in retention, in which we reviewed all 123 people's performance for the year. We then actually put in the succession planning from all our senior managers and our middle managers and our team leaders. So that's now fully done. At the same time, we have a retention toolkit that ensures that people understand why somebody stays with Marks & Spencer. A great example is somebody who was a merchandise payable manager for four years, and now he's moved in to be a non-merchandise payable manager. He's now seen the opportunity from his own personal development and growth. For a long period of time, his development planning was all around visiting depots. It wasn't really the route to go forward.

One of the things we're about to roll out at Marks & Spencer is a revised approach to development. I would like to mention what John F. Kennedy said in 1963. He said, "All of us do not have equal talent, but all of us should have an equal opportunity to develop those talents." That's very, very important. We're all at different levels of understanding the talent, but we should provide everybody with an equal opportunity to develop what they have within themselves. And that's we're doing at Marks & Spencer, because we're setting up four key structures for development. The first two are basics that everybody should have: customer service and finance and accounting knowledge. And then you have a role capability, which we'll work with, and then you have a personal challenge as well. And they will become your four development opportunities for the year.

I always say that if I had one thing to rank first in the budget, it would be training and development because I think that's the key. If we want to drive efficiencies when you see you've no budget for efficiencies, you won't drive efficiencies by investing in travel. You'll get it by investing in people and training and development and culture.

And you see this as a task of the shared services center?
Dan Foley:
Yes. I see it as one of the strategic initiatives that we're doing. The first one is continual constructive challenge, where the culture must change.

And the second one on that stage is all about basically outperforming customer expectations. This basis is that that's what customers expect, and this is where we can do more for them. These are the strategic initiatives that we need to have going.

This was also fully visible in the podium discussion as a differentiator – that they are able to manage this talent pool and provide better education and training. Some of the participants told us they wouldn't have this type of training function in the Shared Services center, but in the line of business. But isn't it crucial that you in the Shared Services center get the right skill sets you needed?
Dan Foley:
You have to go back to capabilities because a lot of people go into jobs, but they don't know why they're there. I think it's almost that people fall into Shared Services centers or want to be an accountant, actually. I don't think people want to be an accountant by trade; they want to be a professional, and accountancy helps them as part of being a good manager through the line. But what I've always found is that you've got to go back to what somebody needs to do the job – what capabilities do they need to do the job? Then you've got to be very honest and measure your own capabilities against that set. The gap then gives you drive to the need, and the need then drives your development plan because you can say, "I need to be very good at managing ambiguity. At this moment I'm beginner, so I've got a gap there. So it's key for me that I go through some development training that helps me manage ambiguity." So something like "I need a personal mentor; I need to get more exposure to a higher stage; I might need to go on a change management course that helps me to understand that and also maybe spend a bit of time in risk management to understand the basis of a risk manager."

The bottom line is that it's okay to do some training to get people to come from the other side and understand it afterwards. I've done a number of presentations on that. One is basically around values, honesty, waving home the flag, timing with a common sense. Every company worldwide has the whole-team development and performance management tools, and I do think the opportunities are there to do it. Also, when you go back you can use different opportunities to do different things. For example, on many occasions we have looked at our team situation, and people were unhappy. So we actually said, "Step back from it. Forget about it. Let's look at a team that doesn't perform." We had an opportunity to look at a video of *Dad's Army* – which is a British TV program, very old-fashioned – to talk about a team of people together, which was good for a different view.

Again, one of the things that I think distinguishes good environments is the winning environment you create. It's creating the winning environment; it's getting those messages out there. A champion is somebody who gets up when he or she shouldn't. You get knocked down, you come back up again, and it's that belief that then moves you to the next stage.

So, is the second the first loser?
Dan Foley:
Yes, and that's pretty true. I think, if I look at some of the stuff over the years, then people do look at it and they do particularly look at it. Those are the differences between leadership and management. All the techniques are there, but you need different leaders for different times.

So for yourself, how would you measure that you are successful?
Dan Foley:
I think there are three types of success. The first one is, have we delivered what we promised? Did we promise to build the best-of-breed shared services? Are we on the right track for that? The answer is yes.

The second thing is, have we delivered on our promise to our people? And I think the answer is nearly yes there. We have a lot to do on that. We've got a lot to do in development. We've got a significant number of people, and we need to focus on the right cultures, the right behaviors, and the right beliefs.

Personally, have I delivered myself? I've got a great sense of satisfaction about what we've done, personally. The fact is that I couldn't have done this without the people around me. I couldn't have done it without the support from my line manager; I couldn't have done it without the actual funding from the finance function; I couldn't have done it without the legal people helping me. The stakeholder piece is huge. But what I would say basically is, at the end of the day, do I sleep happy on a Friday night? Yes, I do. Because I know we've done our best.

That would have been my next question. What keeps you awake?
Dan Foley:
I'll tell you what keeps me awake – there are probably two things. It's ownership. It's about the fact that people need to own issues. They need to take ownership of something and not just pass it over by e-mail to somebody else. Make sure it's closed out. Make sure the customer is satisfied, and go back to the customer and say, "Are you happy with that?"

And the second thing is common sense. Common sense is very hard to find, but in a lot of business processes, common sense is almost the internal control. People would never think of doing some things in life that people do in an operation. For example, contacting the CEO of a company for a purchase order – you would never think of doing that in a normal day-to-day role. Yet some people take that as part of their business.

The last thing for me is that you've got to be happy that you've done your best. And while I'm happy I've done my best, I think, "Is the bar too high? Have we raised the bar too high for some of our staff members?" We've come up fast in seven to eight months.

Is it not too ambitious to expect a single fighter to come in and make this change?
Dan Foley:
I know what you don't want to do: You don't want to lose the team behind you, because sometimes you have to stop. I'll give you a great example. We were very busy in February, and two months ago we decided to stop our work on the strategic initiatives because it was just too much for people. We basically re-launched them today in a staff briefing, and I think people know that this is the right time. The system is better, it's working fine, we're getting better at it, and we've got a lot of opportunities to make it better. Now is the opportunity to deliver more.

Dan, we wish you the best to complete your vision. Thanks a lot for your shared experiences and thoughts.

8.4 Interview: Philips

Interview with Michel de Zeeuw, Senior Vice President Global Finance and Shared Services, Philips International.

Introduction:
Royal Philips Electronics of the Netherlands is a global leader in healthcare, lifestyle and technology, delivering products, services and solutions. Philips is a global electronics company with a multinational workforce of about 121 000 employees. Operations are spread across more then 60 countries. The company is a market leader in medical diagnostic imaging and patient monitoring systems, energy efficient lighting solutions, personal care and home appliances, as well as consumer electronics. Years ago, Philips introduced Shared Services and spend a huge effort in IT systems consolidation to simplify and standardize the system landscape.

Let us start with a very hot topic announced recently, the shared service outsourcing deal between Philips and Infosys. Could you provide some insight into this decision?
Michel De Zeeuw:
It is indeed a very hot topic. We are selling and outsourcing our three Shared Service centers in Poland, India, and Thailand. From October 1, 2007, a bit more than 1450 employees including myself will transfer to Infosys BPO.

What was the major reason for signing the outsourcing deal and doing so now?
Michel De Zeeuw:
We had decided initially to create our off-shore centers ourselves because we had the expertise available, the scale and the local presence to provide support. We believe that we are at a stage now where we need to provide more future to the employees in the service centers and also provide more value to Philips in the long run. In addition we realized some value now by selling the very efficient organization we created.

Was scale the dominant issue?
Michel De Zeeuw:
Yes, scale is very important in this business to generate optimum savings, but also to be able to invest in technology, training and process improvements.

What business functions, such as finance and human resources, do you cover in your Shared Service centers?
Michel De Zeeuw:
We handle finance and accounting, purchasing with requisition handling, catalog management, and supplier negotiations for indirect goods. In finance and accounting, we centrally execute accounts payable, general ledger, fixed assets, travel and expenses, administration tasks, company cards processing, and cash applications.
More directly customer-related processes such as payment collection and relationship management are handled by Shared Services on country level. This is because of language and local regulatory needs. Additionally, we perform some reporting and analytics as well as compliance management tasks. The share of expertise and knowledge-based tasks is a lot lower compared to transactional activities.

You still keep a local Shared Service center for customer-facing activities, while the remaining activities will be executed in your main Shared Service center. With the outsourcing deal with Infosys,

could we say that you will keep the front office under company control, whereas the back-office shared services will be transferred to the external service provider?
Michel De Zeeuw:
Yes, that is how you can describe it. We will have a split of governance and responsibilities. Philips keeps a front office in charge of internal customer relationship management, vendor relationship management, and specific sensitive customer-facing activities.

Shared Services involve the shifting of work from the business to the central Shared Service center. What do you think is the percentage of work which was shifted from the business clients to the Shared Service center?
Michel De Zeeuw:
The percentage varies greatly per process. For example, accounts payable has 10% of work remaining onshore. For accounts receivable and collections, we have retained roughly 75 % locally, and general ledger has a percentage of approximately 40 % that is still kept locally.

What about the human resource functions?
Michel De Zeeuw:
Human resources has taken until now a country per country approach.

Let us pick up the key word "benefit." Looking back to your original goals and business case for Shared Services, did you achieve your key value benefits?
Michel De Zeeuw:
Yes, we achieved our targets for cost reduction. We benchmarked our processes and we are now overall in the first quadrant of the Hackett's cost grid. Our focus now is on business process improvement.

Implementing Shared Services comprises different phases, from preparation and presentation of a business case, implementation and transition of people and IT systems, to stabilization during ongoing optimization. Each of the phases may face different challenges. What were your experiences with implementing and running Shared Services?
Michel De Zeeuw:
I have to admit that it was quite easy for Philips. Of course we experienced some obstacles in convincing stakeholders, especially when it came to onshore-offshore discussions for North America, but everything flowed without disruptions within a normal decision-making process.

We already know that Philips also launched a best-in-finance program. Was this best-in-finance program part of the Shared service initiative?
Michel De Zeeuw:
The shared service project started late 2002 early 2003 and became part of the Best-in-Finance program in 2004. We now have more than four and a half years of operational experience in off-shoring and Shared Services.

What about the people and IT system resources? Many large enterprises struggle with the complexity of their IT system landscape when introducing centralized Shared services. How difficult was it for Philips?
Michel De Zeeuw:
Improving business processes with an IT system landscape that originally had some 220 different IT systems was a difficult task. We are now down to 15-16 instances of SAP and plan on reducing further. To cope with this difficulty we have developed a very unique process harmonization methodology, which proved to be very successful.

How many ERP systems are you ultimately aiming for?
Michel De Zeeuw:
I hope that we can reduce down to one per business, so around four or five ERP systems.

That ratio of reduction of IT systems is impressive. What about the affected people?
Michel De Zeeuw:
Shifting jobs is always an issue in some countries. In Europe, it was less of a problem compared to the United States. In Europe, the finance the accounting teams were already small and fragmented. Many of them found a new job within the Philips organization. In the United States it was different. We had bigger teams there and experienced a large turnover of people after we announced the change. But overall there were no major surprises due to the professionalism of our migration teams and of the retained staff.

Shared Service Organizations and business clients operate on an agreement basis. How formalized are your agreements or relationships between the Shared Service center and the business clients?

Michel De Zeeuw:
We established regional service level agreements (SLAs) with the business units. With our new outsourcing deal with Infosys, we are now also creating a formal SLA between the retained Shared Service Organization and Infosys. Overall Philips remains the owner of the end-to-end processes, and delegates the execution of transactional and rules based tasks to Infosys.

Splitting activities between Shared Service and business units are always a discussion point. How formalized are your work instructions at Philips?
Michel De Zeeuw:
Roles are very well documented in detailed working instructions available for each instance of SAP. We measure the compliance to these working instructions, and have reached a level of 89%. When we started with the centralization process the compliance level was only around 35%, so centralizing has enabled us to harmonize very quickly.

What was your strategy for the implementation? For example, what was your preferred approach: lift-and-shift or transformation and then shifting?
Michel De Zeeuw:
Implementation speed was a crucial factor for us. Of course we did some harmonization work but in general I would say the lift-and-shift approach was our preferred approach.

What was your deployment strategy? Rolling out country by country or going for a roll out function by function?
Michel De Zeeuw:
Our deployment strategy was country by country.

Looking forward to the next five or so years, how do you expect Shared Services to evolve?
Michel De Zeeuw:
I believe there will be a lot more companies going offshore and they will use outsourcing much more. This applies especially to companies with less than €5 billion of revenue. In the long term I hope that level of commoditization of these processes will dramatically increase. For example, accounts payable could become a commodity process across companies. This is a huge value creation opportunity.

Would it be right to say that the next step up in the evolution of Shared Services is to achieve scaling benefits across enterprises on a worldwide level?
Michel De Zeeuw:
Yes, this is what I mean by commoditization.

Finally, what do you have to say to SAP? What do you recommend to SAP as the major provider of solutions for enabling Shared Services and business process outsourcing, with regard to the upcoming challenges of process industrialization and global operations?
Michel De Zeeuw:
SAP has to improve their solutions portfolio to address these new challenges. IT was a key enabler in the past and will be a key enabler in the future in creating standards for business processes.

Thank you for those very useful insights into the potential evolution of Shared Services in the upcoming years. It seems that we can look forward to some intriguing developments. Thank you for your time and all the best in your new role at Infosys.

8.5 Interview: SAP

Interview with Peter Rasper, Head of Finance & Admin SAP responsible amongst others for the European Shared Service Center in Prague, Global Purchasing and Global Facility of SAP.

Introduction:
Serving more than 41,200 customers worldwide, SAP is the world's largest business software company and the world's third-largest independent software provider overall. Today, SAP employs more than 41,900 people in more than 50 countries.

SAP operates several Shared Service Centers. Could you please describe the role of the Shared Service Centers again from the point of view of SAP strategy, and go over the milestones which you have experienced here in Prague?
Peter Rasper:
SAP presented an agenda with objectives for the year 2010. Not only must SAP's agenda for 2010 be supported, it must also be secured massively from a finance point of view and brought forward. Within this context, we need to approach a lot more infrastructure issues, whether it be Global Purchasing, Global Facility or, indeed, the worldwide globalization of financial processes. The finance organization itself must also change dramatically, because it has to support the business during

this company transformation. But it cannot do that with the current portfolio of activities.

We think of the Shared Service itself as a significant motor and catalyst for the change in the finance sector. You can see that in the fact that the skills profiles of the CFOs are changing, the demands made on employees are changing. They are changing because we are extracting the transactional issues out of the activity portfolios of individual employees in our country organizations and are pushing them a bit to make them shift their focus. The whole thing is ultimately a driver for change in the finance sector, but also at SAP, as we get used to working with virtual finance sectors.

The ultimate aim from the CFO point of view is achieving better governance and increased transparency, but quality is also an aspect, of course – we want things to be posted quickly, done quickly, and at the end of the day we want to be as efficient as possible, both in terms of operational excellence and cost. Those are our main drivers, so to speak.

Were these main drivers treated equally? Is it not the case that cost efficiency was the real reason?
Peter Rasper:
Yes, they were treated equally, and, what's more, they are changing a little along the way. The issue of SOX has become more important, of course, now that we have a very large leverage effect via the Shared Center, because we can check things centrally there and only have to do them once, and not thirty or forty times. And then of course there is the finance transformation issue, one which is becoming more and more obvious because it is turning the organization on its head, as well as altering mindsets.

Our building principle was quite simple, in fact. As I always put it, "Be brave, be quick and be pragmatic." That is to say, we put together a Shared Service Center pretty quickly there and – and this is the fourth point – we were able to achieve this because we made sure that the stakeholders were brought along with us. We considered the change management issue to be very important, and we included employees, stakeholders, CFOs and MDs in every phase of the project.

The alignment was achieved with steering committee meetings, advisory council meetings and other measures which we used to inform the stakeholders and include them in decision-making. We started with a small country, that was the milestone as you know, a small willing country, namely Switzerland. Then we quite simply had a proof of concept for Europe. And then we said to ourselves, let's do it on a larger scale, and then essentially included the whole company. It was important to note that critical mass is key. You have to see quickly that you get as much in as possible, so that you can leverage better later.

SAP Business Services has also broadened the number of processes at the same time as the rollout in different countries. Have they always been exactly the same processes, or was the scope widened?
Peter Rasper:
They were exactly the same processes in the first phase. These were general accounting, consulting-billing, education-billing, procure-to-pay and customer-to-cash. This brings us once again to the topic "Be fast" – we spent a very short time setting the standard for these processes. We had two months in total during which a CFO from each country affected had to come up with an acceptable standard for general accounting, P2P or C2C, for example, and sign off on it. The crucial thing was that we could not spend ages refining it: We had to have something quickly which we could start using. So speed is at the top of our list.

How has the service portfolio been developed further?
Peter Rasper:
HR ran in parallel with another approach. We did it country-for-country with the F&A processes, HR started out service-for-service in Europe. We learnt from each other in doing this, and then HR switched to country-for-country too. We co-locate, which is very advantageous as we can move people from one area to another in accordance with their career plans. We can take advantage of the leverage effect from the training measures for other infrastructure issues, or we learn from each other – through the customer surveys, for example – how to approach things, or from customer-facing activities such as the Accounting Interaction Center or HR Interaction Center. This simply makes a great deal of activities easier.

Have you gone as far as having shared first-level support?
Peter Rasper:
That's the next plan. I'm sure we will do that, that's the way we're going.

Which HR processes have you included, and how far have you come by now?
Peter Rasper:
Responsibility for F&A and HR Shared Services are divided in the Business Center. We have two separate divisions, but we work closely

together. In fact, that is an SAP principle: You don't have to centralize all organizations; you merely need to create networks between them. It's the same principle which we already share with the existing Shared Service Centers.

We have a network of Shared Services which are not part of one organization, but which work very closely together and ensure that processes are aligned. Aligned, indeed, with the knowledge that this will help us to reach the IT spending level and that we could send people here and there with it. That is the principle we are working with at the moment, as well as cooperating with the existing Shared Service Centers in Asia Pacific, Latin America and partly in the USA.

This concept of networked organizations with simultaneous cross-location and cross-function is interesting. This is also a bit of a unique characteristic, isn't it, because others do not operate like that; they explicitly create their own organizational units and sometimes even their own companies?
Peter Rasper:
Exactly. It is the balance between diversity gains of decentralize units and central governance - we use this gap as a momentum to allow creativity and innovation in order to have a convergence of best practices. Ideally we would not need a line organization, but we would align along the process chain and create federations of small units, with clear in and output, which optimize themselves and the whole chain.

How advantageous is a shared infrastructure with a single system to SAP?
Peter Rasper:
It's the nuts and bolts of the whole thing. The fact that we're all in the same boat is the basic requirement for being able to work so quickly and not to have to worry about system consolidation or similar problems. We're all in the same boat, as I said. Once a workflow has been defined, it is rolled out worldwide into the various company codes and that's that.

Was that also the motivation for not including BPO? The fact is that it is already such an efficient infrastructure?
Peter Rasper:
Let me put it like this: A Shared Service is always a journey with its own lifecycle. In principle you start by centralizing things, then optimizing and standardizing them. Then you consider outsourcing parts of them. That is exactly our strategy. We transfer certain parts to a third-party provider, for example, after we have optimized them and know exactly

what they are about. At the same time, the Shared Service Center picks up new processes with the bucket which has just been emptied, if you will allow me to take a bucket-wheel excavator as an analogy, and the newly created capacity can work towards standardizing and optimizing these new processes. So it's just like those bucket-wheel excavators which are used in the open-cast mining of lignite, it operates in a cycle.

Would the outsourcing occur under the auspices of the Shared Service Center, perhaps without the end user even noticing it?
Peter Rasper:
That's right; the Shared Service Center is responsible.

A bucket-wheel excavator like the one you mentioned excavates its way across a field, of course. Sooner or later the field will be empty. Where is the limit beyond which outsourcing is not an option, or would you like to leave this completely open?
Peter Rasper:
Well I think that the important thing is to hold on to core competencies – that's kind of my philosophy – the process know-how, for example, the knowledge of how these things are controlled and, ultimately, how they are measured. I also like the idea of arranging it in such a way that, if it should all go wrong, you can in-source it back again. In other words, you don't let the entire know-how out. So that's kind of the building block.

As I said, outsourcing, or, the other way around, SSC is developing more and more into a process know-how carrier, too. And we will not outsource this process know-how. And that's important, as with this process know-how we also achieve some process ownership in the company. In our case that is over and above the competence that a Shared Service Center would get, because they know how travel accounting works, for example.

What are the proportions involved? What would be a headcount of those who remain decentralized in their function and those who go to the SSC and who may then go to outsourcing: Is it 10:90, 30:70 or 50:50?
Peter Rasper:
Well, I cannot make any statement regarding outsourcing, as I said. At the moment we're at about 30:70, but I think that will change again. And you're right; it will probably change in the direction of 20:70:10 or so. And it just keeps moving in that direction. It is also the case, as I said, that we have these transactional services at the moment, but of course it could be other services such as reporting, cost accounting, or whatever.

We have heard that even the international transfers who are processed in the SAP Business Center are in the payroll area. Which are the higher-value services which are now being offered in the Shared Service Center?

Peter Rasper:

Well, HR processes mobility issues. That is something very challenging which was not very easy at the beginning but which is now running well, in my view. This is always the case. For the first year, a Shared Service Center runs in kind of crisis mode, because the organization and the employees of the different organizations and of the Shared Service Center are not yet used to working in this virtual environment. To achieve this, you need completely new skills – in the Shared Service Center, too. You need somebody battle-proven there, as a manager, for example, especially in the initial phase. Somebody who is very accepted in the organization who has both the specific know-how and the potential to push the thing through. But that changes over time, when after two or three years you see that the Shared Service Center has arrived in the organization and conflicts are back on a normal level. From that point of view, then, the level of acceptance is quite different.

Now you need a salesperson more, someone who will see to it that more services are added and that the organization is controlled differently. It's ultimately an evolution of the skills which are needed there. It's important to remember throughout the whole process that the organizations have to be taken on board. We have noticed that it's important not only to look after the F&A organizations during change management, but the organization as a whole must understand that things are now going to be done differently. This change management aspect is a very important one for the organization. For this reason, you can't check often enough that somebody, maybe even a CEO, is paying attention and gives his views on this and similar issues.

As we're on the topic of change management, what was the biggest handicap regarding the changing demands on the employees' skills? Was it the fact that people did not have the right skills and thus needed to be brought up to an acceptable level first?

Peter Rasper:

In principle, the problem was that neither the people who had stayed "at home" in the locations, nor the Shared Service Center employees had ever worked in such an environment. That is to say, virtually, with a lot of cultural differences and now with a new division of labor. The issue of conflict management is a very important one, as is cultural diversity.

People have to accept that others are different, react differently and address others differently.

The type of communication is important: How do I communicate with my colleagues, how do I escalate certain things, how have I determined my communication matrix, and so on? So that was a very significant point, that both sides learnt "Ah, Prague works like that", but Prague also had to understand how the Netherlands or France, or whoever, deal with issues, address issues.

You just mentioned the different skill set which is needed during the different phases of the Shared Service Center. First of all we have the trust-building, well-connected manager, then later more of a sales or service manager. Is that a level below when you consider line management and employee skill? How do you manage higher fluctuation in the long run?
Peter Rasper:
This issue of fluctuation will remain to a certain degree the same, I think. In order to mitigate the risk you have to invest in people. We offer them functional and management career path within the Shared Service and outside and/or develop or certify them over a two year time period as professionals – which helps to improve their market value. Very important is to have a very sound, easy accessible knowledge management with training curriculums and learning tools, which are always up-to-date.
The continuous drive for more standardization is another brick, which helps to solve this issue, as is easier to transfer knowledge and people.

Regarding the fluctuation rate, what kind of calculations should we expect there? In a location like Prague, say.
Peter Rasper:
The issue is the same everywhere. We should take the figure of 20% there, sometimes even higher. That's a fact and it needs to be included in the business plan.

Are there increased efforts to maintain motivation with a permanent training program for this reason?
Peter Rasper:
That's right. We are investing heavily in training, not only within the finance subjects or processes but as well in order to develop the colleagues personally. We offer them career paths, in principle via the different organizational divisions within our Shared Service Center, but also in the Shared Service Center HR. It is important that the strategy is

understood and the SSC is part of this. Therefore we conduct multiple sessions to convey this content to our employees So we are doing quite a lot there to hold on to our employees. On management level we've been very successful in keeping the local management with us, as we invest , trust and connect to them. The employees then group around them, you see.

What would be the career path of somebody in the management of the Shared Service Center? Is that merely a stop-over in the general SAP career path or would you say that being a service manager is a set of skills in its own right?

Peter Rasper:

Well my basic philosophy is that everybody who would like to move up in the finance organization should have worked in the Shared Service Center so that he or she understands how it works and what the issues in there are. For example, I have just transferred an employee with a lot of potential there, as he would like to build a career with us. He will take on management functions there, which is a step towards that.

I think it's very important that you do that. But the career of a Shared Service Center employee is not limited to finance, I think, it could well be in the service area, too. A lot of activities in the service and support area are open to a service manager.

If process know-how is going to be concentrated more and more in the Shared Service Center, isn't that a good reason to send more people through this process know-how?

Peter Rasper:

Yes, exactly. You can also place them in the project management methodologically. They are used to dealing with complex issues, of course, so there are a number of career options open to them.

Let's come to the theme of relationship, business clients and so on. What exactly does the agreement between the Shared Service Center and their customers look like? Is there something formal, something informal, or are there only declarations of intent?

Peter Rasper:

No, the important thing is that it is transparent, and we achieve this transparency by means of KPIs. These KPIs are held in service level agreements in relative detail. They are also in the service item lists, SILs, as we call them, so that they can be tracked precisely. We discuss this every month with the relevant CFOs or F&As on site: They all get a report and have access to a dashboard where they can see the process status. That's important. Then you have a basis for discussion and you can say that we need to do something here and there.

Service level agreements are the basis of the whole thing. At the same time, we also have target agreements jointly set, both in the Shared Service area here in Prague as well as on site. This makes it clear that it is a common issue. DSO, for example, is an issue which needs to be tackled together. A C2C employee has a DSO target for the UK, for example, and an employee in the UK has exactly the same thing. Maintaining team spirit is another important point.

How can you educate your customers so that they can improve the quality of processes, for example the purchase order quota level?
Peter Rasper:
That happens by itself, in fact. That's what I mentioned earlier with the issue of change and when I talked about finance.
In the beginning we didn't struggle with the standard to the last mile. We rather negotiated with those countries before doing the actual migration in order to bring them as close to the standard as possible – e. g. 80%. After go live, the countries realize the effort on both sides for these last 20% and a convergence process to the 100% starts. And so they come of their own accord, which is a better way - the SAP way. The only problem with that was that it took a bit of time and caused partly some friction. This friction led partly to increased fluctuation, which then accelerated the convergence again.

Does every country have its line at about 80/20?
Peter Rasper:
Yes, that was ultimately discussed with each country. I think we have 25 now. A clear gap analysis was done beforehand to see how far they were away from the standard and where the deviations were. And then we sat down with the CFO to discuss how to close the gaps, which were 10% or 20% – not necessarily 20%, but some proportion – and then measures were taken to decrease it and it was decided that that was it. In principle that was a question of compromising, which was the other point, "Be pragmatic"? That only works with the other side's buy-in.

Do you also have a pragmatic limit at which point it makes sense to roll a company into the Shared Service Center?
Peter Rasper:
No. Our approach was to tackle larger countries after a small, willing pilot country. The situation today is that we have the large countries all in. At the moment we're working on bringing in small countries, where

the cost effect is not so great, but the compliance and quality effects are a factor.

OK, I see that that is an important argument. To get back to the up-ramping of the Shared Service Center. What percent of the administrative function, measured as a headcount again, perhaps, is now in the Shared Service Center?

Peter Rasper:

As I said, 70:30. So 70% are in, 30% are still out, and these 30% are still out because of the defined process cut, which leaves work within the local subsidiaries

As you mentioned at the beginning, billing also goes through the Shared Service Center, or are there exceptions to this?

Peter Rasper:

Besides Consulting and Education billing, we only have software billing for indirect distribution for certain countries

Initially we planed to transfer all billing activities. We postponed the Software Billing as it is a complicated, last step with significant interaction within the sales cycle and which can harm the revenue recognition. Therefore we decided to concentrate first on proving the concept with the other processes.

But now some countries are coming and saying that they would like certain processes to be included, and the whole thing has developed its own dynamic because we have shown that we can do it. And because the organization is under pressure everywhere and has to save costs, they are more prepared simply to hand services over to us.

Now a question which touches a bit on technology. How important are productivity tools, actually? As we know, early scanning with automatic invoice parking is used in Prague. Are you already using that to its maximum, or do you have other ideas about how it could be improved?

Peter Rasper:

We use it very intensively – that's a significant point – to make the whole thing more efficient. Especially e-billing and OCR to avoid as much input as possible. Because the less input I have, the less I need to do during the process. Pre-configuring things so that I only need to deal with the exceptions in the Shared Service Center is the decisive moment. That's the basic idea. Other tools are the Duplicate Analyzer, which helps us to make sure that things are not entered twice – or the AIC or Accounting Interaction Center. The AIC is a call center functionality adopted for finance processes and is used for the interaction with our external and internal customers. This tool is essential to organize the helpdesk work and to monitor and optimize issues in all areas.

As stated, we have so far only answered the question of the most valuable process running in the Shared Service Centers from the HR point of view. What would this be in the finance area? Is it reporting for Cost Management?
Peter Rasper:
No and you can not really differentiate as it is a matter of timing and maturity. In the early phase of SSC the most valuable is the most work intensive process – for example, Procure to Pay, Travel accounting or consulting billing. Over time this changes and then the general accounting comes in to the focus as it needs of course a much more sophisticated knowledge.

Are you considering delivering more business analytics? Becoming a service reporting about current figures with a bit of deviation analysis, a center of expertise in the truest sense of the word; or do you limit yourselves to the classic reporting functions?
Peter Rasper:
Well, at the moment we don't have a reporting function, so that's not an issue right now. But it could become one. But our system is designed in such a way that you have a lot of information at your fingertips already. I have my workplace; I can go there and see what I have. I don't really need a lot of analytics behind it.

OK, I suppose you have to understand that. When others consider cost management to be so important and they have to gather the information from decentralized systems. Then it's clear, it's like that because the system is the way it is.
Let's come to the classic closing questions. What keeps you awake at night? What would be the worst-case scenario in the Shared Service Center?
Peter Rasper:
A month-end close or a quarter-end close is no longer an issue. That all runs fine generally. I think the important thing is that Shared Services are a part of the strategy and remain a part of it, to a certain extent, and that the bucket-wheel excavator keeps turning. That's an important point for me and we have to make sure that it happens. Because nothing could be worse for a Shared Service Center than the changes coming to a standstill. You have to change things constantly and keep everybody motivated. There are two sides to it, in a way. First of all there needs to be the

motivation which tells people that they can change something, that they're allowed to change something and that they want to change something, and on the other side there's the possibility of actually getting something moving.

To develop my question: Does that mean that the development of the Shared Service Center will still be going in five years because it is a concept that takes on new issues as the company's strategy changes and adapts?
Peter Rasper:
Exactly, that's how it is. As I said, you take on the issues and condense them to a center of expertise. That means that the issue has been broken down into manageable parts and most parts have been outsourced. You hold on to one part, and that's the center of expertise. That means that you have a lot of condensed COEs afterwards.

That was a comprehensive and clear description. Thank you very much for this interview.

8.6 Interview: Siemens

Interview with Wolfgang Leitmanstetter, Head of Business Development Siemens Shared Service for HR, Siemens AG.

Introduction:
Siemens, headquartered in Berlin and Munich, is one of the world's largest electrical engineering and electronics companies. Siemens provides innovative technologies and comprehensive know-how to benefit customers in 190 countries. Founded more than 150 years ago, the company is active in the areas of Information and Communications, Automation and Control, Power, Transportation, Medical, and Lighting. The company has approximately 475,000 employees working to develop and manufacture products, design and install complex systems and projects, and tailor a wide range of services for individual requirements.

Please would you give a short description of when you started, what processes you use in the Shared Service Center, and what the milestones have been so far.
Wolfgang Leitmanstetter:
Before we start, we need to define what we're talking about. Are we talking about the global Shared Service Center or the national, German Shared Service Center?

I think we should start with the German Shared Service Center and then we can move on to the global topics.
Wolfgang Leitmanstetter:
Then I will only talk about the German one for the moment. We started in 2003. What initiated the whole process was the implementation of a national, comprehensive HCM system in Germany. We used to have, I think, 70 proprietary systems and we merged them using SAP software. That was the impetus behind it all – this common data storage. It made us think: where do we go from here? Then we thought about the Shared Service Center. There was a base-line study to see if it was feasible, if Siemens was capable of implementing something like this. Then in 2003, we finally decided to implement this Shared Service Center in Germany.

What processes did you begin with?
Wolfgang Leitmanstetter:
It was all pure HR – I'm only talking about HR topics here. That means all the administrative processes, including, of course, payroll, recruiting administration, travel expenses administration, and so on. At the same time, we implemented what is normally only done in the second step – we integrated social processes. That means healthcare management, doctors' processes and company social welfare. These were also the two areas we built up with the Global Shared Service Center.

Technically speaking, were you already using the employee interaction center (EIC) at that point?
Wolfgang Leitmanstetter:
At the beginning, we weren't using it. We had a total of 90 locations in Germany and the first step involved reducing them to six. That was a matter of philosophy for us too – do we choose one, two, three, or more locations? And six was the most sensible approach for us, in terms of reorganization costs that are incurred. But also, and this is very important, it was about keeping the know-how. We always considered that if we just chose one location, which is feasible, it would be a risk. We would have lost too much expertise and competence. That's why we went for six locations.
These six locations are responsible for the one-to-one relationship of HR employee to service recipient. Service recipient is the name we give our employees out there, which would be about 170,000 in Germany.

And that is for current employees, not pensioners or anything like that?
Wolfgang Leitmanstetter:

That is just for current employees. Pensioners are also part of the Shared Service Center. There are 150,000 pensioners, so you can add this figure to the one above. Then, of course, there was the question of how do we initiate the first contact between the service recipients and the Shared Service. Ultimately, it was very clear to us that we needed an interaction center. From the very beginning, we had a vision or a concept in mind. We wanted this Shared Service Center to be a factory. That was the concept behind it.

We looked to the manufacturing industry for inspiration. They had done it all before with their industrial processes. We asked ourselves: What are they doing and how can we do it too? We were quick to use the EIC as more than just a call center. We envisioned a complete order management system. And that was implemented relatively quickly with SAP. Within six weeks, I think, we had implemented it. That's must be close to a world record.

It was then further developed. Of course, SAP and Siemens worked on this together. We were one of the first to use EIC in that way, and ultimately all these features like management, ticketing, roll outs, cataloging the individual products, tracking, and all the topics we manage from the EIC came out of it.

Can I ask again how many employees work in the interaction center?
Wolfgang Leitmanstetter:
There are currently 30 employees working there.

And they support 170,000 employees?
Wolfgang Leitmanstetter:
Yes. Let me explain. From the start, we tried to avoid setting up a call center. In other words, we also answer questions. And the number of questions we answer first time round is high. We currently answer approximately 80% of the queries at the first point of contact. We deal with 70,000 a month, which means 70,000 events in this EIC, whether they are queries or orders. That is an impressive number.

Yes, it is impressive. If you have these deployment scenarios, what remains in the Shared Service Center? How much stays in the lines of business?
Wolfgang Leitmanstetter:
The results from our base-line year of 2003 enabled us to find out which services or tasks we could centralize or in other words, incorporate in the

service. We found out that 60% of the HR organization's tasks can be integrated.

But I believe more can be integrated. That figure was too small, and was also influenced by politics. But the ratio then was 60 to 40, 60% was with us, 40% remained with the business partner. And gradually we built up the SSCs, as I said, always keeping this idea of a factory in mind. That is to say, transparency: I know where a ticket is, where it is assigned, to what service unit. In the back office too, I know how long I may need for a process. And with the EIC, we also integrated this service level agreement tracking. That means our factory manager knows where orders are going off course, which ones are classified under the red, yellow, or green traffic lights, and consequently, he can manage his employees, or in other words, control production.

Have you drawn up specific service level agreements with your customers, in other words, the Siemens employees?
Wolfgang Leitmanstetter:
Yes, we have. We have service level agreements for certain products and processes and work packages, they arc discussed with and agreed on by the customer. To us they are the same. Customer A has an identical service to customer B, and we classify our customers under our Siemens areas. They are completely different. Power Generation, which builds power plants, is completely different from Information and Communication Systems. But the service level is the same. Creating an order takes three days, and these three days are part of the lead time. This means the employee contacts the call center, we open the ticket, and from then on the clock is ticking.

How is the call center organized? Is it a separate unit or even a separate company within Siemens?
Wolfgang Leitmanstetter:
No, there is no separate company. We have taken tasks from the HR department and an HR service has been set up in Germany, that's what we still call it today. This 60% of employees I mentioned before has been integrated in the Shared Service area. You have to remember that at the start of 2003, this unit consisted of about 1,500 people. With all the facets it is ultimately only about bundling tasks with the same set up and alignment and putting these into a Shared Service center is difficult. They are, of course, completely different topics that we have to deal with. But in terms of our vision, we had already laid this foundation stone to create transparency. That was a major goal for us. I need to know what we are doing.

So, it's not driven by cost-efficiency, but by quality, rationalization?
Wolfgang Leitmanstetter:
You've always got these three variables. Of course, cost is the main factor when you set up a Shared Service center. By reducing the number of locations from 90 to six, and now we have just two, we have enormous cost advantages. The transparency and economies of scale that allow me to group areas together all results in cost savings. In other words, the cost advantages always took quality and service into account. When you think about these three variables here, you have to really balance them out, so that you can reduce costs, but keep the level of service and quality the same, or even improve it.

Did you ever think about offshoring or nearshoring?
Wolfgang Leitmanstetter:
Yes, that was a topic we looked at, but like I said, for us it is not that easy. The unions and certain other organizations in Germany have a lot of influence at Siemens. We tried one isolated process – a travel expense process – where we tried to build up knowledge. We have off-shored this on a near-shore basis to Bratislava.

We settle approximately 800,000 trips a year there. The whole process, therefore, takes place in Slovakia. Whether or not this process remains a one-off, or whether more will follow, remains to be seen, but I believe there will be more.
Technical support also aids the standardization of processes. One thing you need to remember, and this is where we deviate a bit from your SAP Shared Service Center in Prague, in our case, a lot more is done over the telephone. At your center in Prague I saw that 95% of the contact there is made by e-mail. With us, it is more like 60% telephone calls.

Yes, that is probably due to the SAP culture. We are used to working with people from around the world.
Wolfgang Leitmanstetter:
Yes, exactly. It is also a matter of culture for us too. We have a different culture from SAP. When you set up something like this you need to take into account the culture, including the language. Our employees are used to speaking German, maybe even a specific dialect. And this is something you have to consider.

I don't know if you want to mention figures, but what was your ROI?
Wolfgang Leitmanstetter:
I can be open about that. The figures have been published. Since 2003, we have reduced our cost by 40%. I'll add something there, which is

perhaps of interest to SAP. We didn't stop with the Employee Interaction Center (EIC) order tool. We optimized the workflow systems. It was a long, hard struggle to find the right approach. We have built a type of process engine, or rather, SAP has built it for us.

You need to imagine it lies between a portal, between EIC and the Human Capital Management (HCM) systems, which allows us to map processes even at multiple levels. That means it can also take the pressure off a Shared Service Center. I'll give you an example, if one-time payments arise, management enters the information using a template in the portal and the approval processes then run in the background. From the SAP system to management, everything is managed using the UWL in the portal. If the last reviewer has given their approval, the process is closed, meaning that there is no more work for us in the Shared Service Center.

This means it enters it into the EICsystem, it enters it into the HCM system, it archives it in our electronic system, it generates the letter, it generates a ticket, it does everything. The machine takes care of all the manual work. Today, we do 18 processes like that.

Have these developments been incorporated back into the standard SAP software?
Wolfgang Leitmanstetter:
The SAP development organization has incorporated many of our changes in SAP ERP 2006. This is a very interesting approach. We are definitely well ahead of the game in the German industry.

What are the goals on a global level?
Wolfgang Leitmanstetter:
On October 1, 2006, Siemens AG decided to integrate a global Shared Service here – a place where different faculties can be grouped together. But we have already spoken about HR, and we have already touched on the German delivery. We have a second business area or cluster, as we call them internally, with A&F, a third one with IT, and a fourth with global procurement, mobility services, and all the purchasing topics. These four business areas all belong under the global Shared Service Organization and are going global in late 2007. They offer all the services and products in this area for Siemens internally. We are Siemens' internal service provider; we are not going to go on the external market.

And at the moment you are rolling in the processes?
Wolfgang Leitmanstetter:

We are in the middle of rolling them in. If I can refer to HR again, in 2008 we will have 1,800 employees in this global organization area who will carry out global Shared Service tasks. This is defined in a similar way to the German organization. What are the Shared Service tasks in the HR area? They are payroll services, total rewards administration, employee data management, travel expenses, staff services, and so on.

As I said, these topics are our products. And ultimately we have brought together all the employees from all the different Siemens locations who currently perform these services and placed them in the global Shared Service HR Unit. Our next goal is to do what we did in Germany and reduce 80 locations to four. We are trying to regionalize.

The question is which regional processes can be globalized? Which processes in Europe can be globalized in Europe in one location or even in multiple locations? Can I have a global HCM system in the background for the region at first and then expand it? Can I include Asia Pacific, the United States and Latin America? These are the questions we are currently discussing.

And the whole thing is based on a single SAP instance with the processes you mentioned?

Wolfgang Leitmanstetter:

Yes, that is the goal. The target date is around 2010. We are currently working on the concept that we will position ourselves regionally. For me, one goal would certainly be to have a main system in Europe. In America, PeopleSoft is still very dominant for us, in the Asia Pacific region we have an SAP system, in Latin America we have many different SAP systems – there is still an incredible amount of work to do.

I can explain why this is the case. Until last year, the philosophy at Siemens was “strengthen the countries.” In other words, what we did in Germany, we also did in the other countries. In the end, each country had more or less built up its own Shared Service Center, its own processes with their own systems and their own philosophy. Very little was done on a global scale. Each country was looking out for itself.

And now we want to impose the best practices from the countries at a regional or even global level. And we are speaking about 470,000 employees worldwide. That’s really good – we can use the ABC analysis method. Almost 85% of the employees come from the 12 focus countries. That means we are talking about a lot of relatively small countries too.

Then you have to think about how a small country fits into such a big, complex setup such as the one Germany has. But I don't need to tell you about that. The whole process support, the automation, it just doesn't fit as well in a country like Ireland or Greece with just 600 or 700 employees.

Other companies sometimes try to establish clusters of countries with similar levels of complexity.
Wolfgang Leitmanstetter:
Exactly. We are still in the alignment phase or philosophy phase – what is the best approach? Why are we doing this at Siemens? At Global Shared Service HR, we work under the principle of "leadership in productivity with defined quality and services." Here, too, you can immediately see this is about costs, service, and quality. Once again, you need to take into account the culture at Siemens – our services are not mandatory.

That means that we too have to prove the value of our services and costs and convince the countries to use our services too. Consequently, it is about market share. That sounds a bit stupid for an internal department, but within our internal market we of course want to reach 100% market share. In other words, all these services in this area are delivered by us.

Are you thinking about one day offering these services externally too?
Wolfgang Leitmanstetter:
Perhaps in three or four years. We wanted to do this before in Germany with Siemens Business Services. We wanted to offer them externally, but it failed. Then there was talk that we were going to merge with a large German company to finally get our foot in the door here. I'm sure that made it into the press. At the moment we are focusing on our internal alignment, but as I said, maybe in four or five years.

You manage the HR area in the global Shared Service Center, is that right?
Wolfgang Leitmanstetter:
I am not the head of HR. I have a direct manager who used to be the head of HR services in Germany. Now he has the global role, and I am responsible for Europe. I am responsible for the strategy on a global level, and for its implementation in Europe.

And for financials? I'm just interested in that because we really wanted you to be in this network, regardless of this interview, because you have really pushed financials forward as well.

Wolfgang Leitmanstetter:
A colleague owns the head of Accounting and Finance. He has had a head start because he has had three or four delivery centers for some time. He has one in Prague, one in Munich, one in Singapore, and one in Lisbon. So he is a bit further on because he already has a global data basis with the SAP process in the background. He has already been using an SSC for two or three years. Consequently, he is at least two or three years ahead of us. He would certainly be an interesting contact for you.

It is also interesting that you are already looking to include procurement. Many other SSCs we know have not got that far yet.
Wolfgang Leitmanstetter:
They certainly intend to do it. As I said, at Siemens we did it with these four areas, procurement, mobility, and logistics.

Where is it positioned in the organizational structure? Does it come under the CFO?
Wolfgang Leitmanstetter:
No, it will come under the corporate executive committee.

To return to the subject of building on what's been accomplished in Germany and expanding globally – you have specified 2010 as the target date by which you want to have a standardized system, roll out the processes, and cover approximately 85% of the employees. Where are you heading?
Wolfgang Leitmanstetter:
Sure, but first of all the question is what can actually be centralized from a global perspective? That's an interesting question, followed by do I have to do everything myself? This is also something that will keep us busy for the coming months. It refers to whether or not I can outsource selectively or completely, although there are many question marks here. We mean "selective" in terms of what is the best location, where do I go with these services? Can I really go global if I take the language issue into account? When you look at Europe, you need to offer practically every language from Italian to Flemish (if Belgians are also involved). This makes the options in terms of locations very clear. We'll be able to answer all the questions soon.

What will probably cause us a lot of headache is the topic of benchmarking. Siemens AG wants to benchmark. We want to benchmark ourselves here in Germany first. We want to see where our Shared Service stands in Germany, and of course on a global structure. I don't know what it is like for you, but we are at the beginning. If you read benchmarking studies, regardless of whether they have come from, they very often compare apples with pears, as far as I am concerned. You can interpret how you want, and everyone does well, but you don't get any real concrete information. We want to change this. At least in my area of responsibility in Europe, I want to know where I stand. But I want to compare apples with apples.

We have also used Hackett internally at SAP. It is more of a kind of wake-up call for the board. If you go into the details of the processes, and that's what we did with other companies at some point, Hackett stops. It is also the same in reverse; it involves a lot of analytical work. We did this once for the travel expenses process. We'd be happy to share this with you.
Wolfgang Leitmanstetter:
That would be great. I'd really be interested in that.

We would be very interested in working with you on that. The team that analyzed the travel expenses process included members from SAP, Henkel, Bayer, and DaimlerChrysler I think. It's not something we have right across the board, but our colleagues in the United States have worked with the Americas' SAP Users' Group to try to get detailed benchmark figures, particularly in the supply chain process.
Wolfgang Leitmanstetter:
Benchmarking companies can give you an initial overview. But I believe, and I'll say this bluntly, it's often not worth the paper it's written on. You can use it as a wake-up call, but it's of no help when it comes to making, when I want to know where I stand now. What we are doing now, and it is a very interesting approach, we want to go down to the level of individual services to be able to compare and to create the basis for benchmarking. But we are still in the very early days. What we are looking for are allied companies that want to do this with us.

That would actually be a good starting point. We cannot offer the methodical, statistical scope where everything is proven empirically, as Hackett can. That's the reason we are thinking more along the lines of an exchange of experiences with individually selected companies. This gives you the chance to really go into detail and control the process.
I will discuss it at the Shared Services meeting. People from Shell and BP, for example, also attend, and this idea that six or seven companies actually get together and have their own benchmark is worth a lot more than asking 400 companies in a survey.

Wolfgang Leitmanstetter:
Exactly, that's how I see it.

You have mentioned the processes at Siemens. Where is HR analytics at Siemens? Do you want to also offer more sophisticated processes from the Shared Service Center?
Wolfgang Leitmanstetter:
The topic is a difficult one, but I will say yes to start with. How we will do that is another question. At the moment, for example, we are testing a pilot project in the UK to also offer advisory services for top processes such as for severance pay, semi-retirement, and so on. We are currently setting up a call center in Glasgow with the EIC. We are not doing it for any other countries yet. So, in Germany, if you need advice, you go to your business partner. That is exactly what I was talking about before – this figure of 60% did not go far enough.

That means then in addition to the purely transactional business you also have a competence center under construction that will be based in the Shared Service Center?
Wolfgang Leitmanstetter:
That is our aim. But as I said, the project in the UK is a pilot. We need to see how we can implement it in the rest of the world. Although, of course, we want to do a lot using self services – that is really our philosophy.

That fits together perfectly then – self services, an interaction center, and then process optimization too?
Wolfgang Leitmanstetter:
But you need to know if you are starting on global scale or in one particular country. These are the strategic questions. When do I merge it all in an Human Capital Management system?

You have also mentioned service level agreements. Do you also use tools to manage service levels as contractual obligations?
Wolfgang Leitmanstetter:
No, we don't do that yet. Our service levels are defined with our customers and stored in the EIC for controlling purposes. In this way we can see if we have infringed these agreements and where we stand at the moment. The EIC is also the basis for the reporting. Apart from that, we have no background system.

The last question – what keeps you awake at night when you think about your Shared Service Center?
Wolfgang Leitmanstetter:

If we are talking about Germany, then I can actually say nothing keeps me awake at night anymore. The last sleepless night I had was, I believe, about how we can bring on board the topic of processes. And this struggle with our business partners, because you always have to look after this interface too. Then we have the issue of additional effort: The Shared Service is seen as creating more work – shifting it from the Shared Service to the individual areas – which is of course not true at all. If I used to have to write something down, and today I have to enter it electronically, that does not require any more effort. But our culture presents a problem here: Trying to convince older managers or secretaries that they now have to work on a PC and use the new tools. They get their tasks from the universal worklist. Trying to convince them of the benefits of these changes cost us many sleepless nights in Germany.

Then we have Europe. What is the best way to get a global system at reasonable cost, with PA elements included? How are PA and PY split? What is the best way to split them? These are the questions I am asking myself at the moment. And of course, what can I centralize across Europe? They don't cause sleepless nights, but they are the issues that I'm thinking about at the moment.

Yes, that's what I meant. You have already given us your outlook for the future and topics such as BPO are not in discussion, or at the most, only selectively.
Wolfgang Leitmanstetter:
The complete approach is being discussed. But I have my own opinion about that. As I said, however, we have to ask ourselves the question: Is it only a core business? Can I improve in that area? But I have yet to find a BPO provider that can convince me of that.

I think we have covered all the main questions about your very interesting plans. Thank you for discussing them with us.

8.7 Interview: Solvay

Interview with Guy de Mercier; Head of Shared Service Center Europe.

Introduction:
Solvay, which operates in Pharmaceuticals, Chemicals and Plastics, generated sales from more than 400 units in over 50 countries. About 29000 people service the group's 160000 clients.

Why did you start Shared Services at Solvay?
Guy de Mercier:
We were relatively late to the game of the Shared Services center. Officially we started in 2005, but we started to study it in 2003. The reason it took a little bit longer is that Solvay decided to follow a strategy of BPM, business process management. That means the first priority was put on "redesign first and transform after." We saw many, many experiences of existing Shared Services centers in which they tried to fully centralize or delocalize, and when the process was done, the centers were hoping to be able to optimize. But they didn't have anymore local resources – sometimes not even energy – to do the optimization after the centralization. So at Solvay we followed a strategy of BPM: the first phases, the as-is and the should-be; the implementation of that gap; and then the transfer to the Shared Services center.

So you have been in operation more or less one year?
Guy de Mercier:
Almost three years.

Did you achieve your target, or was it a little bit too optimistic? Did you fulfill everything you thought about?
Guy de Mercier:
It depends on the different processes. I would like to say that in terms of operational and financial targets, we achieved, let's say, 80%. The three conditions in order to be successful when you migrate to a Shared Services center are to have a stabilized and optimized process in place, for it to be fully documented by the people who use it on a day-to-day basis, and for the working language to naturally be English. When that's the case, we were successful within less than three to six months, meaning fully operational from designing the transfer to signing the contracts, hiring the people, training them, and transferring.

Our master data management for customers and vendors, so data maintenance for customer and vendor, was done in three months. We hired four people, we got the blueprint, we defined the service level agreement, we defined the key performance indicators, we trained the people, we transferred the access to documentation, we created the documentation, and we ran the operation in two days. We have between 80 and 100 records on a daily basis with a type of reporting they had never had previously, with full control in segregation of authority.

When you have these three conditions, you are in a perfect position to migrate. Whenever you don't get any of them or when one of them is missing, you pay the price if you don't fix it before the transfer. If you don't have the documentation down because it's unwritten knowledge or a type of process in which the knowledge resides in the people's brains and not on paper – which is often the case for human resources (HR) processes – and/or if English is not the predominant working language – which may be the case in payables and procurement – and/or if your process is not totally redesigned because the transfer to the shared services entity is one of the last triggers to really force and push to this redesign, that means that you are, as a shared services center, in the middle of it, and then you pay the price. For example, accounts payable for Spain took us a year for it to be successful, and we are not yet at the stage of fully validated documentation.

It sounds very difficult to get everything for shared service prepared. Is it because of cultural problems or just from lack of documentation and formalization?

Guy de Mercier:

I do believe the cultural problem is not helping, but the main reason is that the upstream process part, which was the procurement, was not yet in SAP software. They didn't use the workflow in SAP software. So when you are not using the normal procedure for connecting properly to your shared services center, and therefore when you rely on verbal communication, then you are facing significant challenges, because I believe that a Shared Services center is not a tool created for verbal communication. We developed an interaction tool which is very successful, because instead of a call center I put in place an expert contact center, which is charged with solving the problem, not just hitting the contact.

You talked about knowledge-based processes that are in people's heads. In your opinion, do you have today a transactional type of Shared Services center, or are you also starting to go more to the center-of-expertise transformational part of it?

Guy de Mercier:

For us it's very clear: I don't want at all to centralize the expertise. That's a very clear cut-off in the Solvay strategy. I'm very proud to stick to the transactional, to consolidate, to make it ISO-9002-certified, fully and only and exclusively transactional of remote processes. I do believe that it is worth centralizing the knowledge and the expertise also, but not in the same place you centralize transactions. I don't see significant synergy in that, and maybe a little more confusion.

We also have a split process between the business units and the Shared services center. What do you think is the percentage of processes you cover in a shared services center? Let's say accounts payable is very high, or in human resources some payroll is 100% outsourced. What is a rough percentage figure for process split that you have in the shared services center versus what is retained in the organization? Is a high percentage in the shared services center, or is a lot still left in the business units?

Guy de Mercier:

Starting from accounts payable, we are at 90%, and we have 10% remaining in order for goods received and purchase orders to be properly introduced in the system locally. We want to achieve 100% of it because we have an organization, called Strategy Purchasing and Procurement, which is a competence center, and it has the responsibility of managing the upstream procurement part.

On accounts receivable, from a pure cash collection perspective we have 100%. That means we have credit managers in the different regions that report to one central organization. So we have roughly 30 credit managers all over the world working as a front office, but in Solvay they are considered more as a competence center to do credit risk analyses, fix credit limits, discuss with the business, and make large legal recoveries or credit insurance types of strategy and policy. But for the cash collection, going from the collection, reconciliation, and first reminder, we do it 100% from here.

Regarding closing the books, we are, let's say, split 40–45% here and 50% local. We want to grow to 60% here and 40% local, knowing that the local financial manager or controller, will remain in charge of the compliance, governance, and certification of their processes. We don't need here and we will never do so, even if we can. Because following the strategy of a clear split, you need on site the specific business knowledge and legal, local responsibility.

It's very clear, very simple, and I do believe it works well because we have enough saving potential in efficiency to gain with a clear role like that. So I said 90% for account payable, 50% for accounts receivable, 45% for closing the books, travel and expenses 100% here – and that means what? As soon as employees fill in their travel and expense reports locally in a dedicated software application, or in some countries even in Microsoft Excel spreadsheets, they scan their receipts and we control everything here.

On payroll we are doing 15% here and 85% locally, and I don't want to grow more than 25–30% here. And for HR I'm pushing to leave on site a minimum of 70% of the activities. I believe you could transfer 30% to back office. We are not working directly connection with the employee, instead we are working through a service desk through an on-site HR manager. To make it clear, we work for them, not for the employee.

Regarding employees, when you started with Shared Services, did some people move over to the Shared Services center or did you start from scratch locally?

Guy de Mercier:

We started from scratch. But for the building phase I took with me six expatriate directors. That means six senior top experts knowledgeable about every process. That was my agreement with the executive committee that I could choose my people. I've been working with them now for three years – 2005, 2006 and 2007 – and I want to keep them until the optimization phase. They are very senior and wellrecognized as people who know their jobs. For example, a finance manager who is managing 150 financial operators here was the financial director of the biggest Solvay plant; he was on site operating cost accounting in the biggest Solvay plant in France, 2,000 people. So he knows exactly how to close the books and how to do everything. He is a professional.

So I took with me six professionals. And from there I hired all the rest here locally, and I took about three to five people hired through headhunters, who already had a little bit of Shared services experience.

So now looking more at the IT area, it means Shared services, split tasks, processes, involving a heterogeneous system landscape, and so on. What was your environment there? Because, for example, in other companies they started with 220 different systems. There are now about 15 enterprise resource planning systems, and now they're trying to reduce it to three or four. Do you have a similar heterogeneous, fragmented system landscape, and how do you deal with it?

Guy de Mercier:

Not at all. That's the reason Solvay is a little bit late in the game. It's because, as I told you, we not only wanted the process to be redesigned but also stabilized. Stabilized means being run through the same single enterprise resource planning (ERP) platform. We are running everything on SAP R/3 4.6 at the moment. So that's the condition before migrating the Shared Services center. We are running just one single ERP platform for finance; we are running another one for HR, SAP; and we are running

Arinso outsourcing for SAP payroll. We have a dedicated cash management system, CISS, but which is totally integrated in SAP software also. So we enjoy a very stable and harmonized IT environment. My 250 operators here have SAP profiles dedicated to their job descriptions.

You are the first company outside of SAP in Prague that has one single system to run its operations.
Guy de Mercier:
That's very, very interesting to hear. Yes, and that's thanks to our Head of Information and Communication Technology of the Solvay Group, who has invested a lot of effort and money to push SAP for the last 10 years. And now we get the value, sorry to say this, of having suffered that much of SAP; now we know why we had to suffer. The Single Shared services center was the final touch in a long-term strategy to integrate everybody into an integrated system.

Regarding agreements between businesses and shared services centers, do you have a formalized approach or dedicated service agreements?
Guy de Mercier:
It is very, very simple. The agreement is no more than five pages, the same general service agreement. Legally, it's prepared with the legal department and is ready to go to court, if necessary. I want to be ready to send a first reminder, a second reminder, and a third reminder; if one of my Solvay customers is not fulfilling his operating level agreement, I can go for damages in court. So we have legally binding general service agreements. We have dedicated service level agreements by process, which describe the standard way to deliver optimal services. And we have descriptions of all the exceptions that are accepted by the customer business entity and run the processes for a limited period of time.

When I said "legally," that's my intention. Today I'm still very quiet on that, but we have 60 contracts signed; I have a lawyer in Portugal doing that. I'm ready to exclude some certain customers that I don't want to work for.

Moving to the area of implementation, you said you have different phases, and you made it very, very clear that we should transform or stabilize the process first before moving it to a Shared Services center. Did you experience a need for different skills in different phases?
Guy de Mercier:

Yes, we need different skills. I tried to meet the challenge to keep the same people. I want to do that, but I do recognize it's difficult. I believe by keeping the same people you build a real company culture. Speaking two years later, I believe you will be exposed to a risk to have to rebuild your Shared Services culture again and again. And that may be the reason that people, when they go to the next step, are so exhausted to have gone through the first implementation phase that they immediately go for outsourcing. And then the Shared Services center disappears, which I believe is a fundamental mistake.

I'm preparing a vision to keep a Shared services center as an engine, an integration engine, and therefore to keep a company culture of people who are capable to promote the change. So to come back, I do believe you need different skills. I do believe that you need skills for redesign. That means you need dedicated skills on business process management first. From there you need skills in preparing the implementation and migration phase, which takes a very tough project team and change management capability. In parallel, you need entrepreneurs who are ready to build from scratch out of nowhere. So you need self-sufficient, self-motivating people.

Then for the optimization phase you need highly analytical people who are able to grow within the organization up to the certification. This is not for the pleasure of having a certification but to understand that you need to optimize every part of a process in order to have the process optimized. So yes, we need different skills. What we did at Solvay, when I started this project coming from the United States, was that I requested the executive committee to have another project leader besides me to take care of the redesign. He was a top financial guy – he was the #2 in finance just before the chief financial officer – and he worked on that for three years. At the same time I was building the center here, we were reporting together to the executive committee. And the final call was for me. I was allowed to not accept to transfer. So the shape phase, shape and migration, is a dedicated project team. At Solvay we booked seven people in place for two years. Very often, companies underestimate that need, or they hope to have consultants doing that for them. You need a little bit of consultancy to give a push, but you need to do that yourself. Because that phase of knowledge capturing and knowledge transfer is essential.

Let's have a few words on the outlook for Shared Services. What is your opinion on shared services in the future? Will it move to BPO or not?

Guy de Mercier:
I will refer to a statement made by a speaker in a SAP BSAG workshop made last year in Prague. He said to all of us that in the next five years, two-thirds of finance, procurement, IT, and, potentially, HR, transactional activities will be executed one way or another by the equivalent of a Shared Services center. If you look at that, it is quite expensive, quite a lot, two-thirds. At the Shared Services center there is a big future; that's the reason I'm sure you get a lot of support at SAP to do these studies, to look at this market, and so on.

So let me give you an opinion: This market will evolve and will remain. But the players in this market will change. I'm not quite sure an in-house Shared Services center will remain in-house forever, but I'm not quite sure that BPO is the solution either. What I see is a little bit in between. This means that even the big groups, even like Solvay, even those with 30,000 people in the world. You don't get to scale enough worldwide for everything you sell. Impossible. And second, it will never become even part of your core businesses.

For those two reasons, every year you will always have to face certain questions regarding your in-house Shared Services center, "Why we do this ourselves? Isn't it cheaper to do it outside?" The answer is yes, but it depends on what you are talking about. Is it cheaper to do it outside? How do you define the "it," the service itself?

Again, I see two types of Shared Services centers. There is the Shared Services center in-house, which is the one that is the enabler for the transformation. For that, it will remain forever, and you will have top people not being used for core businesses but with likely strong personality. Not to make money, but to be an enabler of fundamental change and integration.

Those Shared Services centers will become like a permanent project team, a permanent experimental line to produce a little bit to understand how to do it and then to work with a partner, which will be your BPO. I do believe that we will see this move for Shared Service centers like SAP Prague and me in three years.

I believe there is potential for a new kind of partnership, an exchange of experience more than simply a forum of best SAP practices. So I believe that in BPO you will have more qualified and more specialized BPO. Maybe a smaller unit in a big BPO's organization – that's where I see the future. So the big BPOs will remain, with all that big machinery, the big workflows, the big volumes. And then I would see the middle office of the success tomorrow. Back office and BPO, no doubt. Front office, customer intimacy within the business, even if it's a BPO organization, its people in the company, in the business. But regarding the middle office, for me the question is where to put it and how to develop it. The people who will take care of the question will give the answer.

From a systems perspective and an ICT enabler perspective (meaning SAP products and solutions), do you have any recommendations to us or to other software providers on where the focus should be to enable the future for the Shared Services business?
Guy de Mercier:
First of all, I was very fortunate to have the Solvay information system. But my recommendation is the following: In the market, there is no one single solution for a Shared Service center. That's very surprising. It is a huge market. Huge! But there is no one single service provider or solution provider or technical provider. When you look around, all the Shared Service centers are struggling to connect fragmented systems everywhere.

When I looked at my experience to start a contact center, I had Siemens proposing a telecom solution through IVR. I had SAP, sorry to say, proposing a complex, sophisticated customer relationship management (CRM) system not adjusted to my simple needs. And finally I found a solution on the Internet through Salesforce.com, which was Internet-based ticket management and CRM sales force support. It is very simple, very basic. So on the market, it's a patchwork, a fragmented solution. You go to telecom, you go to SAP software, or you go to very targeted local solutions through portals.

I believe that in the future a very good solution for SAP would be to approach the Shared Services center by the solution – "what do you need?" – but to do it quicker than in the past. In the past, you did it. I remember Henning had contacted me 10 or 15 years ago on cash management. At that time SAP was starting to develop its treasury module. I was head of the cash center for Solvay Group, and I was dealing with foreign exchange systems, a homemade system, and SAP was calling me as an expert. SAP developed that solution the same way that solutions are still developed today, through an experts' community to gather real specifications of what should be done. But it took SAP three years to develop the treasury module, from the first slide to the first experimental solution. Today the treasury module is working well, but tomorrow, if you take three years, you lose the market.

I agree fully what you said, and I'm lucky that somebody is so precise in his statements to really state the message regarding what the key is behind it, what is driving the wheel, and so on.

Guy de Mercier:

I recommend running your SAP solution by connecting any Bangalore staff to any place in the world. But be aware of what that means: The connectivity is very important. I do believe that was the success of SAP on integration. Integration was really your strength. And you still have great success based on that. And that's necessary for the final solution of a Shared Services center. But sometimes today we need the same force to give up on integration, and you have to play on connectivity. But it should be so well done that people don't see the difference. You have to work connectivity yourself. You have to develop portals yourself.

Thank you for your open opinion on this topic. Your clear opinion on the evolution of Shared Service provides a deep understanding of and insights into Shared Services for many of the readers.

8.8 Interview: Surrey County Council

Interview with Graham White, Head of Human Resources Surrey County Council, UK.

Introduction:

The county of Surrey, in the southeastern UK, is home to one million people. The 33,000 employees of Surrey County Council serve the citizens, providing services such as building and managing schools, social services, road networks, fire services, and public libraries. Surrey has the fifth largest council in the United Kingdom.

Why does your organization decide to set up a shared service center, what were the main drivers?

Graham White:

I think there were two key drivers; one was obviously the service delivery. It was critical that we continue to deliver a service philosophy. And in these days we got to deliver Swedish style services with American prices. In simple terms it means more for less. When we looked at our operations, they were very diverse, very split off, and one of the most obvious solutions was to get things into one place and deliver. And I think the other driver behind it was of course technology itself, it was coming clearer and clearer to us that one of the big 21st-century catalysts of the local government is going to be technology. So we wanted to make sure that we were putting in place all the best practice we can find.

When did you start with the first shared service center?
Graham White:
It formally started around 2004, although really from the day I joined in 2002 we were beginning the process and planning and looking at options. In real terms, up and running well by end 2004, early 2005.

And in the context of that, what services are up and running?
Graham White:
Yes, the high level finance, procurement, ICT, HR, that is the big ones and some elements of property. And of course the whole concept of employee self-service and manager self-service in terms of what that means, there is a whole ring of issues in that.

Let us concentrate on the HR function. What do you cover?
Graham White:
We get to cover virtually every thing from payroll, time recording, holidays and expenses.

What about recruiting?
Graham White:
Recruitmenting, yes. Really just all what we call the transactional activities, but in HR - so anything that has a transactional nature to it or has been moved across organizational management within there as well.

If we move on to benefits, what kind of key value benefits did you prove? So there was cost reduction?
Graham White:
There was, there were significant savings. And some that is of course is what we would call cost avoidance. The cost of delivering local government services has year on year being going up much, much higher than the rate of inflation. And so it wasn't only just about some saving money, it was about stuff in the costs going up anymore. We had pure savings, which of course in HR alone brought in over 9 million pounds and that was mainly around resourcing. In other words, less HR staff do the work. But as well as that we have also been doing a teacher mode to reduce any future project pressure.

So, if we can put a percentage on cost reduction in HR, what would you reckon that cost reduction would be?
Graham White:
It could be anywhere between 50 and 75%. What I mean, my kind of budget is about 5 million pounds, but I have been given new departments in there, so if I tick them out, just about 2 million pounds, it was 9, so

whatever, it is a fraction of 11. So it is pretty impressive. By saying this we didn't just move the budget somewhere else. And we put very, very little into the organization of the shared service center. We are merely 15 or 20 people, but no real costs.

And has there been productivity improvement?
Graham White:
There has. Yes, in a range of areas. The big efficiencies now are really being driven through all the employee self-service. So it's not about HR doing it quicker, it was about HR not doing it anymore. That's where the real savings are.

Excellent. What have been the biggest obstacles and challenges?
Graham White:
Biggest obstacles we experienced were from the line managers. The biggest challenge is to coach the organization, moving it into a culture seeing technology as an advantage, not a disadvantage.

So you did include self services extensively?
Graham White:
Yes, and where we couldn't, because not everybody has a computer, we also put assisted services. That's where they are able to telephone and someone else would do it for them. The saving isn't as great, but you still get some of the economy scale.

What about the IT system landscape? Do you have ERP systems, imaging technology, workflow systems?
Graham White:
Yes, we have all of them and workflow has been the backbone of the success of our SAP system.

In terms of the service delivery model, there are four options. It is a basic model, which you run as a cost center. There is a service quality model, where you run it based on KPIs and all that stuff. There is a market-orientated model, where you have internal, external customer possible and a market model, where you run it purely as an external shared service. Knowing your situation, I would say that you run a model whereby you have KPIs and measurement and penalties and so on against those KPIs, is that correct?
Graham White:
Absolutely. We have three KPIs, focusing on the level of delivery the services.

.

Moving on to that SLA, the contract and service level agreement. So it is a definable, it is a strictly defined service catalogue with well-defined services and so on within a catalogue, is that right?
Graham White:
Absolutely critical, yes. I mean there are some, what we called subjective service standards as well, but at the heart of it, it had to be objective, analytical measures, everything has to have a number behind to make it viable. But as well as that, we also as an organization are developing new values of how we deal which each of our customers, so that was there as well. But the base measure for the effectiveness in the shared service center has always been the KPIs and how we are measuring against that.

And it is a formal, legal, binding agreement between you and the service center provider, is that right?
Graham White:
Yes, as much as we can, we're both part of the same organization, but yes, it is a formal service level, operating level agreement, which outlines the expectations. I have to say, by definition it is an agreement, so it is not only what they must do for me, but it is also what the others must do for them. And that's quite important because, that was a big challenge at the beginning, because everybody wanted to get perfection from the shared service center, but didn't have to want to deliver anything to them in the first place. So, by making an operating level agreement, it is of both sides an operating level.

Okay, if we go to the governance then, the governance is shared between the business unit and the shared service centers?
Graham White:
It is, yes. We form a strategic alliance, where we have a committee or a group that meets once a month to review the working relationships. And there is an escalation process built in around that. Escalations are very rare.

In terms of the implementation, - there is a couple of approaches here. What was your implementation strategy regarding processes?
1. Process standardizing and engineering, then move to the shared service center,
2. Or move existing processes to the shared service center, then clean it up? Which way round did you do that?
Graham White:
We did the first one. But we did it in a laboratory, when it moved, it was already fixed. But we didn't change it and so the instance has moved. We would have blue printed the new solution, but we wouldn't actually have

used it outside of shared service center. But in shared service, where we did move it and the technology wasn't ready, the shared service center would have operated in a sort of invisible manual basis.

Did you do it as a big bang approach, so you did all processes at the same time or did you do in a stepped approach, when you rolled it out?
Graham White:
We did it as a big bang, but we did it some - not right across the as a big bang. We introduced it to the organization service by service. It was a total package each time.

What is the way forward? What are the things you are planning to do, going forward?
Graham White:
Yeah, it is so exciting. We are going for the new upgrade on the technology and we are actually doing a comprehensive review of the whole process again, and overlaying new technology, learning from our mistakes first time round and we think we are facing another, further significant efficiency drive coming on the back of still better technology.

We have talked a couple of times on the people's skills challenges relating to shared services. So, in terms of an HR director, hiring people, putting in processes and getting the right people into the shared service center, then putting the right environment in place from a development etc. point of view....

Maybe let us talk for a couple of minutes about the HR issues and more advice for people on the HR side of the shared service center.
Graham White:
The service team we started out with was to do a twin track approach to recruit externally or new to the organization and at the same time to move across original staff, who have been with us for some time. I mean, with hindsight I'm not sure that was the best solution. I think there were some real stars came across from the organization, but we also inadvertently transferred a lot of old culture and old traditions, which we spent a lot of time trying to fix, which wasn't a good idea. And realistically, I think if I was planning it again, I would far more circumspect how many people I would bring from the old regime into the new. That said, there were still some great people came across, but proportionally I think I would have taken less.

I think in terms of the people that you bring in from outside, it's a whole new skill set. No matter how much you think it's the old way done differently, it's not. It's a completely new skill set and one in which you do need to spend as much time as possible analyzing what it is you're going to be doing and making sure you bring in the sort of people, who will adapt to that role quickly.

And in terms of employee turnover and stuff in the shared service center, how has that been?
Graham White:
We had some of the traditional concerns about turnover. I have to say that it hasn't become intolerable for us. We worked very much on the cultural side of working in the Shared Service Center and build very strong team working, so that people actually enjoy the experience. And we've taken advantage of the fact that some staff like the flexibility and the coming and going within that type of environment. So, on that basis we haven't had any real problems. And to be honest, we should have done, because you know, we built a Shared Service Center, which has virtually zero unemployment.

I wouldn't say it was easy, but we've not had some of the horrendous problems that we've heard from other Shared Service Centers. But I put some of that down to the cultural work we do at the same time as the technical work.

Do you do job rotation within the shared service center?
Graham White:
We do. We do a lot of career success and planning and talent spotting to make sure that people who show a fore take and an opportunity to develop a move within the organization. And because it was the early years, I suppose we've had an excess amount of opportunity, which is meant it was being very easy to motivate staff.

So any sort of final thoughts, any other advice you'd give to anybody who was embarking on a shared service project? What would be your three or four things that you'd tell them to really focus on?
Graham White:
I think number one, stakeholders. You cannot engage enough with stakeholders. No matter how much you think you have engaged, it won't be enough. This is absolutely critical. You've got to do it much, much earlier than you think you should and you've got to keep it going for much longer than you thought you'd have to. I think secondly, in an organization, which is changing from one model to the other, start

communicating with staff as early as possible. For them it is a meteoric change and very challenging for them, and the biggest concerns they always have is, they're not getting enough information.

I think, number three is top level buy in, and not just agreement. They've got to actually become champions of the new model. Because the fourth is really just be on your guard, because the big problem will always be line managers. It's a Machiavellian philosophy. They've been successful under the old regime and they don't actually want to change to a new one.

That's excellent. Thank you Graham.

9 Evolution of Shared Service

One of the most interesting questions for shared services is the question: How does the Shared Service evolve in the future?

The answer to this question is multifaceted. There are distinct areas to look at:

- Shared Service *expand the demand chain* for existing services (increasing scale through going global)
- Shared Service changes into a *different process (service) sourcing delivery model* (outsourcing, self-services, full-automation)
- Shared Service undergoes *processes improvement* process (efficiency, maturity, productivity improvements, effectiveness, optimization)
- Shared Service increases competencies and expertise to *cover more functions or value add* elements of a business processes (increasing scope)
- Shared Service *organizational setup changes* (single global shared service center, virtual shared service centers)
- Shared Service underlying enabling technology (such as ICT systems) landscape will be further *standardized, consolidated and optimized*

Empirical study figures show a shift of priorities. After the initial implementation, operation and stabilizing of Shared Services, the focus shifts to automation, enhancement of the coverage of functional areas (Finance, Human Resources or ICT) and higher value-add services by establishing centers of expertise.

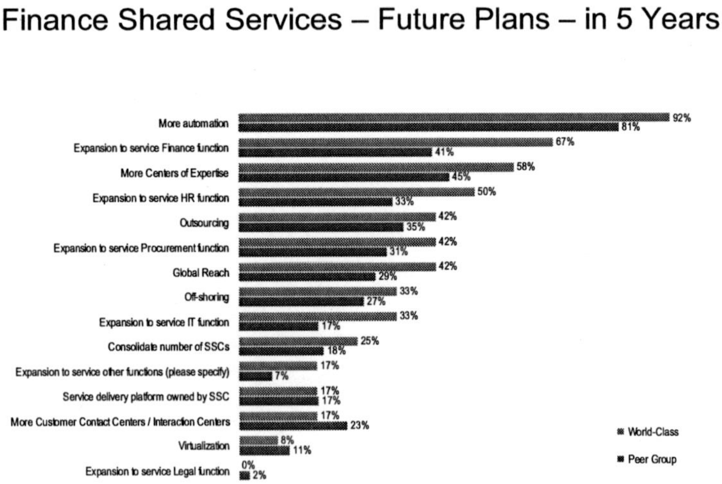

Fig. 100: Finance Shared Services – Future Plans

Source: Hackett/SAP (2007)

9.1 Multifaceted Evolution of Shared Service

The multifaceted approach relates to the different aspects of Shared Services like the demand chain, localization and relocation of resources, process improvements through reengineering and automation, functional scope extension with additional value add services, changing the organizational and managerial structures, taking advantage of emerging technology capabilities and adapting the service delivery concept itself by moving from Shared Services to other delivery models like self-services, business process outsourcing or full-automation.

The current practice of provided Shared Service in Finance is visible from the followed figure.

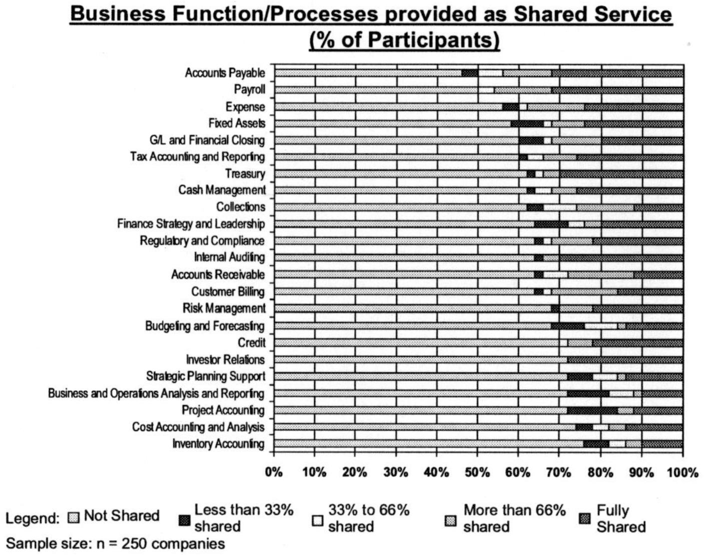

Fig. 101: Business Function/Process provided as Shared Service in Finance

Source: ASUG/SAP (2006)

The degree of Shared Service in Finance varies. In all of the listed Finance sub processes/functions Shared Service has a varying degree of control over the entire shared business process.

9.1.1 Evolution into a Different Service Delivery Model

Adapting the service delivery model is the most important question relating to the future direction of Shared Service. Business process outsourcing (BPO) is not necessarily the logical next step after a Shared Service implementation. Self-services and full automation have to be considered as options as well.

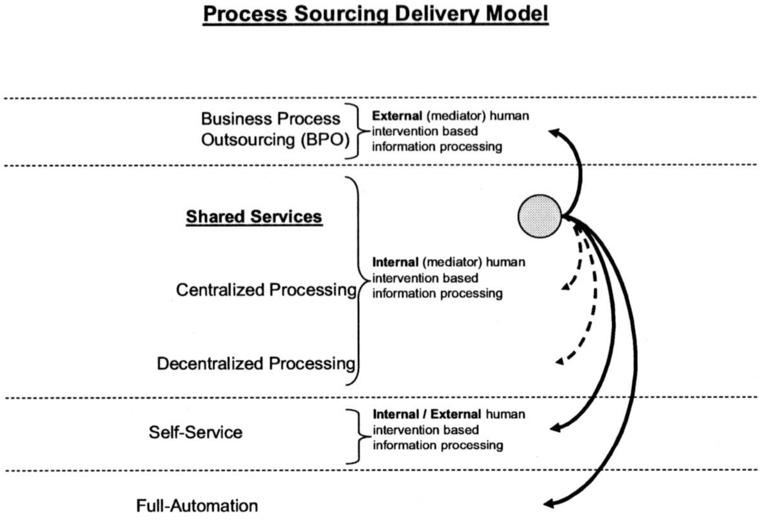

Fig. 102: Evolution of the Shared Service delivery model

The Shared Service concept is based on the assumption that internal Shared Service resources (mainly personnel) are used to support business processes. In all three cases (BPO, Self-Service, Full-Automation) there is a shift of human execution resources *out of the Shared Service organization* for a given workload.

An evolution into different service delivery models will lead to a transformation of the shared service center itself. The shared service center changes from a transactional processing center into a center of expertise/excellence.

Another way of reducing cost is to shift the (same) people workload to cheaper people resources to benefit from *labor arbitrage* effects. Human-based information processing can be performed by internal or external personnel resources. Centralization of the service provision for multiple business clients and allocating the execution to a dedicated independent, *internal organizational unit* are the main characteristics for Shared Services. Reallocating people workload for labor arbitrage lowers the labor cost category. Differences in labor costs are achieved mostly in distant countries (near-shore or off-shore). When it is done within the own corporate umbrella it is called the "off-shore captive" approach. Captive off shored activities are managed internally.

Reallocating the service to an external source is called *business process outsourcing (BPO)*. An external service provider may benefit as well from labor wage differences. But, the decision to move to an external provider implies a change of the coordination model (from hierarchy to network). Additional coordination cost (these are the transaction costs for searching, negotiating, monitoring, adapting, monitoring and adapting) have to be considered and thus compensated by lower service prices.

The use of outsourcing of business functions differs per business function. A recent study carried out by SAP and the American SAP User Group (ASUG) provides a picture of the current state.

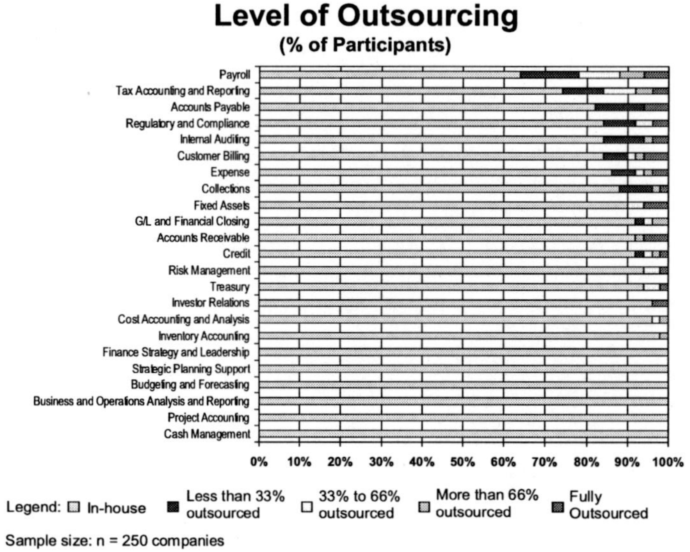

Fig. 103: Level of Outsourcing per business function group
Source: ASUG/SAP (2006)

Other forms of human based information processing are *self-services* where internal (e.g. employees) or external (e.g. customer, vendor, partner) requestors are technically enabled to retrieve and process their information needs by themselves. Self-services are normally not assigned to Shared Services because the personnel execution resource is not part of Shared Service staff.

The current practice views self-services as part of Shared Services. From a terminology point of view, this is not correct. Self-service may exist with or without established Shared Services. For example, business partner (e.g. supplier or customer) uses a self-service offering to update his planning figures in a supply chain network. Self Service is a separate conceptual approach how a service can be delivered. There is still a need for a Shared Service center because it is still necessary to handle exceptions and errors. Additionally it is a lot easier to implement or adapt processes with a central approach than with many decentralized business clients.

Self-services may play a vital role in the combination of different service delivery channels. For example, the first tier of contacts with employee requirement should be handled as self-services, while the upper tiers (with more sophisticated requirements) are routed through to business people with expert knowledge.

Full automation is the third way to evolve Shared Service delivery. Automation is often viewed as the alternative to the movement to lower (people) cost locations. Investing in full automation (straight-through processing, lights-out processing) competes with the alternative of shifting the workload. Increasing the machine workload changes the sourcing structure of the work. People workload will be replaced by machine work. Automation provides more efficiency and consistency of process execution, better governance, control and visibility which leads to an increased compliance to regulatory requirements.

Real world organizational decisions have to assess the different Shared Service delivery models (BPO, self-service, full-automation) for each business process and resource conditions.

9.1.2 Evolution through Process Improvements

Every corporation with Shared Services has its own Shared Service maturity level (design, implementation, operation, optimization phases) and directions. Each phase has its own challenges. When we refer to the evolution of Shared Services, we refer to general company independent future directions.

A company can implement Shared Services using process engineering at any level of maturity. These are the natural stages of a shared business process:

- Transferring *'as-it-is'* processes to Shared Services without any reengineering
- *Simplification* of business processes through harmonization in the Shared Service environment
- *Standardization* of business processes (ideally one common shared business process)

- *Optimization* of business processes (ongoing adaptation to internal and external changes, automation)

Various degrees of automation are part of nearly every process sourcing option. One of the key aspects when we talk about Shared Service is the allocation of workload (service demand). This could include the shift of additional workload (expansion functionally or geographical reach/coverage) to the Shared Service hub and/or shifting workload to different type of execution resources. Those execution resources can be:

- Human workforce, either to the requestor itself (self-services for employees and partners, customers) or to a third party service provider (e.g. outsourcing party). In both cases the "workforce" is outside the Shared Service Organization.
- Technology based (full electronic processing without a human intervention such as full electronic processing of documents or full automation through RFID tags).

Technology-based processing is the ultimate form of information processing (data capturing, more or less sophisticated data execution processing). In general, Shared Service is a special form of organizing the information service execution. Information processing is mostly based on *human execution resources* (plus additional enabling ICT support) for capturing and processing of information/data. On the other hand the information/data processing activities can be entirely based on technology like *information/data tags* (RFID for items). Fully automated object based information processing is the ultimate way of processing information where *no human resource acts as a mediator* to collect and processes data. Most process sourcing solutions have differing portion of automated and human based activities. Thus automation is applicable to any form of information processing where full automation (lights-out, straight-through) is just one extreme of sourcing options.

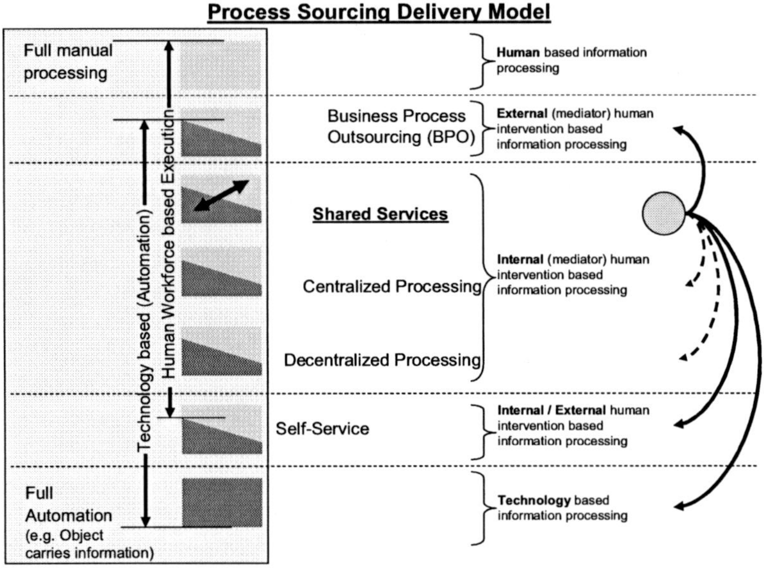

Fig. 104: Service delivery model and sourcing category type

9.1.3 Evolution via Expanding Functional and Value-Added Scope

The term scope indicates different types of business processes. The range of options starts with the expansion of:

- Functional scope (extending the service portfolio by moving into a multi-functional, multi-process coverage, acting more as a business service center with a broader scope)
- Climbing up the ladder to more value-added and expertise based services (transformational services)

There is no single criterion to characterize the level of Shared Services. Business process attributes (transactional/transformational, back/front office, complex/ easy tasks, high/low interactive tasks, high/low risk) *and* execution resources attributes people/technology based, internal/external, location from national – regional – global) are common differentiation criteria to assess future movements in Shared Service. A common approach is to pick one or two characteristics and show the movement over the time axis. The following example shows the focus of selected process characteristics and intensity of technological usage over time.

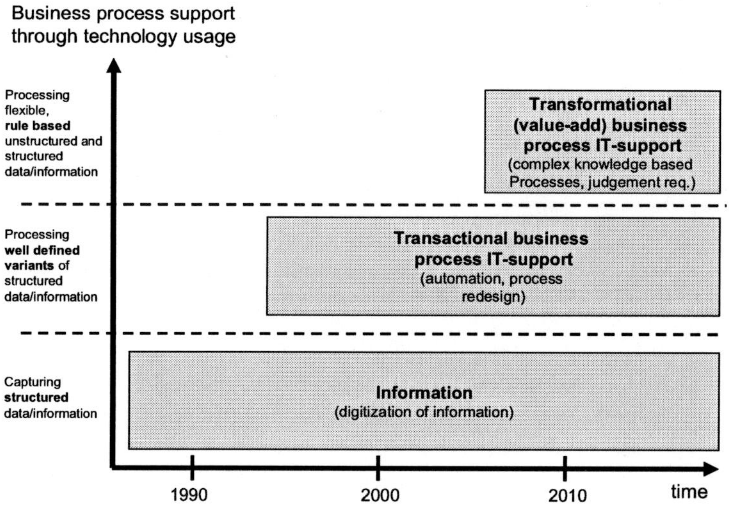

Fig. 105: Example of process support and technology usage evolution over time

Such a pragmatic approach is straight-forward but neglects the complexity of the entire Shared Service picture. There is more than the technology usage involved when it comes to assessing the evolution of Shared Services.

9.1.4 Evolution by Expanding the Demand Chain for Existing Services (Increasing Scale)

The term *scale* refers to the same type of task but with a multiplier. The workload becomes multiplied when expansions occur, such as:

- Geographical reach (such as going global)
- Additional businesses not yet covered in Shared Service (such as other product lines, divisions, business units, associated corporate companies)

In the past local or regional Shared Service centers were in the majority. Improvements in information and communication technology have enabled the implementation of global Shared Service centers. More synergies can be achieved in a global approach, such as higher volume for more scale benefits, a greater worldwide consistency and transparency of business practices, opportunities of low factor cost on a global basis (especially labor costs), taking advantage of potential tax benefits and elimination of expensive costs in cross-border financial transactions.

9.1.5 Evolution through Organizational and Managerial Changes

Expanding the Shared Service concept globally and implementing physical global Shared Service centers are the potential direction of current Shared Service operations. From the organizational perspective, a Shared Service center could operate fully virtual but under strong governance and reporting to a single Shared Service executive. Emerging development of information and communication technologies enables *virtual* Shared Service centers and there is an expectation that this form of delivery will rise in the future.

9.1.6 Evolution through emerging technical capabilities - Information and Communication Technology

Most large global enterprises have implemented a shared service concept. The ICT system landscape is still fragmented and only a few enterprises are in the lucky situation to have only one common ICT shared service platform. Continuous improvement with standardizing, consolidation and optimizing the ICT system landscape is still on the agenda.

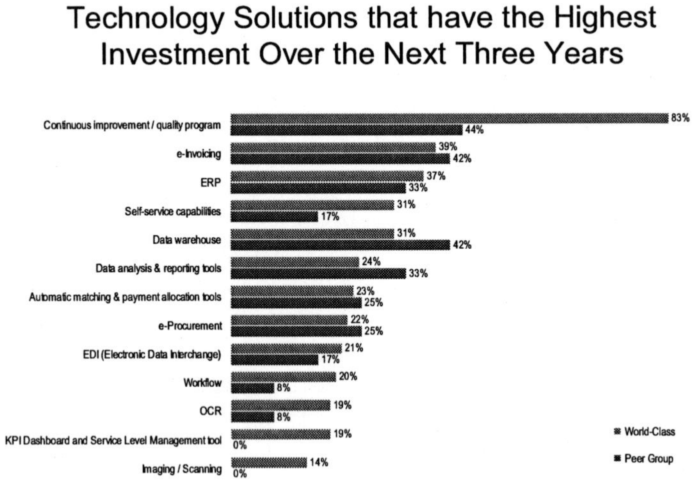

Fig. 106: Investment in technical solutions over the next years
Source: Hackett/SAP (2007)

Emerging business process requirements, such as selective or full outsourcing, require highly flexible ICT systems. Service orientation is the upcoming paradigm how ICT systems will be designed, operated, maintained and supported. *Service Oriented Architectures (SOA)* promise more flexibility at lower cost on the long term basis. Renovation of the existing ICT system landscape according to service oriented concepts would open new opportunities for Shared Services which were constrained by ICT in the past.

9.2 Shared Service Evolution Complexity

A common approach to assess the evolution of Shared Service is to provide an unstructured list of options or to pick one aspect out of a set of characteristics, such as technology usage over time. More sophisticated approaches combine the evolution areas, such as sourcing delivery options *and* process maturity stages.

The following diagram illustrates the grid of business process maturity stages and the process sourcing delivery options (*WHO and WHERE of information processing*) with their impact on potential key value benefits. The evolution of a Shared Service center service portfolio is traceable over time within such a diagram.

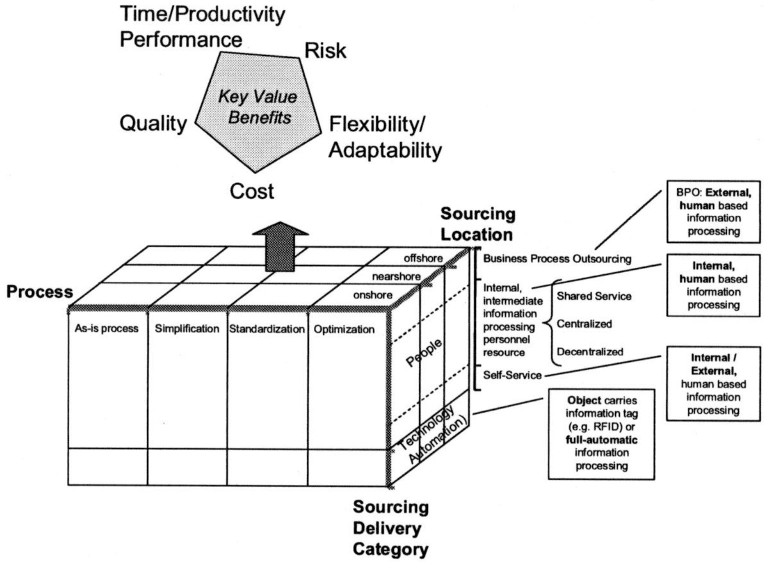

Fig. 107: Process Maturity and Sourcing Grid

A lot more differentiation is needed to assess the evolution of Shared Services. Thus multiple characterizations (profiling) of the business process *and* characterization of the execution resources provide a more realistic picture. Thus, a framework of dimensions with distinct differentiation of dimensional values or groups of values is necessary to form a solid picture. The foundation of our assessment will be based on the roots of *how Shared Service benefits will be achieved* in the following areas:

- Service Demand
  - Geographical Reach
  - Functional/Process Range
- Business Process / Function
  - Core Business Functions
    - Finance & Accounting
    - Human Resources
    - Procurement
    - Information Technology (services)
  - End-to-End Business Process
    - Order-to-Cash
    - Purchase-to-Pay
    - Hire-to-Retire
  - Other Process Characteristics
    - Interactivity
    - Complexity
    - Specialized knowledge/expertise
- Execution Resource:
  - Execution resource category
    - People
    - Technology
  - Location
- Organization/Management of Service Delivery
  - Organization of service delivery
  - Organizational structures, process flows, management of transition, risk management

Evolution comprises the multifaceted view of all major characteristic values. Extracting just one or a few characteristics and neglecting the whole profile simplifies the picture for communicating the results. Evolution occurs for every dimension and not just a single one. The evolution of business process characteristics is an important one. Business process characteristics are described in more bundled measures like 'complexity', degree of 'interactivity', 'specialization and knowledge intensity' and so on.

Those areas will form the *dimension* of the Shared Service assessment framework. Each dimension has some distinct *differentiating dimension values* or a cluster of values.

The determination of the different groups can be based on empirical data or conceptually retrieved. For simplification reasons we limited the dimensional measurement scale to three different dimensional value clusters.

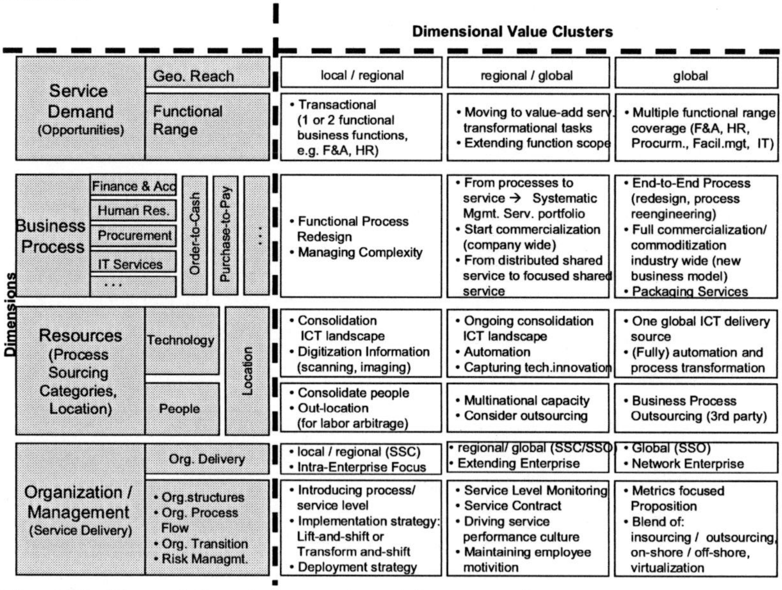

Fig. 108: Shared Service assessment framework

Any assessment based on the differentiation in the dimensions (e.g. splitting resources in people and technology) and/or their values (or cluster of values) lead to a different assessment *profile*. Collecting the profiles from many Shared Service Organizations will provide a statistical picture of the 'as is' or a desired 'will be'.

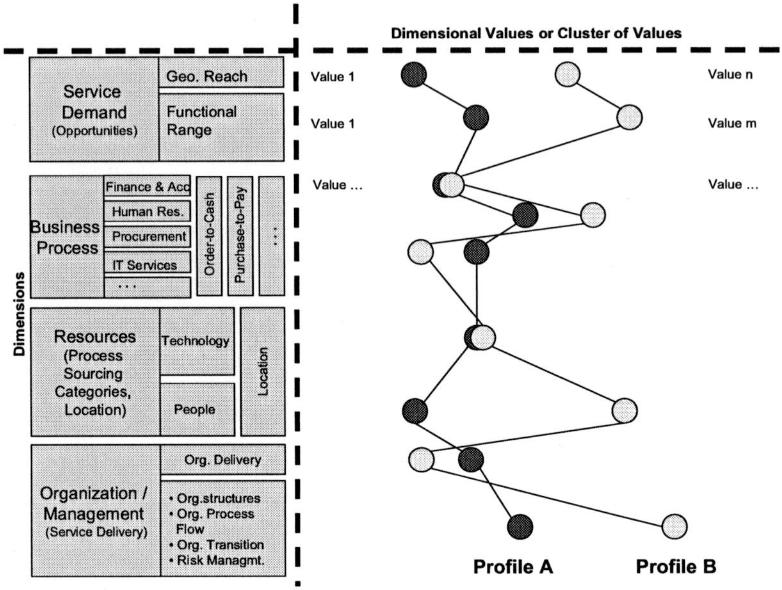

Fig. 109: Profiles of Shared Service Characterization

The prioritization of activities in surveys of Shared Services will indicate a trend to the next stage of the majority of Shared Service solutions. Keep in mind, the company-specific profile and priorities may differ greatly from the average. It could be that a company chooses a different approach in implementing Shared Services. Over time each company will climb (or descend) to a higher (or lower) profile level.

For example, there are the two generic approaches of Lift-and-Shift or Transform-and-Shift, which provide alternative ways to implement Shared Services. Not all companies are moving at the same time in the same direction. If many companies show a similar profile in a certain timeframe we could label it as a *wave (phase, level or generation).*

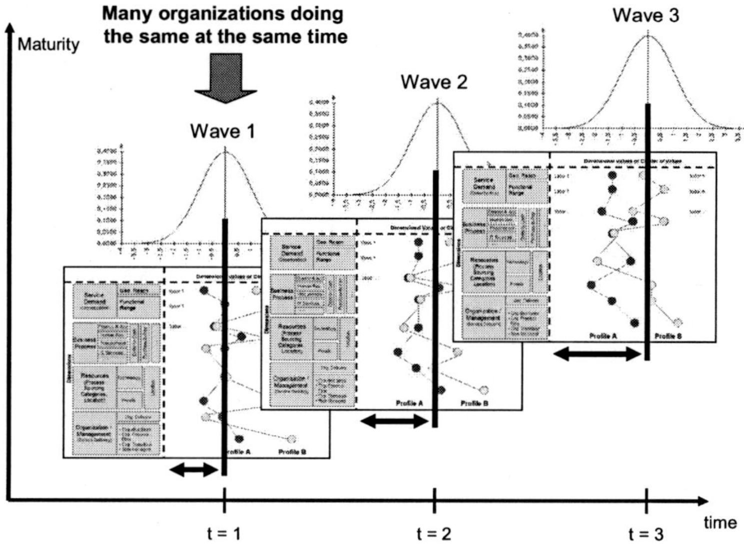

Fig. 110: Waves in Shared Service

Every corporation has its own profile of dimensional value clusters. With the *assumption* that most of the companies implementing and running Shared Services have a *profile close to the three columns of characteristic clusters*, this would indicate the different waves of Shared Services.

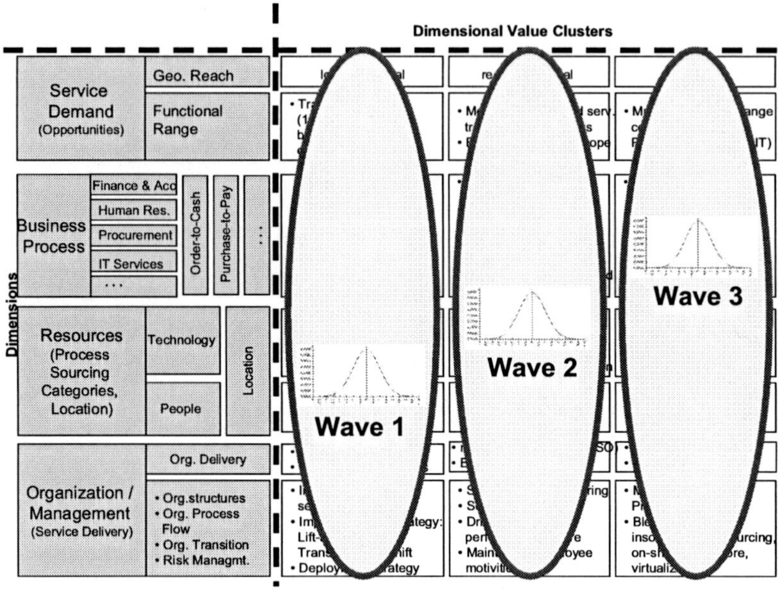

Fig. 111: Shared Service evolution waves

Extracting the most significant difference between the Shared Service waves and labeling it, leads to the following assumptions:

Wave 1: Reorganizing *processes and resource alignment* on enterprise level.

The primary goal is capturing economies of scale, process transformation/ optimization and resource consolidation on *enterprise level*. The major focus is on centralizing and consolidating processes, systems and sourcing locations.

Wave 2: Converting processes into marketable *services (service-products).*

Engineering a process in the way it can be *marketed to internal and external clients* is a step into professionalizing the service delivery. Standardization (further consolidating and harmonizing) of services/processes, policies and systems is mandatory to establish a successful Shared Service Organization. Defining service-products, continuous improvement and ongoing optimization of services/processes, leveraging technology and reassessing sourcing locations is the overall challenge at this stage.

Wave 3: *Industrialization of services* (commercialization/ commoditization).
Further improvements arise from the economies of effects (scale, scope) through process sourcing from *ICT service networks and markets*. A network of internal and external service providers (outsourcing partners) will be established. Location becomes less important. Thus the Shared Service Organization potentially mutates to a virtual Organization.

Summary:
In the chapter of Shared Service Operation Model we discussed a similar differentiation with four basic operation usage models from the *Cost oriented Model* (basic model) up to the more sophisticated *Market model*. Although the different operating models could be used to indicate maturity levels in Shared Service we did not explicitly label them as waves of Shared Service. Waves or generations indicate a common, cross-enterprise situation with organizational independent constraints and opportunities. Thus a fundamental disruptive change or common requirement is necessary to distinguish the waves. The evolution path from *processes* to *services* and from services to the *industrialized services* has some disruptive characteristics.
Shared Service may support any business process. This applies to unique, individualized clients needs up to highly standardized transactional processes. Later ones are of course the primary focus of Shared Service. Potential benefits are limited to the organizational boundary. Therefore simplification, standardization in the area of business processes and execution resources are constrained by the organizational limits. Moving beyond the enterprise implies the distribution of business processes. This can be done in the same approach on a one to one basis. Every business process is in this case on the execution layer unique (individualized). Thus the process flow (business events and activities) and the expected results are unique. Standardizing the process expected results and level of quality leads to *Business Services* in the true sense. Business services decouple the business task from the underlying (mostly technical) service delivery structure. *Marketable business services* are a shared accepted clear definition among (external) business partner community without interpretation or lengthy clarification needs. *Industrialization of business services* implies the standardization of business services cross organizations on the level of business events, flow activities and the target result. The final goal is then sourcing the business service from a market. This will be the ultimate form of commoditization.

Emerging technology (especially ICT technologies), introduction of market oriented organizational and management approaches, globalization of the supply and demand chain, distribution of processes and evolving standardization of business processes will lead to a reduction of transaction cost. The future of business service delivery is based on network arrangements. The following figure shows according to the transaction cost theory the shift to the middle [Picot/Freudenberg 1998, 72f].

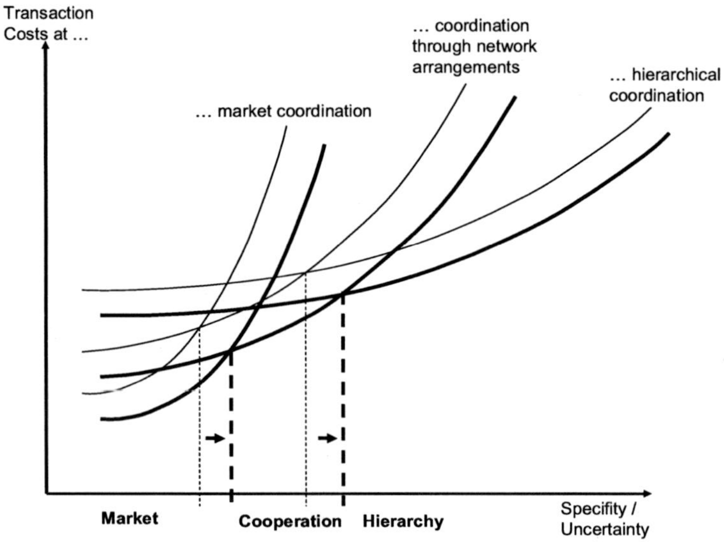

Fig. 112: Changing service delivery coordination form

Source: Keuper et. al. (2006, 406) (own translation)

9.3 Evolution of Shared Services in Different Business Functions

9.3.1 Evolution of Shared Services in Finance & Accounting

Results of empirical studies show the different priorities over time in Finance.

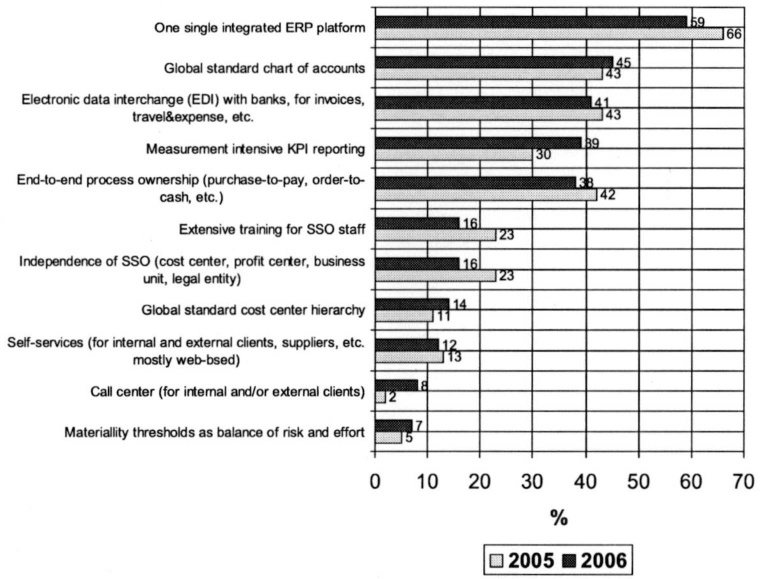

Fig. 113: Shift in Focus of priorities in Financial Shared Services

Source: Values retrieved from: Hackett (2007, 59) and Hackett (2005, 27)

Looking at the results of empirical studies, we can see that the dominant goal over time is to move to one single integrated ERP platform. The goal of having one single source of truth such as a global single chart of accounts is associated with a single ERP platform. Financial transactions (accounts payable and receivable) require the highest amount of administrative activities in F&A. Thus it is clear that electronic processing with financial institutions play an important role in ICT automation of business processes. Most large enterprises with already established Shared Services are trying to stabilize and optimize their Shared Service implementation. Managing shared services with key performance indicators, dashboards and so on, rank as high as the focus on business processes themselves. As more and more processes and sub-tasks are moving to Shared Services, the Shared Service Organization slowly acquires more business expertise and tries to acquire ownership on the end-to-end business processes. Aiming for high value financial services (see the grouping financial processes/functions in the following figure), requires extensive training of Shared Service staff.

illustrative

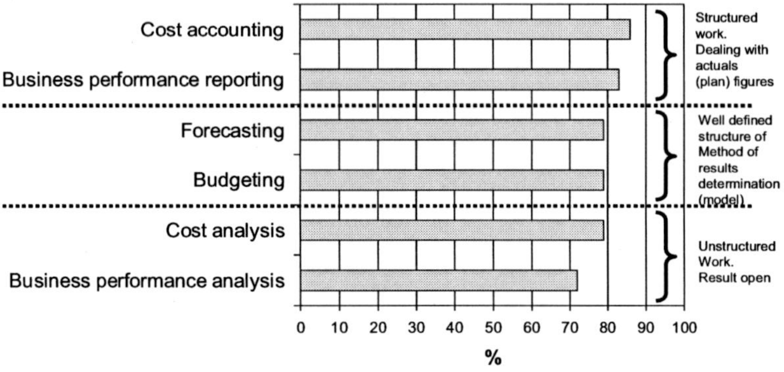

Fig. 114: Finance Processes categorized according to degree of structureness

Financial Shared Services will acquire more processes from decentralized business units, will source more business processes offshore for labor arbitrage, will outsource current shared services and will increase full automation of processes.

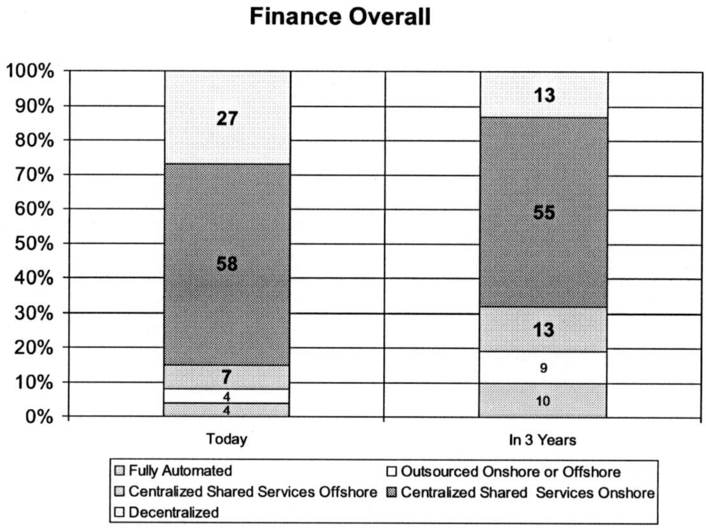

Fig. 115: Expectations of future development of F&A Shared Services

Source: Hackett (2007, 33)

A strong growth is expected for full automation, business process outsourcing and centralized off-shoring finance functions.

9.3.2 Evolution of Shared Services in Human Resources

	MOST LIKELY TO BE TRANSFORMED		
	Internal Process Reengineering	By Consolidation in a SSC	By Outsourcing
Payroll		1	1
Stock option administration			5
Compensation			
Leave			
Training / development	2	4	
Employee communication			
Pensions administration			2
Health & welfare benefits			4
Career & succession planning	1		
Recruitment / selection	4	5	
Assessment / performance appraisal	5		
Expatriate and relocation administration		2	3
HRIS		3	
Entire HR fucntion	3		

Fig. 116: Evolution of Shared Services in Human Resources

Legend: Figures represent range number

Source: ADP (2006)

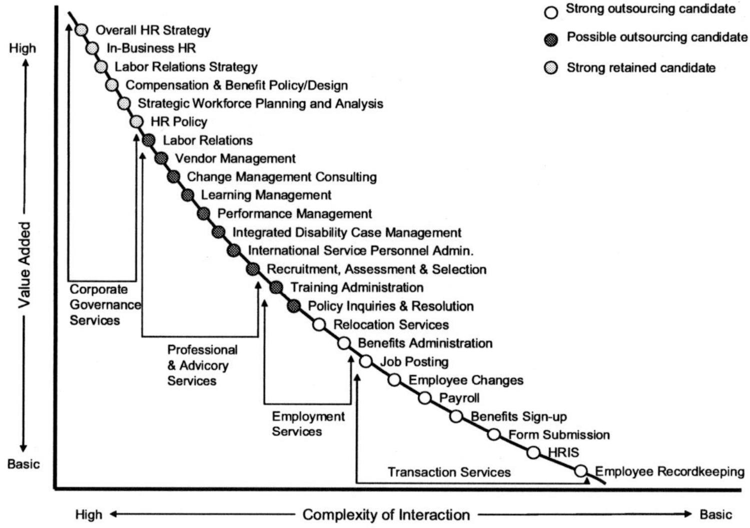

Source: TPI

Fig. 117: Evolution of Human Resources process sourcing

Source: TPI, http://www.tpi.net/services/businesssupport/humanresources/ 22.11.2007

9.3.3 Practice: Future Outlook of Shared Services

Each of the companies interviewed has its own path forward. The directions are determined by the maturity of the Shared Service operations, deployment success, already existing geographical coverage, further standardization and optimization of the business processes, enhancing business process scope and moving up the value chain with value added services, increasing automation, and consolidating the ICT system landscape.

BASF:

BASF plans to close its geographical coverage and optimize the business processes. Dealing with mergers and acquisitions they require an efficient and effective way to roll-in (or carve out) companies to be serviced. BASF tries to provide higher value-add services besides the administrative and supporting processes. Moving up the value chain for Shared Services is one of their main objectives. The lack of availability of experts causes a bottleneck on providing those value-add services, but taking customer orders is already on their radar screen.

"I think we'll be serving all the companies through the business service center. The challenge we'll then face is optimization. I would really like to work on optimizing the procedure, the method itself. In the future, we'll be experiencing more mergers and acquisitions, or even company sales. To do this, we'll need a standardized procedure for how to integrate new companies that are acquired in the future into the BASF business services. A template would enable us to add new companies in the shortest time. This would have to be a relatively fixed procedure. I assume, therefore, that we'll have to build up the relevant expertise for this. These are important points as are, of course, ongoing optimization projects in all areas." [Interview with Hans-Jürgen Seeger, BASF]

Selective business process outsourcing (BPO) for parts of a Shared Service process is foreseeable.
"I could well imagine that we will outsource parts of certain areas, for example the AP area. I'm thinking about sorting the mail; we're already trying to offload certain things." [Interview with Hans-Jürgen Seeger, BASF]

Henkel:
"We are employee-oriented and we don't go faster than our employees are able to go or for which we can find some sort of solution. But as you can imagine, we're not sleeping and we do have to stay competitive, so we obviously have a number of things to keep in mind. …".
"… The real challenge is sustainable reduction." [Interview with Dr. Carlo Mackrodt, Henkel]

Marks & Spencer (M&S):
According to M&S it takes different stages to set up Shared Service centers. The first one is the start-up, the second one implementation and third is the maturity stage, during which Shared service operations are run. . "Based on the maturity phase, the workload will move to business process outsourcing (BPO) with fewer people in the services center, and many more shared service activities will move up the value chain. The role of the services centers transforms into the management of the BPO organization at that stage. And I think that's very key."
"… I see it as one of the strategic initiatives that we're doing. The first one is continual constructive challenge, where the culture must change. And the second one on that stage is all about basically outperforming customer expectations. This basis is that that's what customers expect, and this is where we can do more for them. These are the strategic initiatives that we need to have going." [Interview with Mr. Foley, M&S].

Philips:
"... We benchmarked our processes and we are now overall in the first quadrant of the Hackett's cost grid. Our focus now is on business process improvement."
"I believe there will be a lot more companies going offshore and they will use outsourcing much more. This applies especially to companies with less than €5 billion of revenue. In the long term I hope that level of commoditization of these processes will dramatically increase. For example, accounts payable could become a commodity process across companies. This is a huge value creation opportunity."
"SAP has to improve their solutions portfolio to address these new challenges. IT was a key enabler in the past and will be a key enabler in the future in creating standards for business processes." [Interview with Michel de Zeeuw, Philips]

SAP:
"… A Shared Service is always a journey with its own lifecycle. In principle you start by centralizing things, then optimizing and standardizing them. Then you consider outsourcing parts of them. That is exactly our strategy. We transfer certain parts to a third-party provider, for example, after we have optimized them and know exactly what they are about. At the same time, the Shared Service Center picks up new processes with the bucket which has just been emptied, if you will allow me to take a bucket-wheel excavator as an analogy, and the newly created capacity can work towards standardizing and optimizing these new processes. So it's just like those bucket-wheel excavators which are used in the open-cast mining of lignite, it operates in a cycle."
"As I said, outsourcing, or, the other way around, SSC is developing more and more into a process know-how carrier, too. And we will not outsource this process know-how. And that's important, as with this process know-how we also achieve some process ownership in the company. In our case that is over and above the competence that a Shared Service Center would get, because they know how travel accounting works, for example."
"… I think the important thing is that Shared Services are a part of the strategy and remain a part of it, to a certain extent, and that the bucket-wheel excavator keeps turning. That's an important point for me and we have to make sure that it happens. Because nothing could be worse for a Shared Service Center than the changes coming to a standstill. You have to change things constantly and keep everybody motivated. …
As I said, you take on the issues and condense them to a center of expertise. That means that the issue has been broken down into manageable parts and most parts have been outsourced. You hold on to

one part, and that's the center of expertise. That means that you have a lot of condensed COEs afterwards." [Interview with Peter Rasper, SAP]

Solvay:
"So let me give you an opinion: This market will evolve and will remain. But the players in this market will change. I'm not quite sure an in-house shared services center will remain in-house forever, but I'm not quite sure that BPO is the solution either. What I see is a little bit in between.
For those two reasons, every year you will always face, regarding your in-house shared services center, "Why we do this ourselves? Isn't it cheaper to do it outside?" The answer is yes, but it depends on what you are talking about. Is it cheaper to do it outside? How do you define the "it," the service itself?
Again, I see two types of shared services centers. There is the shared services center in-house, which is the one that is the enabler for the transformation. For that, it will remain forever, and you will have top people not being used for core businesses but with likely strong personality. Not only to generate cost savings but also to be an enabler of fundamental change and integration.
Those shared services centers will become like a permanent reengineering project team, a permanent experimental line to produce in-house part of the re-engineered processes to understand how to do it and then to work with a partner, which will be your BPO.
I believe there is potential for a new kind of partnership, an exchange of experience more than simply a forum of best SAP practices. So I believe that in BPO you will have more qualified and more specialized BPO. Maybe a smaller unit in a big BPOs organization – that's where I see the future. So the big BPOs will remain, with all that big machinery, the big workflows, the big volumes. And then I would see the middle office of the success tomorrow. Back office and BPO, no doubt. Front office, customer intimacy within the business, even if it's a BPO organization, it's people in the company, in the business. But regarding the middle office, for me the question is where to put it and how to develop it. The people who will take care of the question will give the answer." [Interview with Guy de Mercier, Solvay]

Regarding the Shared Service enabling ICT system landscape Solvay would suggest a broader dedicated view on the enabling technology with a speedier delivery to the market.
"First of all, I was very fortunate to have the Solvay information system. But my recommendation is the following: In the market, there is no one single solution for a shared services center. That's very surprising. It is a huge market. Huge! But there is no one single service provider or solution

provider or technical provider. When you look around, all the shared services centers are struggling to connect fragmented systems everywhere.

When I looked at my experience to start a contact center, I had Siemens proposing a telecom solution through IVR. I had SAP, sorry to say, proposing a complex, sophisticated customer relationship management (CRM) system not adjusted to my simple needs. And finally I found a solution on the Internet through Salesforce.com, which was Internet-based ticket management and CRM sales force support. It is very simple, very basic. So on the market, it's a patchwork, a fragmented solution. You go to telecom, you go to SAP software, or you go to very targeted local solutions through portals.

I believe that in the future a very good solution for SAP would be to approach the shared services center by the solution – "what do you need?" – but to do it quicker than in the past. In the past, you did it. I remember Henning had contacted me 10 or 15 years ago on cash management. At that time SAP was starting to develop its treasury module. I was head of the cash center for Solvay Group, and I was dealing with foreign exchange systems, a homemade system, and SAP was calling me as an expert. SAP developed that solution the same way that solutions are still developed today, through an experts' community to gather real specifications of what should be done. But it took SAP three years to develop the treasury module, from the first slide to the first experimental solution. Today the treasury module is working well, but tomorrow, if you take three years, you lose the market."

The connectivity is very important. I do believe that was the success of SAP on integration. Integration was really your strength. And you still have great success based on that. And that's necessary for the final solution of a shared services center. But sometimes today we need the same force to give up on integration, and you have to play on connectivity. But it should be so well done that people don't see the difference. You have to work connectivity yourself. You have to develop portals yourself." [Interview with Guy de Mercier, Solvay]

9.4 Epilogue – A Glance into the Crystal Ball

Shared Service Optimization is neither a status of actual system consolidation nor a people/organization cleansing. It is an ongoing *Change Management Process* in an organizational life cycle. When you have standardized, consolidated, automated (and optimized) the process you may give it back to organizational units or outsource it under a new strong governance framework.

A typical step after Shared Service optimization is commoditization and consequently outsourcing. Very few Shared Service Centers continue to provide optimized services to third parties. A similar destiny for ICT Services is foreseeable.

All corporate processes (business processes in a corporation) are evaluated to run as Shared Services, except strategy planning and decision support which is close to production and customer. So the implementation of Shared Services is a sustainable step towards commoditization and a result of industrialization. With the potential of industry standards, more and more industries may move forward to more industrialization of the whole industry.

Abbreviations

ABC	Activity Based Costing
AP	Accounts Payable
APH	Application Hosting
AR	Accounts Receivable
ASP	Application Service Provider
ASS	Applied Software Service
ASUG	American SAP User Group
A2A	Application-to-Application
BPM	Business Process Management
BPO	Business Process Outsourcing
BPS	Business Process Sourcing
BU	Business Unit
B2B	Business-to-Business
B2C	Business-to-Consumer
CD	Compact Disk
CEO	Chief Executive Officer
CFO	Chief Financial Officer
CIO	Chief Information Officer
CRM	Customer Relationship Management
DSO	Day Sales Outstanding
EBPP	Electronic Bill Presentment and Payment
EDI	Electronic Data Interchange
EIRO	European Industrial Relations Observatory
ERP	Enterprise Resource Planning
F&A	Finance and Accounting
FA	Fixed Assets
FSCM	Financial Supply Chain Management
FTE	Full Time Equivalent (human resource)
GA	General Accounting
GAAP	General Accepted Accounting Principles
GDS	Global Distribution Systems
GL	General Ledger
GRC	Governance Risk Compliance
HCM	Human Capital Management
HTTP	Hyper Text Transfer Protocol
HTTPS	Hyper Text Transfer Protocol Secure
HR	Human Resources
IAS	International Accounting Standards (now IFRS)
ICT	Information and Communication Technology
IFRS	International Financial Reporting Standards
IQPC	International Quality & Productivity Center
ISO	International Standard Organization
IT	Information Technology
ITO	Information Technology Outsourcing
KPI	Key Performance Indicator
MBO	Management by Objectives
MIME	Multipurpose Internet Mail Extension
M&A	Mergers & Acquisitions

NAFTA	North America Free Trade Agreement
NPV	Net Present Value
OCR	Optical Character Recognition
OTC	Order-to-Cash
PDA	Personnel Digital Assistant (Device)
PO	Purchase Order
PTP	Purchase-to-Pay
PWC	Price Waterhouse Cooper
RFID	Radio Frequency Identification Number
ROI	Return on Investment
SaaS	Software-as-a-Service
SBPOA	Shared Service and Business Process Outsourcing Association (now: SharedXpertise Forums)
SFTP	Secure File Transfer Protocol
SLA	Service Level Agreement
SOA	Service Oriented Architecture
SOD	Software-on-Demand
SOX	Sarbanes Oxley Act
SRM	Supplier Relationship Management
SS	Shared Service
SSC	Shared Service Center
SSO	Shared Service Organisation
TCO	Total cost of ownership
T&E	Travel and Expense
XML	Extensible Markup Language
X.400	A specific Message Handling System (MHS) an E-Mail System and an alternative to Internet E-Mail

Tables

Figures

Bibliography

ADP (2006) N. N.: Survey 200 decision-makers, Global Organizations, Q3-4 2006. 2006.

AMEX/ATKearny (2003) N. N.: European Expense Management Study, Eds.: AMEX / A.T. Kearny: European Expense Management Study 2003. 2003.

ASUG/SAP (2006) N. N.: Benchmarking Study May 2006, Eds.: ASUG / SAP: ASUG/SAP (American/SAP User Group), Benchmarking Study May 2006. 2006.

Bangemann (2007) Bangemann, Tom Olavi: Best Practice Benchmarking (Finance Example). Eds.: SharedXpertise Finance Forum: Finance Transformation Europe 2007. Brussels, 2007.

Bangemann (2005a) Bangemann, Tom Olavi: Benchmarking - Shared Services & World Class Finance, SAP CFO Round Table. Eds.: SAP Business Solution Architects Group: SAP BSAG - CFO Roundtable. Budapest, 2005.

Bangemann (2005) Bangemann, Tom Olavi: Shared Services in Finance and Accounting. Burlington, Gower Publishing Company, 2005.

Bergeron (2002) Bergeron, B. P.: Essentials of Shared Services. John Wiley & Sons, Inc., 2002.

Bread et. al. (2004) Bread, M. ; Rupp, T.: Moving Towards Global Shared Services. Eds.: JP Morgan / McKinsey: Total Working Capital Study. 2004

Coase (1937) Coase R.H.: The nature of the firm. Economica. 1937, *4:16*, p.386-405.

Daley (2003) Daley, J.: Moving from Shared to Managed Services. Eds.: Read, C., Scheuermann, H.-D.: The CFO as Business Integrator. Chichester (West Sussex), et. al., John Wiley & Sons, 2003.

Dressler (2007) Dressler Sören: Shared Services, Business Process Outsourcing und Offshoring. Wiesbaden, Gabler, 2007

Glahn (2006) Glahn Carsten von ; Oecking Christian: Transition and Transformation von Shared-IT-Services - Gestalterische Prämissen zur Einführung eines standardisierten IT-Service-Portfolios im Konzern. Eds.: Keuper F., Oecking C.: Corporate Shared Services. Wiesbaden, Gabler, 2006.

Hackett (2005a) N. N.: Fourth Annual European Finance Shared Service Organisation Study 2005, Eds.: The Hackett Group: Fourth Annual European Finance Shared Service Organisation Study 2005. 2005

Hackett (2007a) N. N.: ROI in Technology: The Key to World-Class Performance, Eds.: The Hackett Group: 2007 Book of Numbers ™ Research Series. Vol. 11. 2. 2007

Hackett (2007) N. N.: Globalization: The New Horizon for European Finance Shared Services, Eds.: The Hackett Group: 2007 Book of Numbers ™ Research Series. Vol. 11. 1. 2007

Hackett (2004) N. N.: 3rd Annual Financial Shared Service Organization Study 2004, Eds.: The Hackett Group: 3rd Annual Financial Shared Service Organization Study 2004. 2004

Hackett (2005) N. N.: 2005 Optimizing a Return on Business Complexity: Performance Metrics and Practices of World-Class Companies, Eds.: The Hackett Group: 2005 Book of Numbers © Research Series. Vol. 5. 2 2005 p. 43.

Hackett (2005c) N. N.: World –Class Defined: Realized Performance Based on Proven Best Practices 2005 Optimizing a Return on Business, Eds.: The Hackett Group: 2005 Book of Numbers © Research Series. Vol. 5. 1 2005.

Hackett (2005b) N. N.: 2005 Performance Metrics and Practices of World-Class Finance Organizations, Eds.: The Hackett Group: Book of Numbers™ Research Series. Vol. 6. 1 2005

Hackett (2005d) N. N.: 2005 Performance Metrics and Practices of World-Class Companies, Eds.: The Hackett Group: Book of Numbers™ Research Series. Vol. 5. 3. 2005

Hackett (2005e) N. N.: 2005 Performance Metrics and Practices of World-Class Human Resources Organizations, Eds.: The Hackett Group: Book of Numbers™ Research Series. Vol. 7. 1. 2005

Hackett (2006) N. N.: European Finance SSO Study 2006. Eds.: The Hackett Group: 2006

Hackett (2005e) N. N.: 2005 Performance Metrics and Practices of World-Class Human Resources Organizations. Eds.: The Hackett Group: 2005 Performance Metrics and Practices of World-Class Human Resources Organizations. Vol. 7. 1, 2005 p.13.

Hackett/SAP (2007) N. N.: 2007 Market survey Shared Services, 2007 (August – September 2007)

HROA (2006) N. N.: HR Transformation Survey - A global vision. Eds.: HROA in association with ADP: 2006 p.17.

HROA (2007) N. N.: HR Transformation - Myth or Reality. Eds.: HROA Europe and ScharedXpertise Forum in association with TPI: TPI Report. 01/2007, 2007 p.15.

Janssen et. al. (2007) Janssen, M.; Ramirez, J.; Dorr, E.: Balancing Business Process Globalization and Transformation. Eds.: The Hackett Group: FAO Today, Excerpt research from The Hackett Group. 2007.

Keuper et. al. (2006) Keuper F.; Oecking Christian. Eds.: Corporate Shared Services. Wiesbaden, Gabler, 2006.

Köhler (2002) Köhler Frost W.: Grundlagen des Application Service Providing. Eds.: Köhler-Frost W.: Grundlagen des Application Service Providing. Berlin, KS-Energy-Verlag, 2002.

Kris (2002) Kris A.: Shared Service Forum 18-19. April 2002. Eds.: Andersen: Andersen Shared Service Forum. Berlin, 2002.

Mercer (2002) N. N.: Shared Service Centers in Multi Country Regions. Eds.: Mercer Human Resource Consulting HR: Shared Service Centers in Multi Country Regions. 2002

Ortwein (2006) Ortwein T.: Sourcing – die neue Kernkompetenz der IT. Eds.: Pierre Audoin Consultants (PAC): PAC Inform. 2006, *2*.

Picot/Freudenberg (1998) Picot A., Freudenberg H.: Neue organisatorische Ansätze zum Umgang mit Komplexität, in: Adam D. (Eds.) Komplexitätsmanagement, Schriften zur Unternehmensführung, Vol 61, Wiesbaden 1998, 68-86

Picot/Reichwald/Wiegand (2001) Picot A., Reichwald R., Wiegand R. T.: Die grenzenlose Unternehmung, Wiesbaden, 2001

Quinn et. al. (1999) Quinn, Barbara; Kris, Andrew; Cooke, Robert S.: Shared Services - Mining for Corporate Gold. Financial Times Prentice Hall, London, 1999

Quinn et. al. (2000) Quinn, Barbara; Cooke, Robert; Kris, Andrew: Shared Services - Mining for Corporate Gold, London et. al., 2000

SAP (2004) N. N.: White paper – Financial Supply Chain Management with SAP. Walldorf. 2004

SBPOA (2004) N. N.: SBPOA Shared Service Week 2004, Main Conference 18th & 19th May 2004, Manchester (UK). Eds.: SBPOA (Shared Service and Business Process Outsourcing Association): Shared Services Week 2004. Manchester, UK, 2004

SBPOA (2002) N. N.: SBPOA Shared Service Survey 2002. Eds.: SBPOA Shared Service and Business Process Outsourcing Association: SBPOA Shared Service Survey 2002. 2002

Searl (2006) Searl, P.: F&A Transformation Survey - How shared services and outsourcing are impacting the F&A operation. Eds.: SharedXpertise / Hewlett Packard: 2006.

TPI (2007) N. N.: Human Resources. Eds.: Technology Partners International(TPI): Human Resources. 2007, http://www.tpi.net/services/businesssupport/humanresources/. 22.11.2007 07:40.

Ulrich (1995) Ulrich, D.: Shared Services: From Vogue to Value, in: Human Resource Planning, Vol. 18, 1995, 12-23

Weller (2007) Weller, P.: World-Class Finance Shared Services. Eds.: IMA Annual Conference: Phoenix (Arizona, US), 2007.

Wikipedia: Shared Services (2007) Wikipedia: Shared Services. http://www.en.wikipedia.org/wiki/Shared_services. 14.07.2007 11:25.